Arts & Crafts Movement

Text: Oscar Lovell Triggs

Page 4:
First row (from left to right):
Richard Norman Shaw (architect), main staircase, 1883-1884.
Cragside House, Garden and Estate, Rothbury.

M. H. Baillie Scott,
window for the Music Room of Dr. R. K., Manheim, 1902.
Museum Künstlerkolonie, Darmstadt.

William Morris (original design),
Philip Webb (modification) and
Dante Gabriel Rossetti (painting of the original three doors),
settle and bookcase.
The Red House, Bexleyheath, London.

Second row (from left to right):
Phoebe Anna Traquair,
"Angel" Chalice, 1904-1905.
Victoria & Albert Museum, London.

Alexander Fisher,
The Peacock Sconce, c. 1899.
Victoria & Albert Museum, London.

Charles Robert Ashbee (for the design),
the Guild of Handicraft (for the manufacturing),
decanter, c. 1904-1905.
Victoria & Albert Museum, London.

Third row (from left to right):
William Morris (design) and **Morris & Co.** (production),
Strawberry-Thief, 1883.
Victoria & Albert Museum, London.

William Morris,
Tulip and Trellis, 1870.
Victoria & Albert Museum, London.

William Morris,
Single Stem, c. 1905.
Victoria & Albert Museum, London.

Layout:
BASELINE CO LTD
33 Ter – 33 Bis Mac Dinh Chi St.,
Star Building; 6th floor
District 1, Ho Chi Minh City
Vietnam

ISBN: 978-1-84484-622-1

Printed in India

Oscar Lovell Triggs

Arts & Crafts Movement

PARKSTONE
INTERNATIONAL

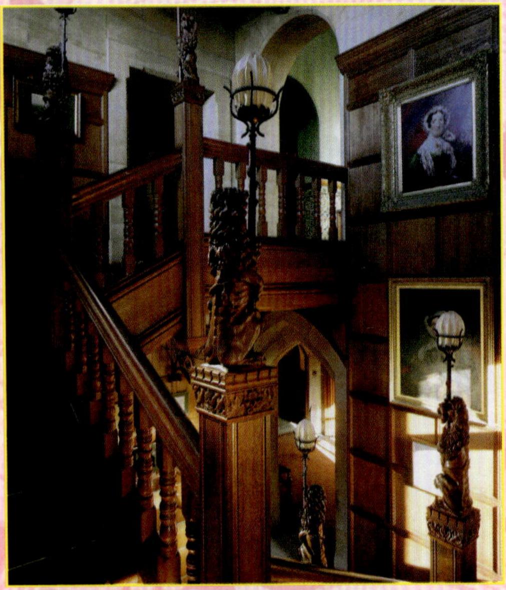
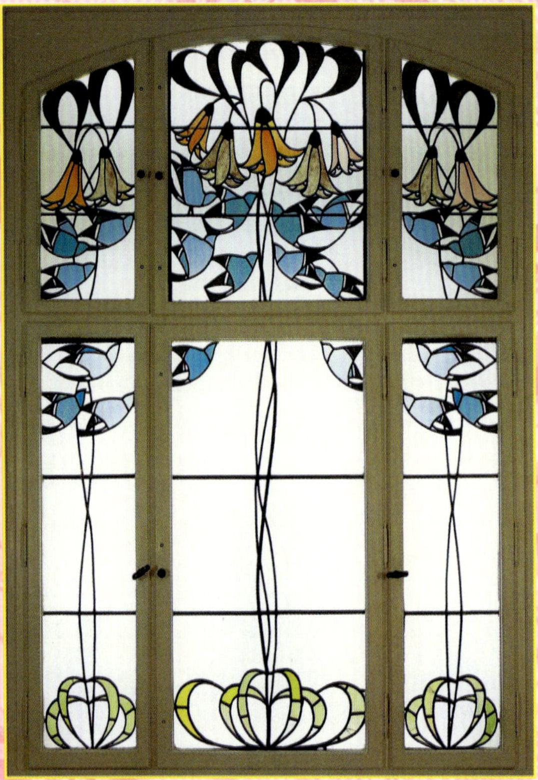
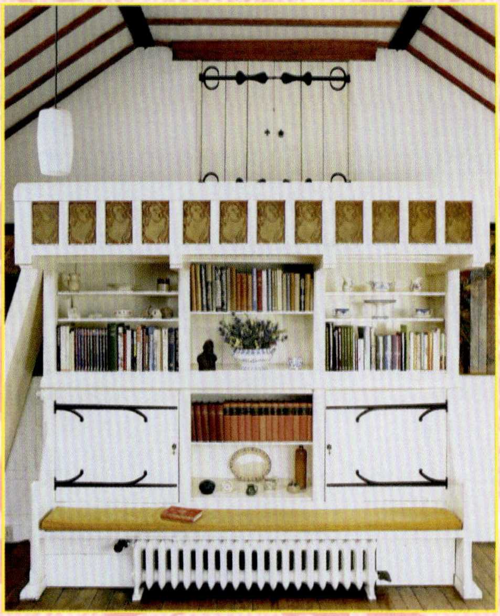
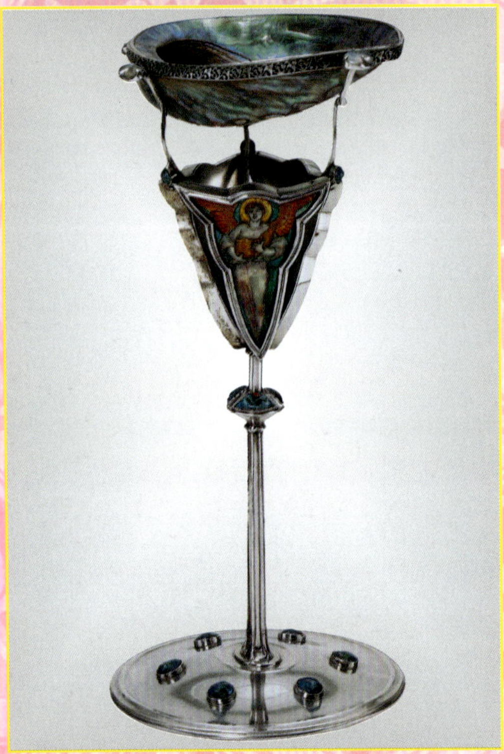
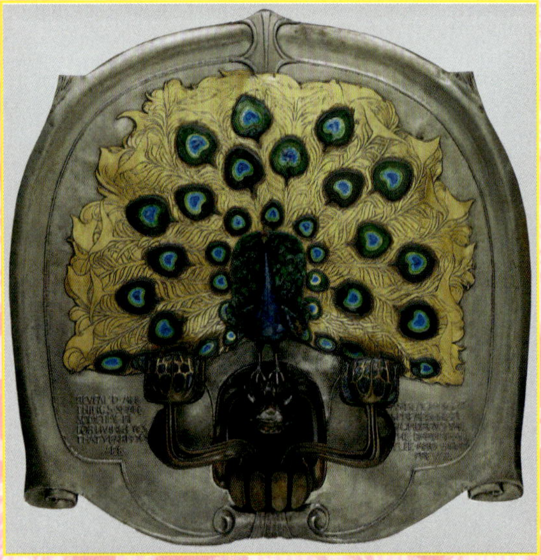
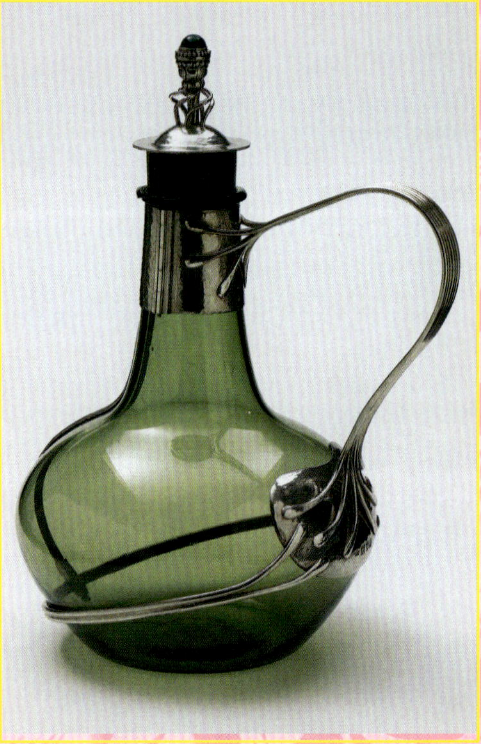
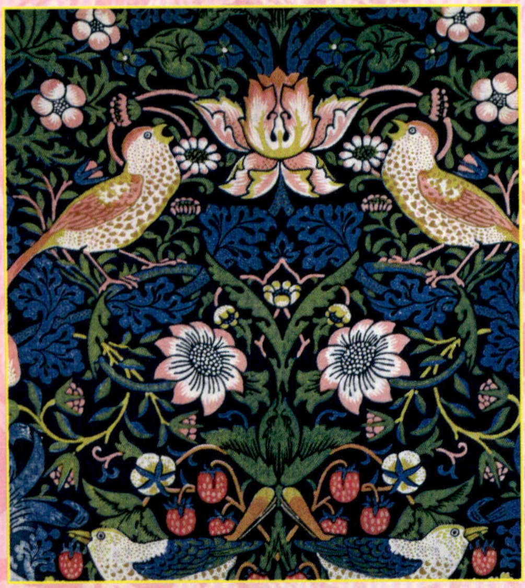
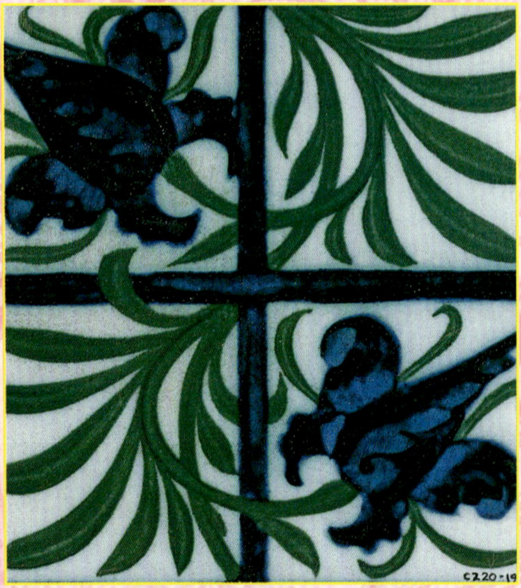

CONTENTS

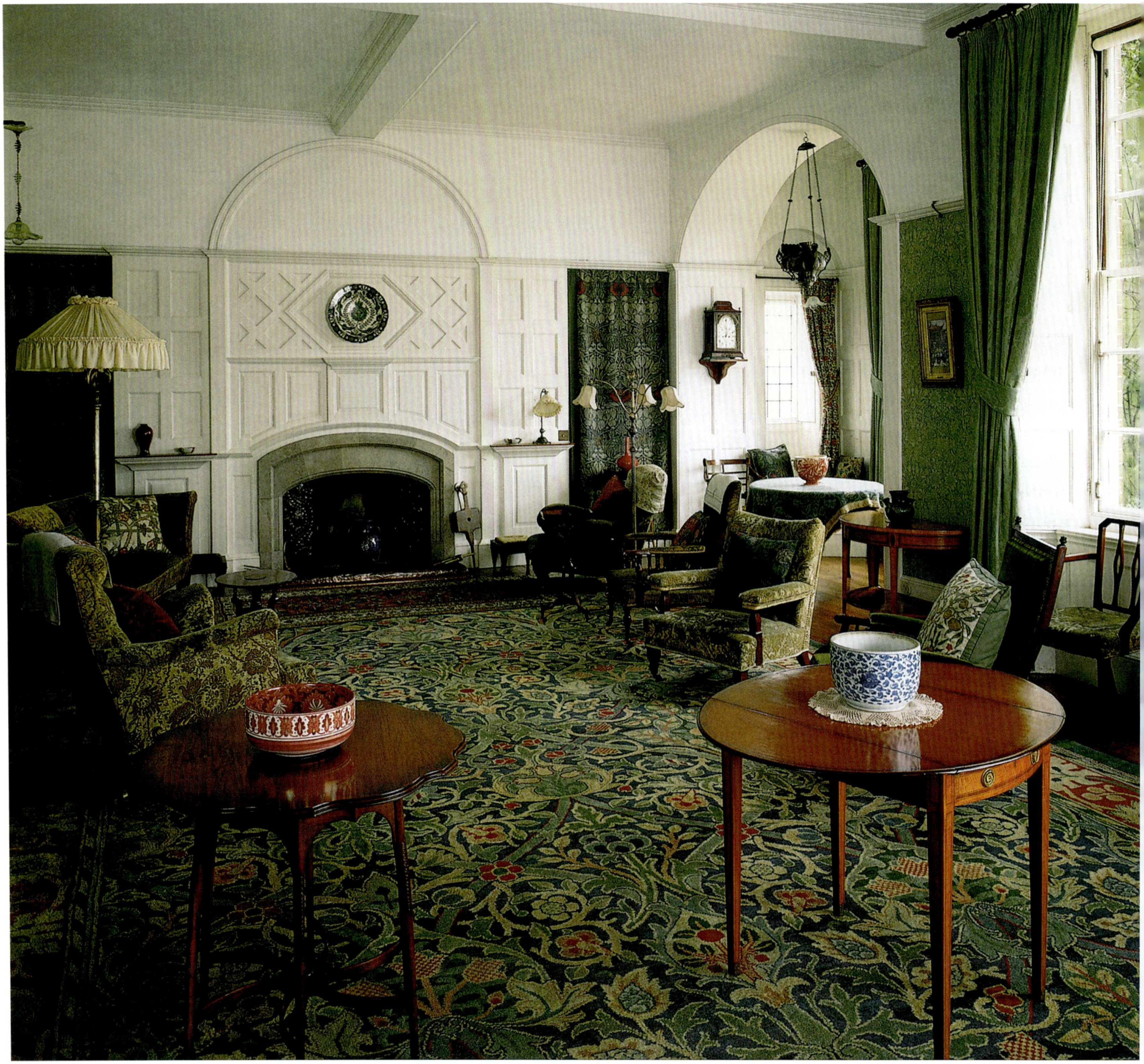

1 - Ruskin's Contribution to the Doctrine of Work

"Art is no recreation, it cannot be learned at spare moments, nor pursued when we have nothing better to do. It is no handiwork for drawing-room tables, no relief for the ennui of boudoirs; it must be understood and undertaken seriously or not at all. To advance it men's lives must be given, and to receive it, their hearts." John Ruskin, *Modern Painters*, 1843.

The primary motive of the Arts and Crafts movement was, as the name implies, the association of art and labour. Initially an English movement, it slowly emerged from the general industrial field over about forty years, though its differentiation into a distinct phase of industrialism belonged to the last ten years. The year 1860 was counted as the approximate year of its beginning, when William Morris built his famous Red House on the outskirts of London, and served his apprenticeship to the industrial arts by designing and executing the decoration and furniture of his home. The Arts and Crafts theory appeared before 1860 though, through the writings of Ruskin and Morris.

The story of John Ruskin's pilgrimage, his passage from naturalism to artistic interests, and thence to socialism, is one of the most significant life histories of the nineteenth century. In all his early writings on nature and art it was the relation of these to man for which he cared. Ruskin's moral sentiments were the element that differentiated him from other art teachers and thus marked him early for the mission of social reform. He declared himself that the beginning of his political economy is to be found in the assertion in *Modern Painters* that beautiful things are useful to men because they are beautiful, and for the sake of their beauty only, and not to sell, or pawn, or in any way turn into money. We are fortunate also to have Ruskin's own statement of the purpose of his art studies, following upon *Modern Painters.* He told an audience at Bradford:

"The book I called *The Seven Lamps* was to show that certain right states of temper and moral feeling were the magic powers by which all good architecture, without exception, had been produced. *The Stones of Venice* had, from beginning to end, no other aim than to show that the Gothic architecture of Venice had arisen out of, and

Philip Webb and **Morris & Co.**,
The Victorian Drawing Room,
c. 1892-1894.
Standen, East Grinstead.

indicated in all its features, a state of pure national faith and of domestic virtue, and that its Renaissance architecture had arisen out of, and in all its features indicated, a state of concealed national infidelity and of domestic corruption."

The recognition of the relations between art and national character signifies the social bearing of these volumes. Concerning the *Stones of Venice*, W. G. Collingwood makes the following comment:

"The kernel of the work was the chapter on the nature of the Gothic, in which he showed, more distinctly than in *The Seven Lamps*, and connected with a wider range of thought, suggested by Pre-Raphaelitism, the great doctrine that art cannot be produced except by artists; that architecture, in so far as it is an art, does not mean the mechanical execution, by unintelligent workmen, of vapid working-drawings from an architect's office; that, just as Socrates postponed the day of justice until philosophers should be kings, and kings philosophers, so Ruskin postponed the reign of art until workmen should be artists, and artists workmen. . . Out of that idea the whole of his doctrine could be evolved, with all its safe-guardings and widening vistas. For if the workman must be made an artist, he must have the experience, the feelings, of an artist, as well as the skill; and that involves every circumstance of education and opportunity which may make for his truest well-being. And when Mr. Ruskin came to examine into the subject practically, he found that mere drawing-schools and charitable efforts could not make an artist out of a mechanic or country bumpkin; for wider questions were complicated with this of art – nothing short of the fundamental principles of human intercourse and social economy. Now for the first time, after much sinking of trial-shafts, he had reached the true ore of thought, in the deep-lying strata; and the working of the mine was begun."

The volume entitled *A Joy Forever* being the substance of lectures delivered in 1857 on the political economy of art – the title is significant – marks definitely the parting of the ways, and his intention thereafter to speak out openly on social themes.

William Morris (for the design) and **Morris & Co.** (for the production), *Tulip and Willow*, 1873 (design) and 1883 (printing). Pattern for printed fabric, block-printed and indigo discharge on cotton, 135.5 x 93 cm. Victoria & Albert Museum, London.

As an economist Ruskin inaugurated three departures from teachings of the time, the first relating to general political economy, the second to the theory of beauty, and the third to the doctrine of work. Ruskin's divergence from the economical teaching of his day was not wider than his difference from contemporary aesthetics. The term "aesthetic" had been first used by Baumgarten in the eighteenth century to designate the science of beauty, meaning by the term that the beautiful made its

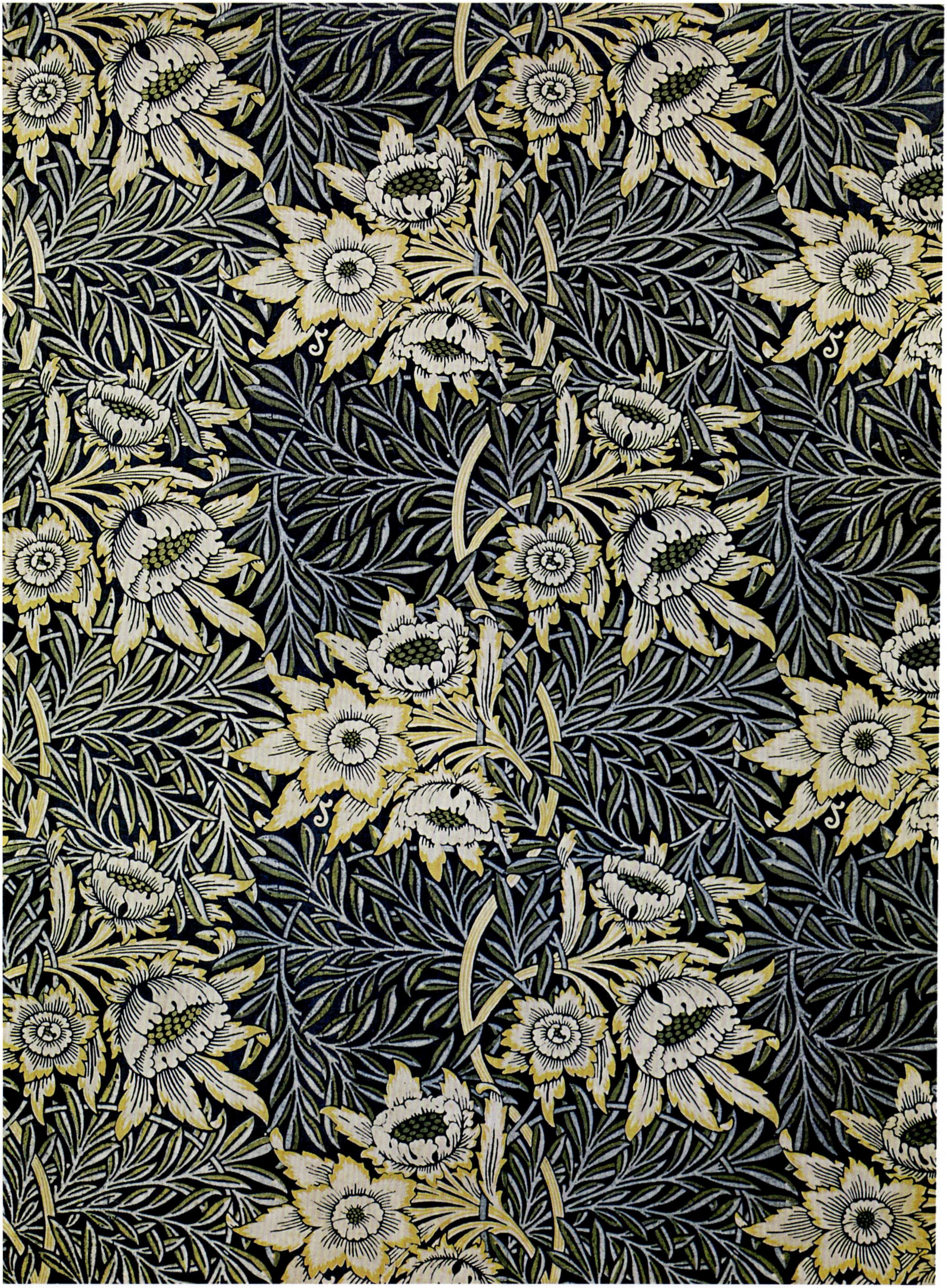

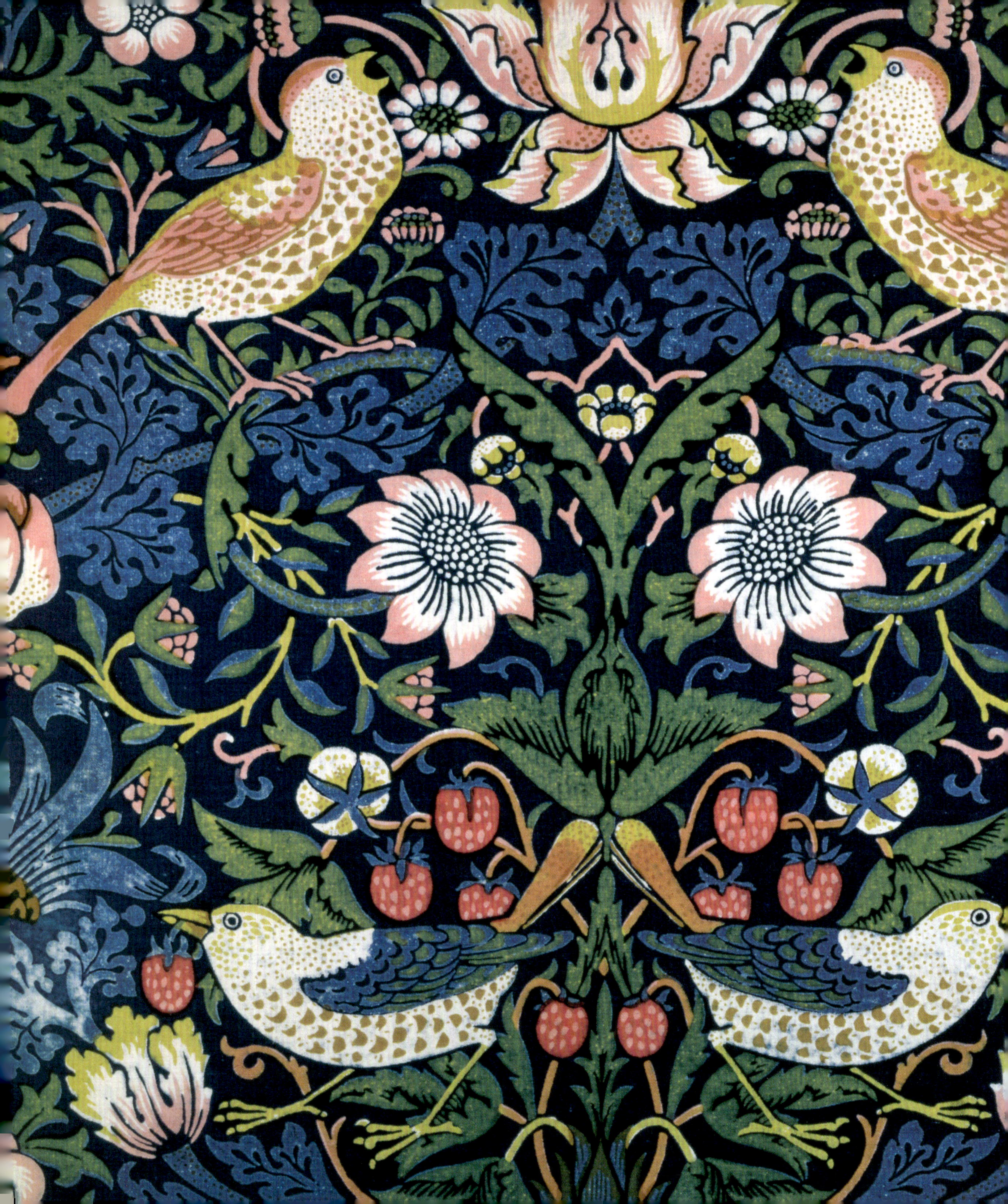

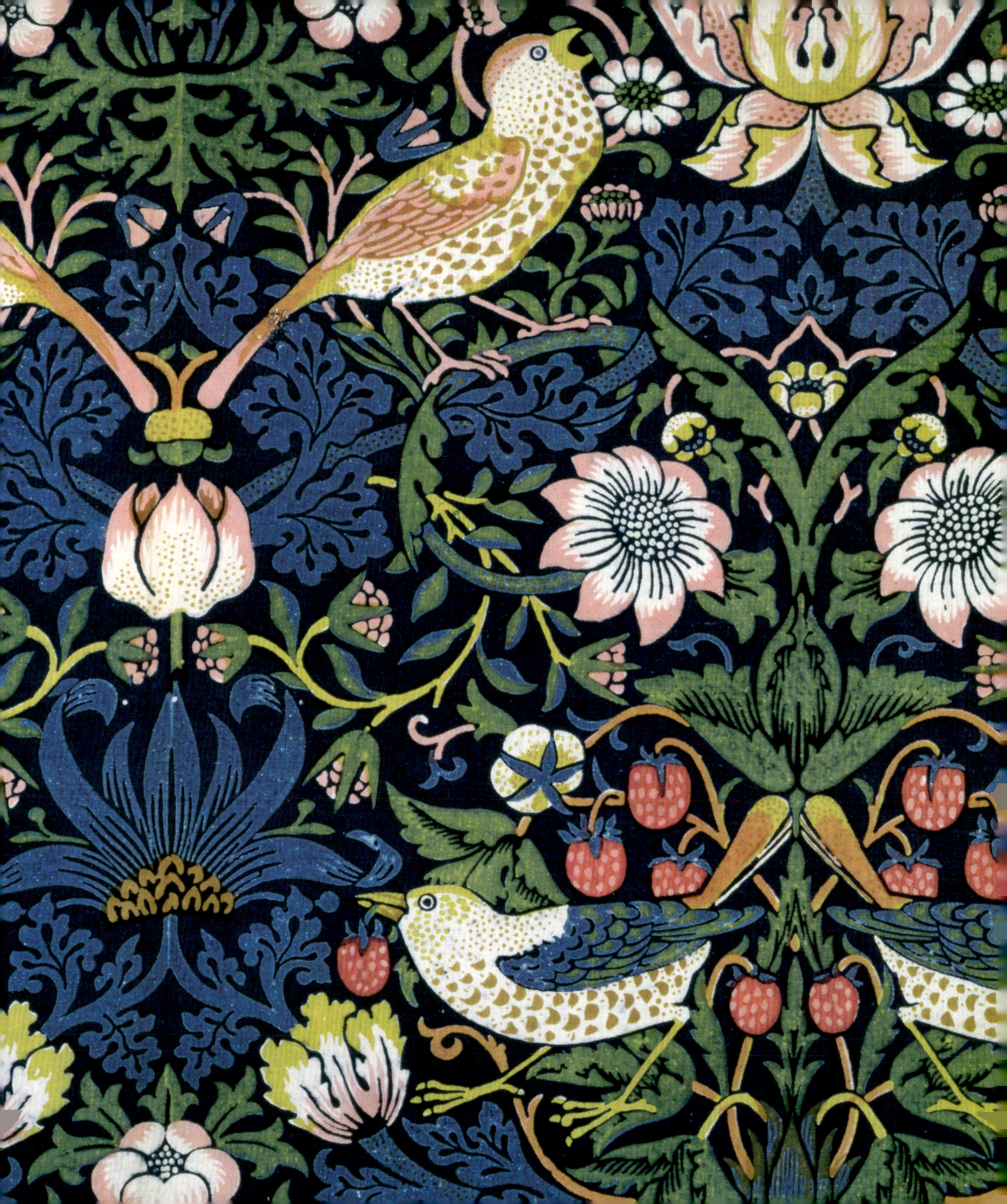

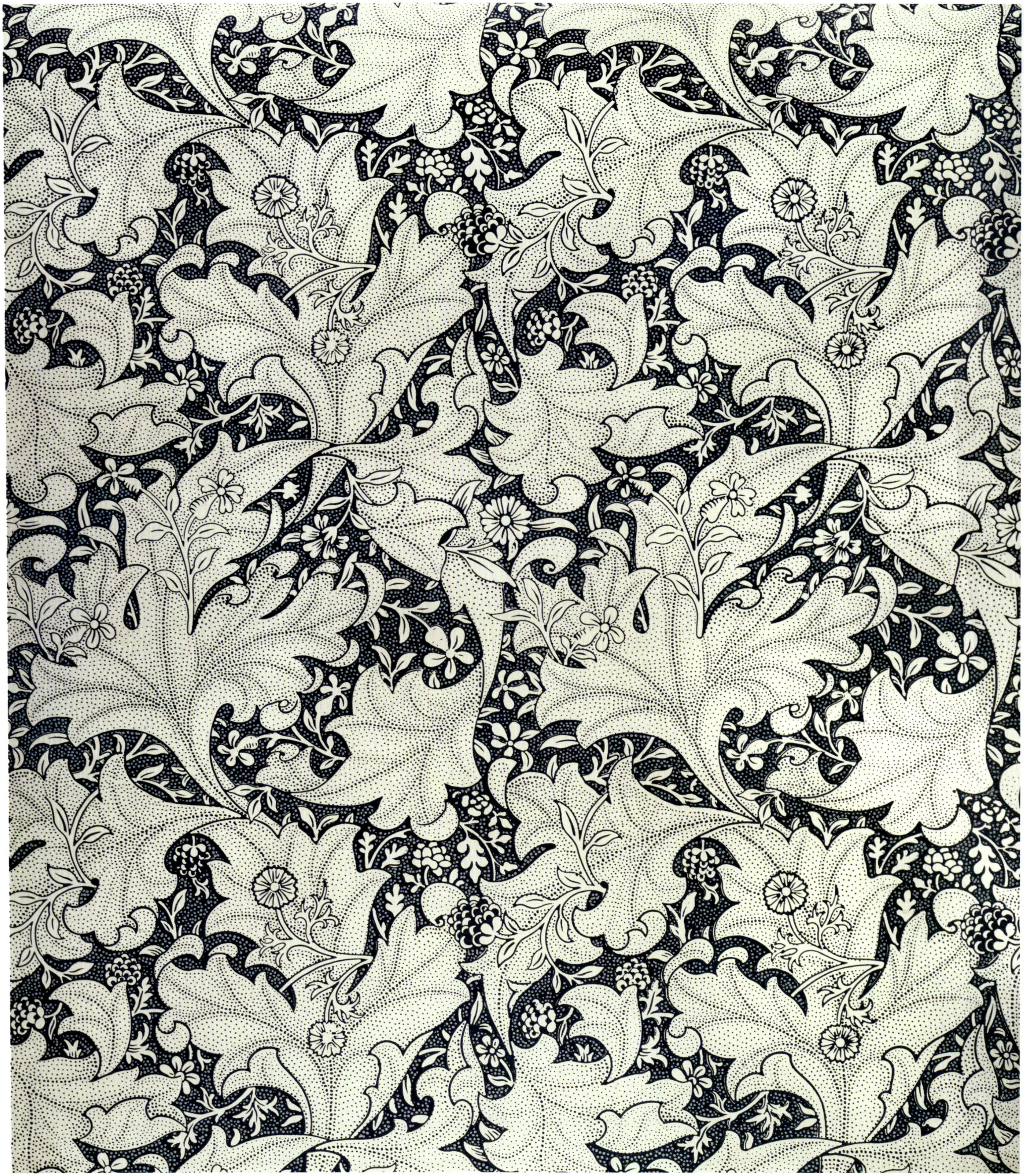

primary appeal to sensation, as distinguished from the good and true, where perception was interior. In making beauty "the perfection of sensuous knowledge," the field of aesthetics was demarked plainly from that of logic and ethics. These distinctions prevailed in philosophy up to the middle of the nineteenth century, with the result of fashioning a school of art that laid stress only upon sense effects, and, advocating "art for art's sake," had so far withdrawn from life that art had become merely a means of amusing and entertaining the upper and leisure classes. Against this aesthetic Ruskin set his face, affirming that the impressions of beauty were not of sense, or wholly of mind, but more essentially moral or social. The test he applied to art was its degree of social usefulness. He would never even use the term "aesthetic" except to refute its implications. The art of any country is seen to be an exact exponent of its ethical life: "You can have noble art only from noble persons." When writing the *Stones of Venice*, he examined each structure with reference to its capacity for fulfilling expressional purposes. In his more technical lectures on art at Oxford it was noticed that he touched constantly upon the problems of life. His exposition of the art of engraving, for instance, was as much a treatise on line in art as on line in conduct. His characterisation of the art of engraving, in the course of these lectures, is quite typical of his attitude: "It is athletic; it is resolute; it is obedient." In *Aratra Pentilici*, speaking of sculpture, he said: "Its proper subject is the spiritual power seen in the form of any living thing, and so represented as to give evidence that the sculptor has loved the good of it and hated the evil." The laws which he deduced for sculpture are wholly untechnical: (1) That the work is to be with tools of men. (2) That it is to be in natural materials. (3) That it is to exhibit the virtues of those materials, and aim at no quality inconsistent with them. (4) That its temper is to be quiet and gentle, in harmony with common needs, and in consent to common intelligence. From such discussion the definition is soon reached that art is expression.

As art, then, is not an entity distinguished by a quality called beauty, but a mode of expression, allied to all other forms of expression, and so marked by characteristics that may be termed moral or social, it follows that the chief test of art is its inclusiveness, its lowly origin, its universality, its serviceability, its degree of satisfying genuine social needs. The general proposition underlying *Modern Painters*, *Stones of Venice*, and his other art studies is this: "Great art is nothing else than the type of strong and noble life." A sense for the noble in life is something quite different from the "taste for beauty" developed by the opposite aesthetic. The false sense for art is known by its refinement, its fastidiousness, its preciosity; purity of taste is tested by its universality. Hence Ruskin told his students to beware of the spirit of choice, saying, "It is an insolent spirit, and commonly a base and blind one, too." He told them also that the main business of art was its service in the actual

William Morris (for the design) and **Morris & Co.** (for the production), *Strawberry-Thief*, 1883.
Pattern for printed fabric, block-printed and indigo discharge on cotton, 60 x 95.2 cm.
Victoria & Albert Museum, London.

William Morris, *"Wallflower"* design.
Private collection.

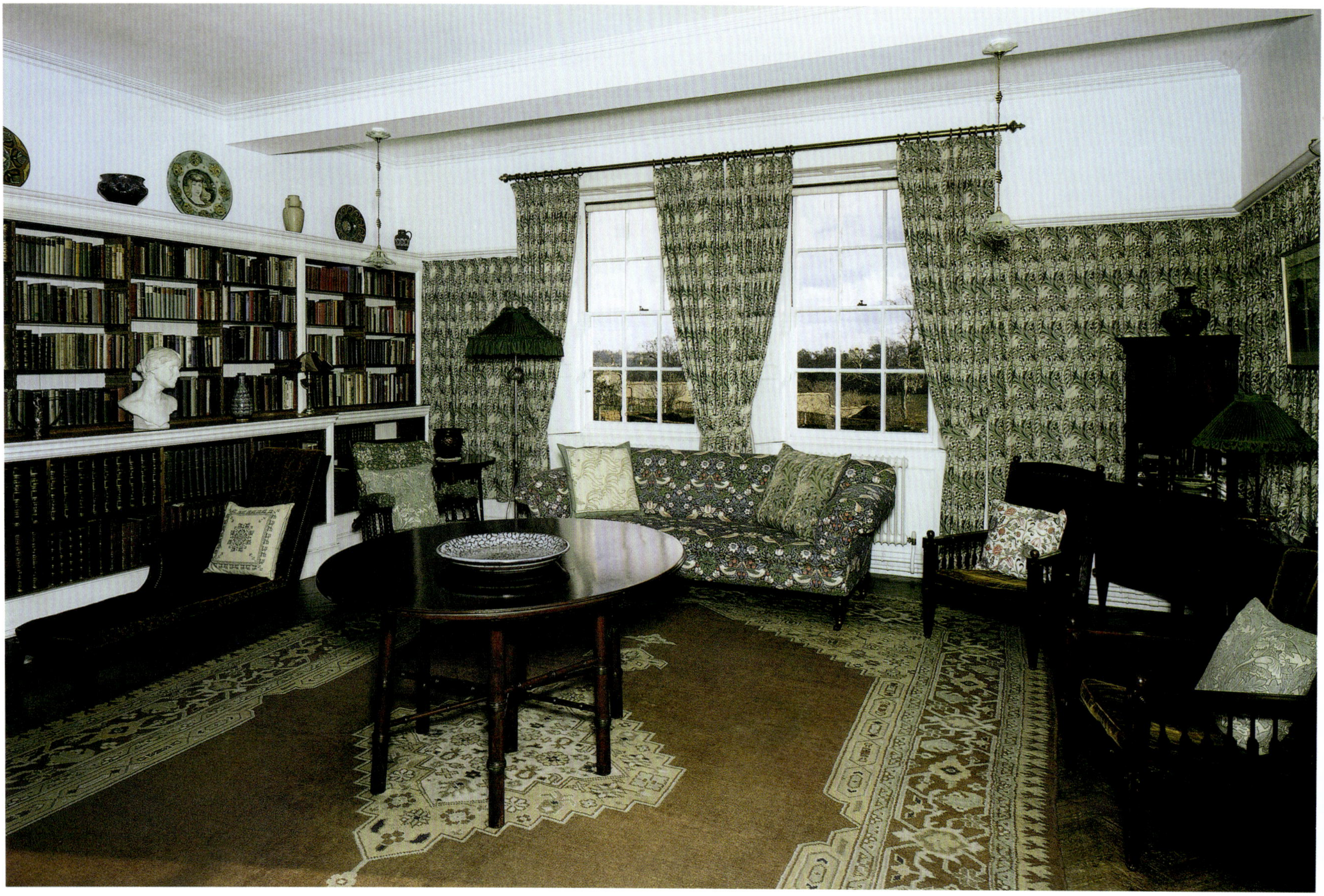

Philip Webb and **Morris & Co.**,
The Morning Room, c. 1892-1894.
Standen, East Grinstead.

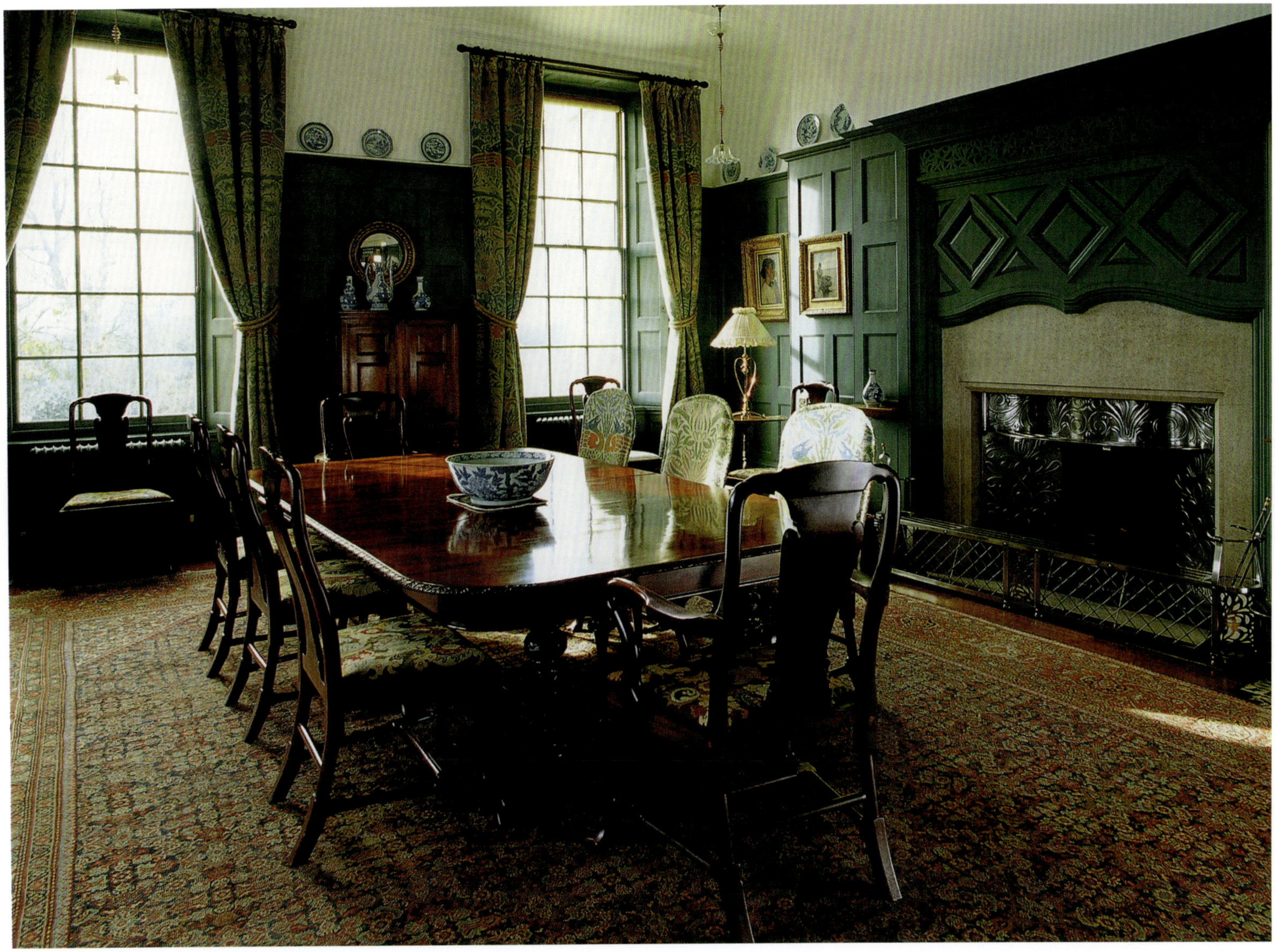

S. & H. Jewell & Co. (for the table and Queen Ann chairs) and **Philip Webb** (for the fireplace design), *The Dining Room*, 1896 (furniture). Standen, East Grinstead.

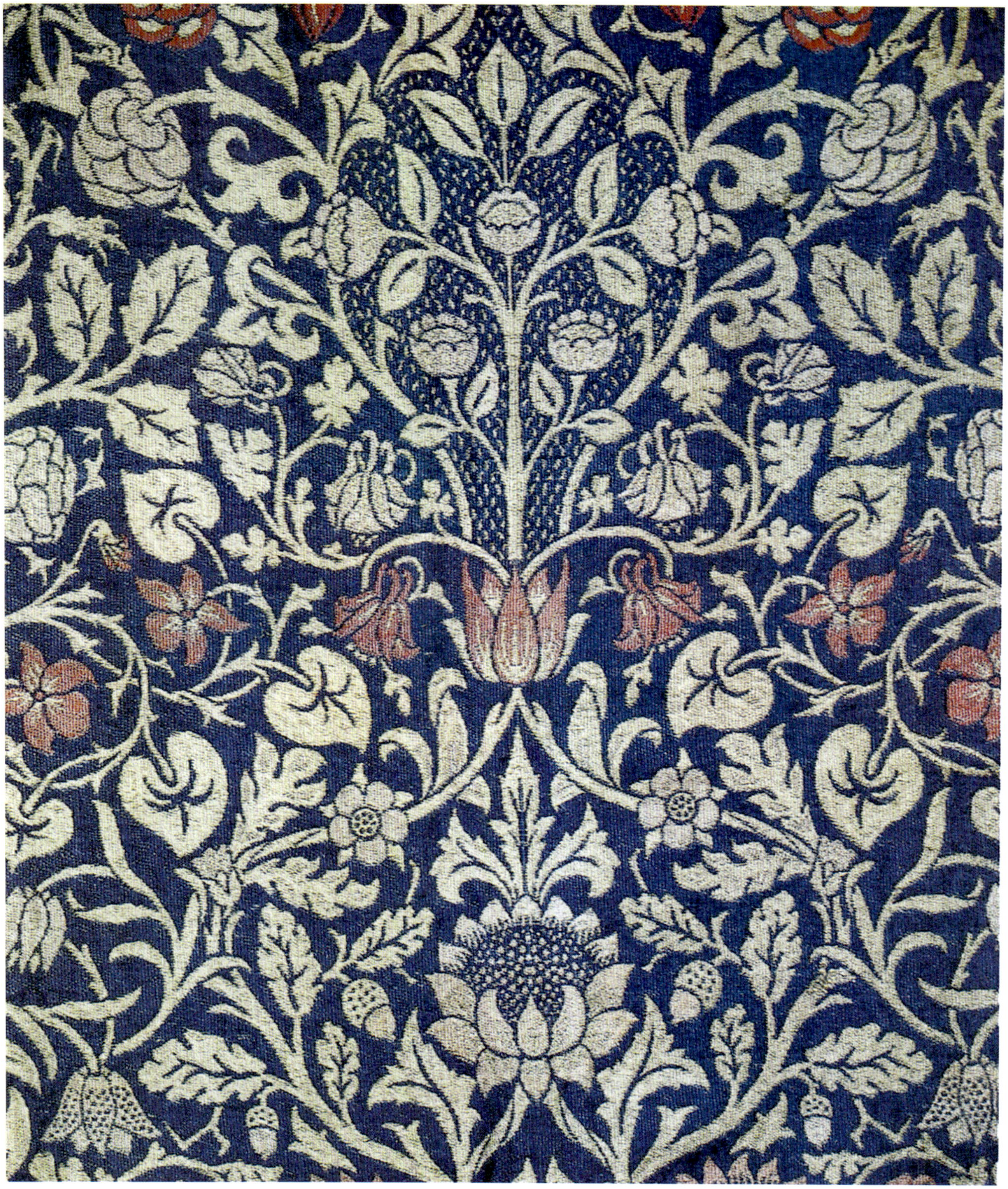

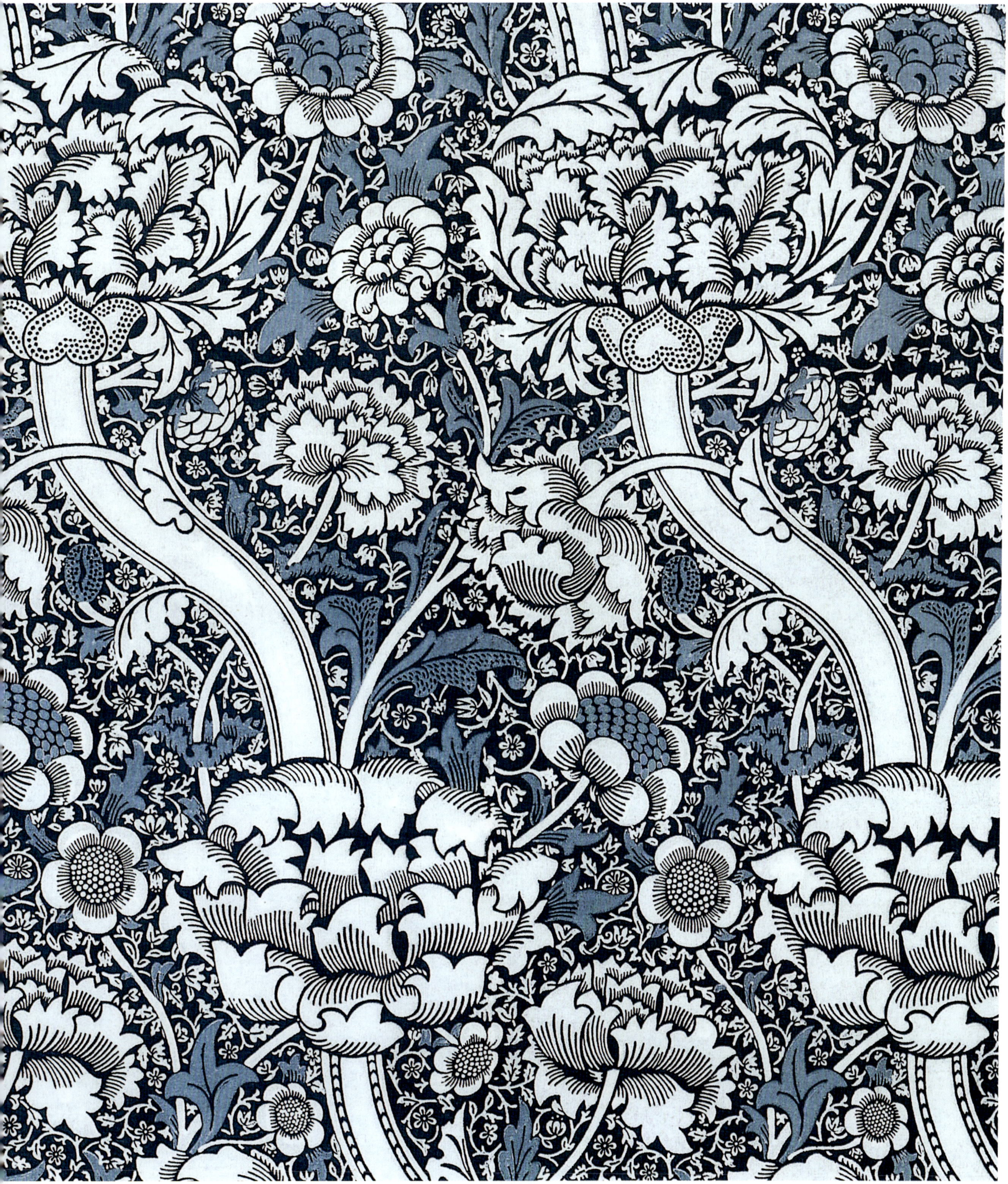

uses of daily life, and that the beginning of art was in getting the country clean and the people beautiful. He pointed then to the fact that all good architecture rose out of domestic work, that before great churches and palaces could be built it was necessary to build good doors and garret windows. The best architecture was simply a glorified roof. His own statement runs: "The dome of the Vatican, the porches of Rheims or Chartres, the vaults and arches of their aisles, the canopy of the tomb, and the spire of the belfry are art forms resulting from the mere requirement that a certain space should be strongly covered from heat and rain." In the *Crown of Wild Olive* we meet the startling statement that the builders of the great medieval cathedrals corrupted Gothic architecture – they corrupted it by forgetting the people and devoting it to priestly and aesthetic needs, until, losing its vitality, it declined in expressiveness and ultimately ceased to be. From these and other instances, Ruskin deplored the tendency of art to narrow its appeal and to become the object of the educated classes.

However attractive much of the art of the Renaissance was to him, he yet saw that it had for foundation nothing but the pride of life – the pride of the so-called superior classes. His strongest statement on this point occurs in *The Two Paths*:

"The great lesson of history is, that all the fine arts hitherto, having been supported by the selfish power of the 'noblesse', and never having extended their range to the comfort or the relief of the mass of the people – the arts, I say, thus practiced, and thus matured, have only accelerated the ruin of the states they adorned; and at the moment when, in any kingdom, you point to the triumph of its greatest artists, you point also to the determined hour of the kingdom's decline. The names of great painters are like passing bells: in the name of Velásquez, you hear sounded the fall of Spain; in the name of Leonardo, that of Milan; in the name of Raphael, that of Rome. And there is profound justice in this; for in proportion to the nobleness of the power is the guilt of its use for purposes vain or vile; and hitherto the greater the art the more surely has it been used, and used solely, for the decoration of pride or the provoking of sensuality. We may abandon the hope – or if you like the words better – we may disdain the temptation of the pomp and grace of Italy in her youth. For us there can be no more the throne of marble, for us no more the vault of gold; but for us there is the loftier and lovelier privilege of bringing the power and charm of art within the reach of the humble and the poor; and as the magnificence of past ages failed by its narrowness and its pride, ours may prevail and continue by its universality and its lowliness."

The beauty which is to be "a joy forever" must be a joy for all.

William Morris,
Violet and Columbine, 1883.
Pattern for woven textile.
Private collection.

William Morris,
Wandle (name of the river next to Morris' workshop), 1884.
Pattern for printed fabric, block-printed and indigo discharge on cotton, 160.1 x 96.5 cm.
Victoria & Albert Museum, London.

John Henry Dearle (for the design) and **Morris & Co.** (for the production),
Iris, 1902.
Wallpaper.
Private collection.

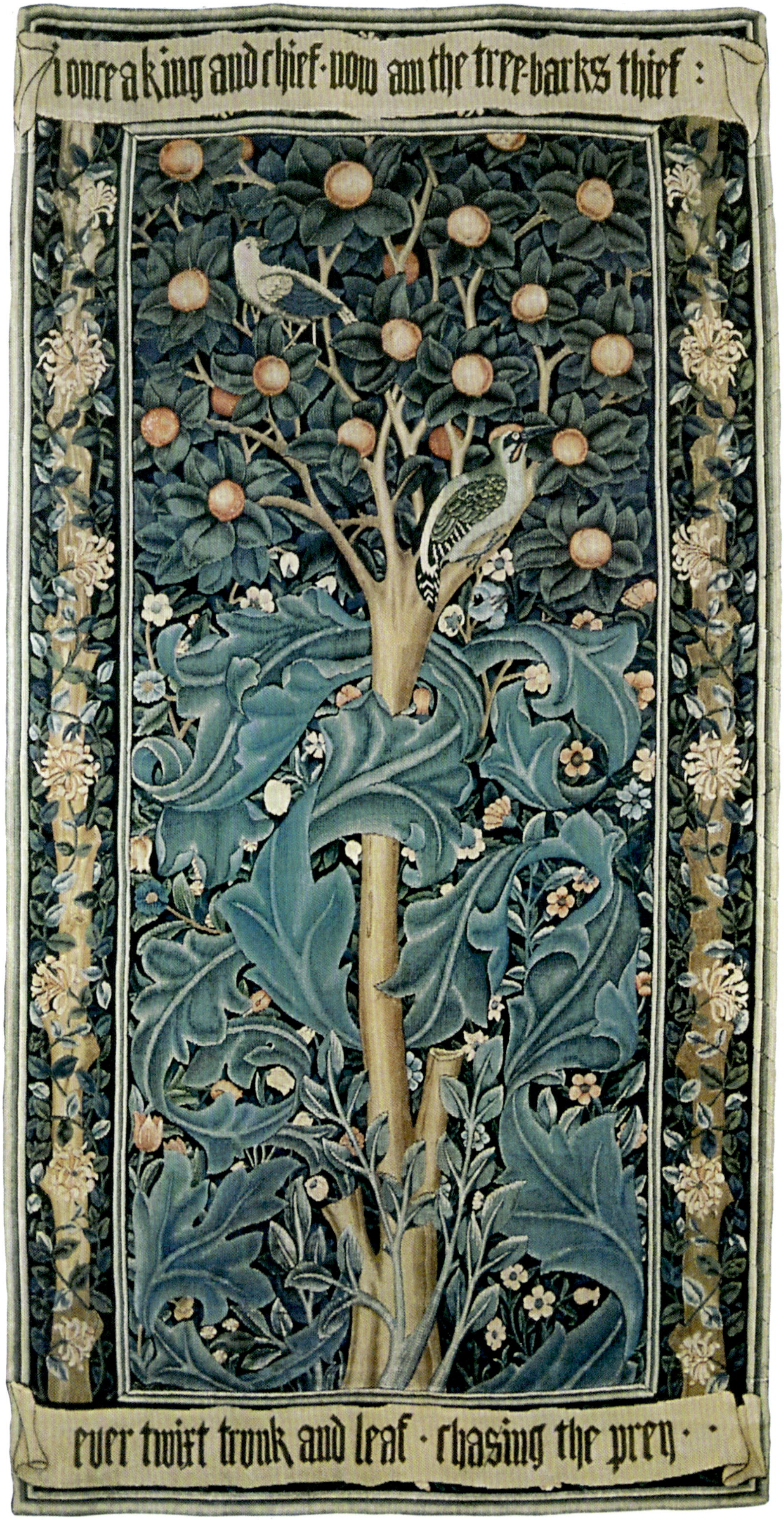

William Morris,
The Woodpecker, 1885.
Tapestry.
William Morris Gallery, London.

Edward Burne-Jones and
William Morris (for the design) and
Morris & Co. (for the production),
Pomona, 1885.
Tapestry woven wool, silk and mohair on a cotton warp, 300 x 210 cm.
The Whitworth Gallery,
University of Manchester, Manchester.

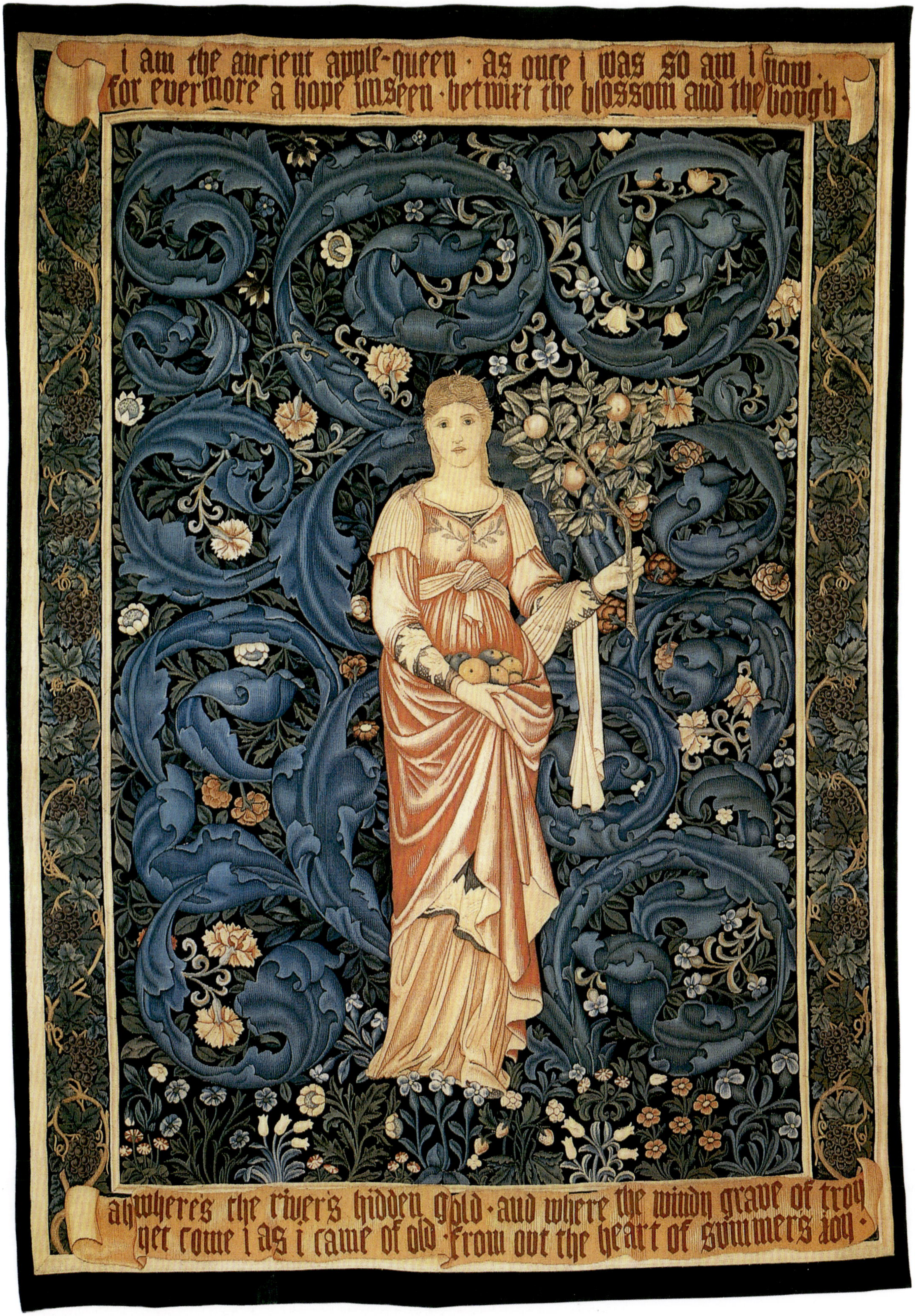
i am the ancient apple-queen · as once i was so am i now ·
for evermore a hope unseen · betwixt the blossom and the bough ·
ah wheres the river's hidden gold · and where the windy grave of troy
yet come i as i came of old · from out the heart of summers joy ·

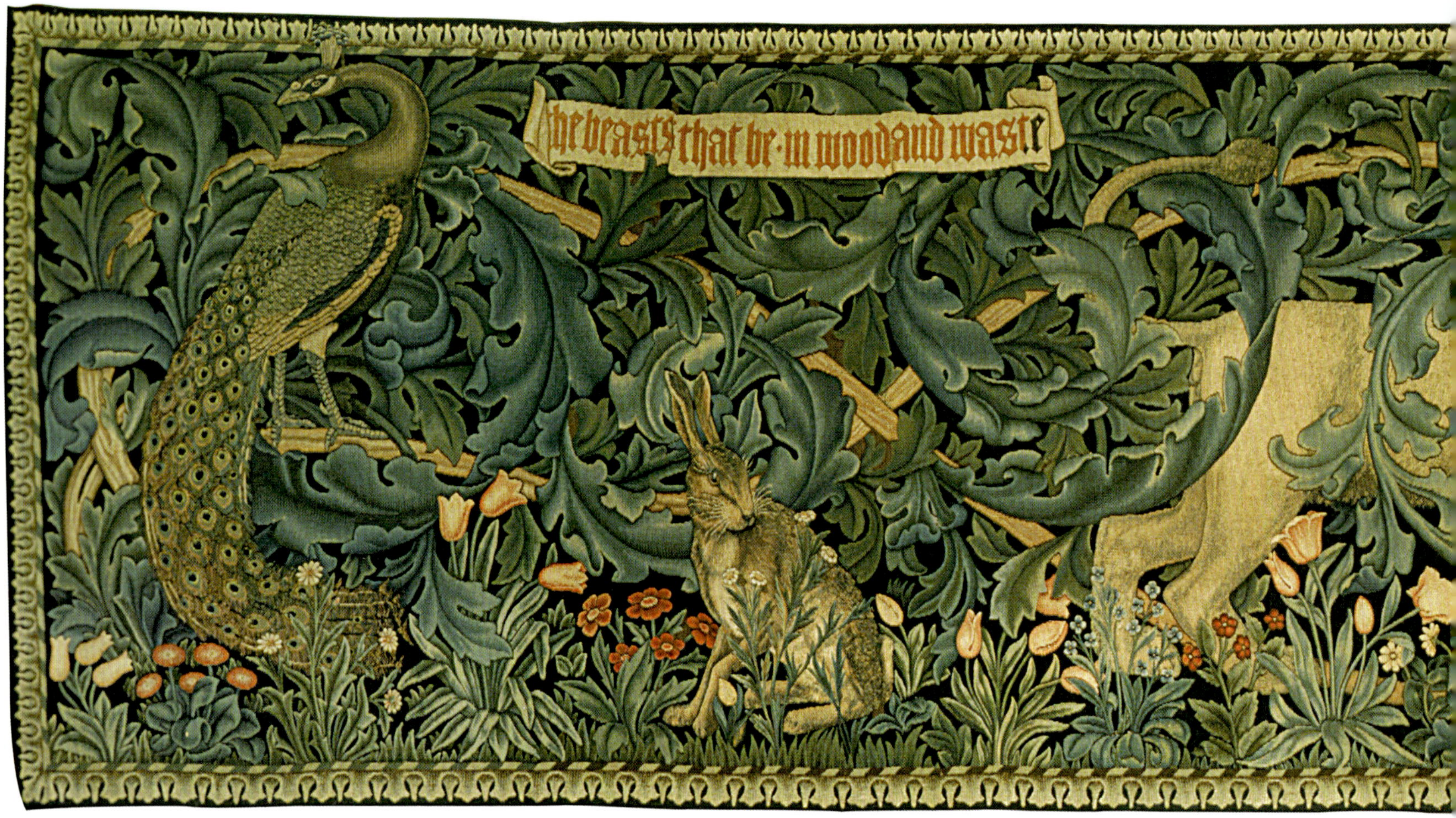

The ground is now cleared for understanding Ruskin's teachings respecting industry. He had proclaimed that art must spring from the people, that its test was its lowliness and its universality. He now reversed the proposition, and announced the necessity of ennobling the people through association with art – an association to be attained by means of their labour. The separation that had occurred between the artist and the artisan had worked injury to both kinds of products. The artists had become effeminate because they were not used to handling rough materials; workmen had become debased because they could not exercise their faculties in designing. The problem was to universalise art and to ennoble labour. Whether labour was dignified or not depended upon its character; whether rough and exhausting or with elements of recreation; whether done under conditions of slavery or freedom. Some work is degrading by its physical conditions; other work is dangerous to health; still other work destroys moral character. Labour can be dignified only as it has the character of dignity. In *The Seven Lamps* it is written that "objects are noble or ignoble in proportion to the amount of the energy of that mind which has visibly been employed upon them." But fullness of life involves a large degree of freedom.

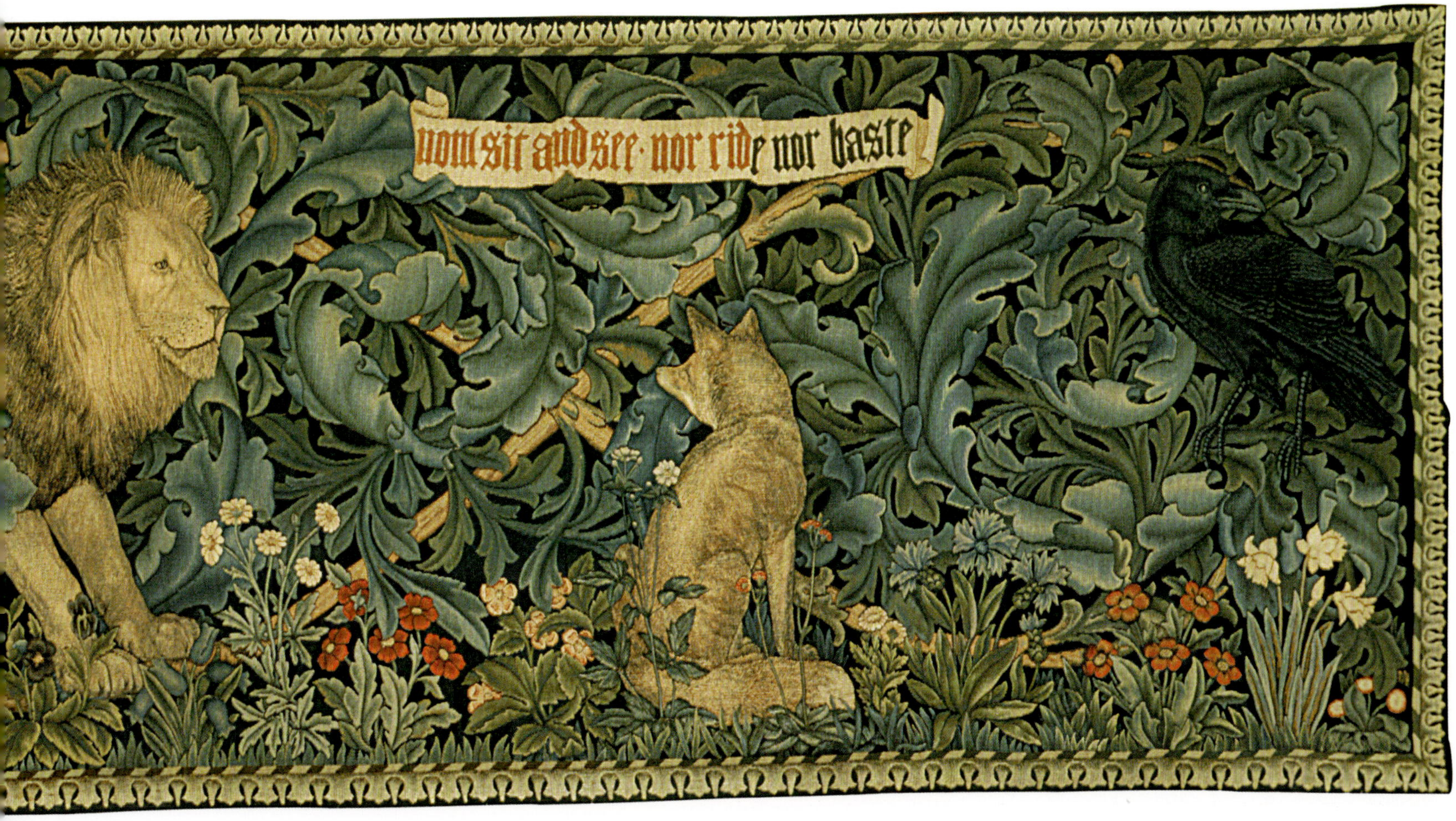

The sight of a degraded workman caused Ruskin the deepest gloom, while that of a free workman aroused his highest enthusiasm.

He observed and commended in the free workman the hand's muscular firmness and subtlety, the brain's instantaneously selective and ordinant energy, the will's unceasing governance, and the whole being's joyful play and exertion – a joy such as the eagle seems to take in the wave of his wings. His defense of Gothic architecture as against the Greek is based upon the nature of the Gothic as involving the liberty of the workman in its design and execution, and he went so far as to assert that, in order to raise up the workman of the present day into a living soul, the whole system of Greek architecture as now practised – the system, that is, of ordered and deindividualised work – must be annihilated. To produce a free workman education and science should strive, for surely these are made for man and not man for them. The modern industrial problem is to decrease the number of employments involving degradation, and to raise the character of others by allowing the utmost possible freedom to the workmen.

William Morris, **Philip Webb** and **John Henry Dearle** (for the design) and the **Merton Abbey Workshop** (for the production),
The Forest, 1887.
Tapestry, woven wool and silk on a cotton warp, 121.9 x 452 cm.
Victoria & Albert Museum, London.

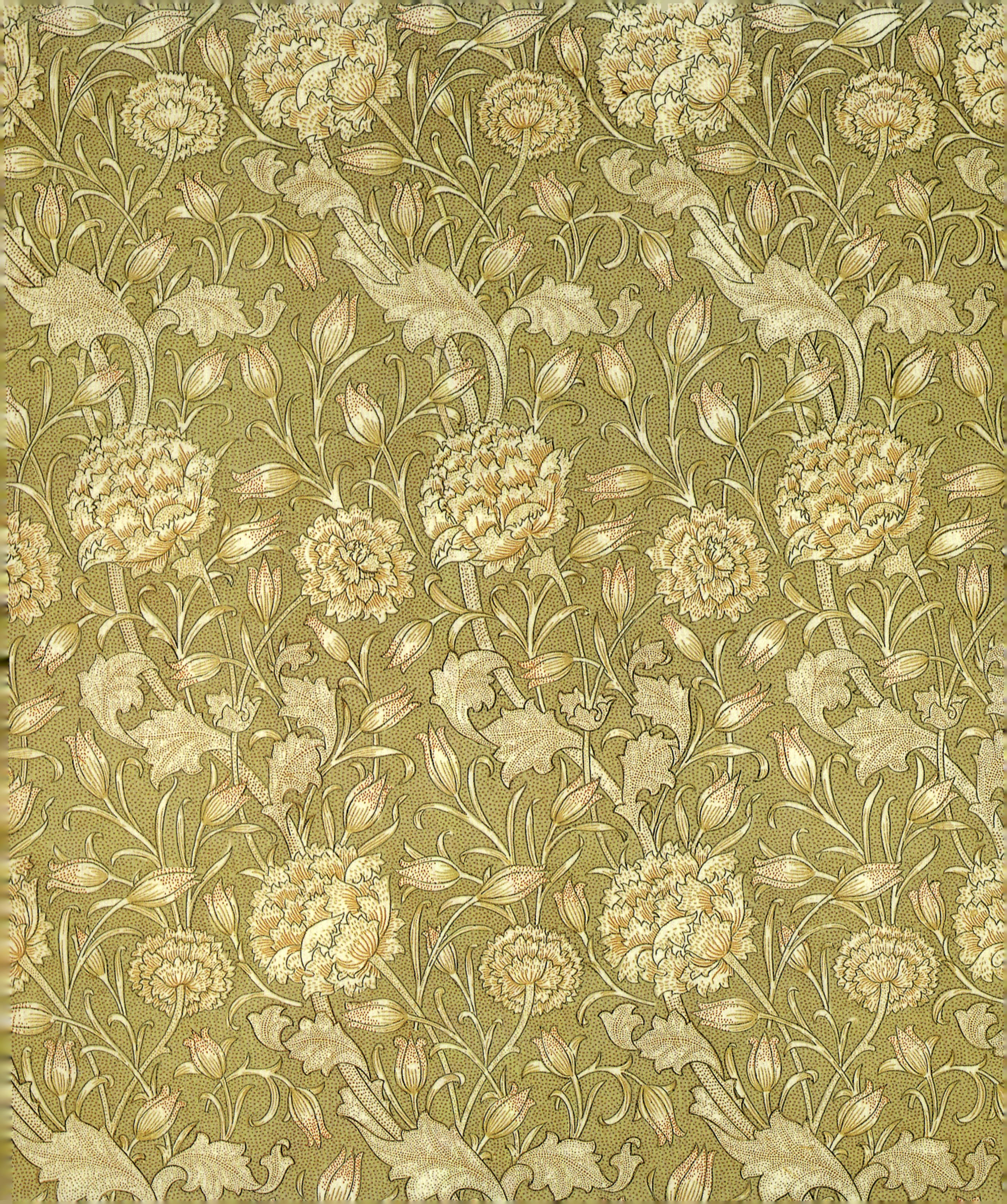

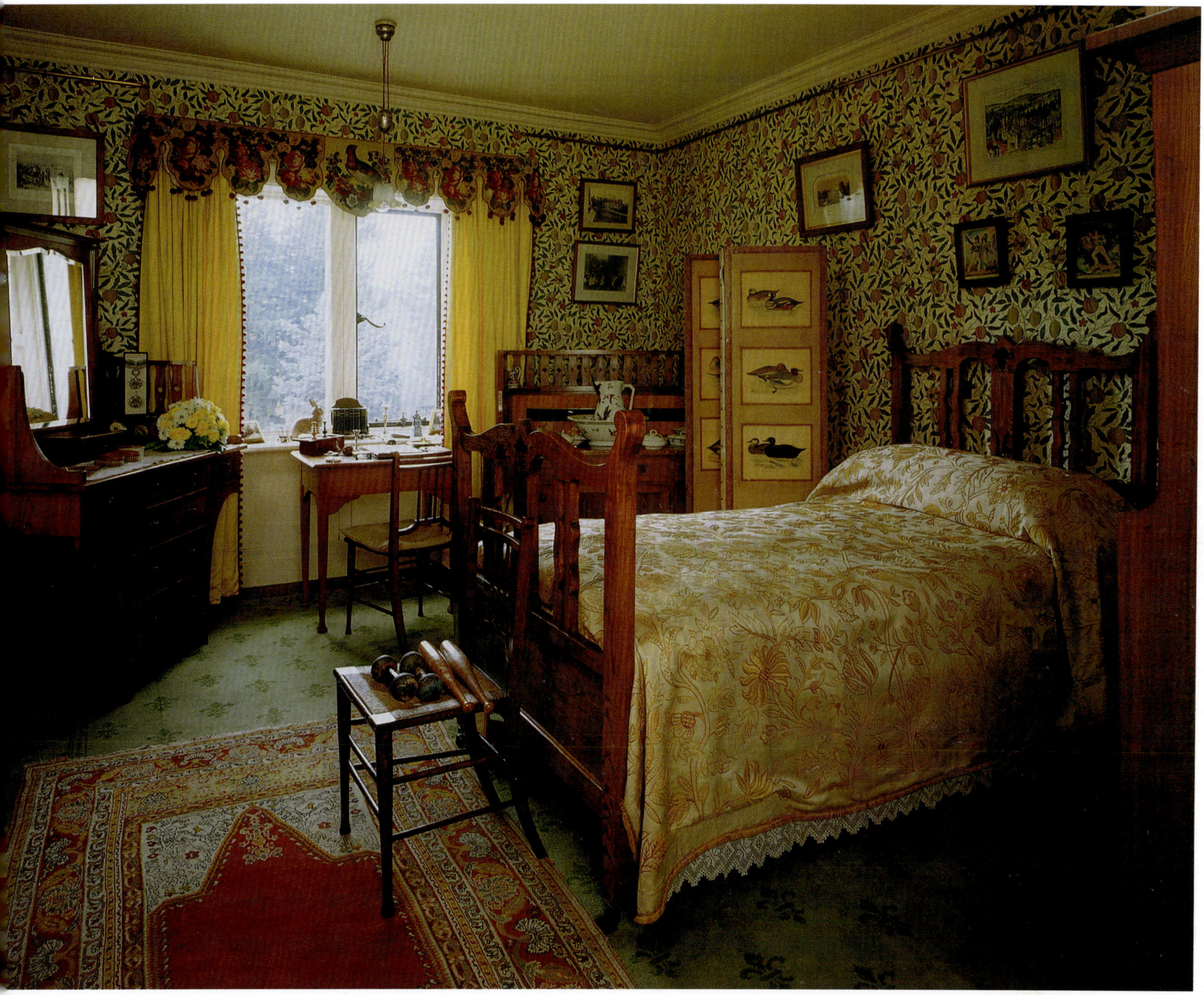

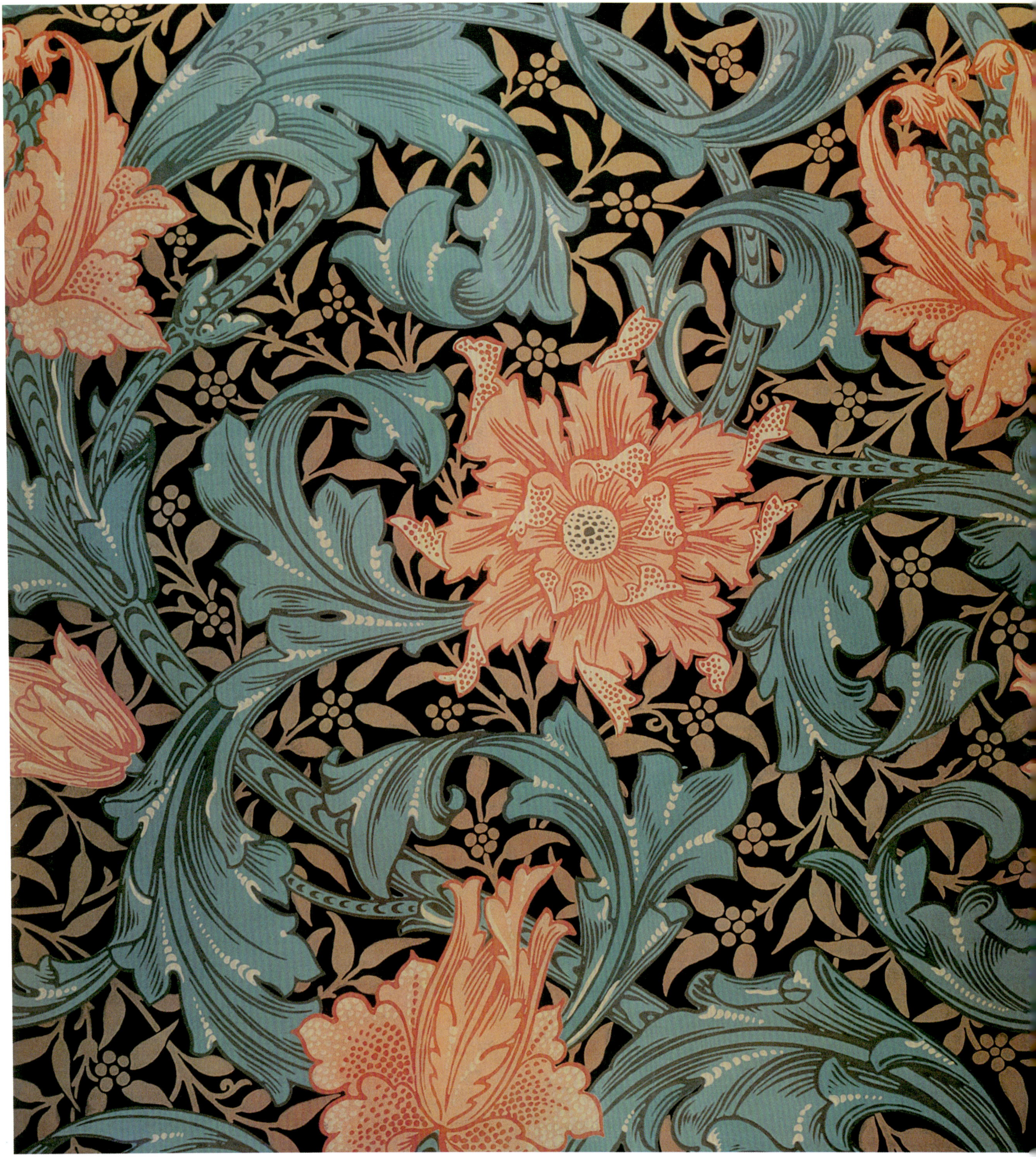

Another fundamental proposition in Ruskin's theory of industry is that all good work must be free hand-work. Probably Ruskin would admit to himself that his antagonism to the machine was too extreme; but to cry out against the machine is one way of insisting upon the value of human life. If the machine was always employed in the service of man, to relieve him of drudgery and of all work debasing in its nature, if it always did work for him, and produce the things he needed, little could be said against it. But in the service of mammon and greed, compelling men to be its slave and lackey, it is anything but a lovely spectacle, and to Ruskin's eyes it appeared in the guise of a monster and not of a minister. And there is this to be said, that as soon as the principles of art are applied to industry the machine ceases to have much importance, and we can agree with the twenty-fifth aphorism of *The Seven Lamps*, that "All good work must be free hand-work."

The social wrong wrought by division of labour is another phase of Ruskin's arraignment of current industrialism. A profitable device from the point of view of production, considered as mere quantity, division of labour, especially in association with machinery and forced by competition, does injury to the producer and eventually to the consumer. It is a social wrong to the workman because it tends to degrade him to a mechanism, exercises but a single set of faculties, and dissociates him from the completed product, a knowledge of which alone makes his labour rational. "It is not the labour that is divided, but the men – divided into mere segments and crumbs of life." It is a social wrong to the consumer because production, though increased in quantity, is lessened in quality, and the true utility of the goods is correspondingly lowered. In other words, the mercantile value of machinery and division of labour does not coincide with their social value, which is the true economy. "It comes to this," says J. A. Hobsors, remarking upon this point, "that only good work can produce real utilities; excessive division of labour, in degrading the character of labour, degrades the quality of commodities, and a progress estimated quantitatively in increase of low-class material forms of wealth is not true progress." The demand of art is for a whole man, a rational process, and a valuable result. Its expression is qualitative and not quantitative. And this explains why artists and those associated in art production are the first to protest against an industrial system that enforces bad workmanship.

Other aspects of his doctrine of work are presented in an early essay on pre-Raphaelitism and though this special passage was written with reference to the artist, it applies to all workers:

"It may be proved, with much certainty, that God intends no man to live in this world without working; but it seems to me no less evident that he intends every

William Morris,
Wild Tulip, 1884.
Pattern for wallpaper.
Dining Room, Wightwick Manor.
Wightwick Bank.

Richard Norman Shaw (architect) and **various designers,**
The Yellow Bedroom, 1883-1884.
Cragside House, Garden and Estate, Rothbury.

William Morris,
Single Stem, c. 1905.
Wallpaper, colour print from woodblocks.
Victoria & Albert Museum, London.

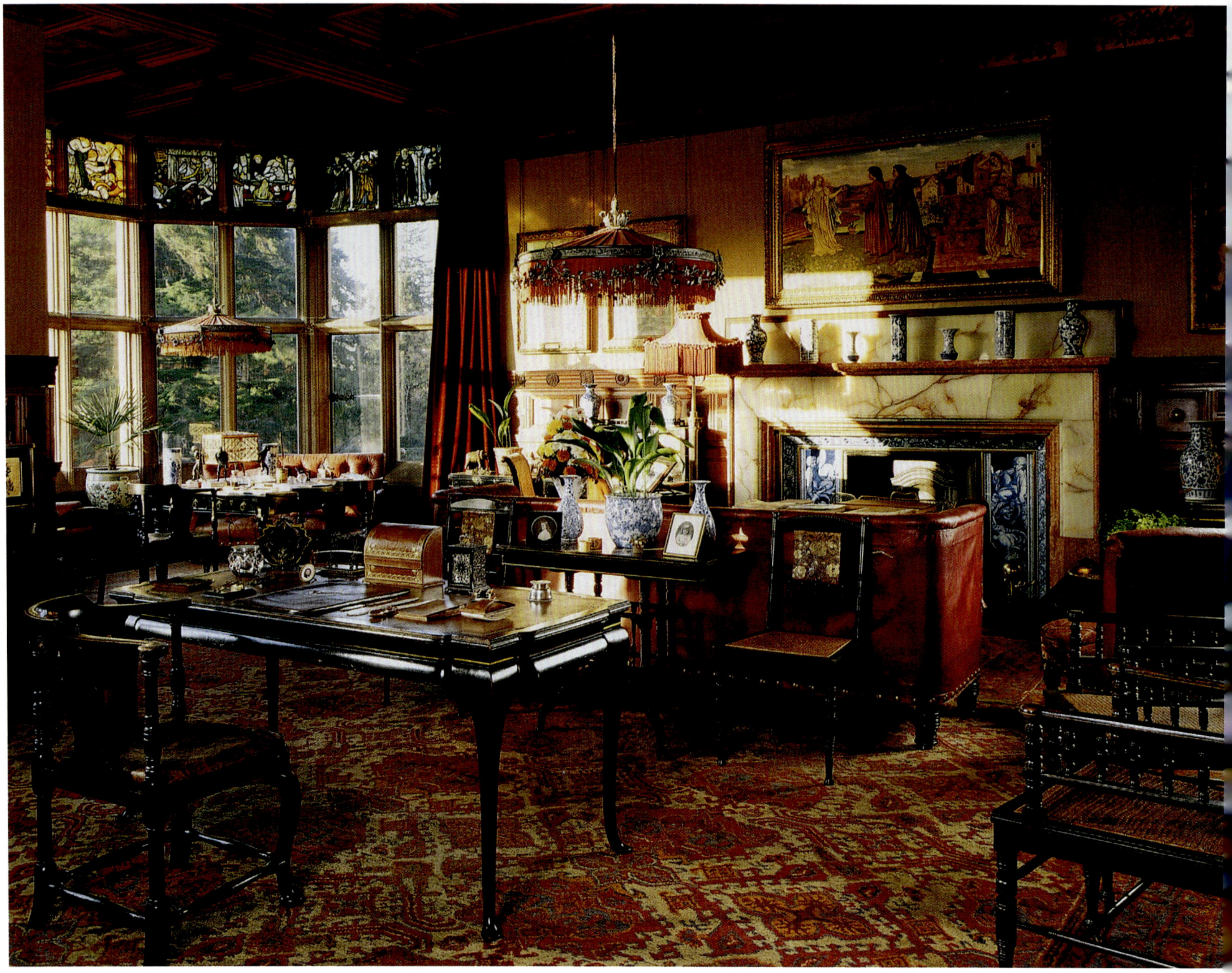

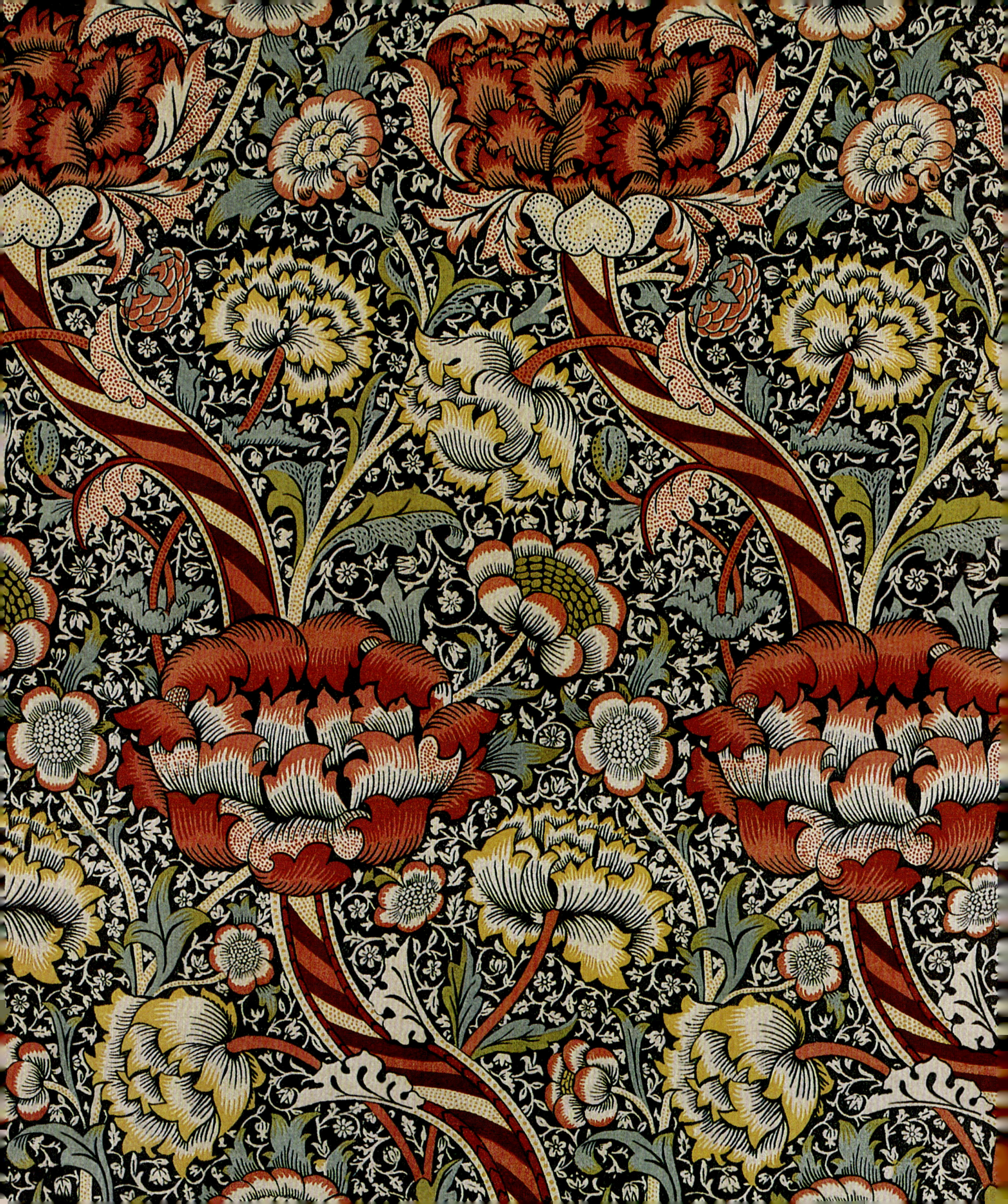

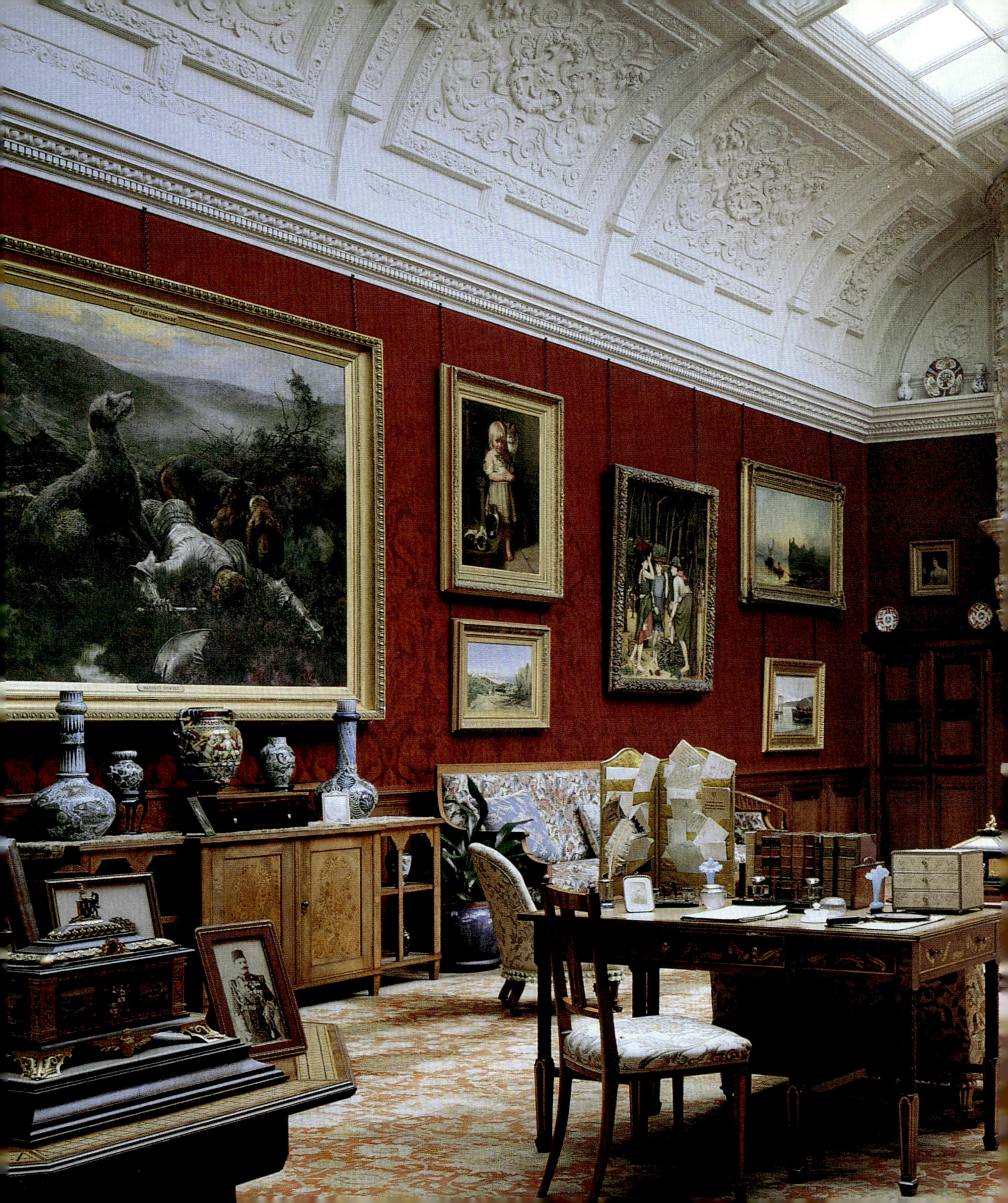

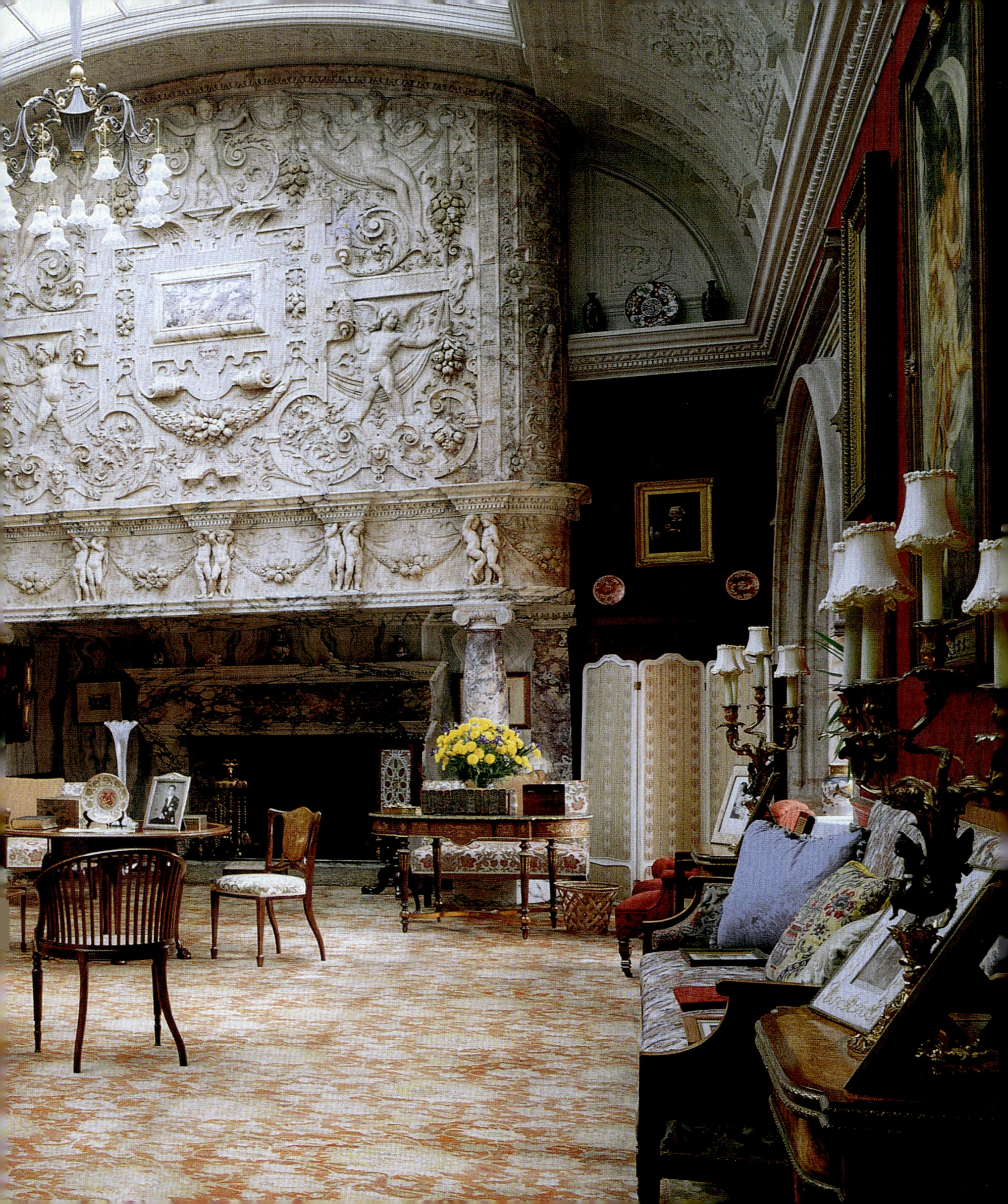

man to be happy in his work. It is written, 'in the sweat of thy brow,' but it was never written 'in the breaking of thine heart,' thou shalt eat bread; and I find that, as on the one hand, infinite misery is caused by idle people, who both fail in doing what was appointed for them to do, and set in motion various springs of mischief in matters in which they should have had no concern, so on the other hand, no small misery is caused by overworked and unhappy people, in the dark views which they necessarily take up themselves, and force upon others, of work itself. Were it not so, I believe the fact of their being unhappy is in itself a violation of divine law, and sign of some kind of folly or sin in their way of life. Now in order that people may be happy in their work, these three things are needed: they must be fit for it; they must not do too much of it; and they must have a sense of success in it – not a doubtful sense, such as needs some testimony of other people for its confirmation, but a sure sense, or rather knowledge, that so much work has been done well, and faithfully done, whatever the world may say or think about it. So that in order that a man maybe happy, it is necessary that he should not only be capable of his work, but a good judge of his work."

In other words a certain amount of leisure, a certain amount of skill, and a certain amount of intelligence, are requisite for the best work. Given, then, ideal conditions for work, what profits should a man have for his labour?

The essential reward lies naturally in the happiness which the work engenders. Labour that is wholesome exercise, involving the skill and intelligence and character of the individual, is not really labour in the Ruskinian sense, for there is in it no expense of life. By the recognition of the human values of labour the question of wages is rendered of secondary moment. The real demand of workmen who have not been degraded or corrupted by the mammonism of the day is not for higher wages but for better conditions of labour. The assumption that a man is a repository of energy to be elicited by wages alone is unworthy any observer of men. The wage system is simply one stage better than the slave system it superseded, and wages high or low is still a token of industrial bondage. The distinguishing sign of slavery, Ruskin said, "is to have a price and to be bought for it." The best work of artists, poets, and scientists is never paid for, nor can the value of toil in these fields be ever measured in terms of money. "The largest quantity of work," our economist declares, "will not be done by this curious engine (the Soul) for pay, or under pressure. It will be done only when the motive force, that is to say, the will or spirit of the creatures is brought up to the greatest strength by its own proper fuel, namely, by the affections." Could workmen today direct their united energies toward self-education, so that the nature by which they are surrounded and the life with which they are connected might mean more to them, and so that the things they possess might be more highly valued; could employers understand that work is done

Richard Norman Shaw (architect) and **Morris & Co.** (for the stained-glass windows), library, 1883-1884. Carved oak ceiling and wainscoting. Cragside House, Garden and Estate, Rothbury.

William Morris,
Wandle (name of the river next to Morris' workshop), 1884.
Indigo-discharged and block-printed cotton, 165 x 92 cm.
Victoria & Albert Museum, London.

Richard Norman Shaw (architect) and his assistant, **W. R. Lethby** (for the design of the chimneypiece), drawing room, 1883-1884.
Carved Italian marble inglenook and fireplace.
Cragside House, Garden and Estate, Rothbury.

Morris, Marshall, Faulkner & Co.,
Moon, 1866-1868.
Panel.
The Green Dining Room,
Victoria & Albert Museum, London.

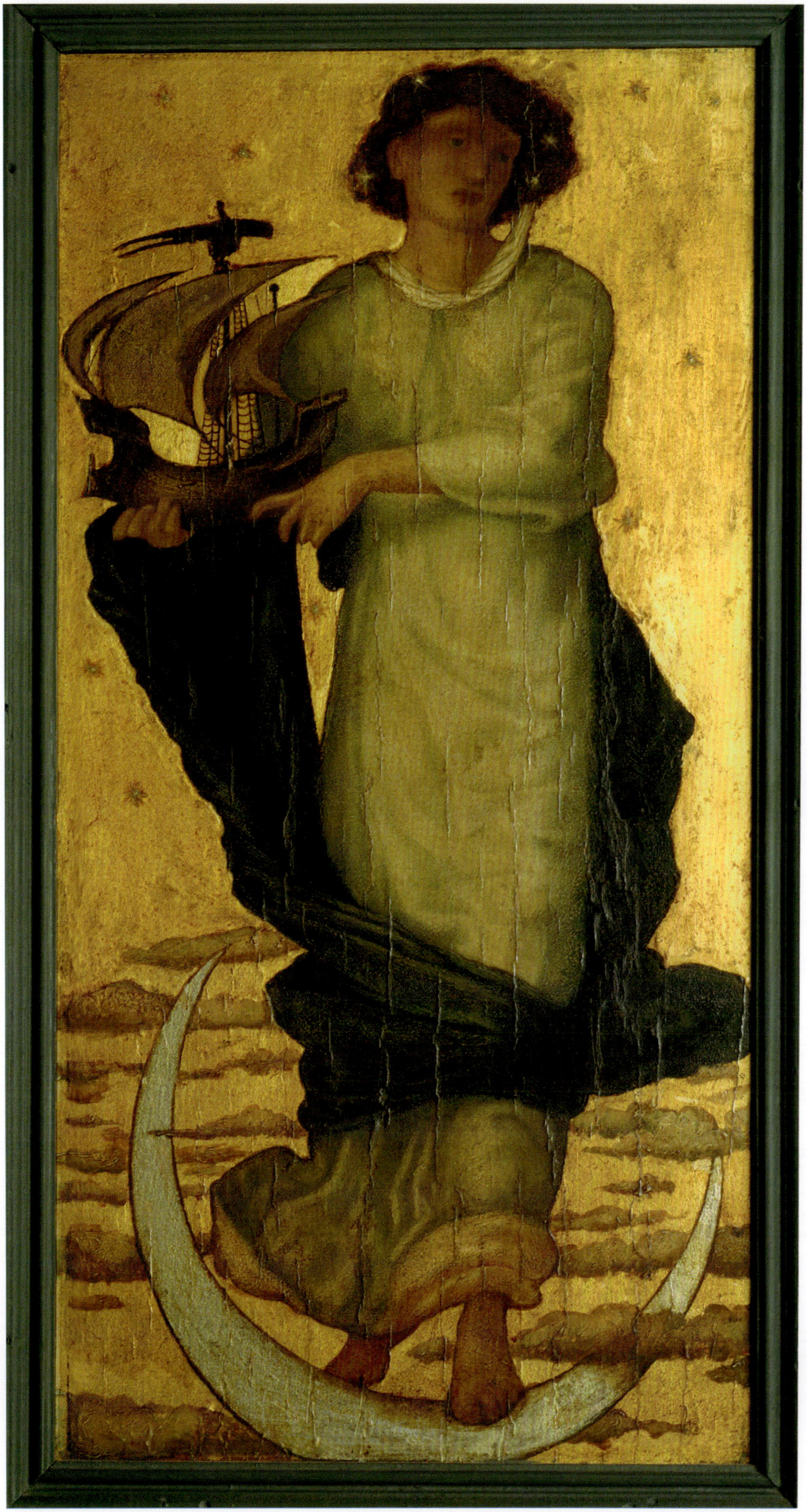

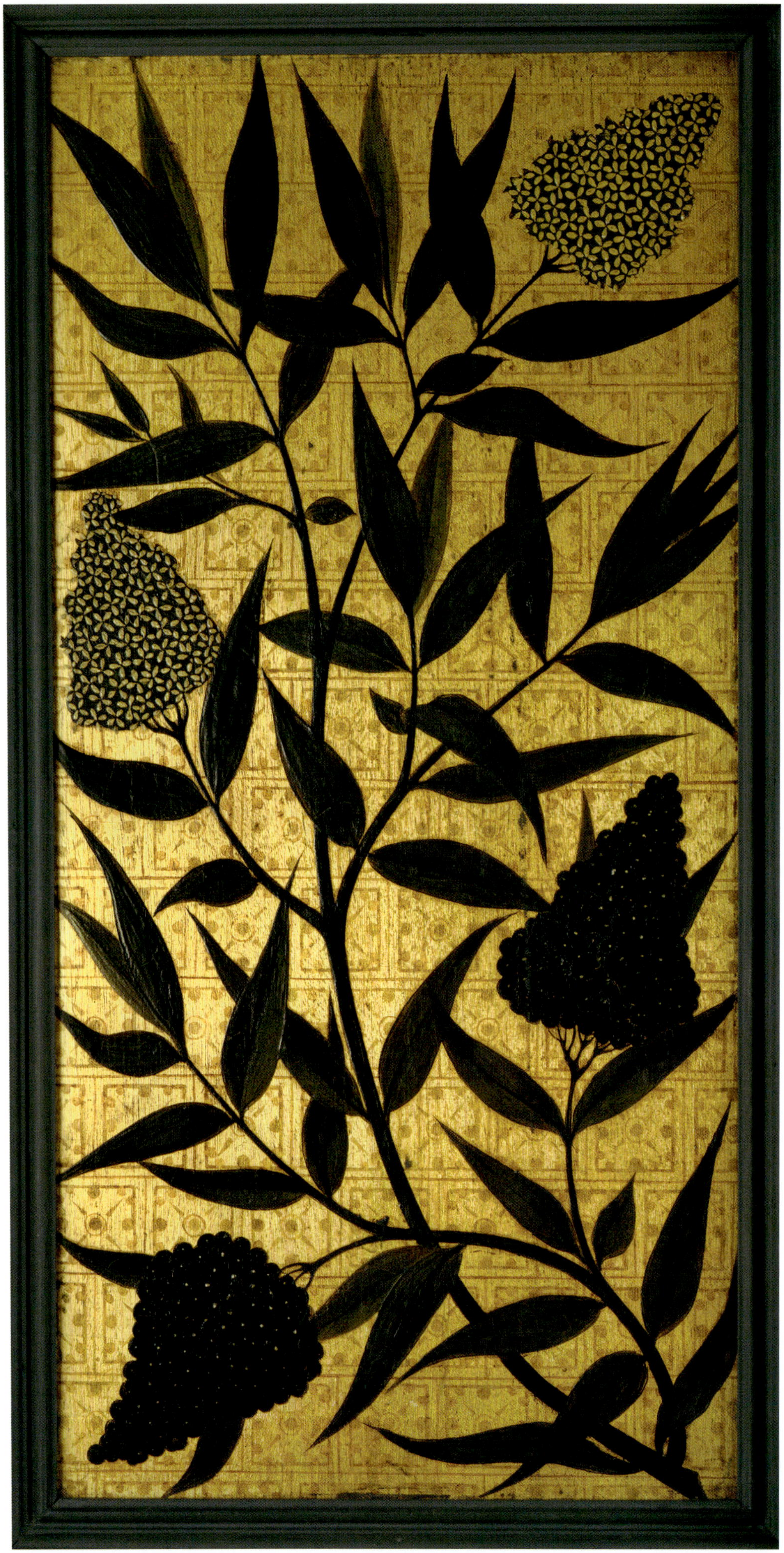

well only when it is done with a will and that no man has a thoroughly sound will unless he has character and is contented, knowing he is what he should be and is in his place; could this higher ideal of labour be generally accepted and acted upon, then would the battle between those who have and those who have not be speedily ended. The real labour problem is not that of shorter hours or of higher wages, but it is to change the character of work so that work will be its own reward. It will be remembered that Ruskin promised as the fruit of ideal labour a crown of wild olive, symbolising by this token grey honour and sweet rest. "Free-heartedness, and graciousness, and undisturbed trust, and requited love, and the sight of the peace of others, and the ministry of their pain; these – and the blue sky above you, and the sweet waters and flowers of the earth beneath; and mysteries and presences, innumerable, of living things – may yet be your riches, untormenting and divine; serviceable for the life that now is; nor, it may be, without promise of that which is to come."

Ruskin wrote a pamphlet pleading for the preservation of the great buildings of the past, then neglected and falling to ruins, and out of this suggestion came the Society for the Preservation of Ancient Buildings, in the work of which William Morris figured so conspicuously. As a writer, manufacturer, and distributer of books, he tried to apply the principles of commercial integrity and honour he had advocated. He would not advertise; he employed no middlemen; he gave no discounts; he engaged in no competitive struggle for a market; he looked out for the welfare of the workmen employed in manufacture; he used the best paper he could procure, and took extraordinary care with the printing; he began the sale of his books from a little Kentish village, at one price, and without credit. Of like nature was his experiment with a London tea-shop: putting a salaried servant in charge, he built up a successful business in tea, without advertisement or any trick of the trade, and was enabled later to turn the shop over to Miss Hill as a part of his good-tenement scheme. He was not above street-cleaning or road-making, as was shown by his forming a company to keep a certain length of London street "clean as the deck of a ship" for a given season, and by his joining in with Oxford undergraduates in mending the Hinksey road. The most considerable of his practical schemes for reform was the St. George's Company, which began to take definite shape about 1875. The general purpose of this company or guild was to socialise both capital and labour, and incidentally to demonstrate two economic propositions – one, that agriculture formed the only genuine basis of national life, and the other that happiness was derived from honest and contented co-operative labour. It was his object to collect from persons of means a fund of money sufficient to buy land, at first for a small colony of Ruskinites, who should form an ideal nucleus of perfectly just persons, and from whom the idea of justice should radiate, until the whole social body was shaped to its image. As the idea of a perfect

Morris, Marshall, Faulkner & Co.,
Elderflowers, 1866-1868.
Panel.
The Green Dining Room,
Victoria & Albert Museum, London.

Morris, Marshall, Faulkner & Co.,
The Green Dining Room, 1866-1868.
Victoria & Albert Museum, London.

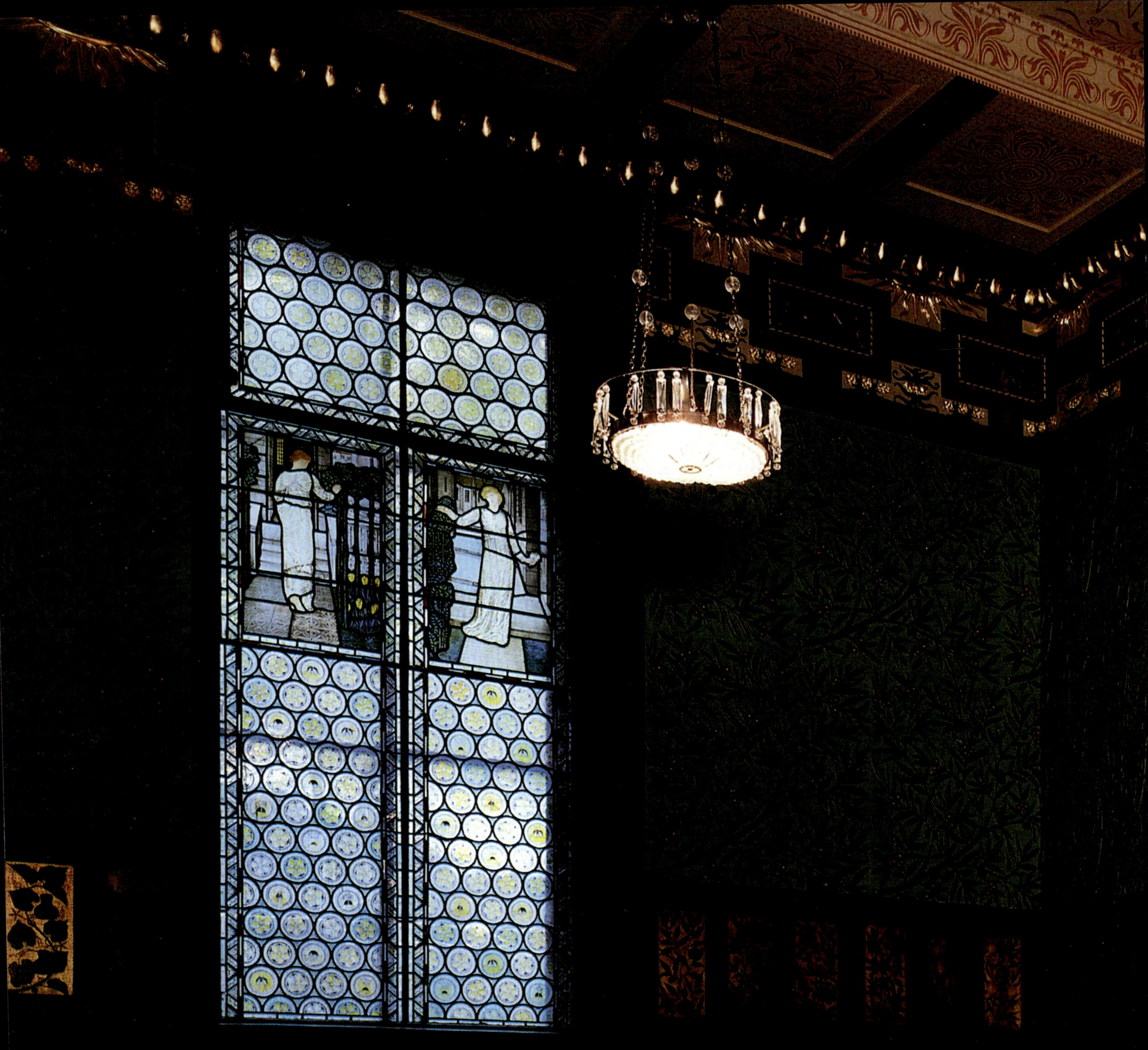

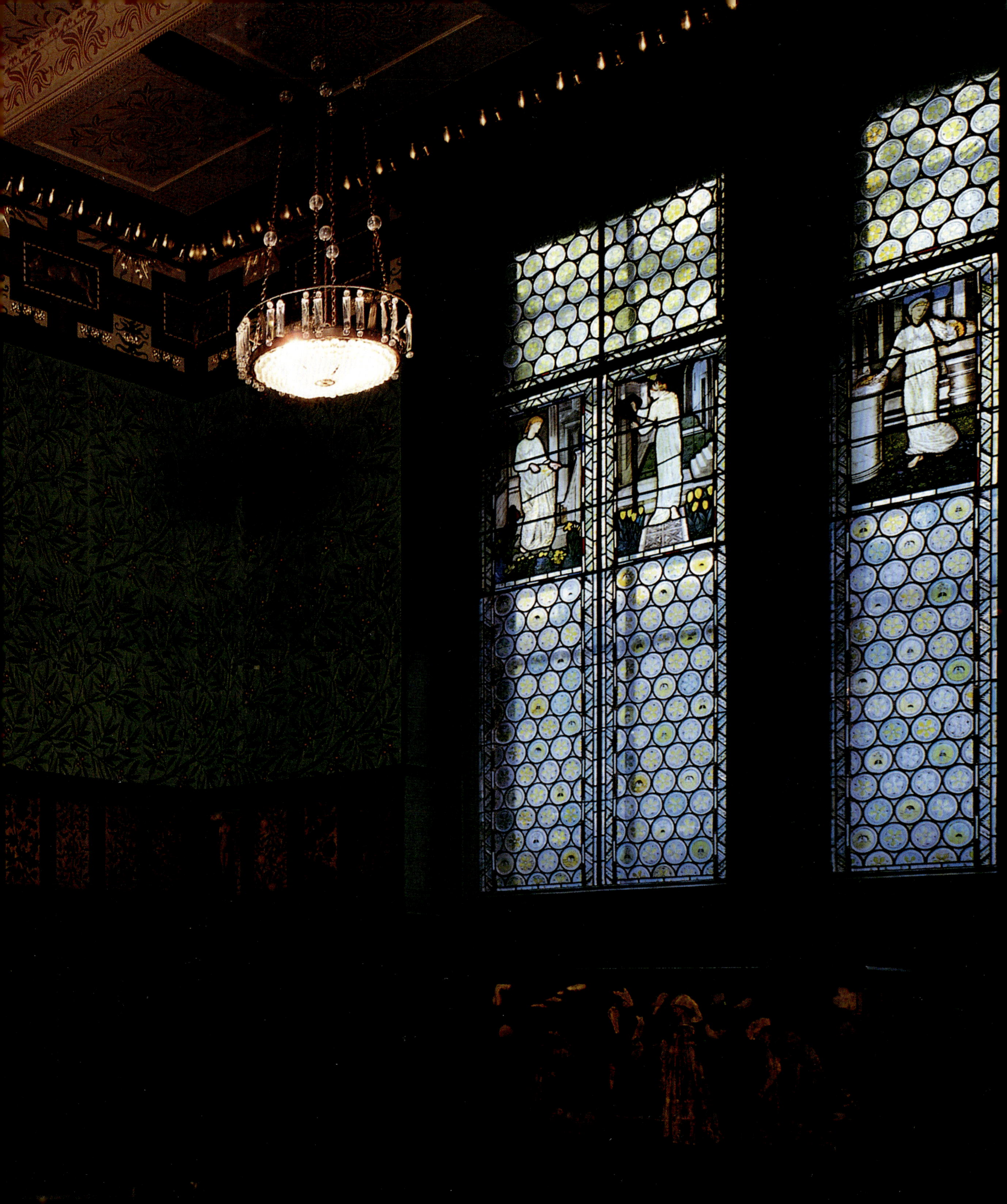

social order matured in Ruskin's mind he turned his thoughts more and more to the possibility of showing to the world, in the St. George's Guild, a copy of his vision of the new feudalism. With insufficient means for the experiment, and with no marked public approval, there was no opportunity in Ruskin's lifetime for the dream to be realised. Like many another social dream, the St. George's Guild remains a paper Utopia – though its conception by no means lacks potential for the future. As the agricultural proposition could not be proved, the guild funds were devoted to the establishment of the Ruskin Gallery in Sheffield, originally called the Museum of St. George. As this museum embodies certain of the master's ideas on education, thus much of his original plan may be said to be realised. The finer examples of man's and nature's created forms are here placed in view with reference to their ethnic, scientific, and artistic significance, and the museum is so conducted that the objects displayed minister at once to delight and instruction. With this museum as a nucleus, and with the many societies organised in England and America for the study of Ruskin's writings, the general ideal, if not all the specific ones, of the St. George's Guild may yet be realised. Already the modern revival of various home industries, particularly in spinning and weaving, is due directly to Ruskin's teachings. It was one of his opinions that workers should engage in some useful craft under wholesome and humane conditions, and another that the people, the consuming class, should have the opportunity of using sound and serviceable goods instead of being compelled to buy what Carlyle called "cheap and nasty" ones. He thought that home industry might still exist by the side of the machine-driven factory. Two opportunities for reviving the spinning and weaving industries presented themselves in Ruskin's lifetime – one on the Isle of Man, where the industry was languishing, and another among the Westmoreland cottages, where the art had long since passed away. The successful revival of these local industries was the initial phase of a general economic movement that had for social support the Home Arts and Industries Association, now the Art Workers Guild, which has succeeded in establishing many of the handicrafts on a permanent economic basis. This movement is not to be understood as a fanatical protest against machinery, and not as a return to the abandoned domestic system of mediaeval days, but rather as a modern conscious effort to advance a step beyond the factory stage of industry, and to inaugurate a new industrialism wherein the interests of both the producing and consuming classes are guarded – the one class demanding the opportunity of individual expression, and the other the satisfaction of its higher wants. So it is today that in nearly every instance of organised effort to create better industrial conditions the informing mind of Ruskin is somewhere apparent. In whatever direction, one advances it is discovered that this pioneer mind has gone on before – and as the world advances but slowly it will be long before he can be passed by.

Edward Burne-Jones
(for the design and decoration),
Ladies and Animals sideboard, 1860.
Pine painted in oil paint, with gold and silver leaf,
116.8 x 152.4 x 73.7 cm.
Victoria & Albert Museum, London.

Charles F. A. Voysey,
The Donnemara (signature Donegal Carpets design).
Carpet, 622.9 x 465.2 cm.
Private collection.

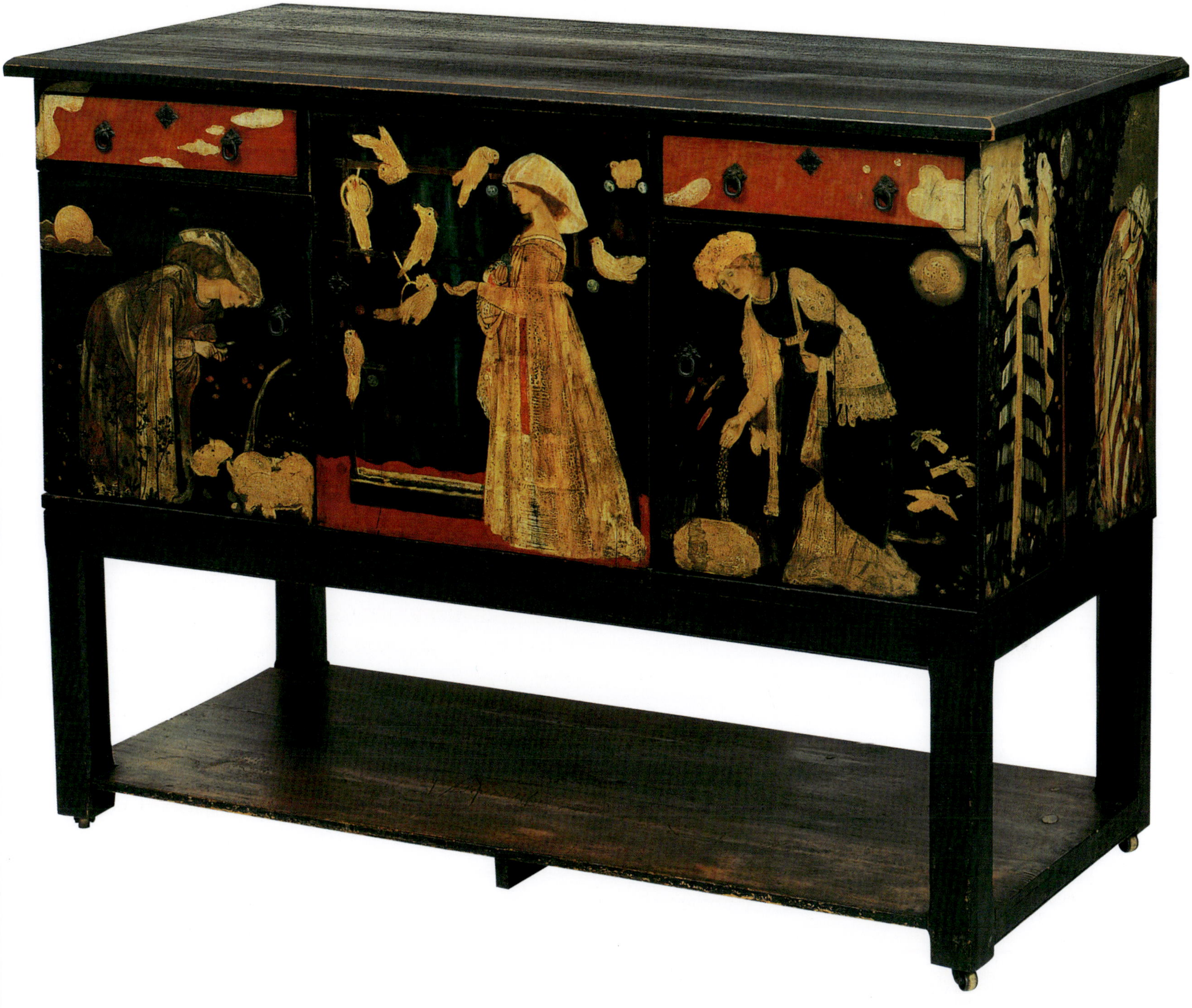

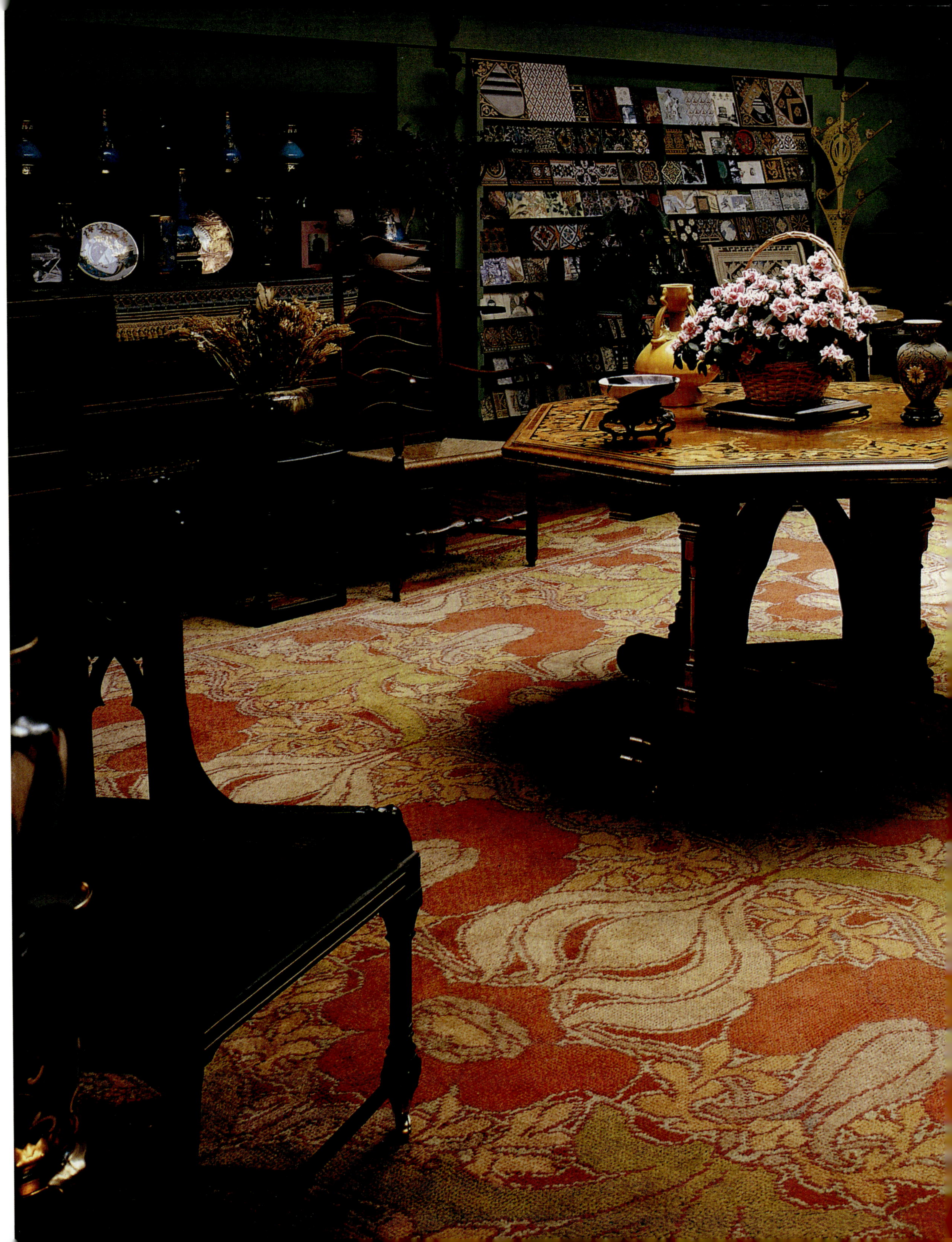

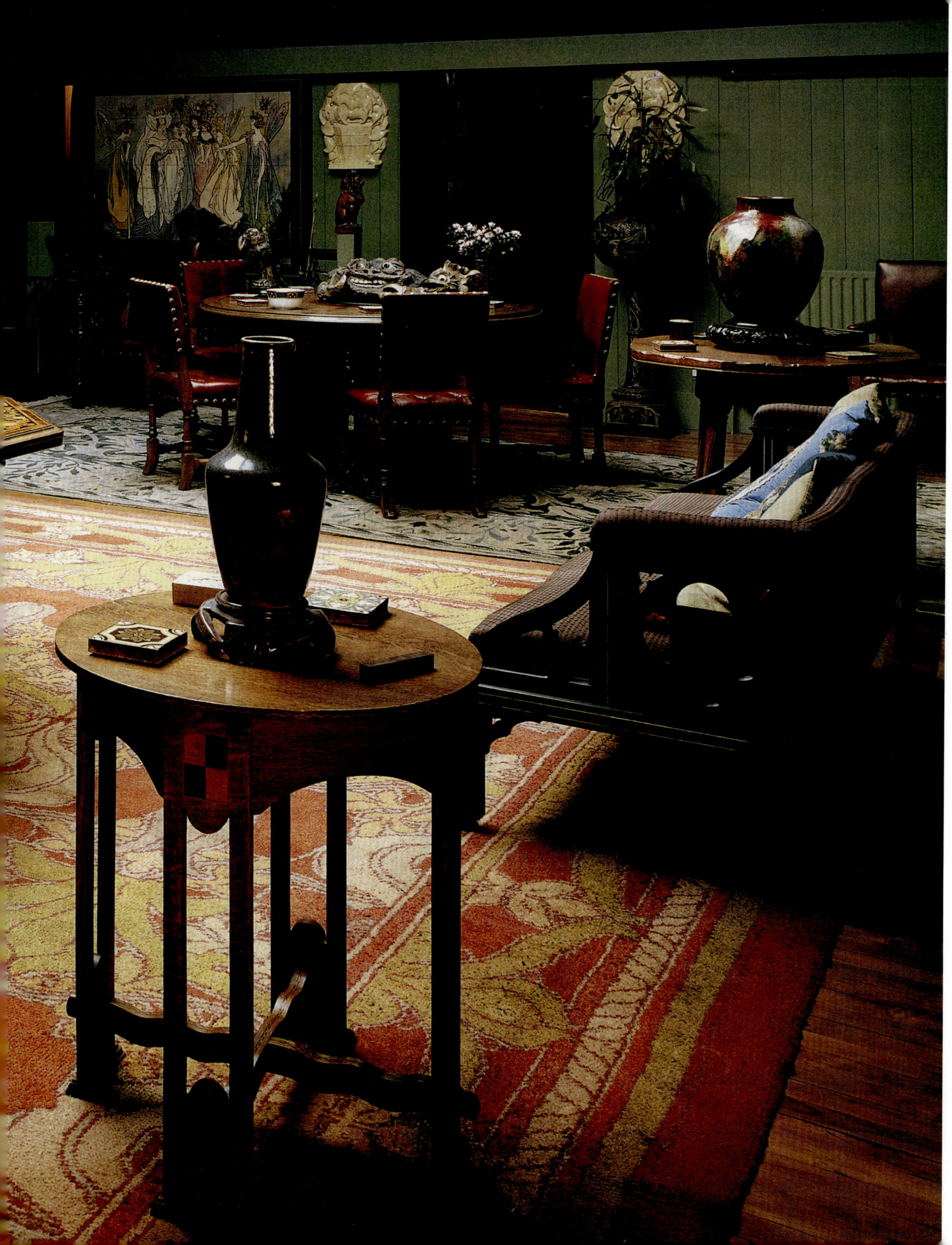

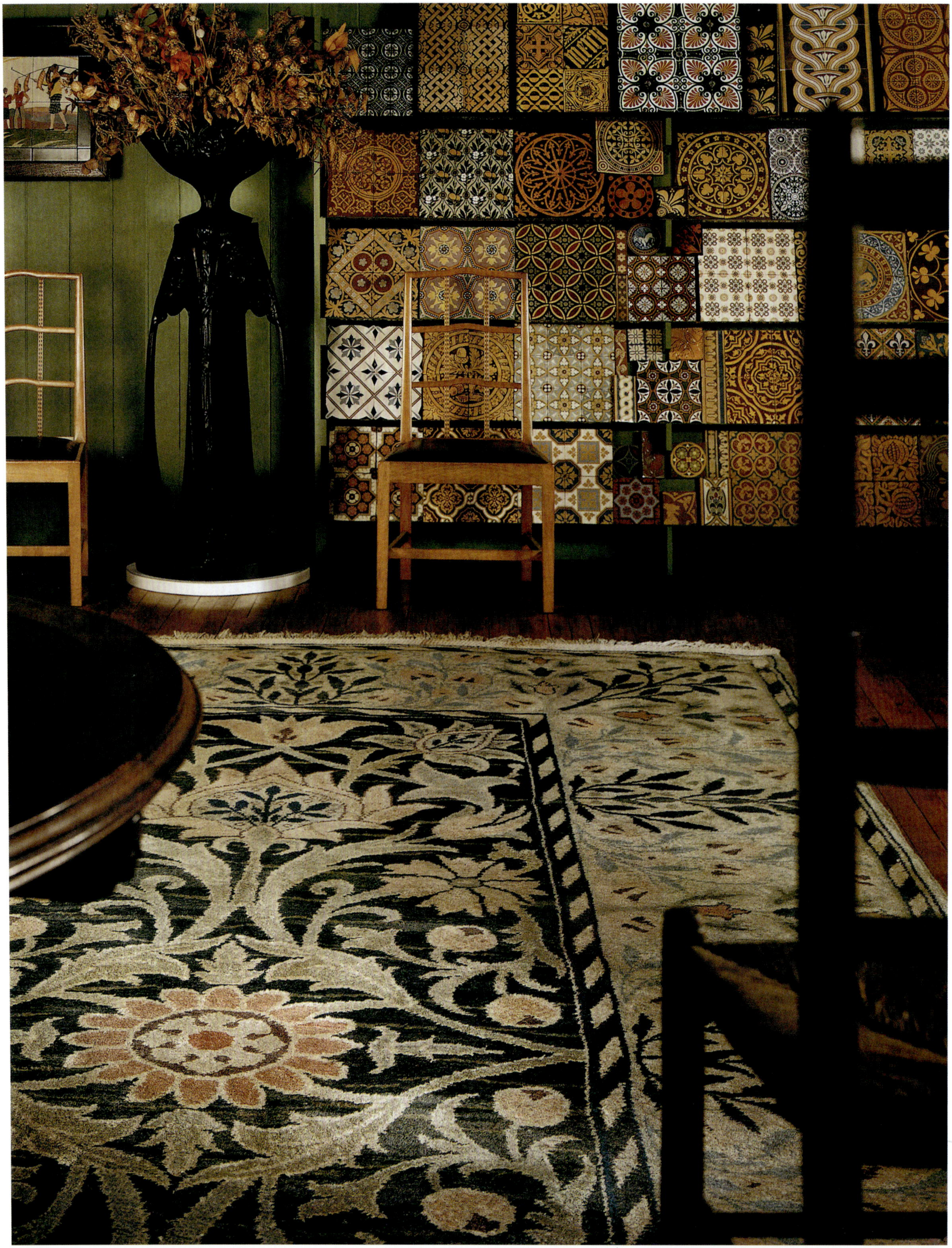

2 - Morris and his Plea for an Industrial Commonwealth

"The growth of decorative art in this country [...] has now reached a point at which it seems desirable that artists of reputation should devote their time to it."

Morris, Marshall, Faulkner & Company, *Prospectus*, 1861

By the middle of the century Ruskin, following the tracks of Thomas Carlyle, had created a certain discipleship, and were receiving the unbounded admiration of young men of fervent and poetic temperament, who were probably drawn at first by the splendid rhetoric of *Past and Present* and *Modern Painters* without examining very closely their social implications. Chief among the admirers of Ruskin was William Morris, his junior by fifteen years. Morris was just entering Oxford as Ruskin was publishing the *Stones of Venice*, the book that first kindled in Morris his social beliefs, to which he always referred as the first statement of the doctrine that art is the expression of man's pleasure in labour. He reprinted the chapter *On the Nature of the Gothic* forty years after its first publication as one of the first products of the Kelmscott Press, to stand in testimony of the abiding influence of the master-thinker. Of narrower range than Ruskin, but more intensive in his own direction, Morris gave his life to the determination of the relation between art and labour, and made himself, therefore, the chief exponent of the idea of the Arts and Crafts. Ruskin theorised; Morris demonstrated: henceforth the problem of other workers is that of extension and inclusion.

"Poet, artist, manufacturer, and socialist" – these terms describe the life-work of Morris in in its three-fold aspect of artist, craftsman, and social reformer. The history of handicraft shows no life more eventful than Morris's, nor more filled with notable achievements. As a boy his hands were always active, net-making being a favourite diversion. It was foreseen that he would take up the pencil and the engraver's tool at the earliest opportunity of instruction, although he was matriculated at Oxford for holy orders. His college chum, Burne-Jones – also intended for the church, but even then practicing the art through which he was to become famous – taught him drawing and engraving. The two artists were soon considering the advisability of giving up the church and devoting their lives to art – the one aspiring to be a painter, the other an architect. To architecture forthwith Morris turned his attention, and while he never

William Morris,
Hammersmith carpet.
Private collection.

Charles F. A. Voysey (for the design) and **Donegal Carpets** (for the production),
The Rose, Donegal carpet, 1899.
Wool.
Private collection.

The Silver Studio (for the design) and woven for **Liberty's**,
The Fintona, Donegal carpet, c. 1902.
Wool.
Private collection.

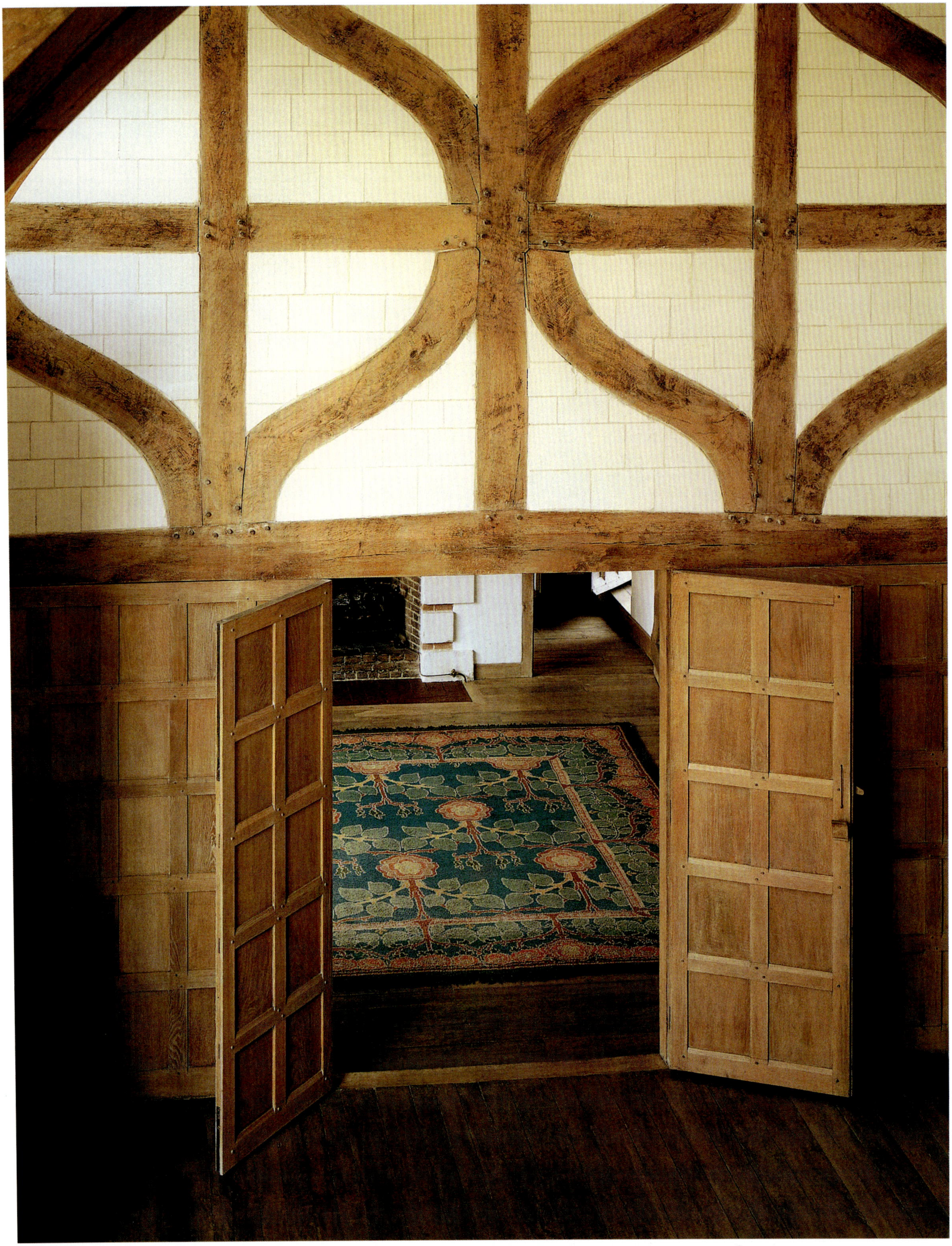

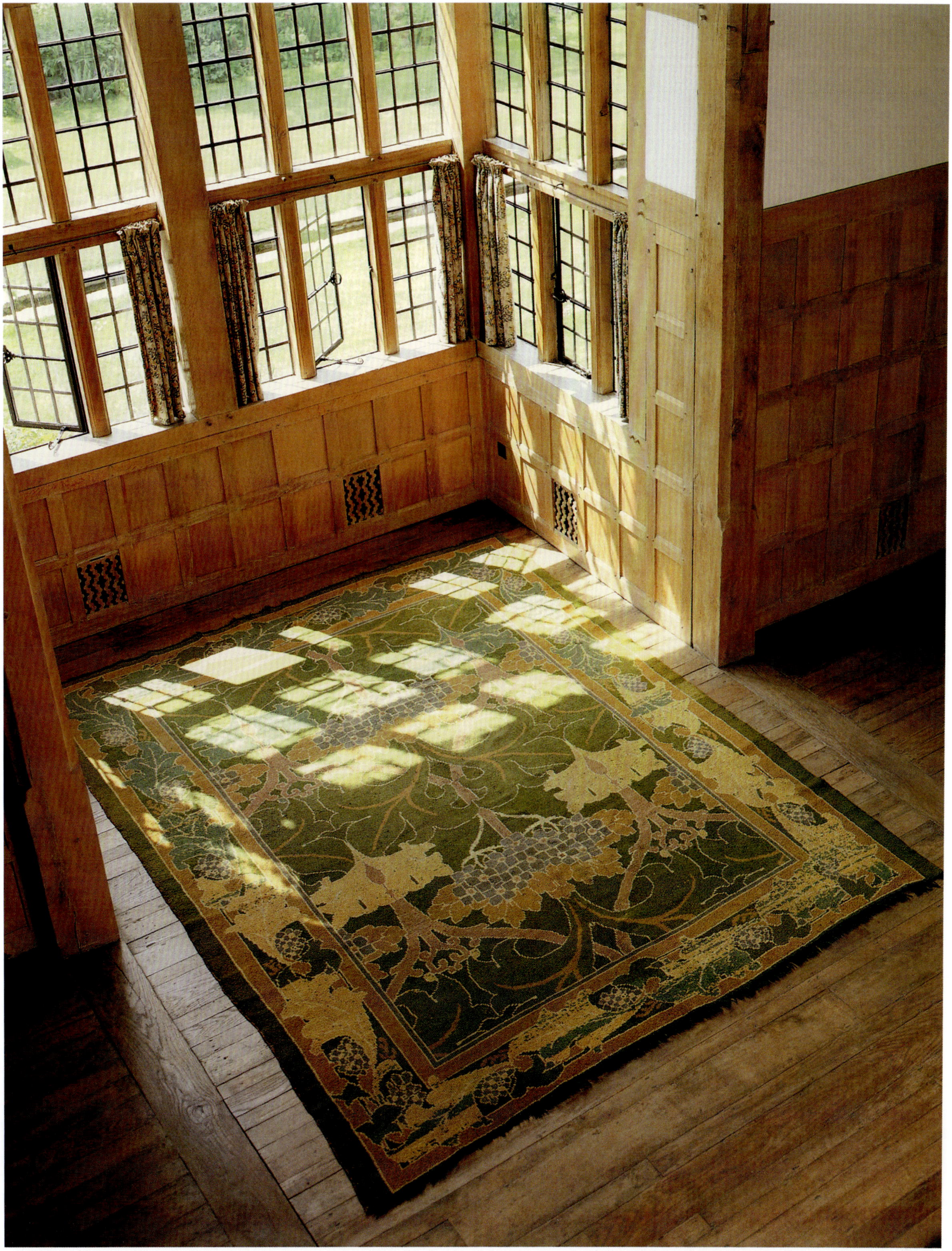

worked professionally as an architect, his studies at this time were of immense service in clarifying his thought and concentrating his energies. While in the office of Mr. G. E. Street, and pursuing his studies in architecture, he began the practice of more than one handicraft – clay-modelling, wood and stone carving, manuscript illumination, window-designing and embroidery, and these occupations were soon to fill his days even to the exclusion of painting, which Rossetti had taught him, and of poetry, which was his native expression.

The beginning of Morris's work as a professional decorator and manufacturer occurred in 1857. Practicing painting under the Pre-Raphaelite Dante Gabriel Rossetti's direction, experimenting in mural decoration on the walls of the Oxford Union Society, feeling his way in various arts and handicrafts, preparing also *The Defence of Guinevere* for publication, here was evidence of a splendid general culture, which, when specialised, was destined to accomplish grand results. In 1859 and 1860 Morris and Philip Webb, just out of the architect's office, built the famous Red House in an orchard and meadow plot near London, carrying out in practice for the first time their theories of domestic building and decoration. These first steps were so important that Morris's biographer J.W. Mackail's account of the house may be quoted in full:

"It was planned as an L-shaped building, two-storied, with a high-pitched roof of red tile. The beautiful oak staircase filled a bold projection in the angle, and corridors ran from it along both the inner walls, so that the rooms on both limbs of the house faced outward onto the garden. The two other sides of this half-quadrangle were masked by rose-trellises, inclosing a square inner court, in the middle of which rose the most striking architectural feature of the building, a well-house of brickwork and oak timber, with a steep, conical, tiled roof. Externally the house was plain almost to severity, and depended for its effect on its solidity and fine proportion. The decorative features it possessed were constructional, not of the nature of applied ornament: the frankly emphasised relieving arches over the windows, the deep cornice moulding, the louvre in the high, open roof over the staircase, and the two spacious recessed porches. Inside, its most remarkable feature was the large drawing-room, which filled the external angle of the L on the upper floor. It looked by its main end window northwards toward the road and the open country, and a projecting oriel on the western side overlooked the long bowling-green, which ran, encircled with apple-trees, close under the length of that wing. The decoration of the room, and of the staircase by which it was reached, was to be the work of several years for Morris and his friends, and he boldly announced that he meant to make it the most beautiful room in England. But through the whole house, inside and out, the same standard was, so far as possible, to be kept up.

Probably created by **Gavin Morton**, Donegal carpet with a Turkish inspired design, c. 1899. Private collection.

Charles F. A. Voysey (for the design) and **Ginzkey** (for the production), design for a carpet. Printed card.

William Morris, bed cover, c. 1876. Linen embroidered with silks, 190.5 x 166.4 cm. Victoria & Albert Museum, London.

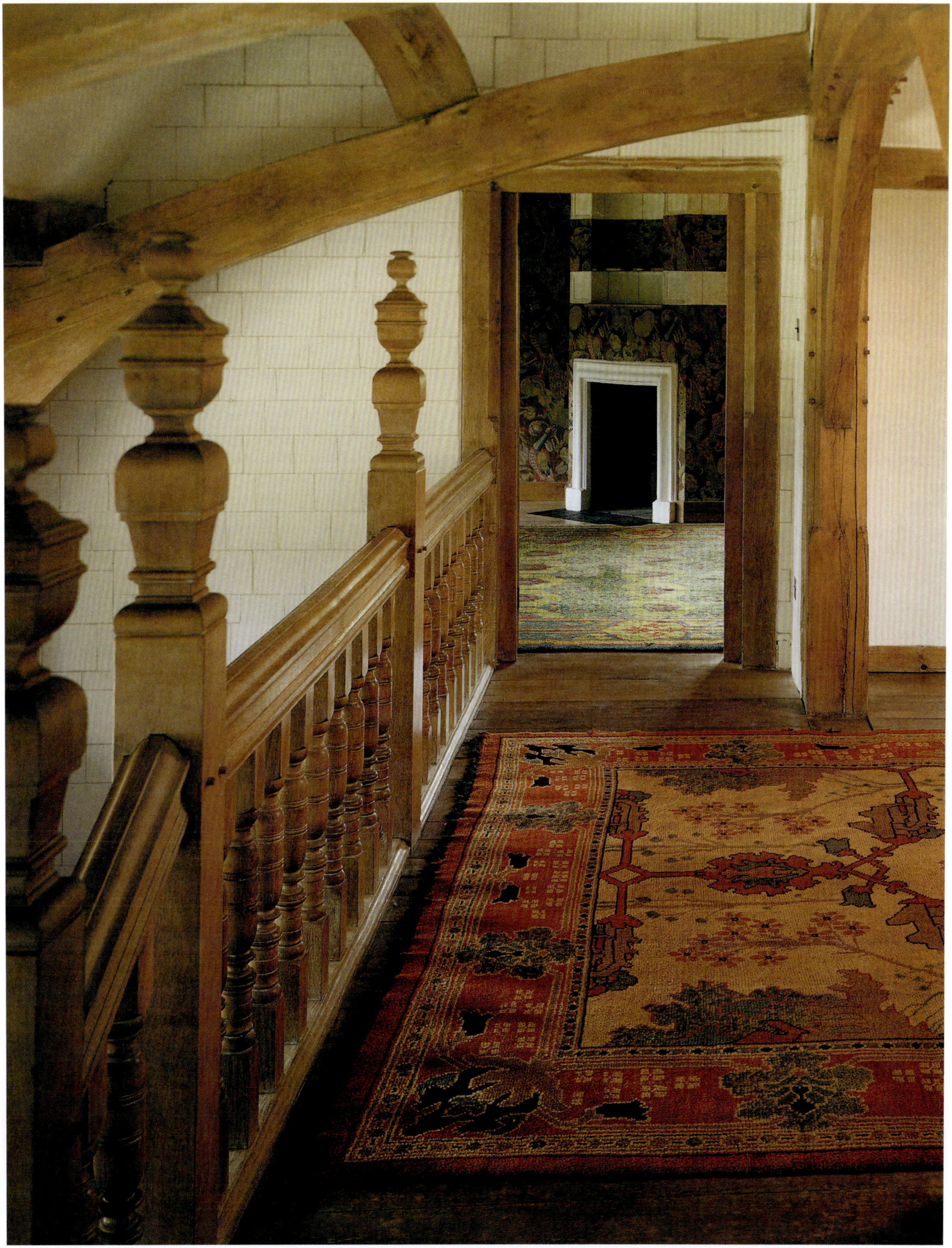

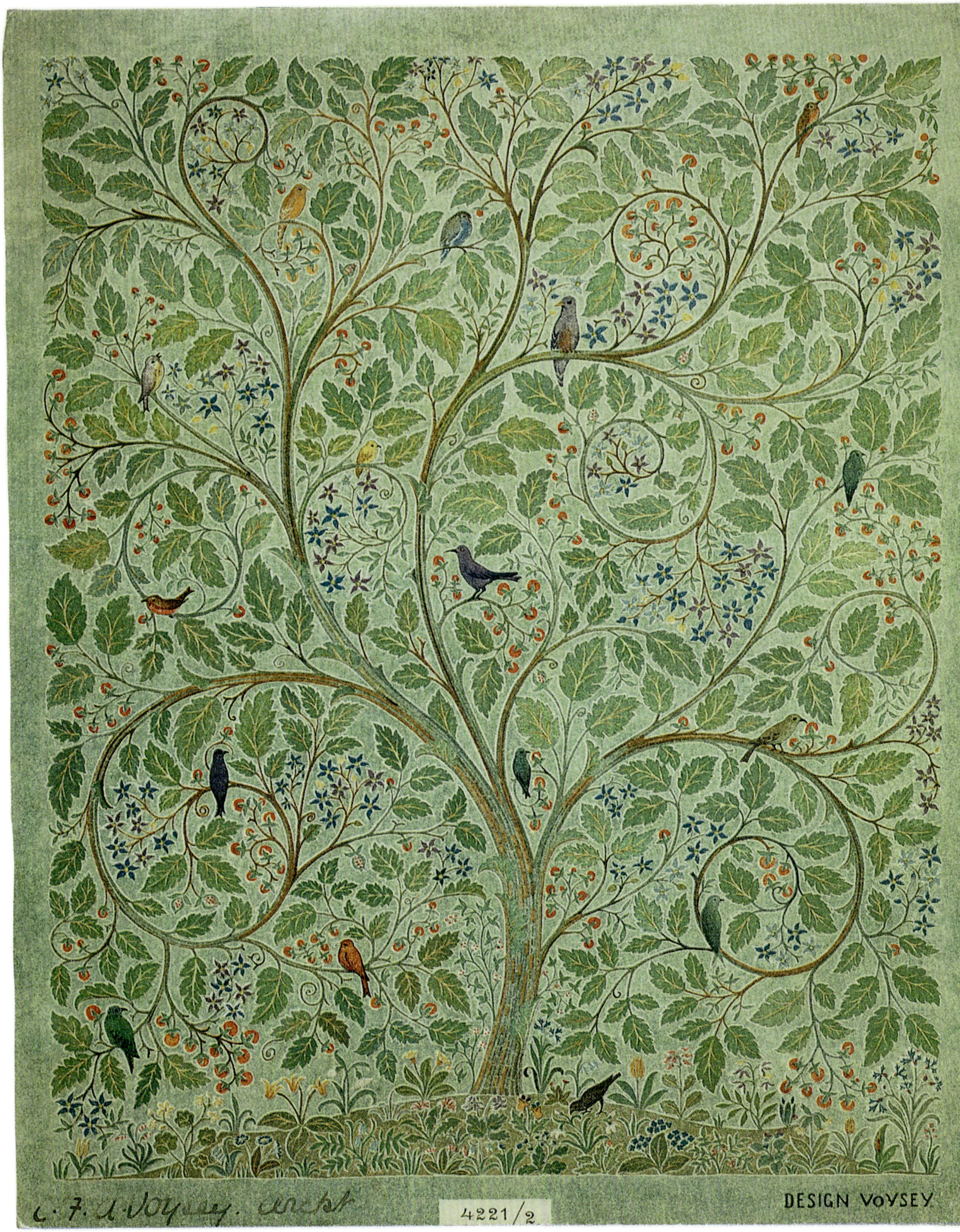

4221/2
DESIGN VOYSEY

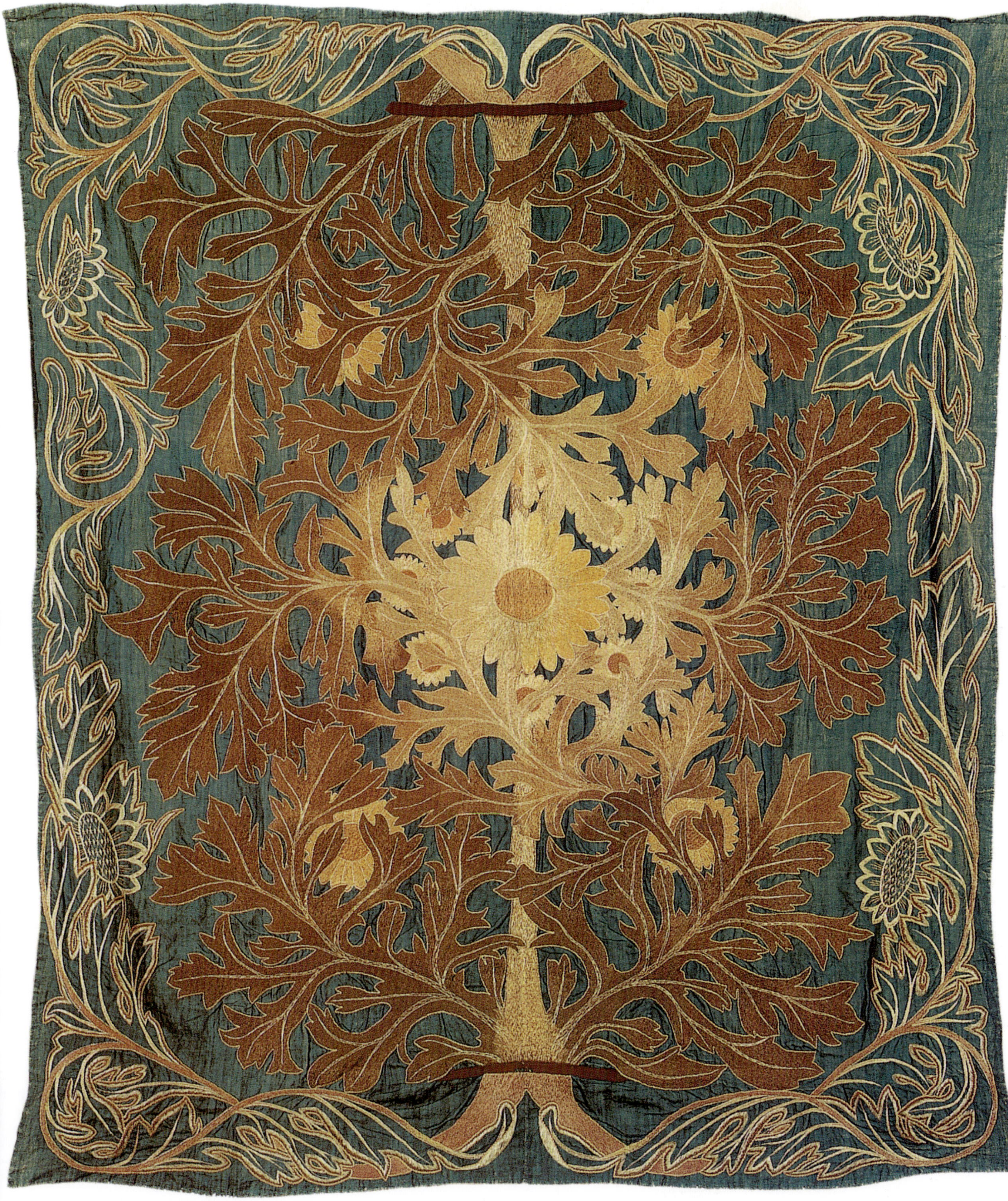

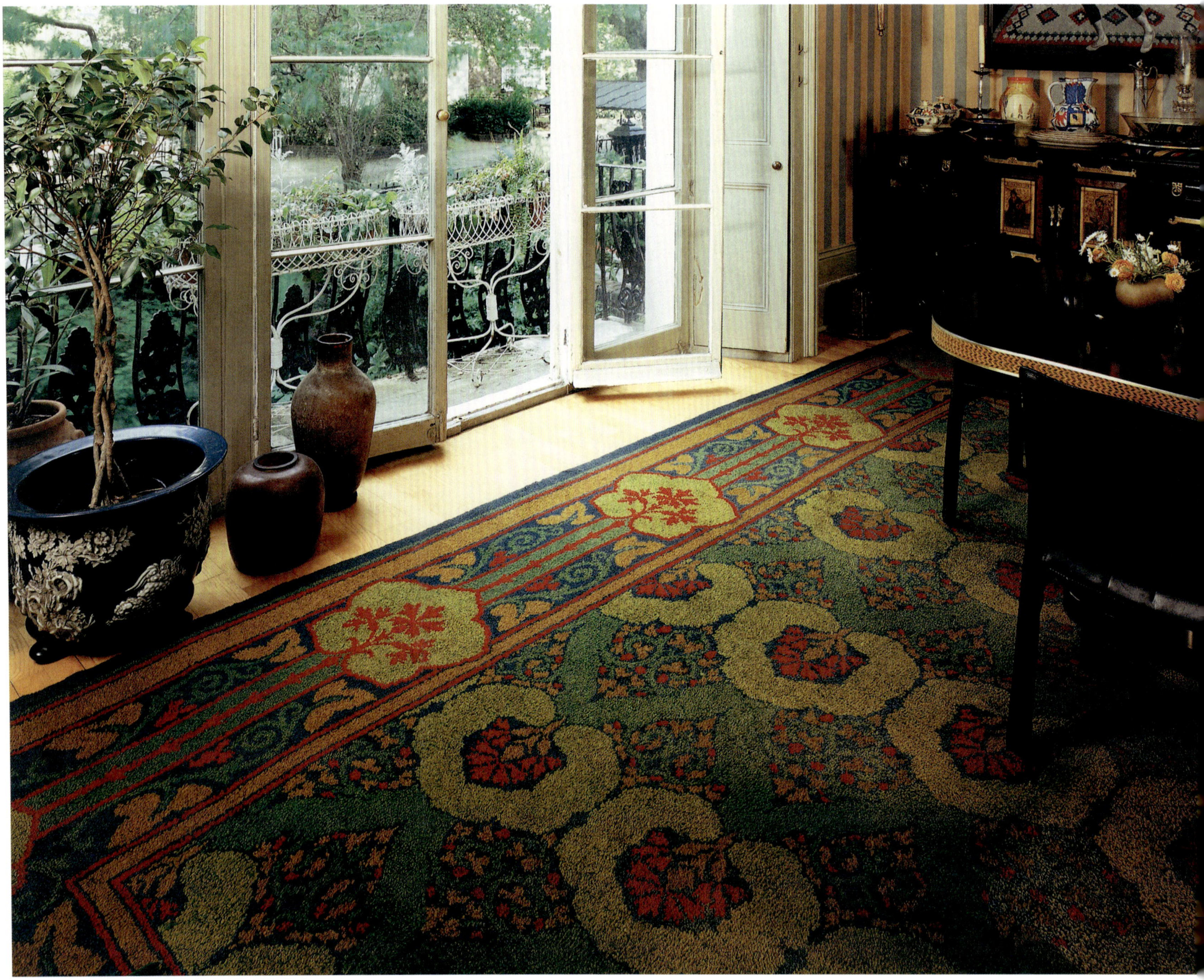

It was at this point that the problem of decoration began. The bricklaying and carpentery could be executed directly from the architect's designs. But when the shell of the house was completed, and stood clean and bare among the apple-trees, everything – or nearly everything – that was to furnish or decorate it had to be likewise designed and made. Only in a few isolated cases, such as Persian carpets and blue china or delft for vessels of household use, was there anything then to be bought ready-made that Morris could be content with in his own house. Not a chair, or table, or bed; not a cloth or paper-hanging for the walls; nor tiles to line fireplaces or passages; nor a curtain or a candlestick. These had to be reinvented, one might almost say, to escape the flat ugliness of the current article. The great painted settle from Red Lion Square was taken and set up in the drawing room, the top of it being railed in so as to form a small music gallery. Much of the furniture was designed by Webb and executed under his eye: the great oak dining table, other tables, chairs, cupboards, massive copper candlesticks, fire-dogs, and table glass of extreme beauty. The plastered walls and ceilings were treated with simple designs in tempera, and for the hall and main living rooms a richer and more elaborate scheme of decoration was designed and gradually executed. The garden was planned with the same care and originality as the house; in both alike the study of older models never sank into mere antiquarianism or imitation of obsolete forms. Morris's knowledge of architecture was so entirely a part of himself that he never seemed to think about it as anything peculiar. But in his knowledge of gardening he did – with reason – pride himself. It is very doubtful whether he was ever seen with a spade in his hands; in later years at Kelmscott his manual work in the garden was almost limited to clipping yew hedges. But of flowers and vegetables and fruit trees he knew all the ways and capabilities. Red House garden, with its long grass walks, its midsummer lilies and autumn sunflowers, its wattled rose-trellises inclosing richly flowered square garden plots, was then as unique as the house it surrounded. The building had been planned with such care that hardly a tree in the orchard had to be cut down; apples fell in at the windows as they stood open on hot autumn nights."

Into this house the Morrises moved during the summer of 1860, and after two years of residence the house was practically completed. "The garden, skilfully laid out amid the old orchard, had developed its full beauty, and the adornment of the house kept growing into greater and greater elaboration. A scheme had been designed for the mural decoration of the hall, staircase, and drawing room, upon various parts of which work went on intermittently for several years. The walls of the spacious and finely proportioned staircase were to be completely covered with paintings in tempera of scenes from the War of Troy, to be designed and executed by Burne-Jones. Below them on a large wall space in the hall was to be a great ship carrying the Greek heroes. It was designed, as the rest of the Troy series were also to have been, in a frankly medieval spirit; a warship indeed of the fourteenth century, with the shields of the kings hung

Charles F. A. Voysey,
The Glenmure, Donegal carpet, 1903.
Kidderminster's Carpet Heritage,
Kidderminster.

Charles F. A. Voysey,
The Donnemara
(signature Donegal Carpets design).
Wool, 345.2 x 315.2 cm.
Private collection.

William Morris,
Hammersmith rug, c. 1880.
Cotton, undyed.
Private collection.

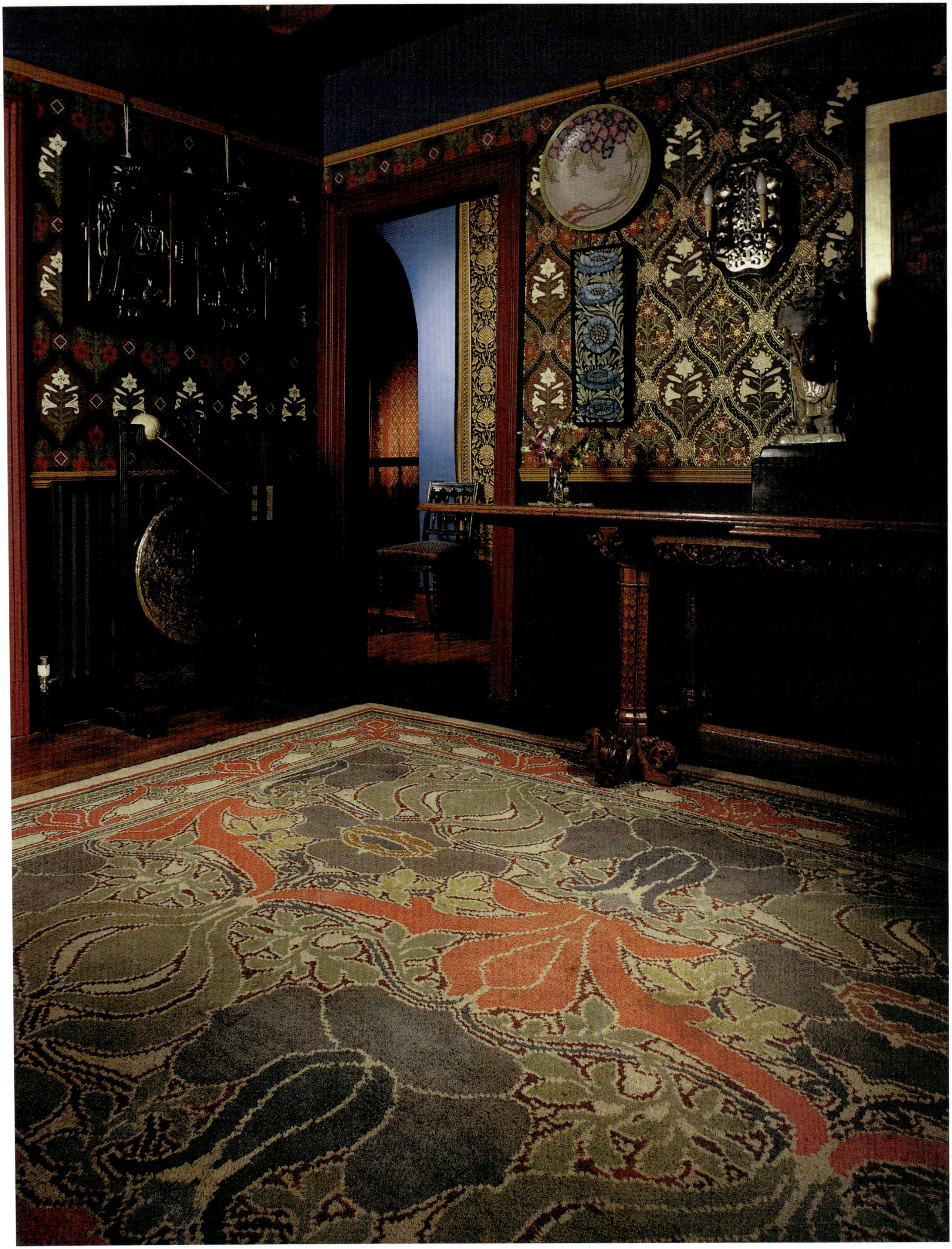

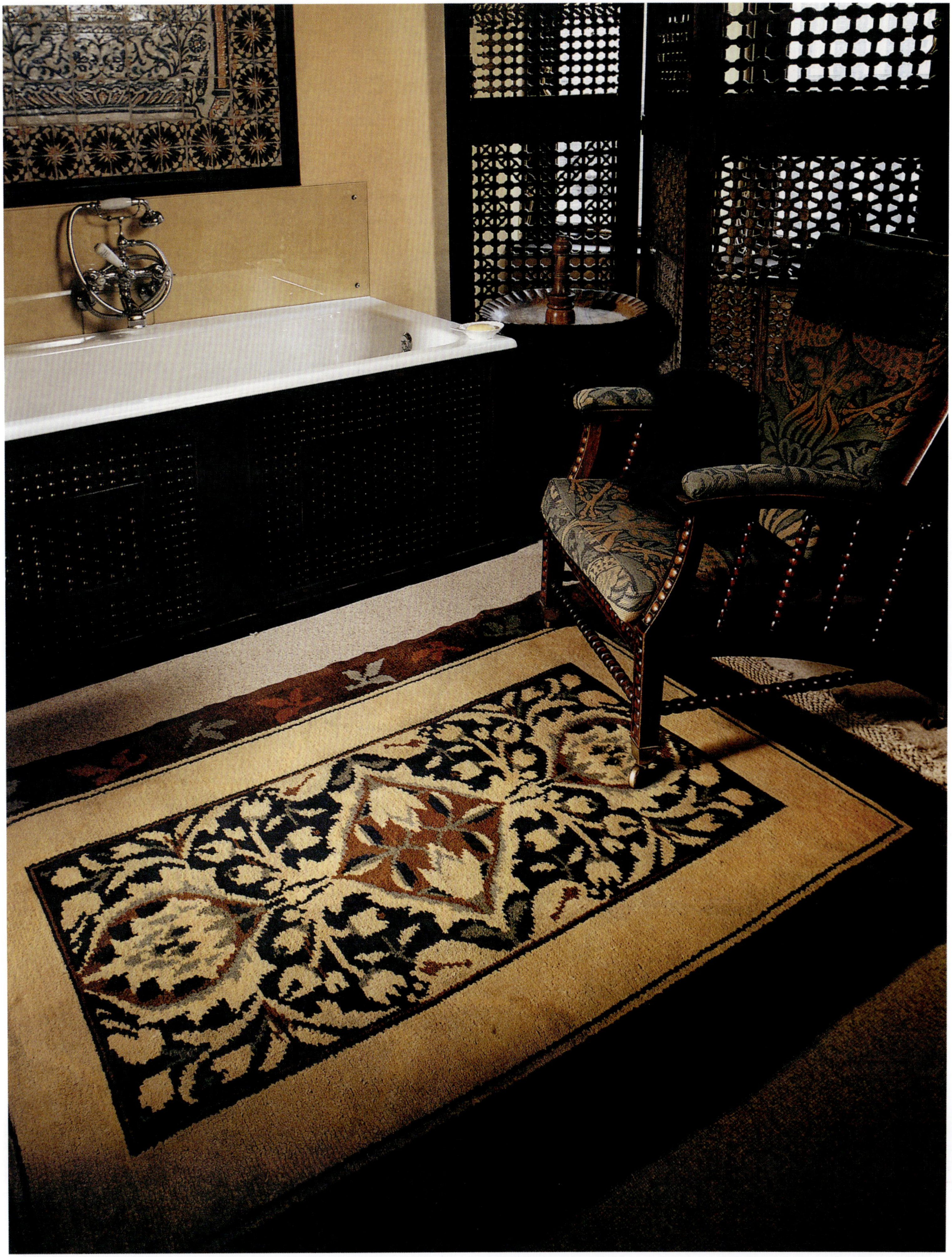

over the bulwarks. Round the drawing-room, at a height of about five feet from the floor, was to be a continuous belt of pictures, the subjects of which were scenes from the fifteenth-century English romance of "Sir Degrevaunt". Three of them were executed by Burne-Jones, and remain on the walls today. Below them the wall was to have been covered with magnificent embroidered hangings. The principal bedroom was hung with indigo-dyed blue serge with a pattern of flowers worked on it in bright-coloured wools. For the dining room embroidered hangings of a much more elaborate and splendid nature were designed and partly executed, in a scheme of design like those of his later tapestries when he revived the art of tapestry-weaving, of twelve figures with trees between and above them, and a belt of flowers running below their feet. Yet another hanging, executed by Morris with his own hands, was of green trees with gaily coloured birds among them, and a running scroll emblazoned with his motto in English, "If I can." The same motto in French reappeared in the painted glass with which a number of windows of the house were gradually filled, and on the tiles which lined the deep porches. In the hall a second great cupboard began to be painted with scenes from the Niebelungenlied. There were no paper hangings in the house. The rooms that had not painted walls were hung with flower-embroidered cloth worked from his designs by Mrs. Morris and other needlewomen. Even the ceilings were decorated with bold, simple patterns in distemper, the design being pricked into the plaster so as to allow the ceiling to be re-whitewashed and the decoration renewed [...].

Out of the building and furnishing of this house Morris's work as a manufacturer sprang. He had felt the joy of workmanship, he had been made aware of his wonderful faculty of designing, and he now understood the need by the public of artistic furnishing. Early in the year 1861 the firm of Morris, Marshall, Faulkner and Company – made up of seven members – was formed, with the purpose of designing and manufacturing fine art fabrics. The circular sent out to the public announcing the work of the company is one of the most important documents in the history of the modern revival of handicraft. It reads in part as follows:

"The growth of decorative art in this country, owing to the efforts of English architects, has now reached a point at which it seems desirable that artists of reputation should devote their time to it. Although, no doubt, particular instances of success may be cited, still it must be generally felt that attempts of this kind hitherto have been crude and fragmentary. Up to this time the want of that artistic supervision which can alone bring about harmony between the parts of a successful work has been increased by the necessarily excessive outlay, consequent on taking one individual artist from his pictorial labours. The artists whose names appear above hope by association to do away with this difficulty. Having among their number men of varied qualifications, they will be able to undertake any species of decoration, mural or otherwise, from pictures, properly so-

William Morris,
Orchard, c. 1880-1890.
Curtain.
Victoria & Albert Museum, London.

Gavin Morton and **G. K. Robertson**,
Donegal carpet, 1899.
Private collection.

William Morris,
Bullerswood, 1889.
Woven wool carpet on cotton warp, 764.8 x 398.8 cm.
Victoria & Albert Museum, London.

Charles F. A. Voysey (for the design) and **Yates & Co.** (for the production),
The River Mat, 1903.
Private collection.

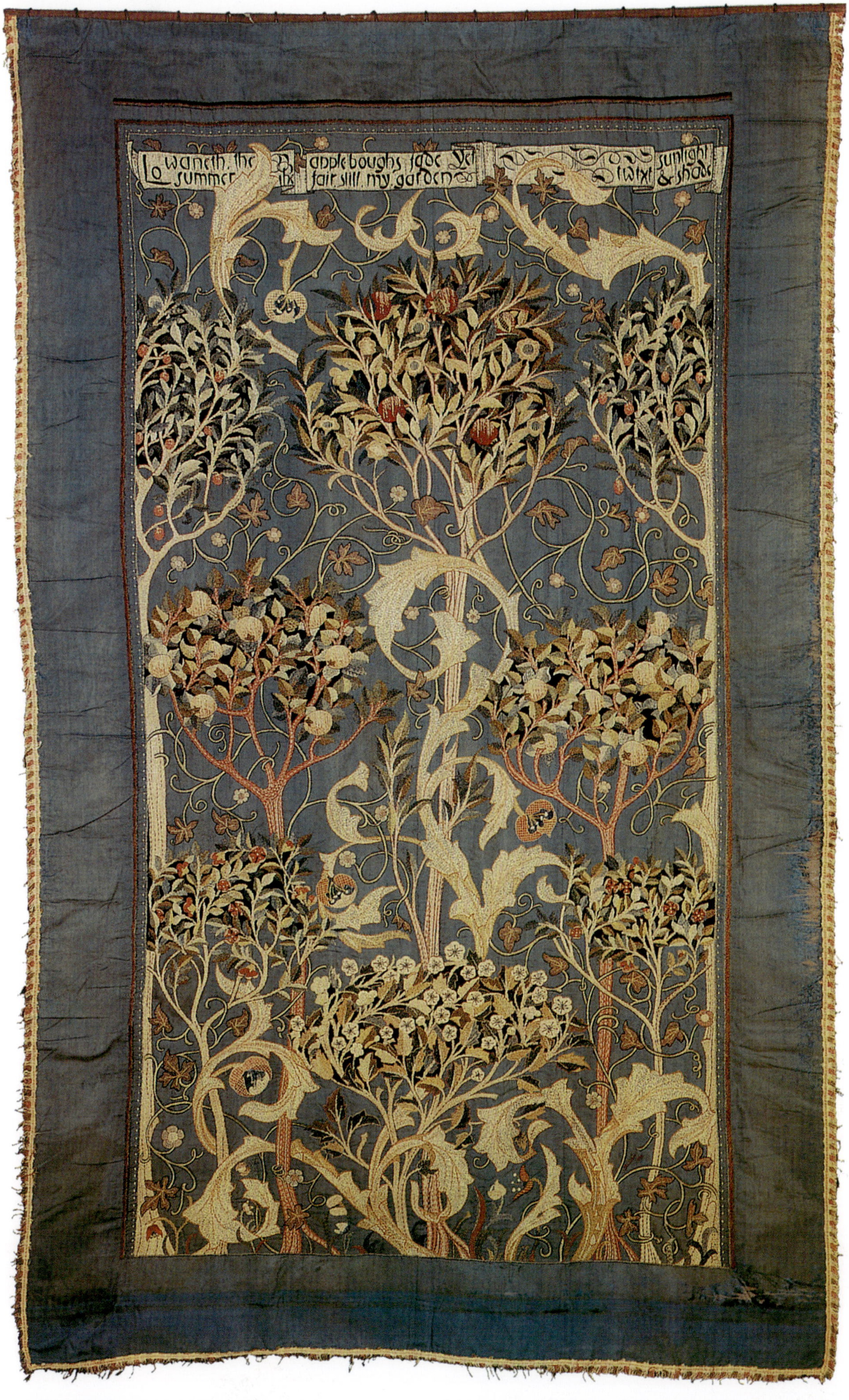
Lo
waneth the
summer
apple boughs fade yet
fair still my garden
twixt
sunlight
& shade

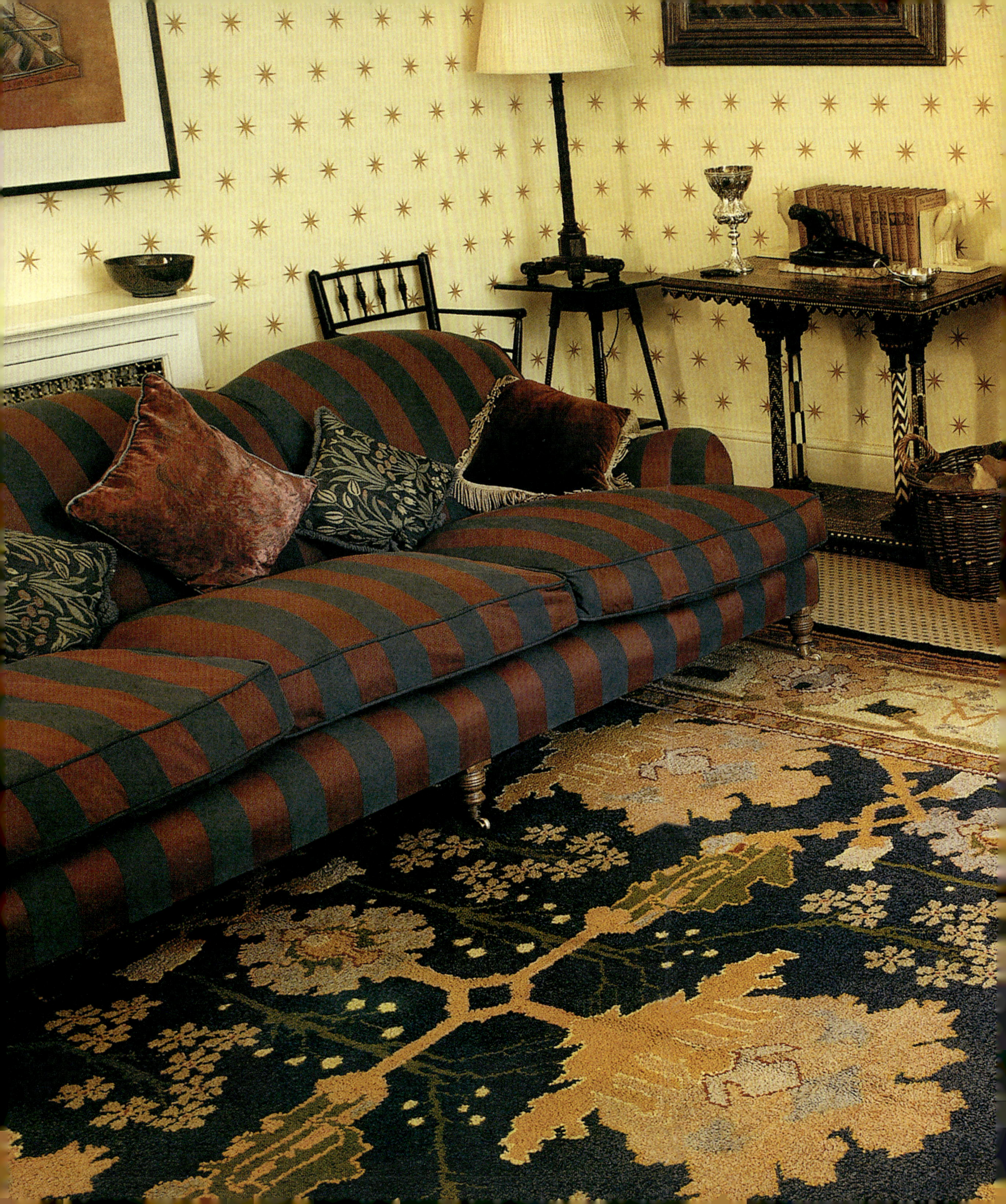

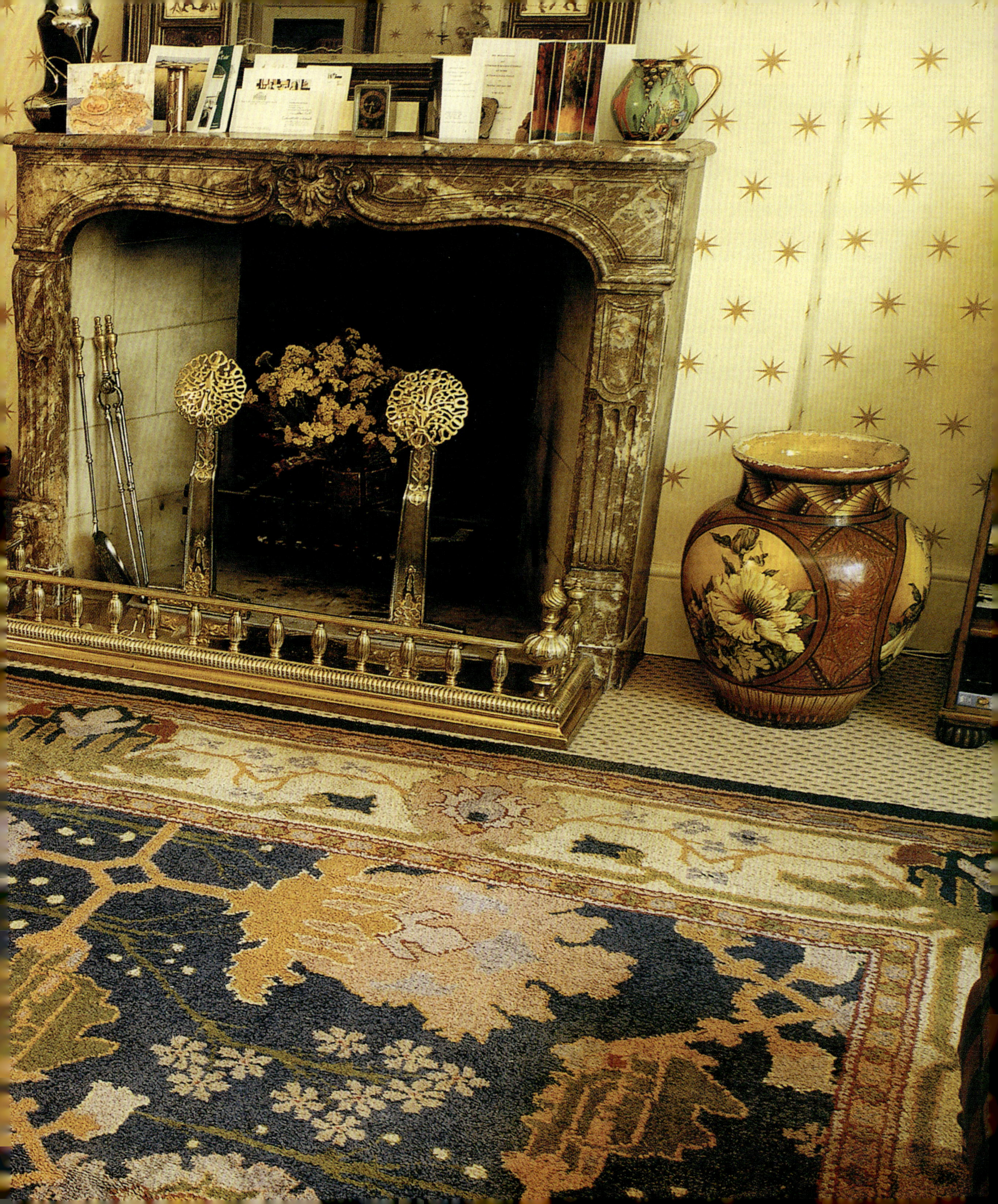

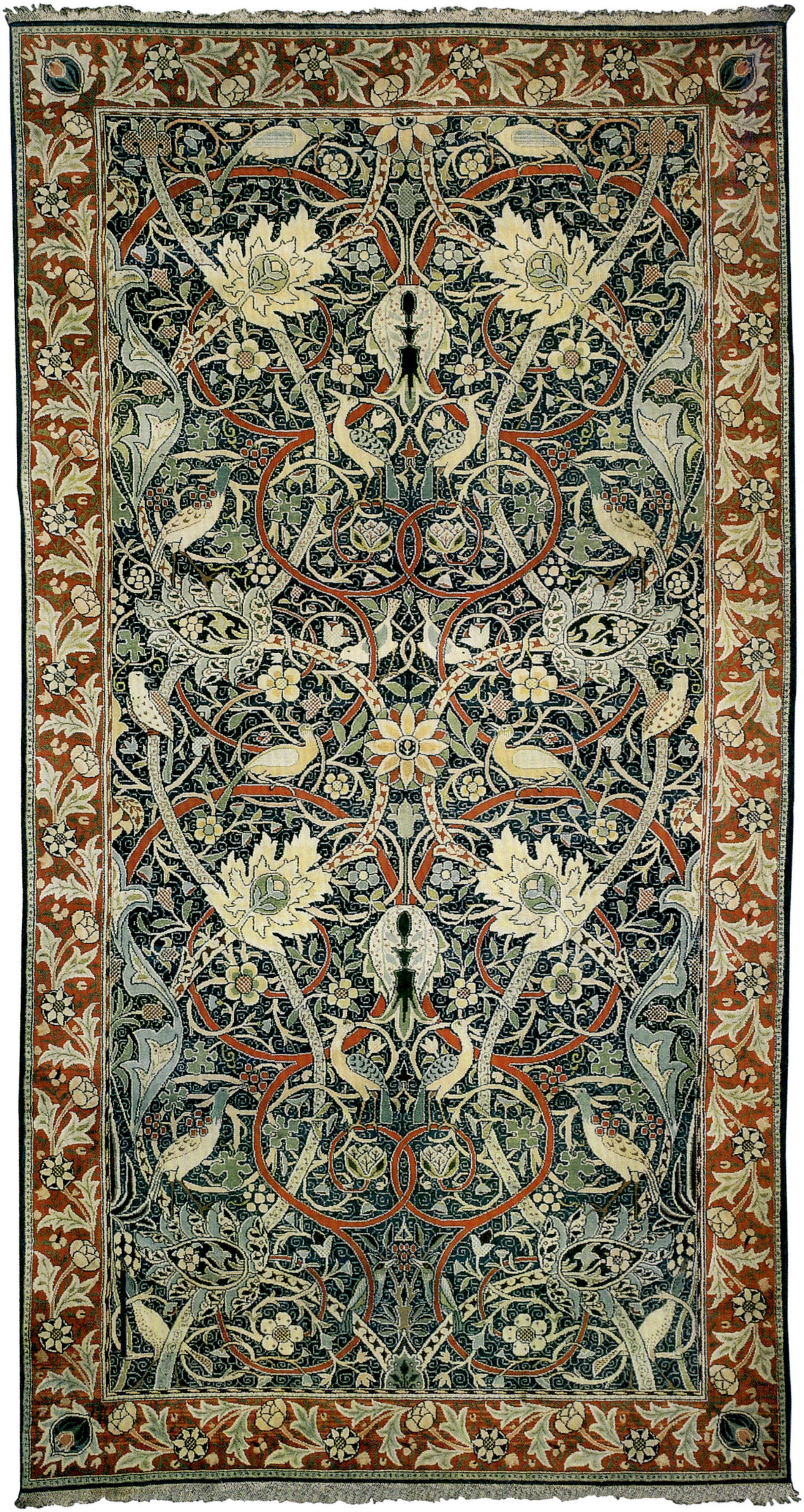

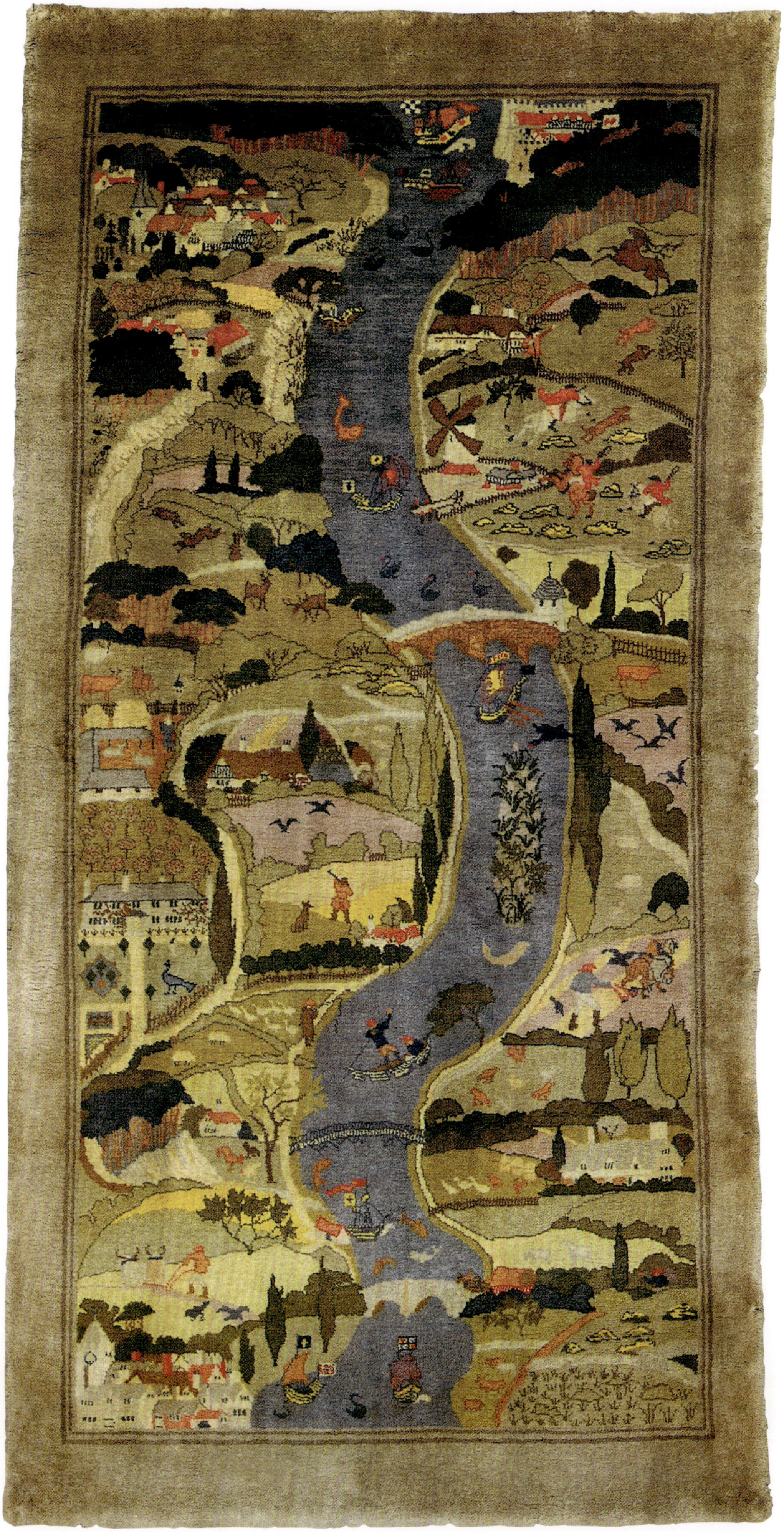

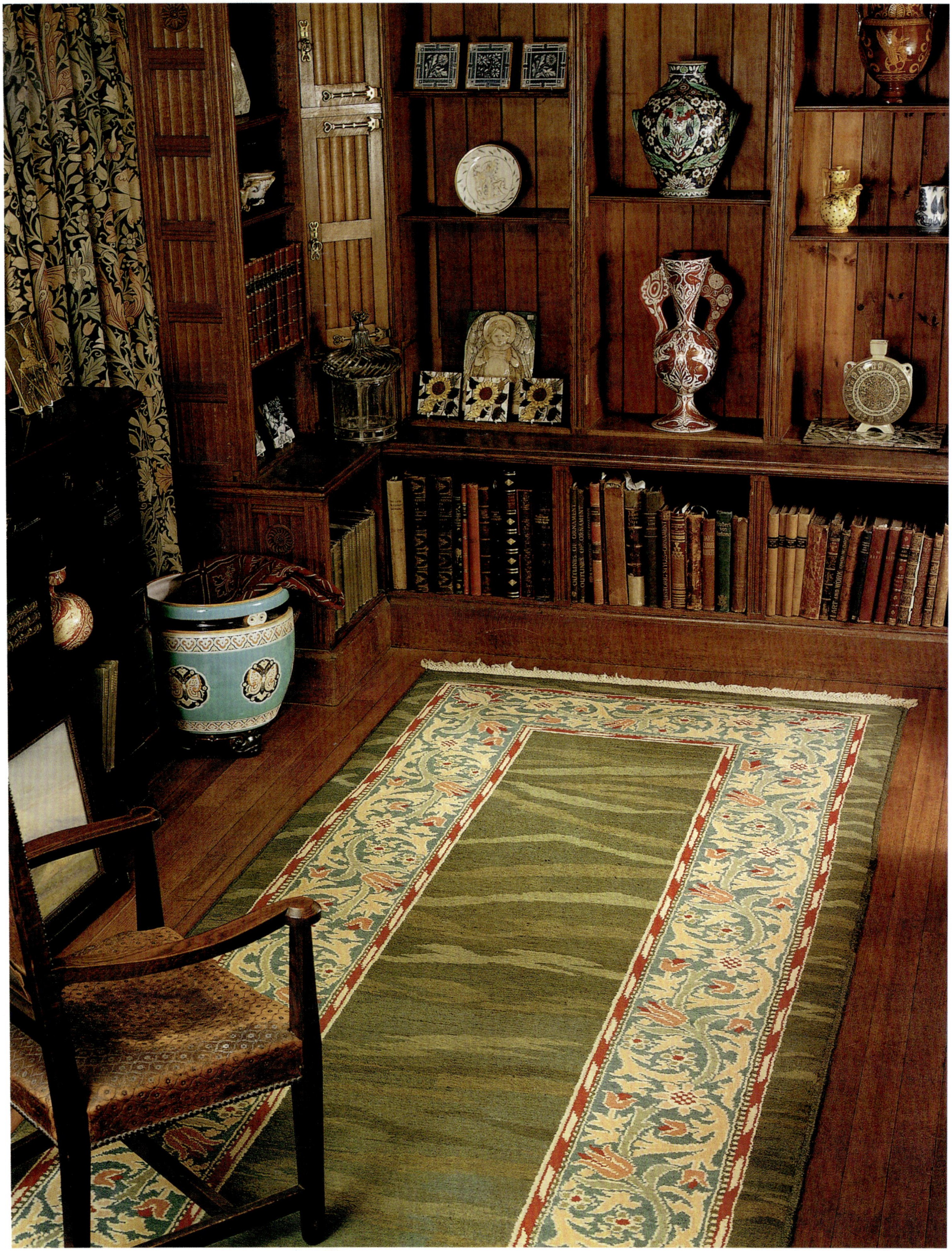

called, down to the consideration of the smallest work susceptible of art beauty. It is anticipated that by such co-operation, the largest amount of what is essentially the artist's work, along with his constant supervision, will be secured at the smallest possible expense, while the work done must necessarily be of a much more complete order than if any single artist were incidentally employed in the usual manner. These artists having for many years been deeply attached to the study of the decorative arts of all times and countries, have felt more than most people the want of some one place where they could either obtain or get produced work of a genuine and beautiful character. They have therefore now established themselves as a firm for the production, by themselves and under their supervision, of:

I. Mural decoration, either in pictures or in pattern work, or merely in the arrangement of colours, as applied to dwelling-houses, churches, or public buildings.
II. Carving generally as applied to architecture.
III. Stained glass, especially with reference to its harmony with mural decoration.
IV. Metal work in all its branches, including jewellery.
V. Furniture, either depending for its beauty on its own design, on the application of materials hitherto overlooked, or on its conjunction with figure and pattern painting. Under this head is included embroidery of all kinds, stamped leather, and ornamental work in other such materials, besides every article necessary for domestic use.

It is only requisite to state further that work of all the above classes will be estimated for, and executed in a business-like manner; and it is believed that good decoration, involving rather the luxury of taste than the luxury of costliness, will be found to be much less expensive than is generally supposed."

Into the work of this manufactory Morris entered with his customary energy and sagacity. He was the practical manager of the firm's business and did more work himself than all the other "artists" together. He was equipped for every craft, even to the stitching of embroidery, and as the "firm's poet" wrote verses for tile decoration. The business rapidly developed, the demand for stained glass windows and embroidered textiles, owing to the revival of ritualism and Catholicism, being considerable. One of Faulkner's letters, written in 1862, gives a pleasant picture of the inner company of workers, and indicates also something of the progress of the business the first year. Thereafter, their affairs increased so rapidly that in 1865 the work of the firm was carried to larger quarters in Queen Square, Bloomsbury. Morris gave up the Red House and came to live in London, the premises at Queen Square being his headquarters for thesubsequent seventeen years. In 1875 the firm was dissolved, then reconstituted with Morris as manager and Burne-Jones and Webb as assistants. Morris invested all his means in the business, and depended upon it for his income. With greater opportunities, and inspired with success, he pursued his labours with unremitting diligence. His restless fingers were fairly itching for work.

William Morris,
Hammersmith carpet with a plain centre.
Private collection.

After 1870 his history may fairly be divided into periods, according to his interest in new crafts. In 1870 he took up the art of illumination, and executed several painted books, including the *Rubaiyat of Omar Khayyam*, the *Odes of Horace*, and his own *Cupid and Psyche*. The *Rubaiyat* is thus described by Mackail:

"This manuscript may take rank, by its elaborate beauty, as one of his chief masterpieces. It was finished on the 16th of October, 1872, after being a year and a half in hand. On its tiny scale – twenty-three pages, measuring six inches by three and a half – it is a volume of immense labour and exquisite workmanship. On eighteen of the pages the illumination is confined to a central space less than three inches by two, with a title in gold above each. In that central space, alongside and between verses, is a running ornament of flowers and fruits. On the other five pages the margins are completely filled with floriated designs among them, which are minute but beautifully drawn and coloured figures, the lower half of the last page being also filled by a design of two figures holding a scroll. The treatment or the fruit and flower work is an admirable adaptation of an almost Pre-Raphaelite naturalism to the methods and limits of ornamental design.

Work in dyeing and weaving soon put a stop to illumination. Working over the dye-vat in the cellar at Queen Square, and at Leek on a larger scale with Mr. George Wardle, he restored old and long-lost methods of dyeing. Once this was done, looms were set up in the top story of the workshop, and weaving in silk and wool went on with great energy. On moving to Hammersmith, in 1878, a tapestry-room was built into his bedroom so that he might work at the first dawn, and the new house was hung with his own tapestries. By 1880 the carpet and rug weaving had progressed so successfully that a public exhibition was held at the salesroom in Oxford street, the circular announcing that this was "an attempt to make England independent of the East for carpets which may claim to be considered works of art."

Concerning his love for the Middle Ages, Morris was not controlled by an unreasoning medievalism, but he sought out the lost threads of the various crafts, and wherever an art had reached its highest development, there Morris directed his studies. It happened that many of the crafts were at their best estate in certain countries of Europe in the early Middle Ages, but if Turkey, or Persia, or India, could furnish a better practical example of any craft, Morris's "medievalism" did not prevent him from sitting at the feet of these teachers also. It is clear, too, that he was not a mere copyist of ancient or foreign excellencies, but that his purpose was to discover the principles of a craft by a study of its best examples, and to work therefrom in the modern spirit.

In 1881 occurred the removal of the manufactory to Merton Abbey, a village near the Thames, some seven miles from Charing Cross. The advantages at this location were far

William Morris,
Small Barr.
Hammersmith carpet,
hand-knotted wool.
Wightwick Manor, Wightwick Bank.

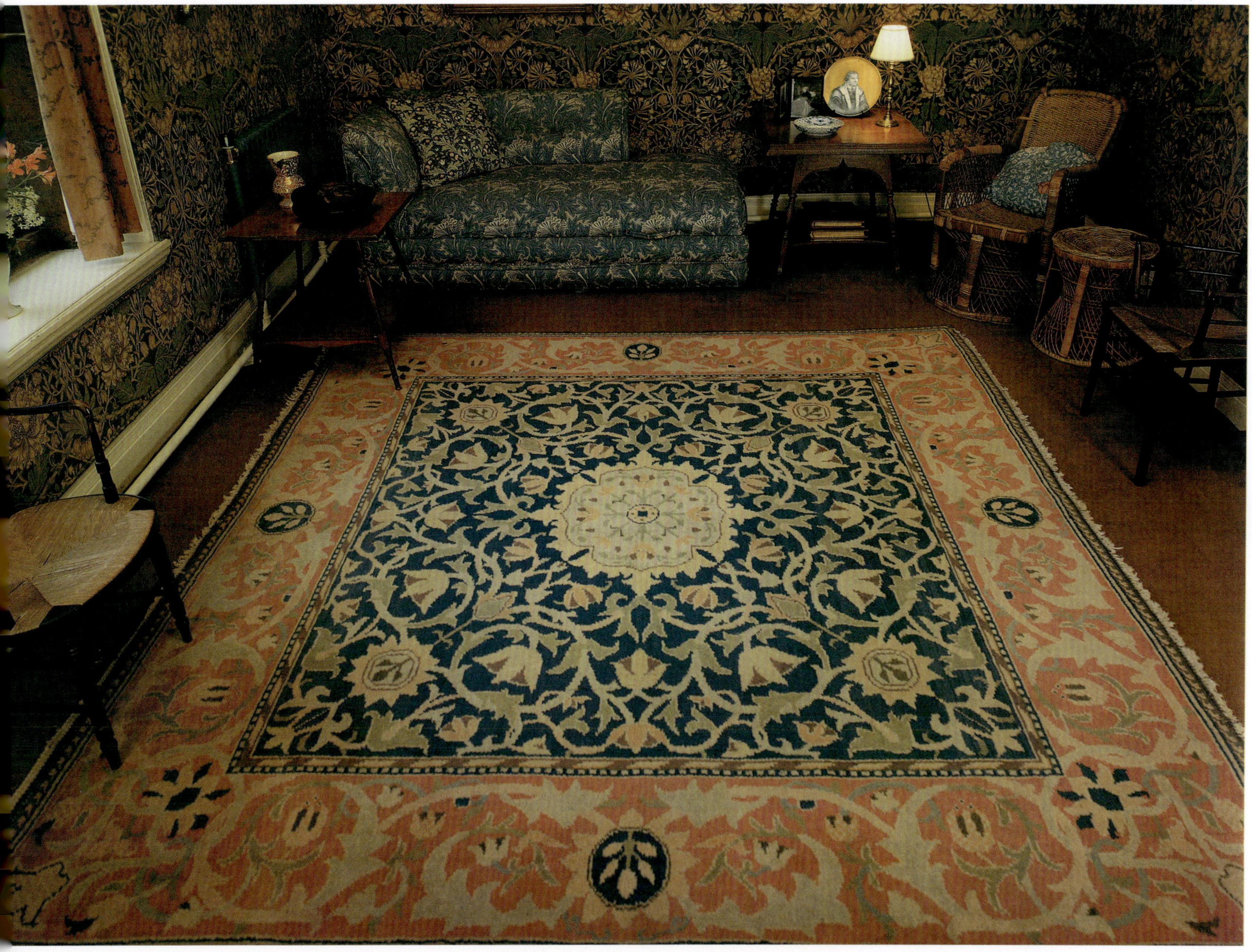

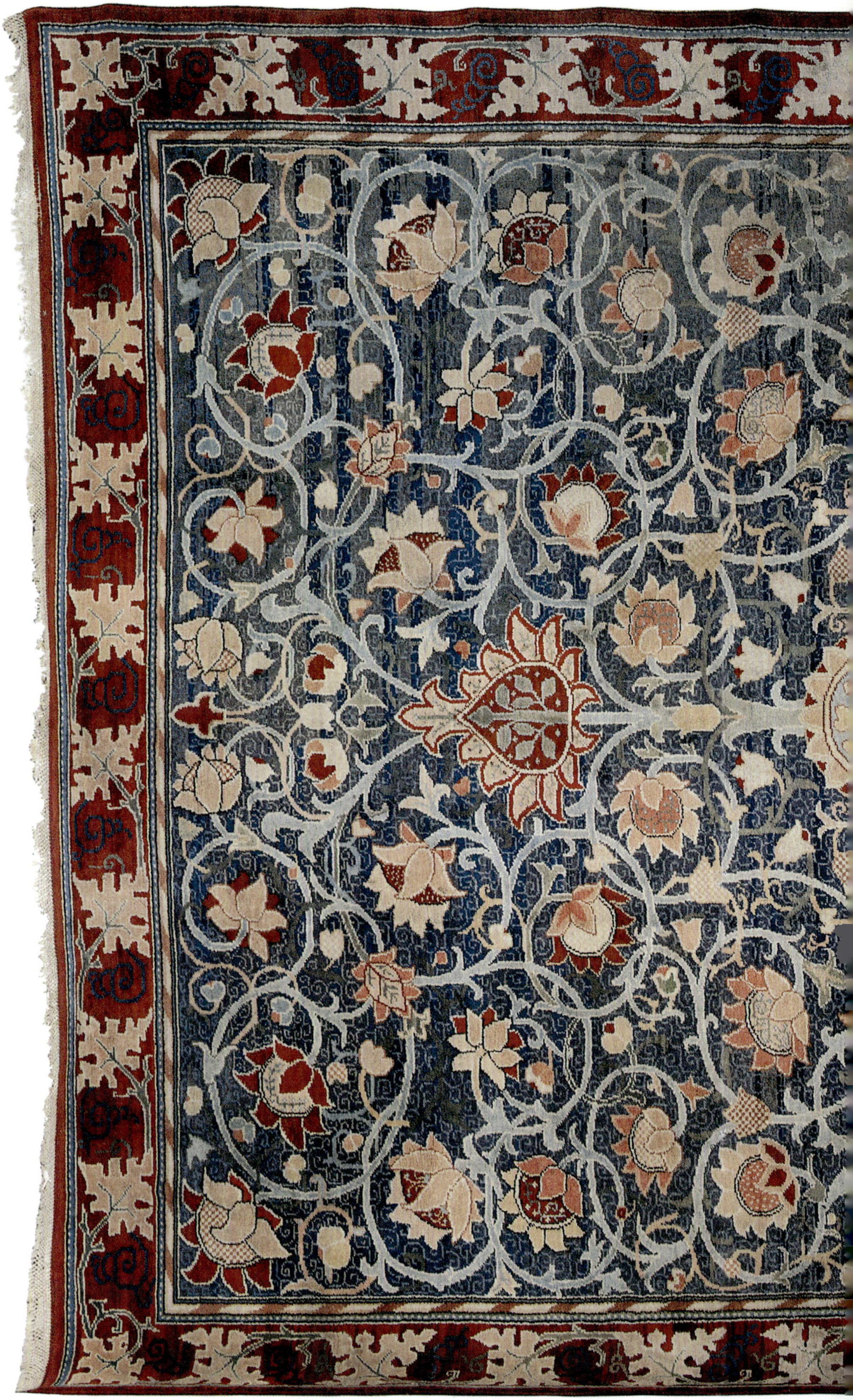

William Morris (for the design), *Holland Park*, 1883.
Hammersmith Carpet,
475.4 x 412.7 cm.
Private collection.

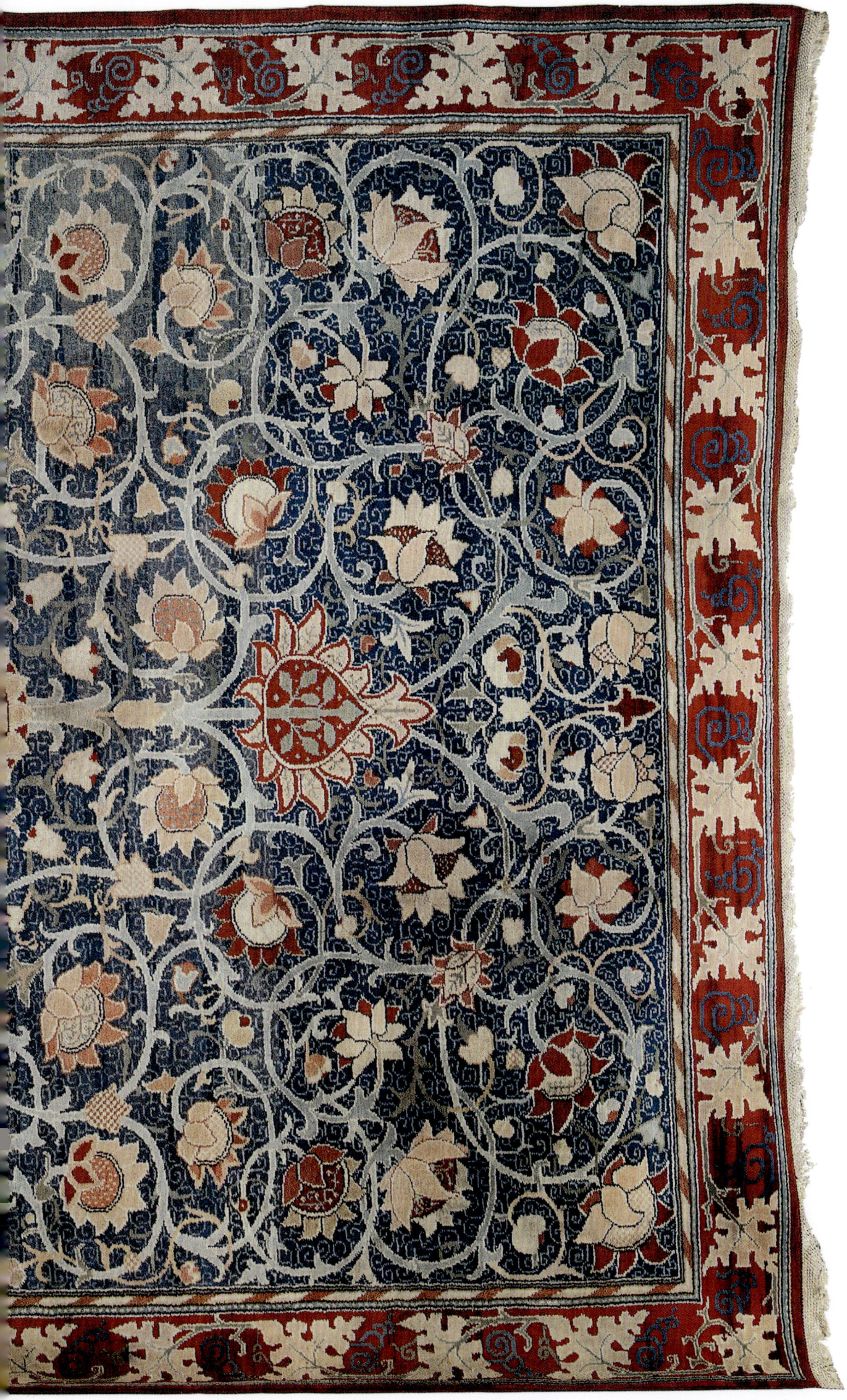

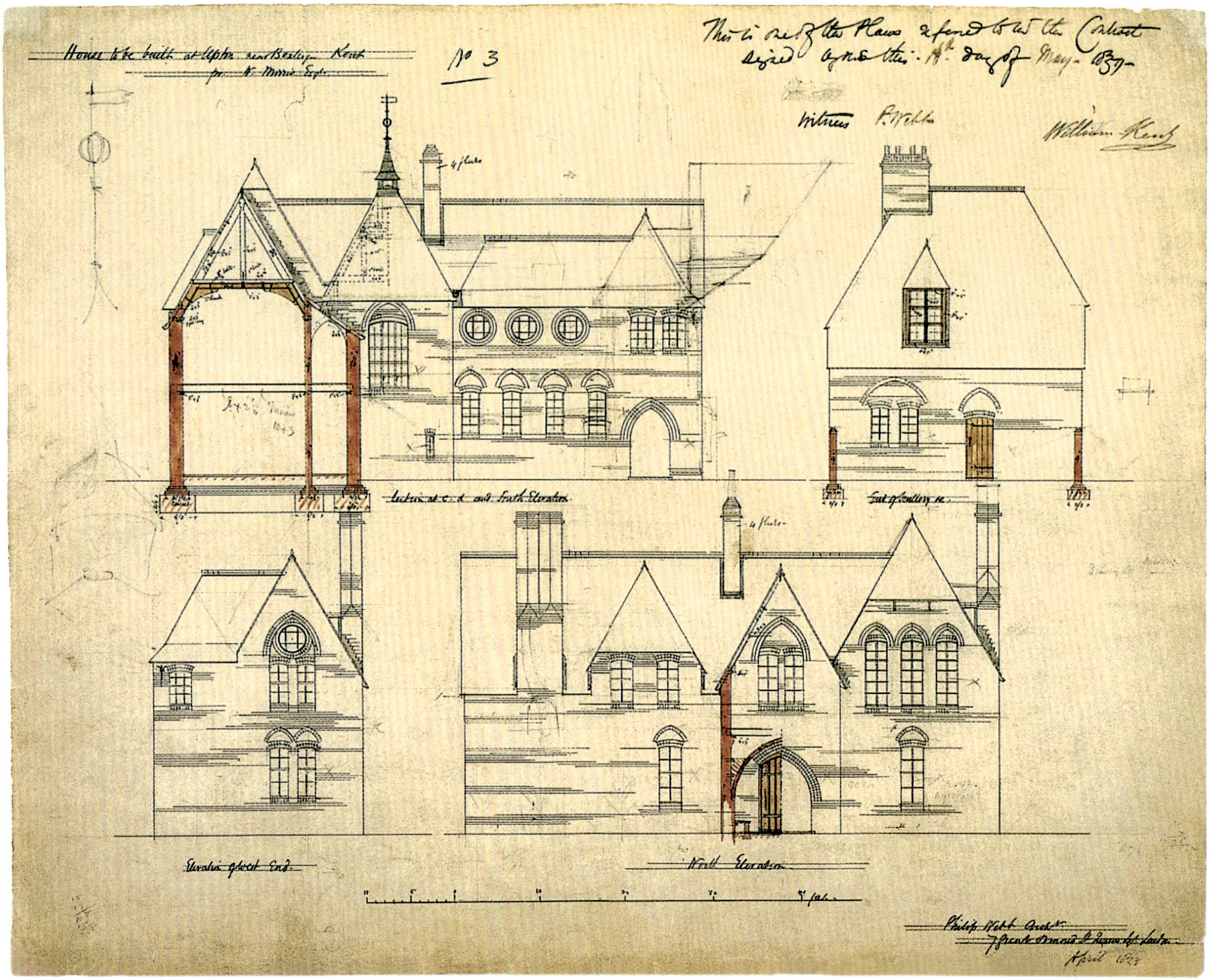

Philip Webb,
architectural drawing for the Red House (north and south elevations and details), 1839.
52.1 x 63.5 cm.
Victoria & Albert Museum, London

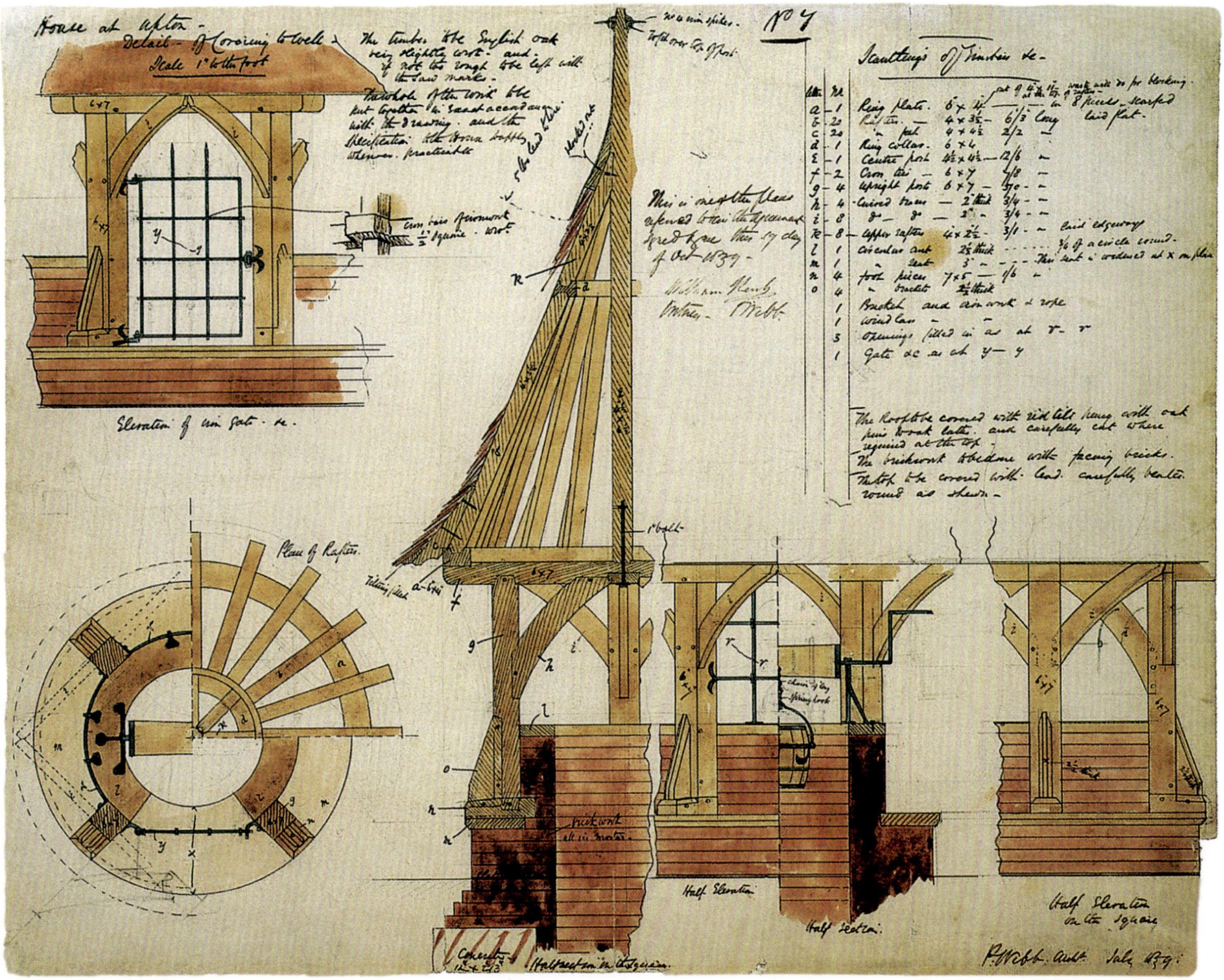

Philip Webb,
architectural drawing for the Red House (details of the roof over the well), 1839.
53 x 65.8 cm.
Victoria & Albert Museum, London.

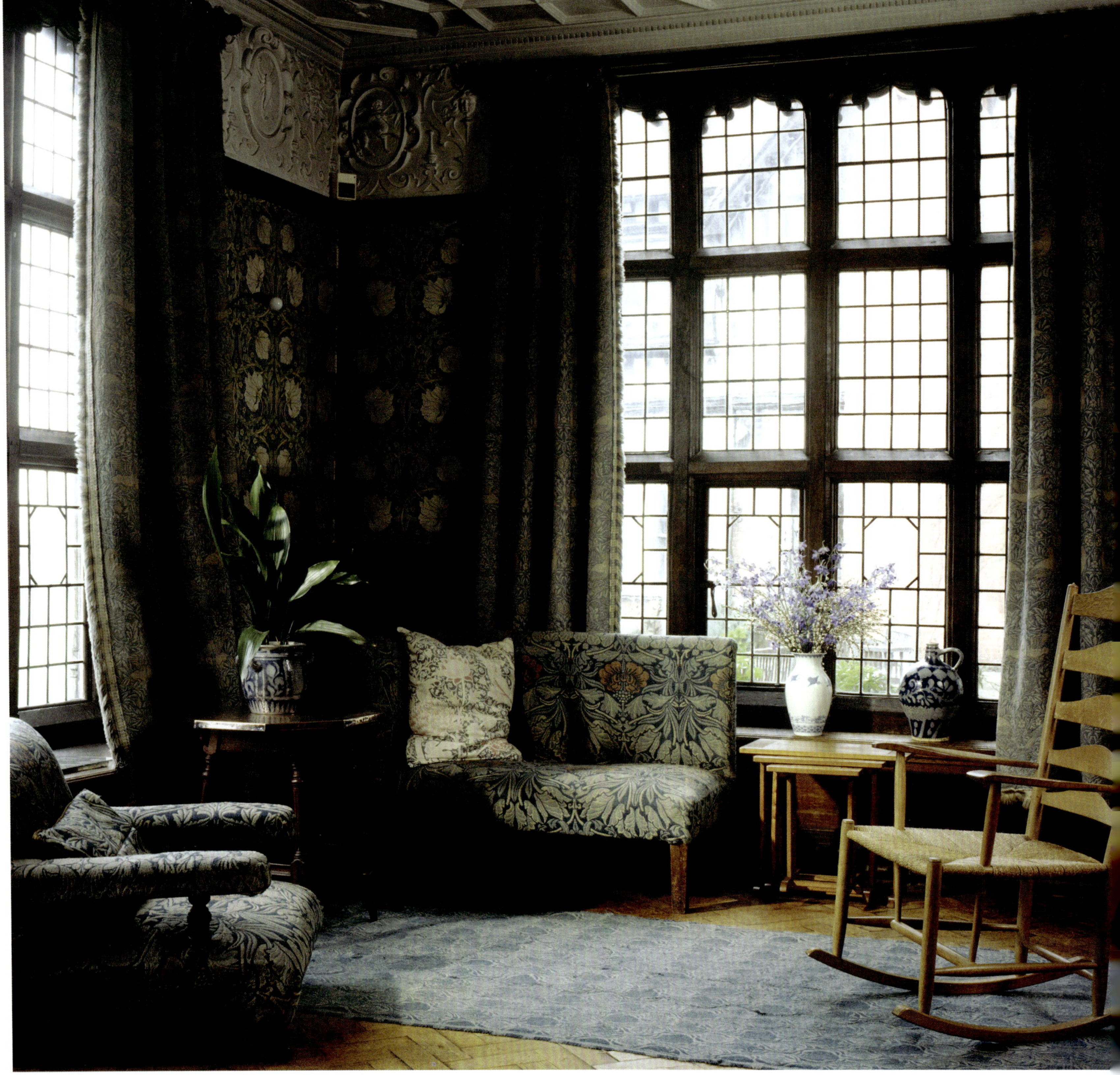

superior to any they had enjoyed. The capacious sheds of disused print-works, with some modification, gave room for designing, weaving, and cloth-printing. A running stream furnished water for dyeing. There was space for gardens. The grounds were free from noise and dust and distraction. There were birds' songs and the full sunshine. Under these conditions the work of the firm rapidly developed, the most important new line undertaken being the printing of "chintzes". Their new circulars advertised twelve different kinds of work: painted glass windows, arras tapestry, carpets, embroidery, tiles, furniture, general house decoration, printed cotton goods, paper hangings, figured woven stuffs, furniture velvets and cloths, and upholstery. Aside from the continual expansion of the work already undertaken there is little more to record on the side of Morris's practical craftsmanship. He had initiated a genuine revival of art industry, and was now instrumental in forming a school of designers and makers.

The Arts and Crafts Exhibition Society, which was started in London in 1888, may be taken as the type of result springing from the economic teaching of Ruskin and the example of Morris. Artists working in the decorative and applied fields had been pressing for recognition at the doors of the Royal Academy, but when their claims were refused they organised a separate exhibition. Such an exhibition had been suggested by Ruskin as early as 1878, and was now carried into effect by the new group of craftsmen, the most prominent of whom were Walter Crane, C. R. Ashbee, T. J. Cobden-Sanderson, and the Morrises, but numbering altogether over a hundred. The association was first known as The Combined Arts, but later, at the suggestion of Mr. Cobden-Sanderson, adopted the name of Arts and Crafts, as signifying more specifically the union of art and industry, for which the society stood. The exhibitions of the society increased yearly in value and importance, and they later became the most conspicuous evidence of the modern revival of handicraft. The volumes of essays upon the crafts which the society published contain the most advanced technical instruction in the applied arts to be found in English. The papers by Morris represent his final thought upon the crafts he practised, and contain his last protest against the "reckless waste of life in the pursuit of the means of life," which the current system of economy had countenanced. Walter Crane, acting as spokesman of the society, expressed his belief that the true root and basis of all art lay in the handicrafts. "If there is no room or chance of recognition," he argued, "for really artistic power and feeling in design and craftsmanship – if art is not recognised in the humblest object and material, and felt to be as valuable in its own way as the more highly rewarded pictorial skill – the arts cannot be in a sound condition; and if artists cease to be found among the crafts, there is great danger that they will vanish from the arts also, and become manufacturers and salesmen instead."

The last art which Morris attempted to master was that of printing. His interest in printing dates back to 1867, when he attempted to issue *The Earthly Paradise* in costly

William Morris,
The Billiard Room.
Bird tapestry weave curtain,
Pimpernel wallpaper and *Lily Kidderminster* carpet.
The Red House, Bexleyheath, London.

Philip Webb (for the design),
the Red House, 1860.
Bexleyheath, London.

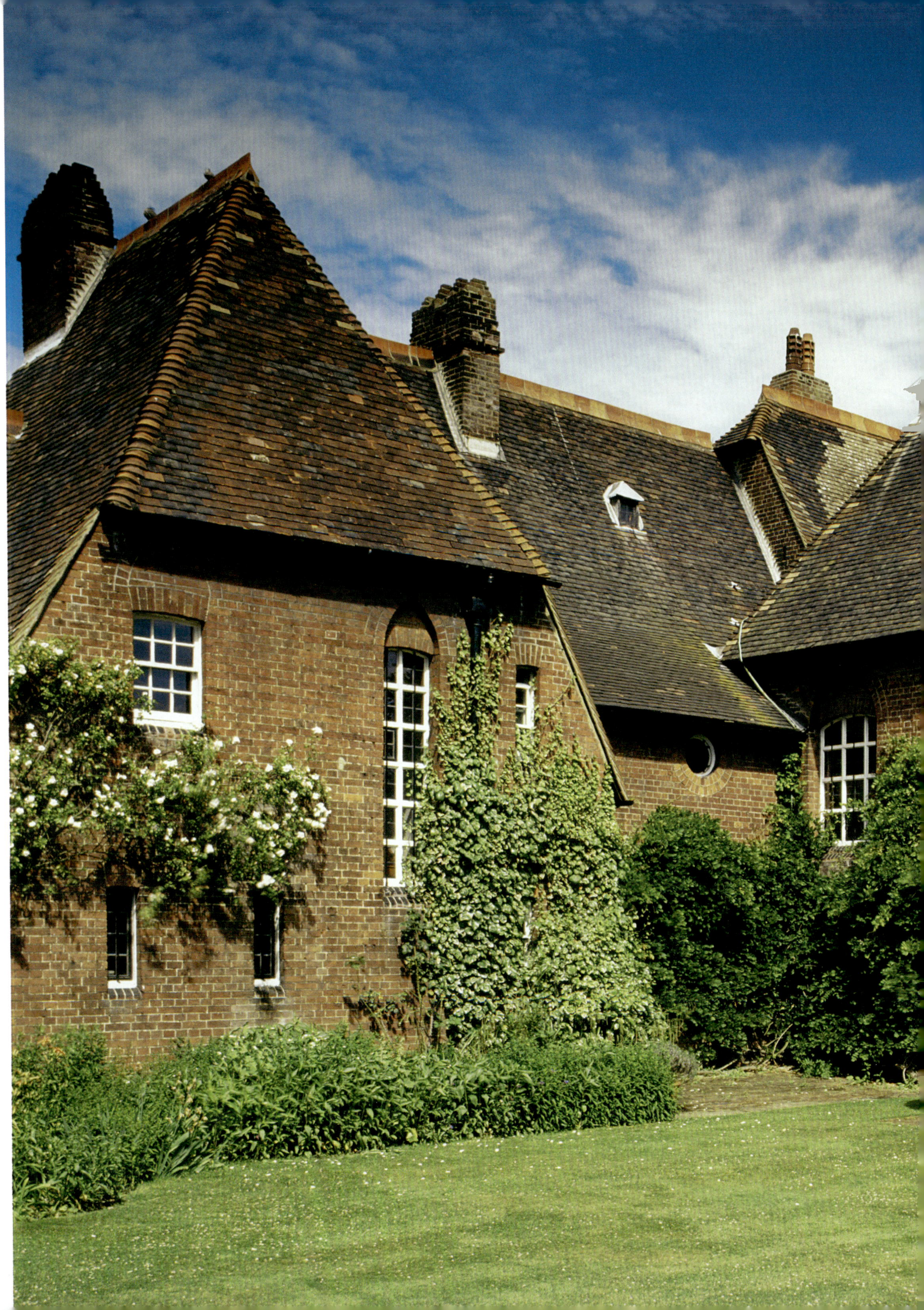

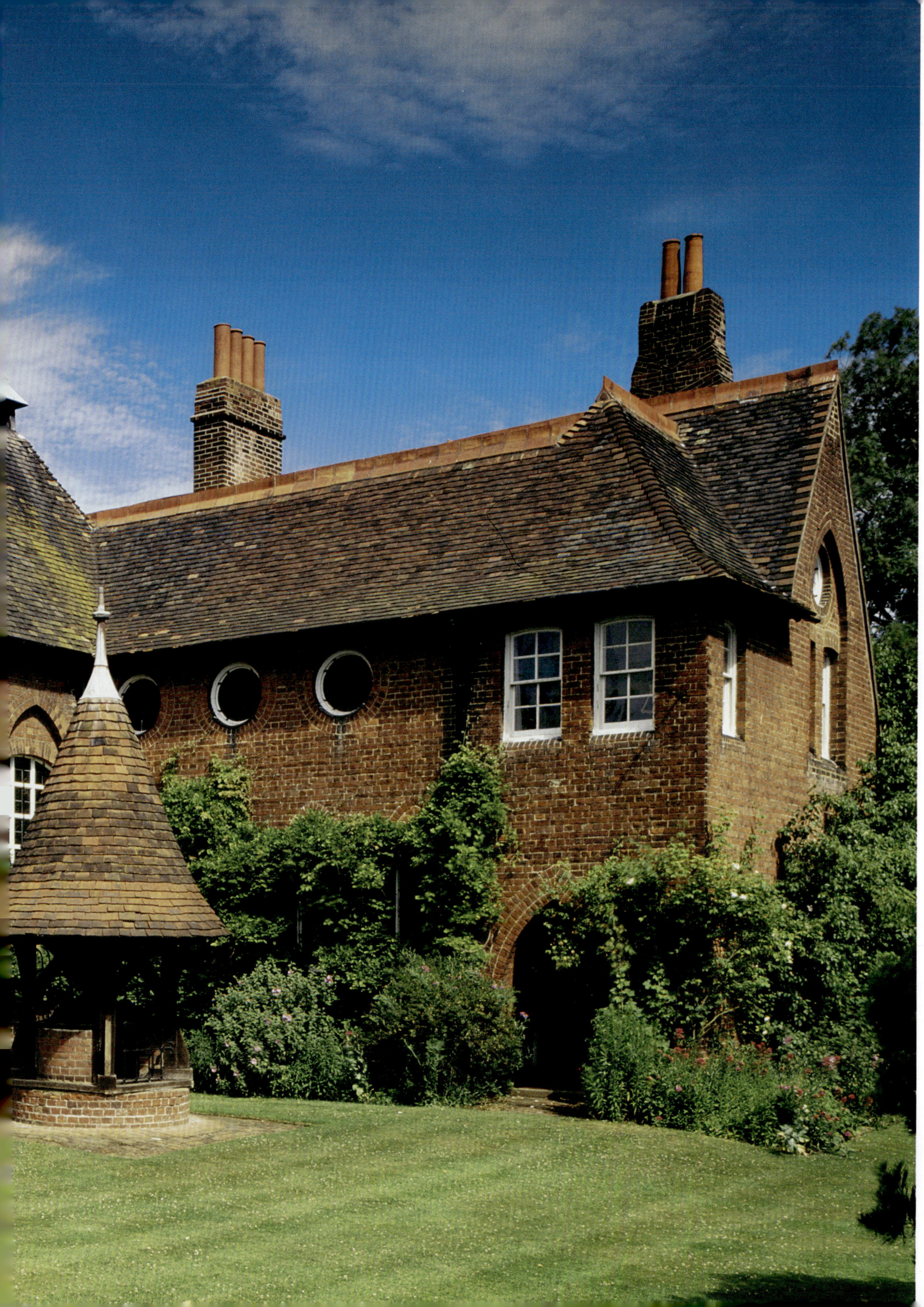

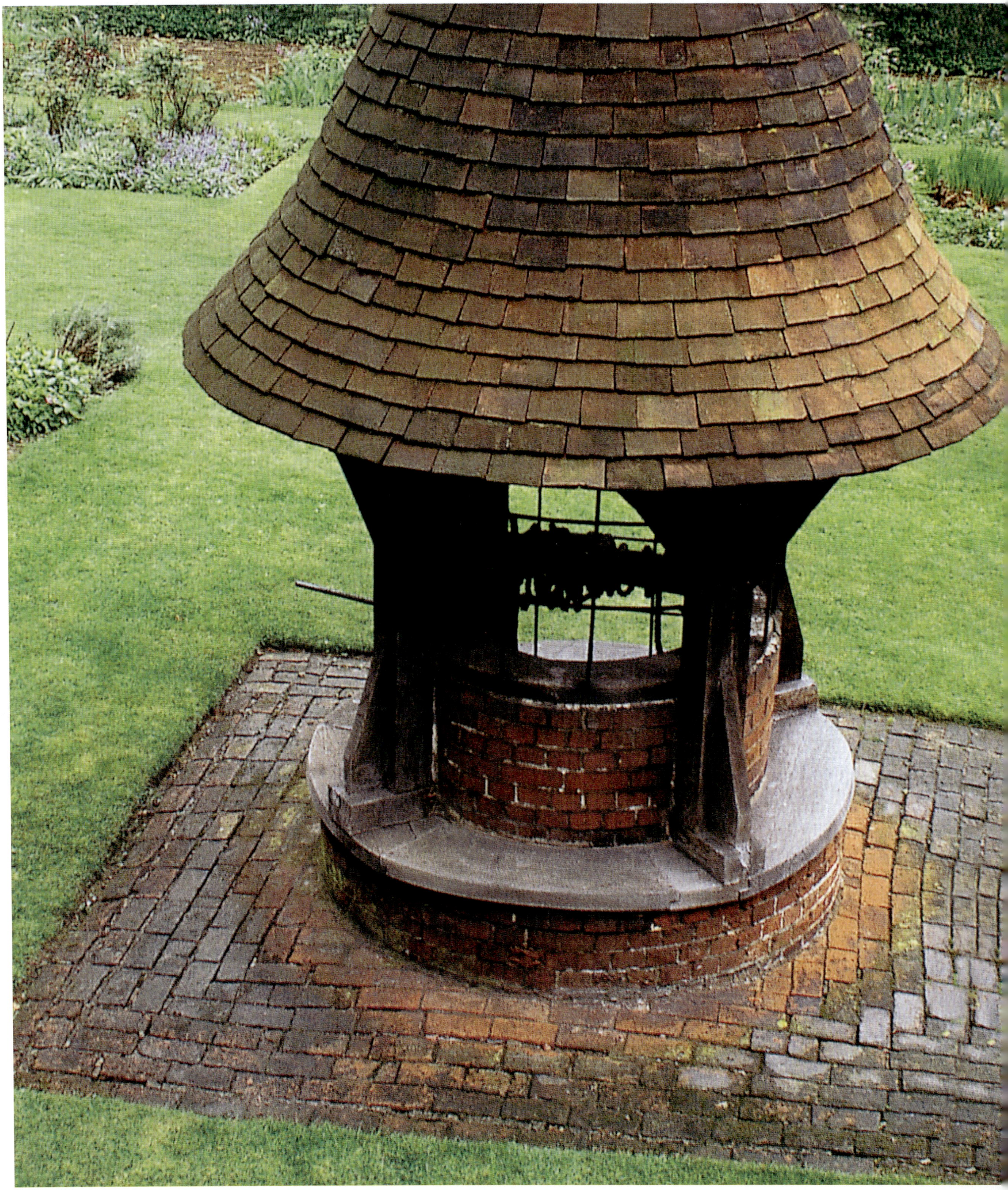

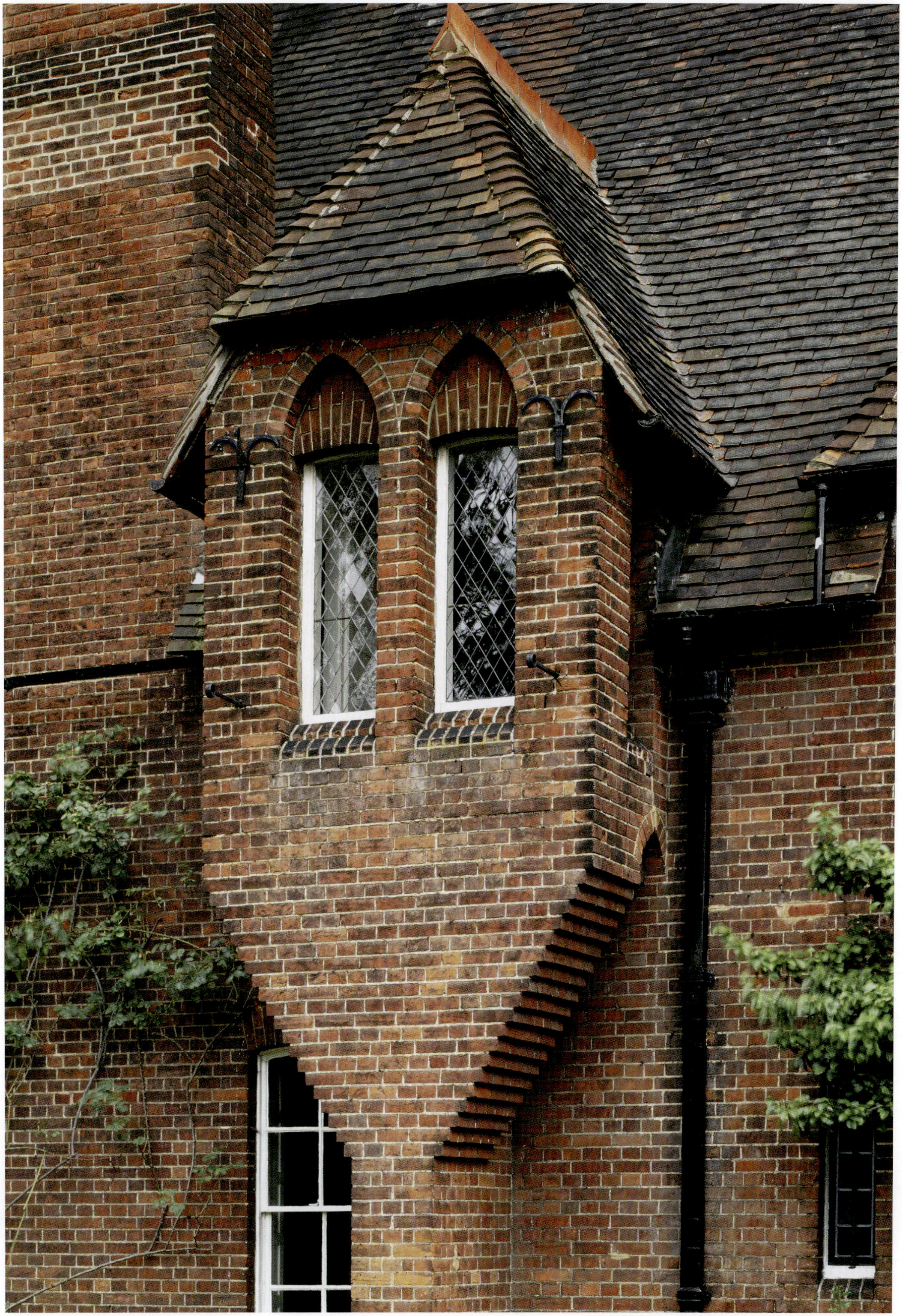

form and failed when faced with the difficulty of getting satisfactory printing and illustration. Now that he was writing again, and his zest for socialism being on the wane, he wanted to issue *The House of the Wolfings* and *The Roots of the Mountain* in attractive typography and took up once more the study of type and book-making in all its modes. For a time his work in connection with the Kelmscott Press, which was established in 1891, took him away from all other crafts. The letter he wanted was "pure in form; severe, without needless excrescences; solid, without the thickening and thinning of the line which is the essential fault of the ordinary modern type, and which makes it difficult to read; and not compressed laterally, as all later type has grown to be, owing to commercial exigencies." He found the perfected Roman type in the printing of Nicholas Jenson, one of the Venetian printers of the fifteenth century, and upon this type he based his own. In all he constructed three new types. He drew practically all the letters, stops, initials, borders, and ornaments which were used in his book-making, The Press continued for seven years, and in that time fifty-two works in sixty-six volumes were issued. In every respect – as printer, binder, and publisher – Morris advanced the art and craft of the book. Certainly his great Chaucer, finished just before his death, after more than three years of labour, is one of the most notable books in the world.

The socialism that lay at the base of Morris's handicraft may now be set forth. An implicit socialism may be understood as always abiding at the heart of his life. Exclusive and aristocratic though he was in his early youth, there was ever the larger sense for unity, and like Ruskin in similar circumstances, he yearned for social contact. The first manifestation of a community spirit was at the formation by the young men of Morris's group at Oxford of the Brotherhood, conceived in the beginning as a semi-monastic order, devoted to the higher life, but gradually changing to a social crusade against the age, with Carlyle and Ruskin as their accepted leaders. During the year 1856 the Brotherhood published the *Oxford and Cambridge Magazine*, which was intended to be the organ of the new thought. Ruskin promised something for its columns, but Morris was the chief contributor and its financial support. The essays were of a literary and social nature, but there was little grasp of the realities of the social problem. When Morris left Oxford for the architect's office the magazine languished, and was not issued a second year. The Oxford Brotherhood came to its real fulfilment in the business firm of Morris, Marshall, Faulkner and Company, which was in a rather vague way socialistic in its motive, certainly ideal in its tendency. The work of the manufactory was carried on in protest against the current economic and business methods of the day. In the first place, Morris made goods, not because he wanted to make money, but because he wanted to do the thing he was doing. He would not waste life in getting the means for living. He would take pleasure in his work, and make goods that were serviceable to others. Above all, he stood for the integrity of work, and would not himself make a design he could not execute, or with reference to materials he did not know.

Philip Webb (for the design), view from the Red House, 1860. Bexleyheath, London.

Philip Webb (for the design), the Red House (detail of windows on the west front), 1860. Bexleyheath, London.

William Morris, *The "Chèvrefeuille" Room*, 1887. Wightwick Manor, Wightwick Bank.

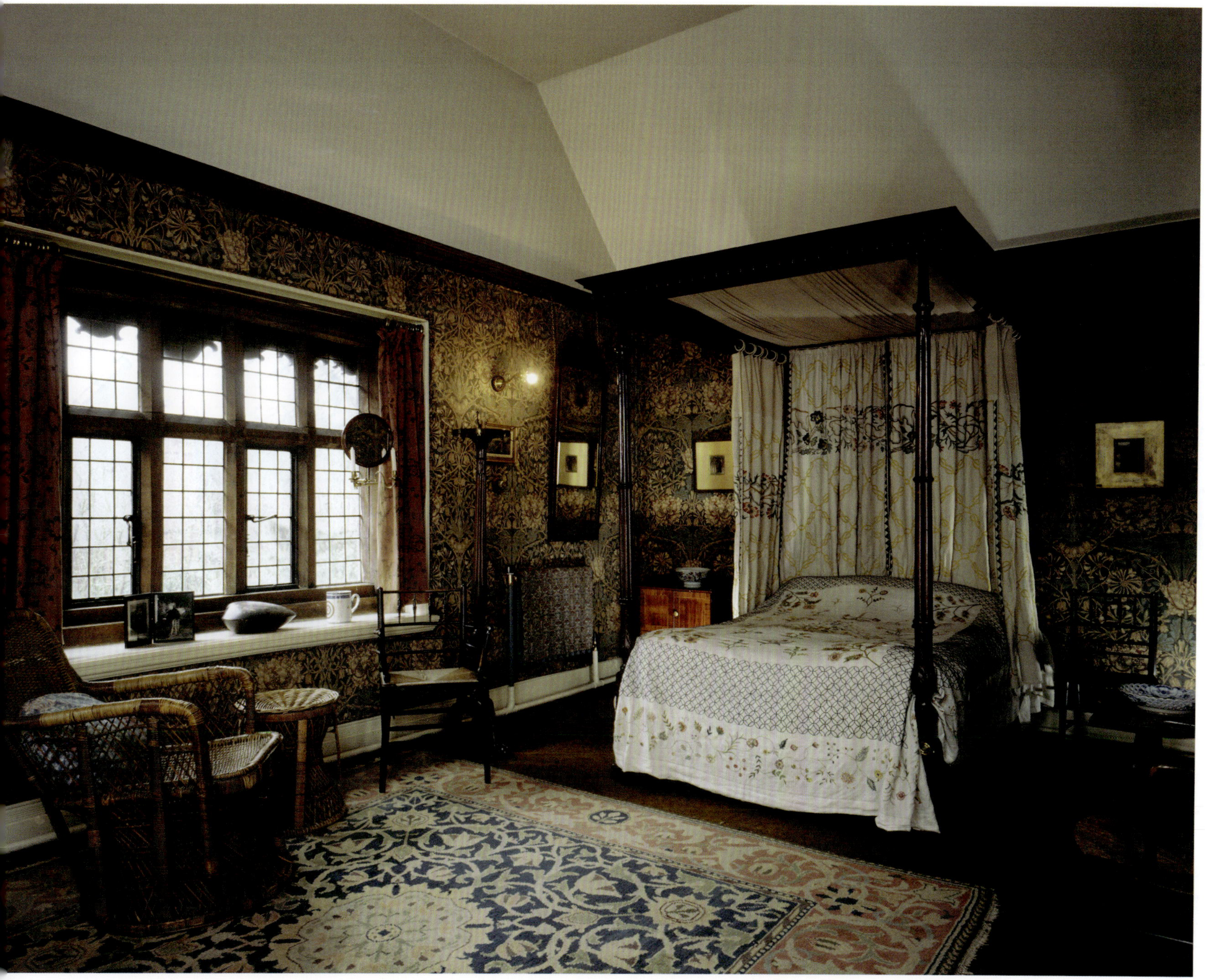

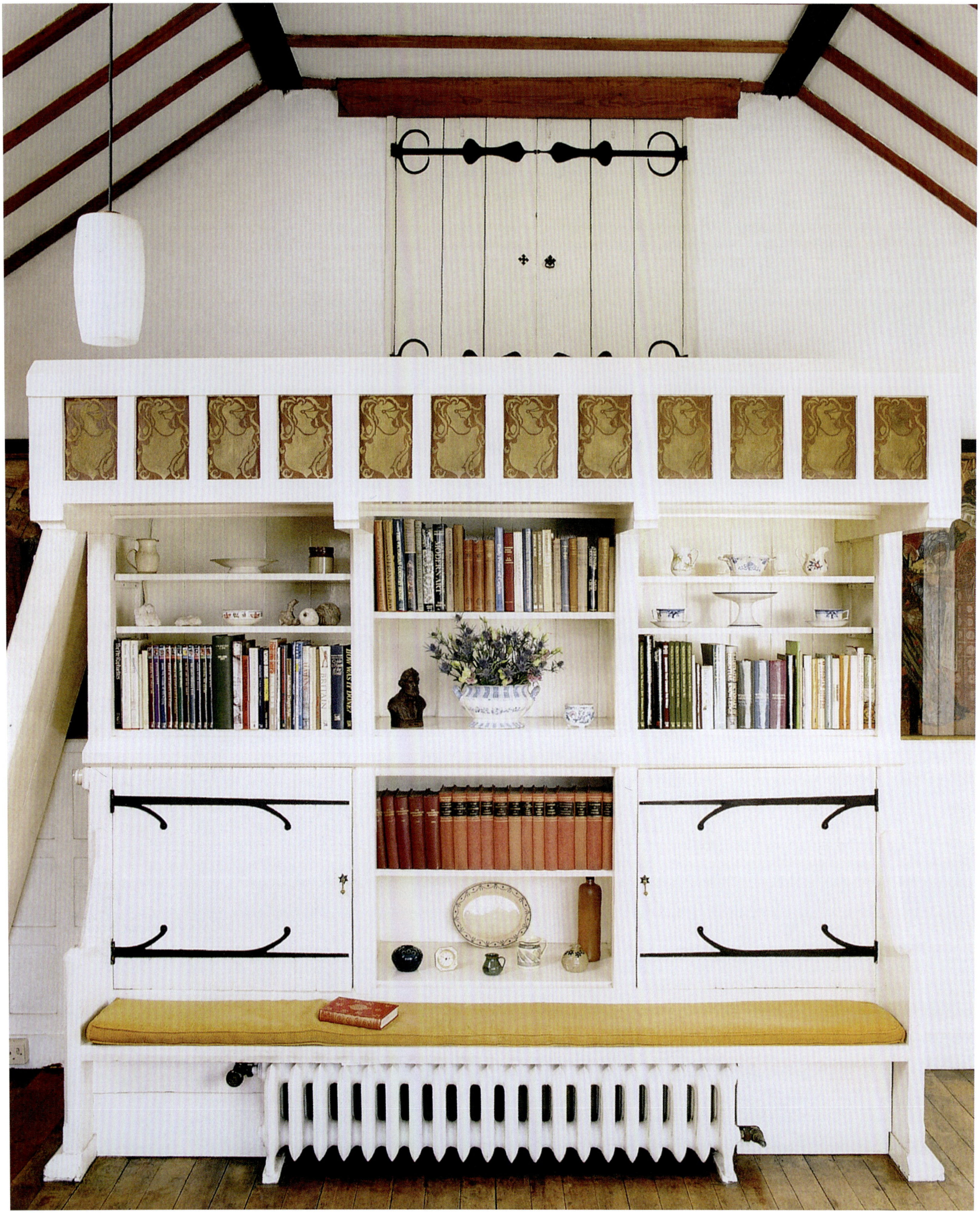

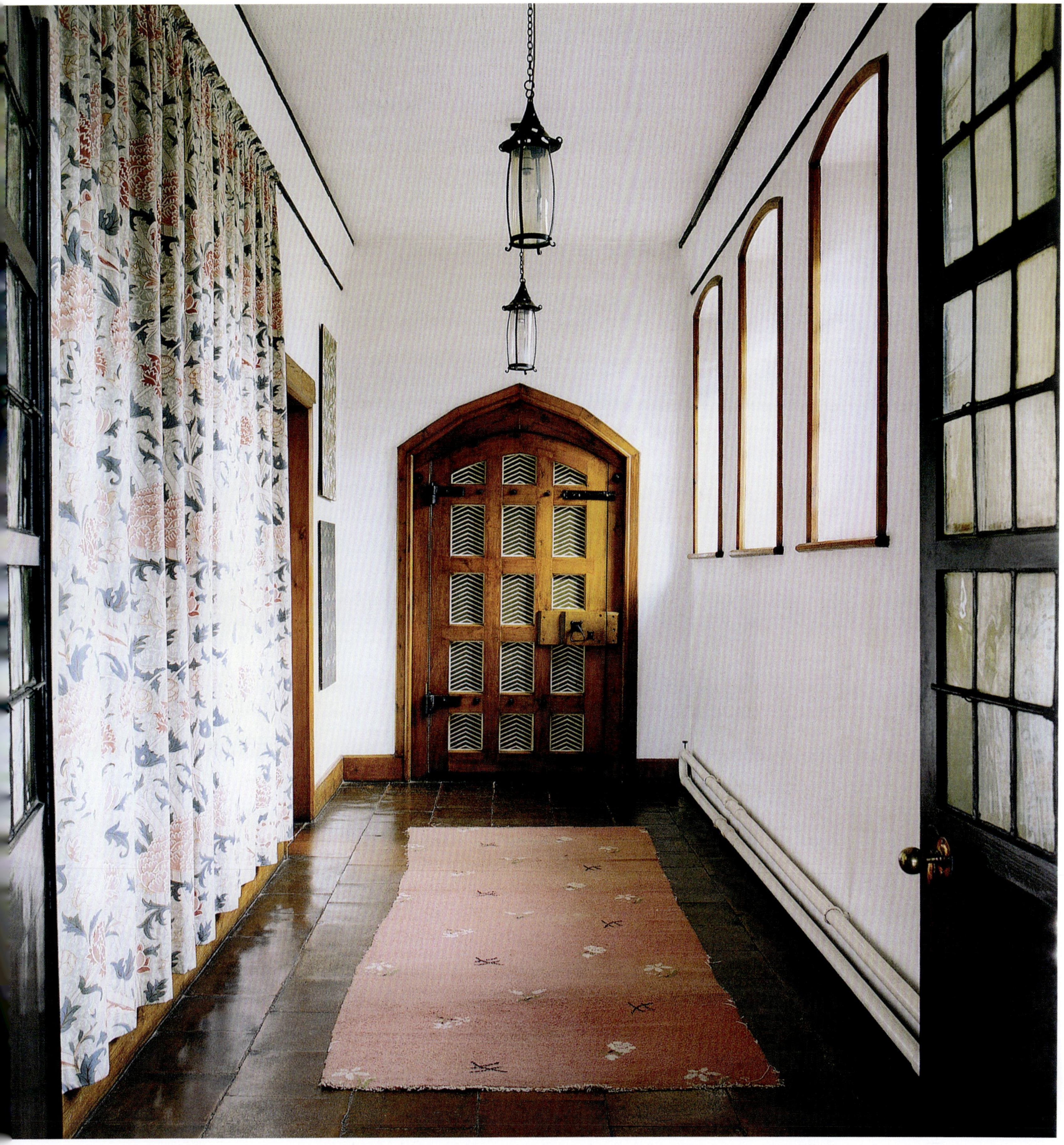

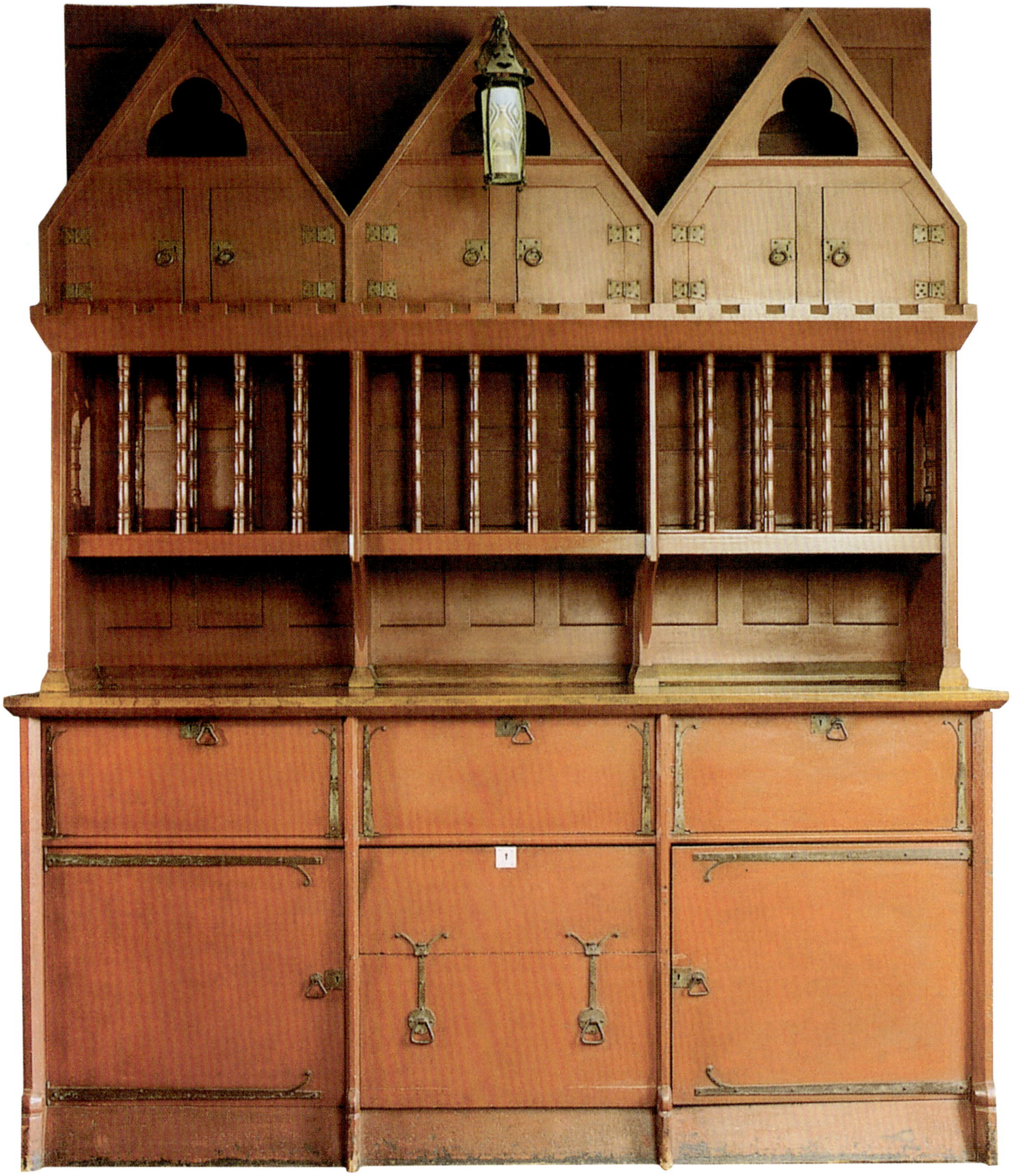

For himself, he wanted "money enough to keep him from fear of want or degradation for him and his; leisure enough from bread-earning work to give him time to read and think and connect his own life with the life of the great world; work enough and praise of it, and encouragement enough to make him feel good friends with his fellows; and his own due share of art, the chief part of which will he a dwelling that does not lack the beauty which Nature would freely allow it, if our own perversity did not turn Nature out of doors." Inevitably the work he was doing forced him to think of the conditions of labour in the capitalistic régime, yet for twenty years – or from about 1860 to 1880 – he saw no way of effecting revolution save by example. He was content to labour in his own field, in his own way, choosing poetry as one means of expression and craftsmanship as another. In politics he would be described as a Liberal, but passive in his attitude.

But in 1877 Morris was listening to the call to larger social service. That year he was instrumental in forming two social organisations, one the Society for the Protection of Ancient Buildings, out of his interest in which grew his active instruction in art, and the other the Eastern Question Association, a devotion to which led to his militant socialism. His most active propaganda for the Society for the Protection of Ancient Buildings was carried out in 1880, when it was learned that sweeping restorations were in progress at St. Marks, Venice. Morris wrote and spoke unceasingly in protest against the proposed demolition, the cause taking him to Oxford to appear there for the first time in a public capacity. He felt real heart sorrow at the loss that seemed eminent – the loss "of a work of art, a monument of history, and a piece of nature." Notwithstanding all discouragements, Morris persisted in preaching this lesson of the beauty of the earth and of man to the end of his days, and in his feelings toward the earth and man's historic monuments we may find the ground of much of his socialism.

The object of the second organisation Morris was interested in at the beginning of his active socialism was to prevent the war in the East. Morris was again chosen to write the manifesto for the society, and addressing "the workingmen of England", used these words:

"Workingmen of England, one word of warning yet: I doubt if you know the bitterness of hatred against freedom and progress that lies at the heart of the richer classes in this country; their newspapers veil it in a kind of decent language; but do but hear them talking among themselves, as I have often done, and I know not whether scorn or anger would prevail in you at their folly and insolence. These men cannot speak of your order, of its aims, of its leaders, without a sneer or an insult; these men, if they had the power (may England perish rather!), would thwart your just aspirations, would silence you, would deliver you bound hand and foot forever to irresponsible capital. Fellow citizens, look to it, and if you have any wrongs to be redressed, if you cherish your most worthy

William Morris (for the original design), **Philip Webb** (for the modifications) and **Dante Gabriel Rossetti** (for the painting of the original three doors), settle and bookcase.
The Red House, Bexleyheath, London.

Philip Webb (for the design), passage of the Red House opening to the servant's room, 1860.
The Red House, Bexleyheath, London.

Philip Webb,
Gothic dresser.
The Red House,
Bexleyheath, London.

hope of raising your whole order peacefully and solidly, if you thirst for leisure and knowledge, if you long to lessen these inequalities which have been our stumbling block since the beginning of the world, then cast aside sloth and cry out against an unjust war, and urge us of the middle classes to do no less."

Before an Exeter Hall audience gathered to protest against the government, Morris made his first appearance as a writer of political verse, with a ballad, entitled "Wake, London Lads," anticipating there the later "Chants for Socialists."

In 1877 Morris became treasurer of the National Liberal League, an organisation made up of workingmen in opposition to the Eastern policy of the government, but when a later election placed the Liberal party in power, and Morris saw that hope rested in neither Tory nor Whig, he withdrew from party lines and worked for the actual reconstruction of society. In December of the same year, 1877 – the year that marks the beginning of Morris's widening social interests – he delivered his first lecture on the decorative arts before the Trades Guild of Learning, and when published immediately in pamphlet form, the essay became his first prose contribution to socialistic literature. This essay (afterward reprinted in the volume entitled *Hopes and Fears for Art*, under the head of *The Lesser Arts*) contains some pregnant sentences relative to his social hopes and motives. He was here speaking to craftsmen, and he addressed them familiarly and with deep feeling, lamenting the decay of art, but hoping for its revival again under better social conditions. The decay of the lesser arts – the arts, that is, of use – had come about through the withdrawal of the fine artist from the field of handicraft and his attachment to the leisure classes. As the arts sundered into the greater and the lesser, contempt was begotten on one side and ignorance on the other. The artist left the craftsman without hope of elevation; he himself was left without the help of intelligent sympathy. Both classes have suffered, but the workman more than the artist. Commerce also has fallen more heavily upon the craftsman than upon the artist; he has been forced into the field of competition, a competition not of excellence, but of cheapness, and the things he makes are veritably "cheap and nasty", and as they were without pleasure to the maker, so they give no pleasure to the user.

An address in 1881 on "Art and the Beauty of the Earth" is well said to be the "sum of all his earlier and the germ of all his later doctrines." With that complete historic knowledge which characterises all his writings, he distinguished between the times that cultivated art and those that neglected it. For example, he spoke of the art in the Middle Ages and mentioned the freedom of the arts at that period. He also discusses the theme of the machine. It is possible that nearly everything needed by man can be made by machinery. "I myself," Morris said, "have boundless faith in their capacity. I believe machines can do everything except make works of art." The second clause in Morris's indictment of his times referred to the ugliness of the environment: "Of all the things

William Morris,
unfinished painting on the cupboard in the hall of the Red House, 1860.
The Red House, Bexleyheath, London.

Morris & Co.,
The Great Parlour, 1893.
Polychrome timber ceiling and furnitures provided by Morris & Co. and seventeenth and eighteenth-century pieces.
Wightwick Manor, Wightwick Bank.

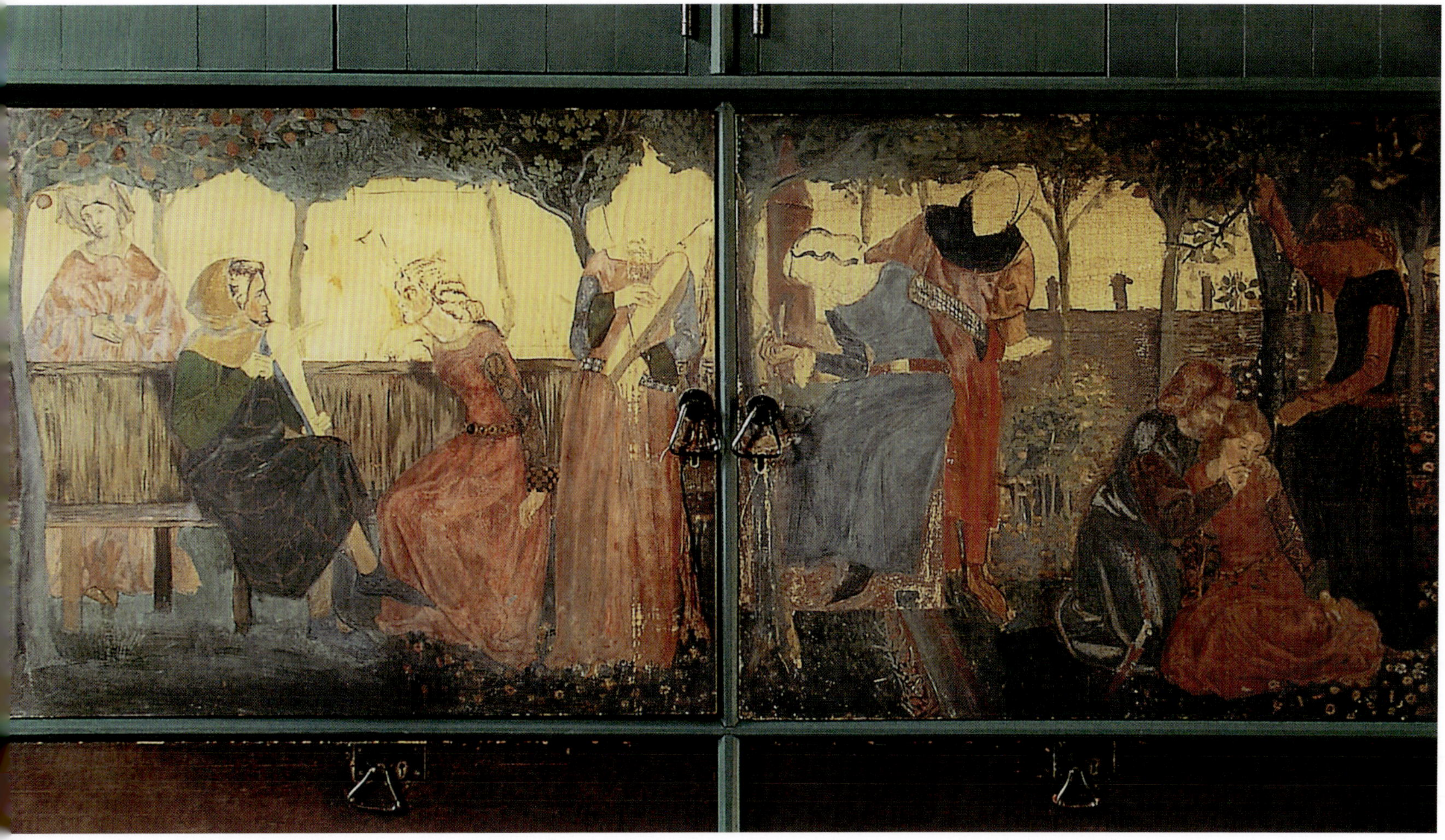

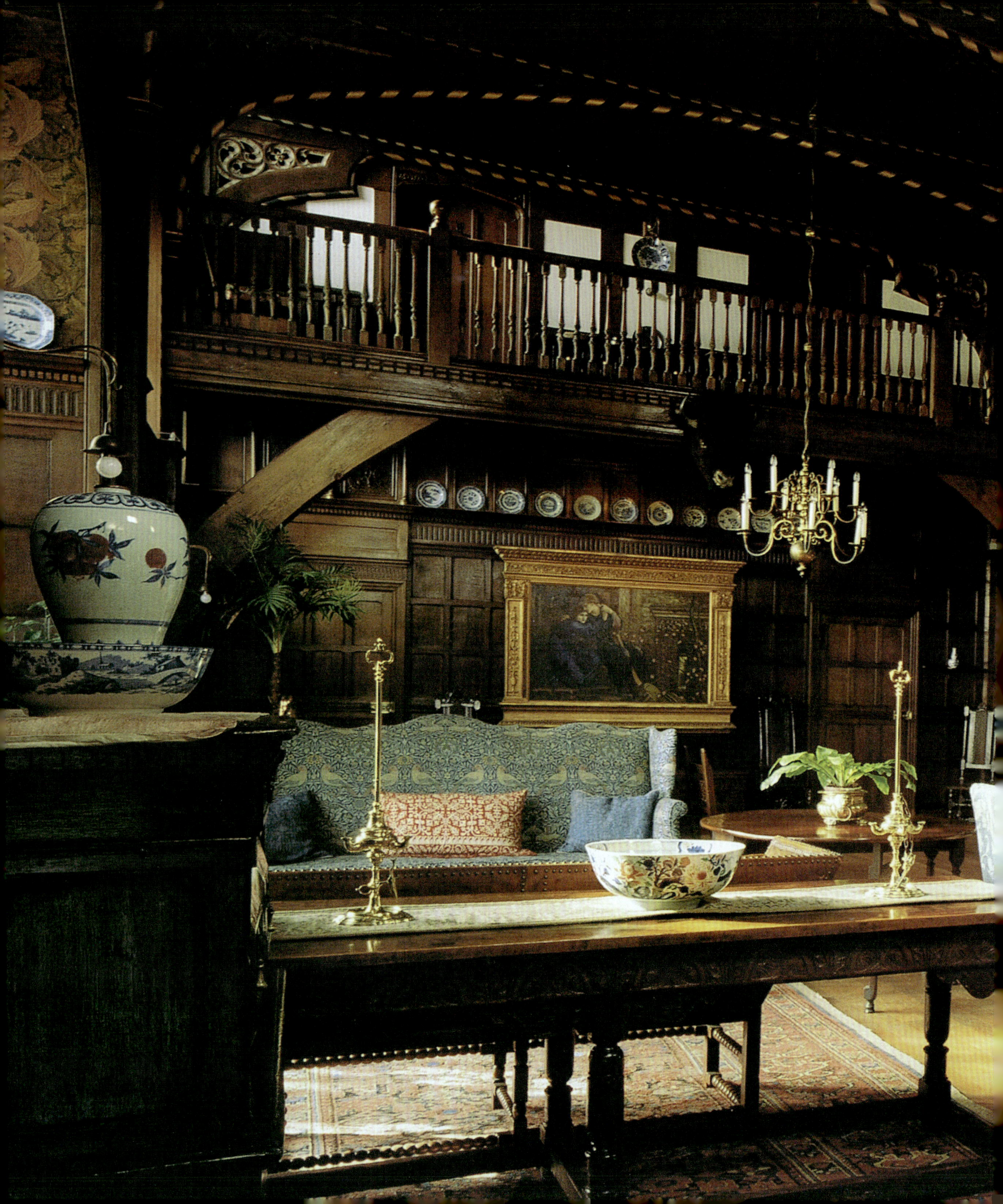

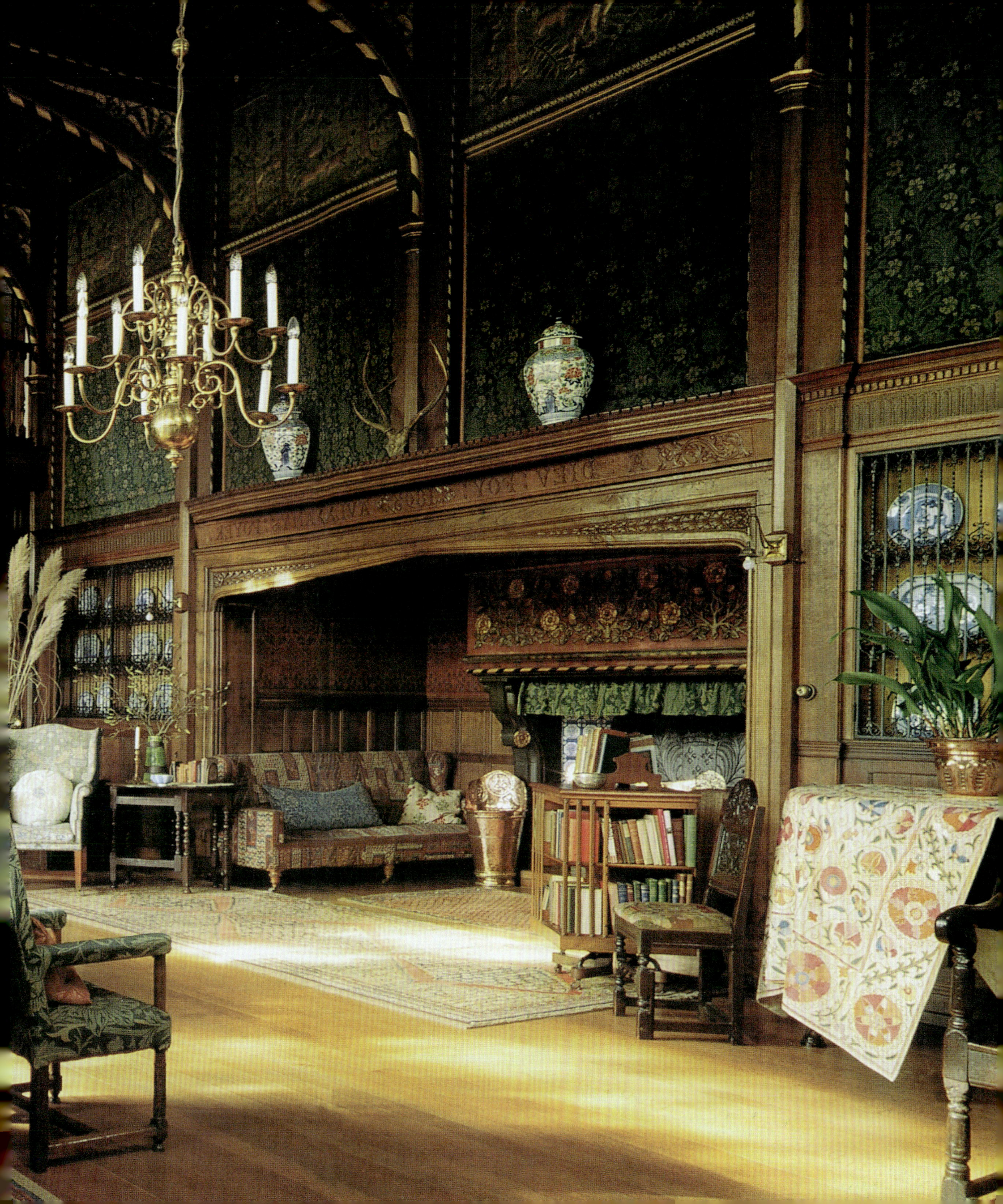

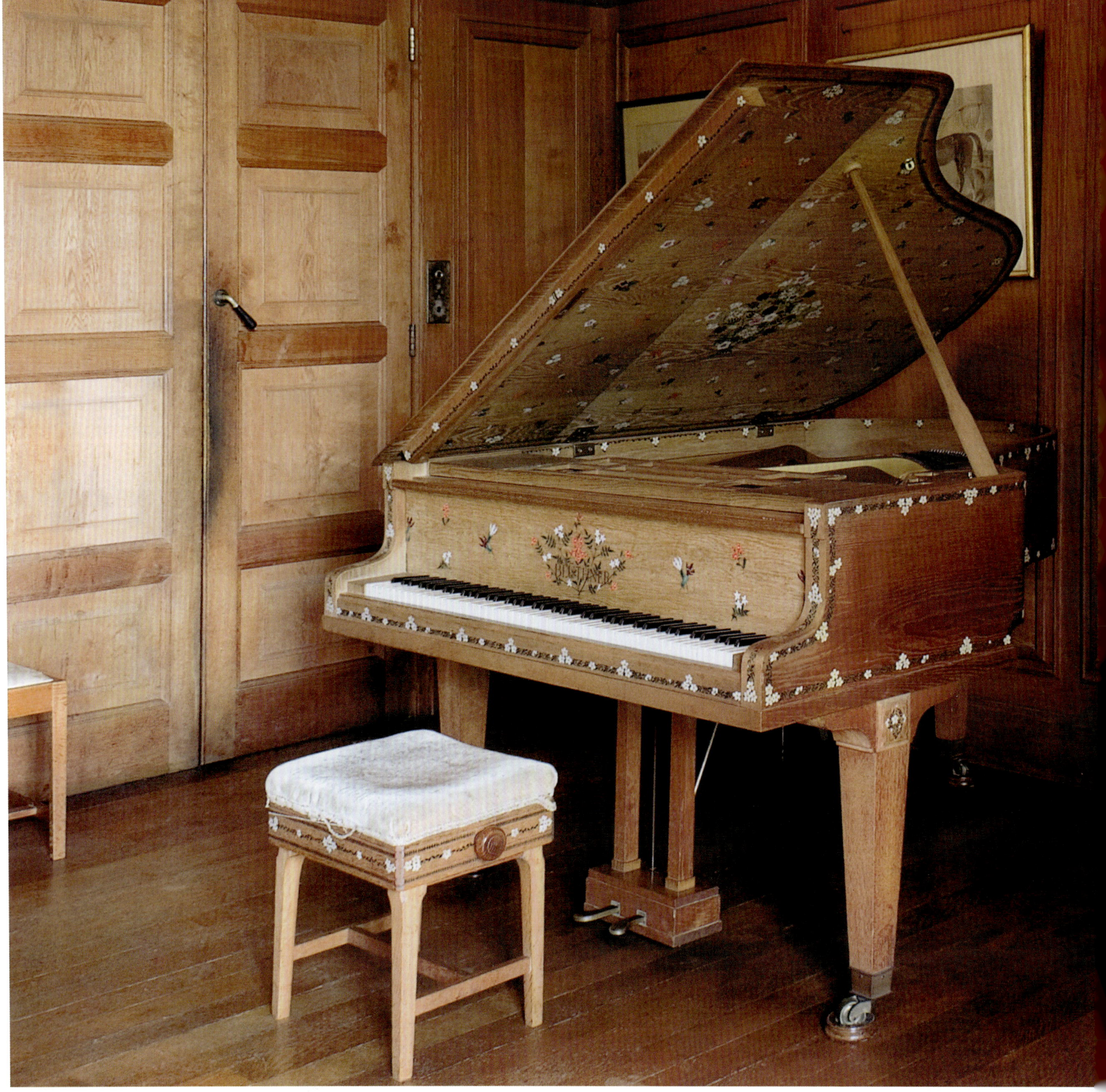

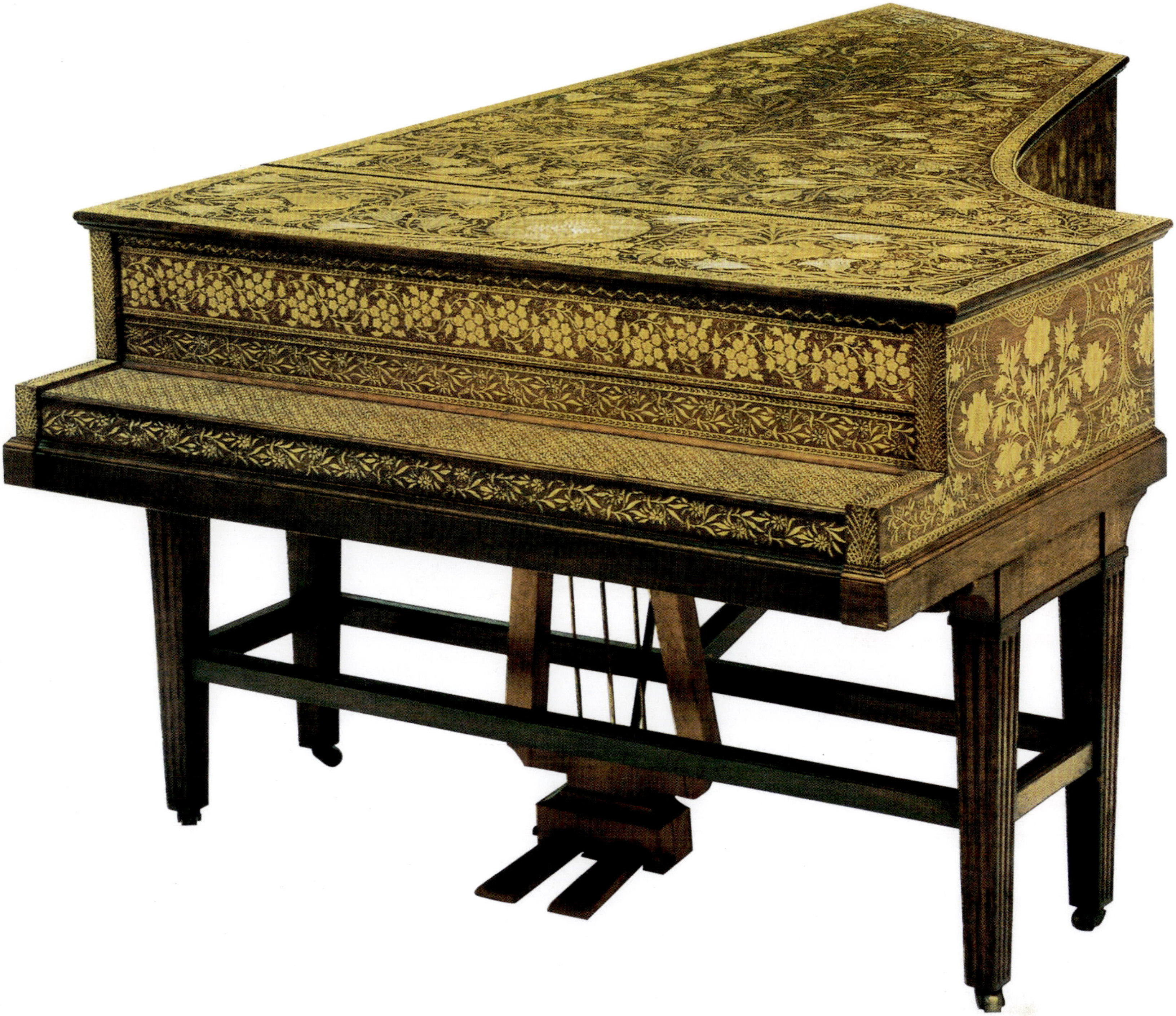

that are likely to give us back popular art in England, the cleaning of England is the first and most necessary. Those who are to make beautiful things must live in a beautiful place." For an art which is to be made by the people and for the people two virtues are necessary: honesty and simplicity – honesty as opposed to injustice, and simplicity as opposed to luxury. On both of these topics Morris wrote many passages. His golden rule of house-furnishing was, "Have nothing in your houses which you do not know to be useful or believe to be beautiful." He claimed that all art started from this simplicity, and the greater the art the more noticeable was its simplicity. But this virtue appealed to him not merely because simple art was more beautiful than sumptuous art but because it was more social. Luxury is an outgrowth of and is accompanied by slavery; it means the piling up of possessions, the spoil of the earth, and for the owner a chain of pompous circumstance which checks and annoys him at every step. Finally he stated definitely in this volume what the "Cause" is for which he strives: "That cause is the democracy of art, the ennobling of daily and common work, which will one day put hope and pleasure in the place of fear and pain, as the forces which move men to labour and keep the world a-going."

After the publication of this volume Morris's socialism became more and more political and actively militant. With his conscience touched, and hoping something practical might be done to relieve the social situation, Morris gave up his half-hearted political radicalism and joined the Democratic Federation, contributing time and money to its publication, *Justice*. He conceived that by state socialism something of change could be effected, and for several years, particularly during 1883 and 1884, he gave most of his time and energy to socialistic propaganda. When his friends expostulated that the lectures he was delivering, and the leaders and "Chants for Socialists" he was writing did not compensate for the poetry he was neglecting, and that his work as a socialist was less effective and valuable than his designing and weaving, he answered, "I cannot help acting in this matter." How seriously the times were pressing upon him is indicated by a letter dated 1883: "I have long felt sure that commercialism must be attacked at the root before we can be on the road for those improvements in life which I so much desire. A society which is founded on the system of compelling all well-to-do people to live on making the greatest possible profit out of the labour of others must be wrong. For it means the perpetuating the division of society into civilised and uncivilised classes. I am far from being an anarchist, but even anarchy is better than this, which is in fact anarchy and despotism mixed. If there is no hope of conquering this – let us eat and drink, for tomorrow we die."

At this time Morris was firm in the belief that the reorganisation of society was practicable, and that if it could be effected the misery of the world would speedily come to an end. In writing the manifesto for the Hammersmith branch of the Democratic Federation, he

Louise Powell,
piano.
Rodmarton Manor, Cirencester.

Edward Burne-Jones and **Kate Faulkner** (for the design) and **John Broadwood** (for the production),
grand piano, 1883.
Oak, stained and decorated with gold and silver-gilt gesso,
266 x 140.5 x 45.7 cm.
Victoria & Albert Museum, London.

Edward Ould (architect) and **Charles Eamer Kempe** (stained glass design), entrance hall alcove, built in 1887-1888.
Wightwick Manor, Wightwick Bank.

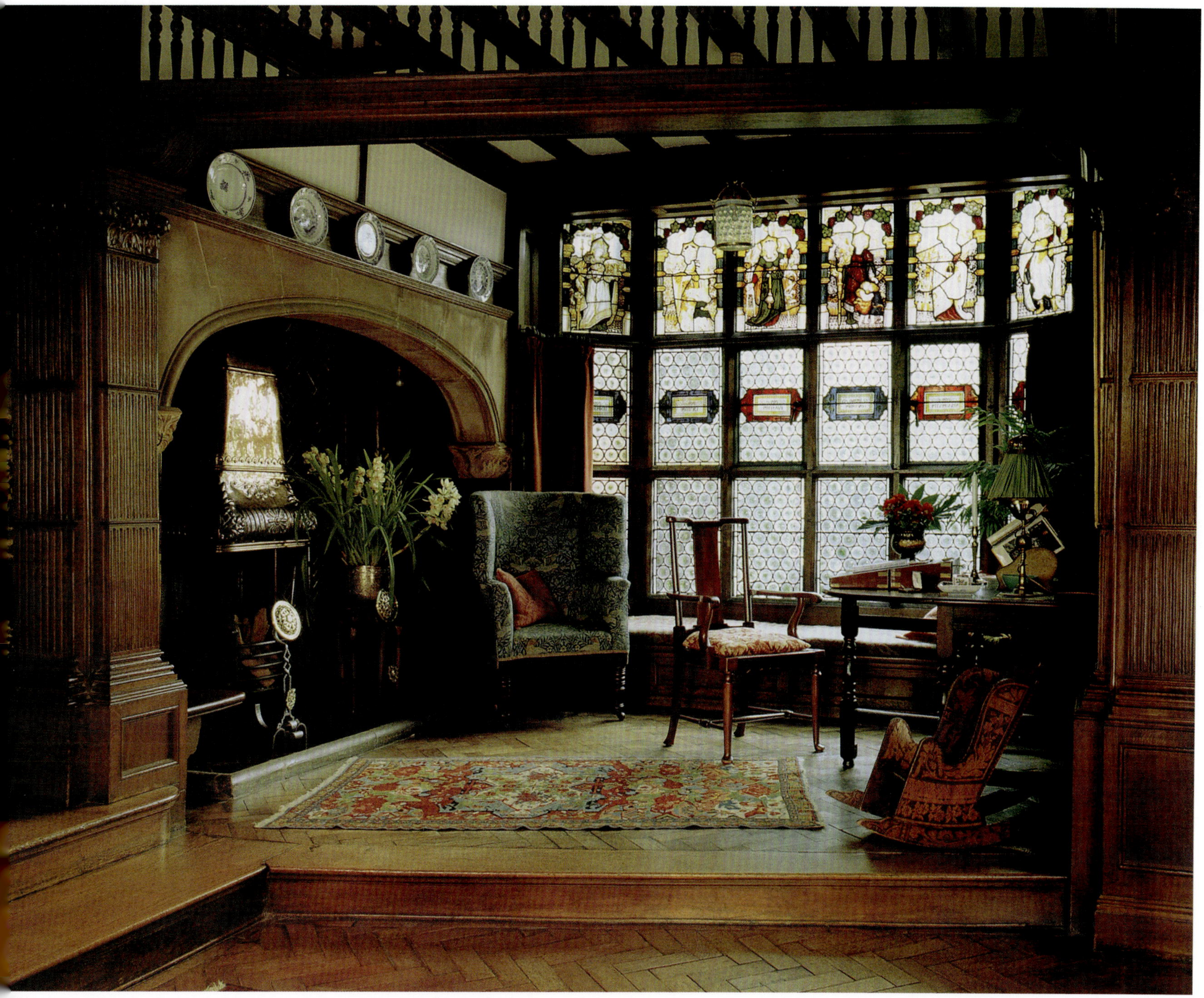

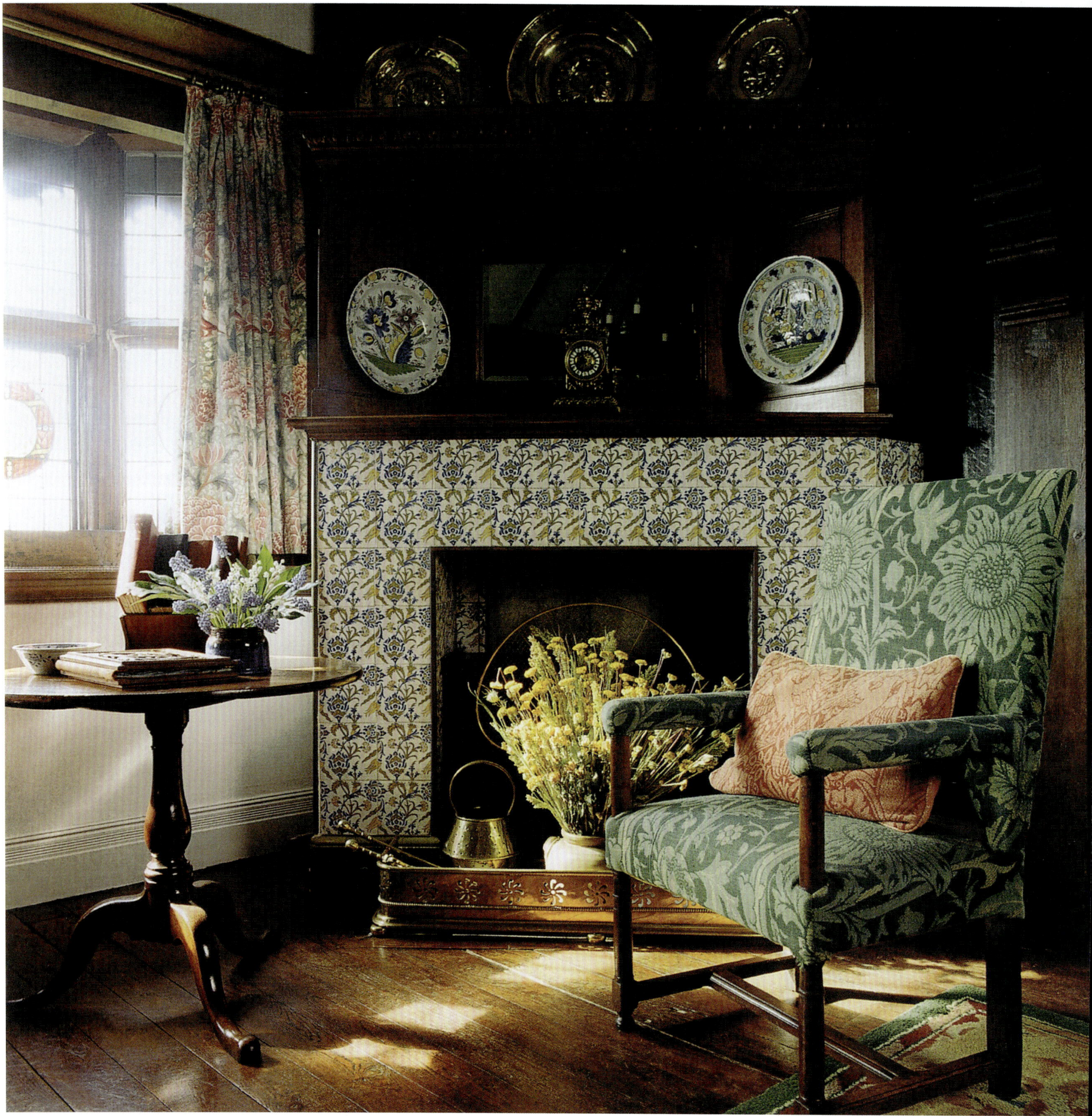

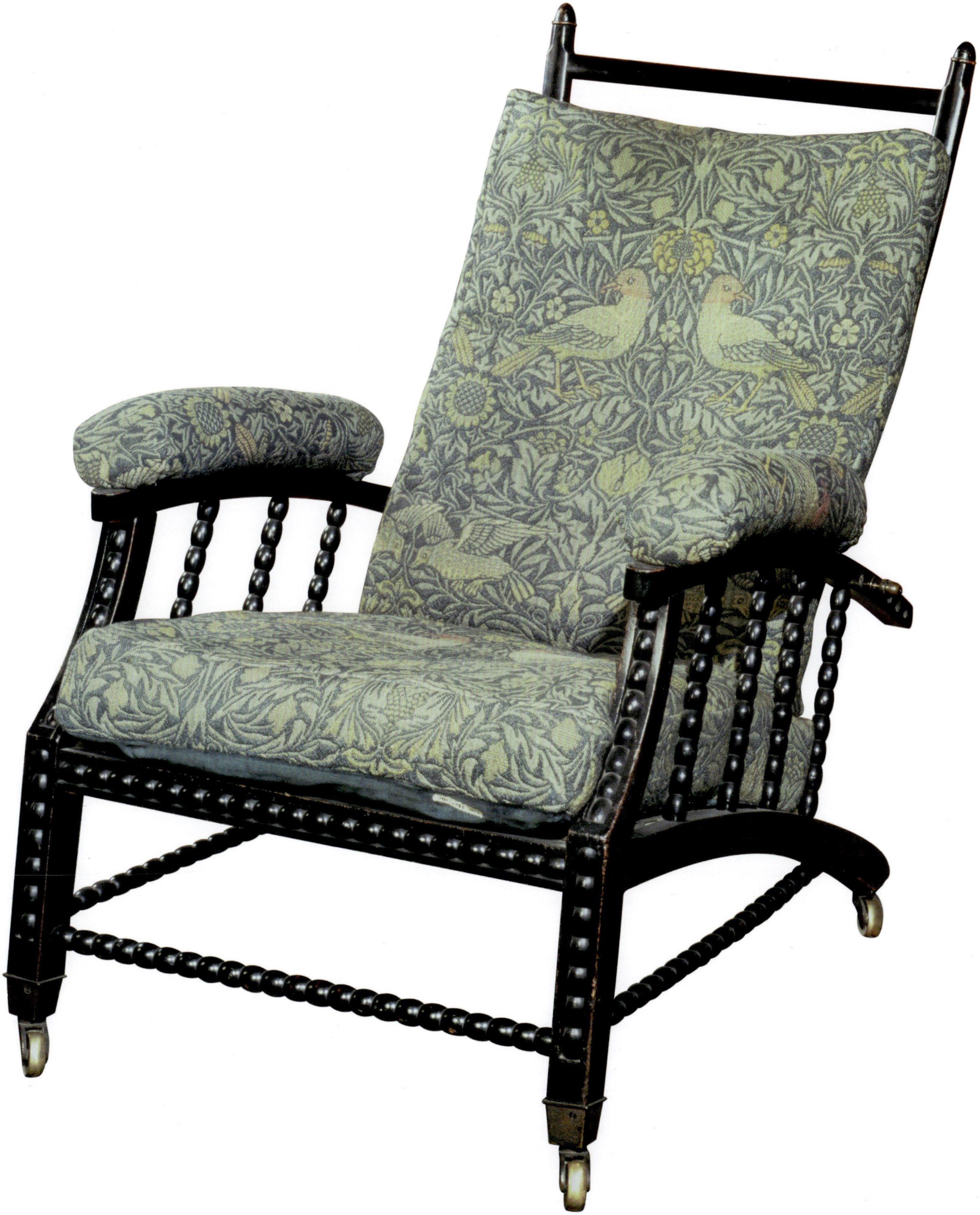

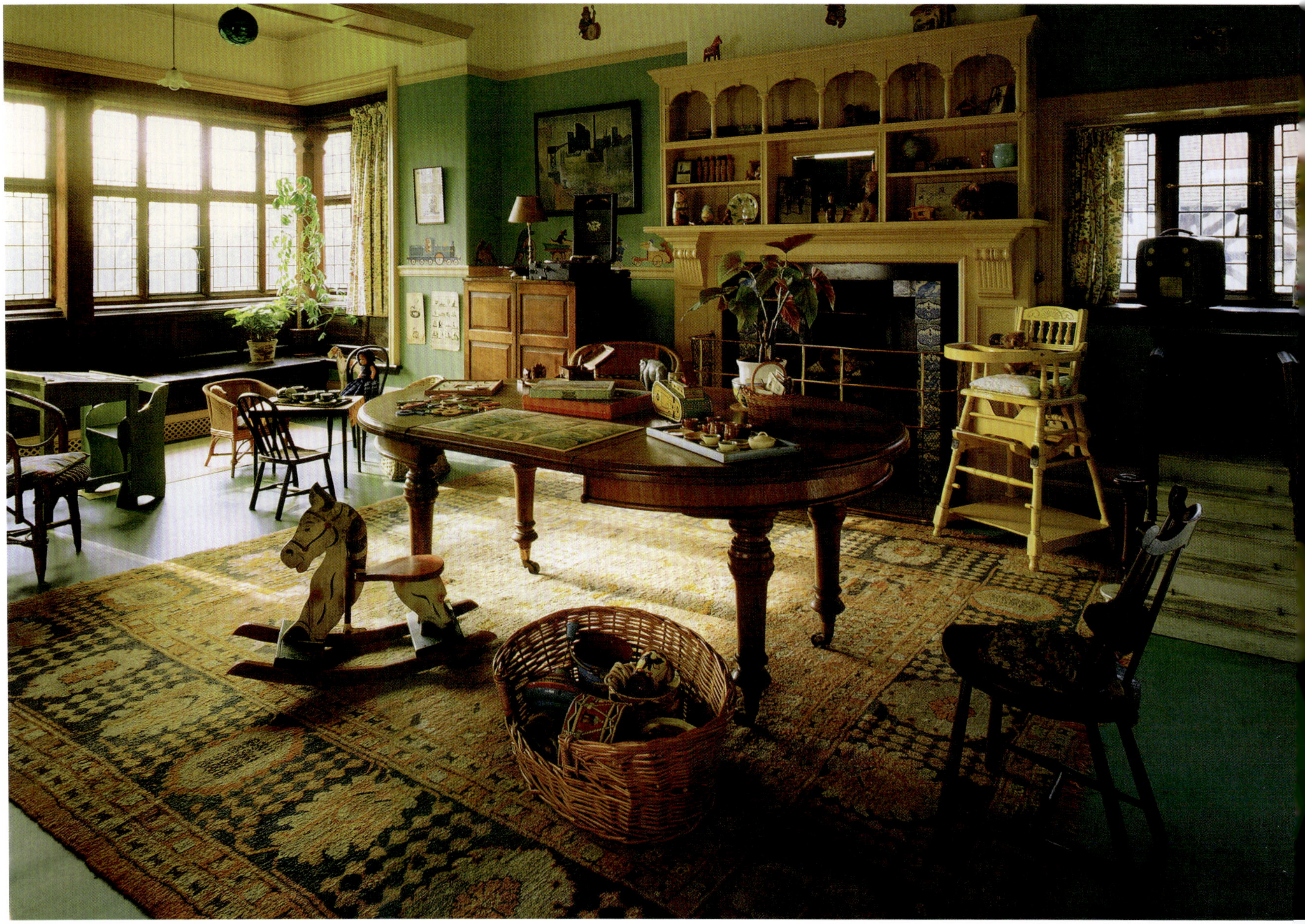

referred again to the war between capital and labour, and declared: "Socialism will end this war by abolishing classes; this change will get rid of bad housing, underfeeding, overwork, and ignorance." He believed this so thoroughly that when the Democratic Federation was disrupted – owing to the bickerings of members – Morris was prominent in organising at once the Socialist League and in conducting its paper, *The Commonweal.* The manifesto of the new league, dismissing as useless all temporary and partial changes, declared for a complete revolution in the basis of society. Filled with loathing at the "cannibalism" of society, Morris wrote at this time: "One must turn to hope, and only in one direction do I see it – on the road to revolution; everything else is gone now." Yet after 1886 Morris gradually withdrew from the more violent members of his party, and announced that the revolution must come by education: "Education towards revolution seems to me to express in three words what our policy should be." Consequently he took less and less interest in the active propaganda of the day, and turned again to literature, publishing, in 1886, *The Dream of John Ball*, socialistic in its motive, to be sure, but tempered by reflection and imagination. In 1890 he contributed to successive numbers of *The Commonweal* his socialistic romance, *News from Nowhere*, written in opposition to Bellamy's *Looking Backward.* Morris here proposes a simple, pastoral life, motived by co-operation in labour, incentive to which is pleasure in life itself, as against Bellamy's complex state socialism, centralisation, and machinery. Finally, in 1890, the affairs of the Socialistic League having gone from bad to worse, Morris resigned from the organisation.

Soon after withdrawing from the league, Morris organised the Hammersmith Socialist Society, with the object of "making socialists" and spreading the principles of socialism. The meetings were held weekly at Morris's house on the Upper Mall, and by lectures, street-meetings, and publications the work of the society was carried on its "Statement of Principles".

During the remaining years of his life Morris was active in many directions – writing, working, lecturing, equally interested in life and in the arts of life. To the ending of the day of commercial selfishness, and to the dawning of the day of peace and good will, Morris ever looked forward, with the same feeling as when, in Sigurd, he pictured the twilight of the old gods and the rising of the sun of Balder, the Beautiful.

The Sixth Exhibition, in 1899, of the London Arts and Crafts Exhibition Society was made notable by a memorial exhibition of works by William Morris. One room of the new gallery was devoted to a collection of his more intimate and personal work, comprising over one hundred and fifty of his original drawings for fabrics, stained glass, wall-paper, and printing, and the products of the Kelmscott Press. To the catalogue of this exhibition Mr. Walter Crane contributed a note in memory of the former president of the society, which, as one of the most adequate estimates made of the great designer, may be quoted:

Edward Ould (architect) and **Morris & Co.** (for the furniture and textiles), *The Oak Room*, built in 1887-1888. Fireplace lined with Dutch "Persian Flower" tiles and carved with lines from Samuel Taylor Coleridge's *The Rime of the Ancient Mariner.* Wightwick Manor, Wightwick Bank.

William Morris, adjustable-back chair, upholstered in original *Bird* woollen tapestry, 1870-1890. Ebonized wood with Utrecht velvet upholstery. Loose covers of wool tapestry, 97.8 x 71.1 x 91.4 cm. Victoria & Albert Museum, London.

Edward Ould (architect) and **Morris & Co.** (for the furniture and textiles), nursery, built in 1887-1888. Wightwick Manor, Wightwick Bank.

"Three years have passed since, on the eve of the opening of our Fifth Exhibition, on October 3rd, 1896, William Morris, our late president, died. It seems fitting, therefore, in inaugurating the Sixth Exhibition of the Society, to offer a word to the memory of the great designer and craftsman, poet and social reformer, who has been so potent an influence in the movement of revival in the handicrafts which has characterised the later years of our century. Looking at the evidence of his extraordinary energy and power of concentration spent upon the details of so many different crafts, one is struck no less by the vigour and strength of his work in each as by the care and taste displayed. William Morris's unerring instinct for decorative beauty in surface ornament allowed him to be exuberant and profuse, rich and intricate, or, as in the earlier work, frank and simple. One sees an English taste and reserve united with a luxuriant and almost Oriental fancy. Yet through them all one feels the spirit of the romantic and narrative poet refining and informing every detail, as one may see the sunlight illuminating the leafy meshes of a wild wood. In the same way, as we wander through the poet's own garden in *The Earthly Paradise*, we feel the spirit of the artist and craftsman dwelling lovingly upon the beauty of carved pillars and inlaid floors, the wonders of the loom, the vessels of brass, and of silver and gold, which become parts of that rich mosaic of romance which he himself wove in his verse and prose tales, so glowing with colour and pattern as scarcely to need the illuminator's gold and blue and scarlet, which again, in the literal sense, no one knew better how to use than William Morris. Strictly reserved and formalised as his drawing and designs were, in adaptation to printing; and weaving, his treatment of natural forms shows the close observer and student of structural line and form, as well as the artist's delight in them. An ardent enthusiast for the character and beauty of medieval art, deeply penetrated with its spirit, while possessing a profound knowledge of its letter, he wrote and designed freely in what some thought the disguise of a past age, but it was as an *artist*, not as an archæologist, and he was strengthened in all his work by his knowledge and love of architecture, by which all the arts are united. So that, although we may trace the sources of his inspiration and the various influences under which he lived, the total impression of the work of William Morris, regarded as a whole, is that of the full and free expression of a powerful personality; and it was by the force of that personality that he was able to inspire and direct others with so much success and to leave behind him a living tradition. Again, in his social work, it was his passion for beauty, and love of a simple and wholesome life, however refined, which drove him to revolt against the gloomy conventions, the pretenses, the meanness and shabbiness of so much in the aspects of modern existence. Although, with his usual thoroughness and power of concentration, he pursued the matter to its roots in the economic system, his artistic instincts, as well as his reason and humanity, made him a socialist; and beyond the din of controversy, he took care to record his own conception of an ideal state, in his Utopian romance, 'News from Nowhere.'"

Morris & Co.,
dining room, built in 1893.
Panels in unpolished walnut and ornate plaster frieze and ceiling.
Wightwick Manor, Wightwick Bank.

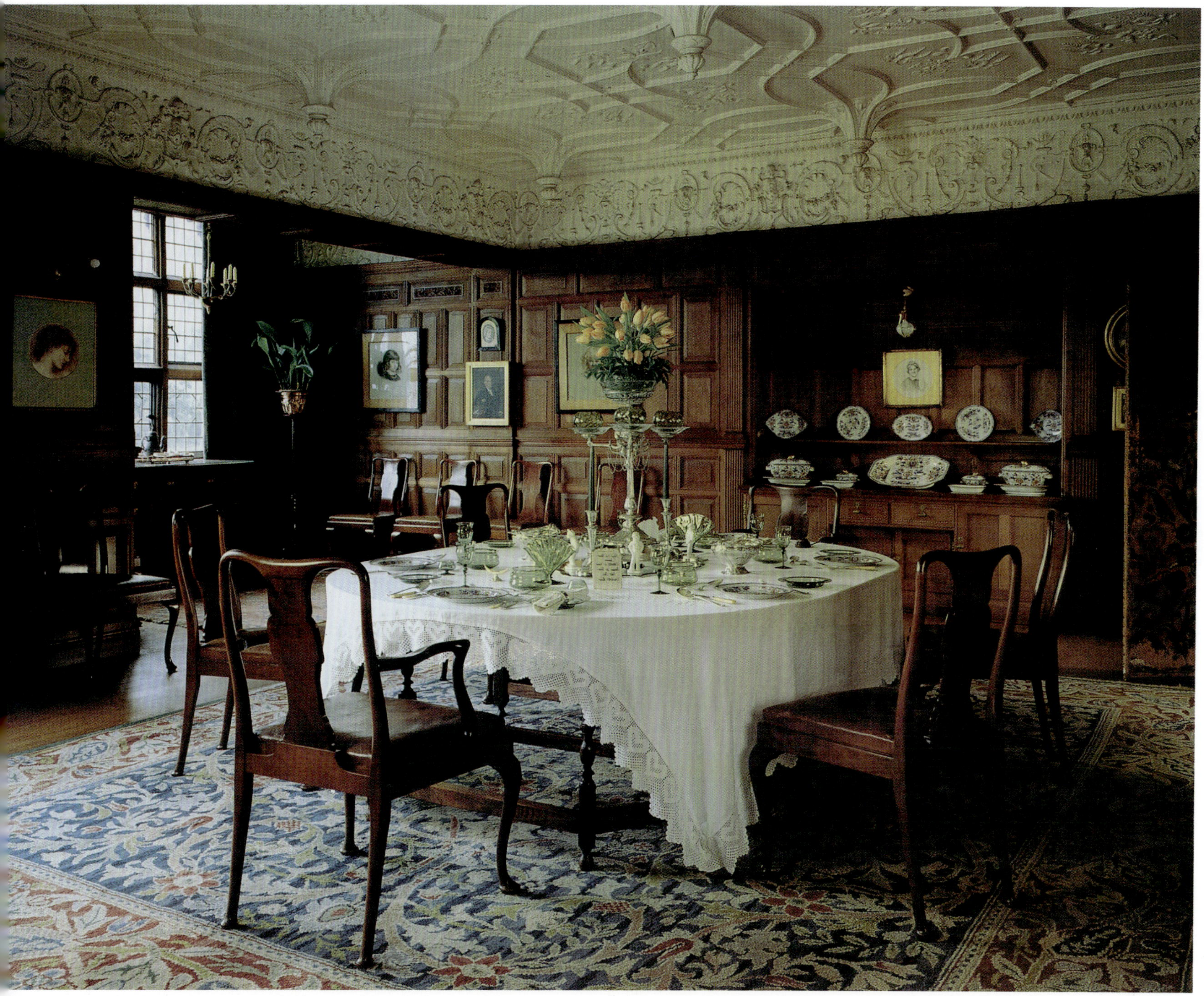

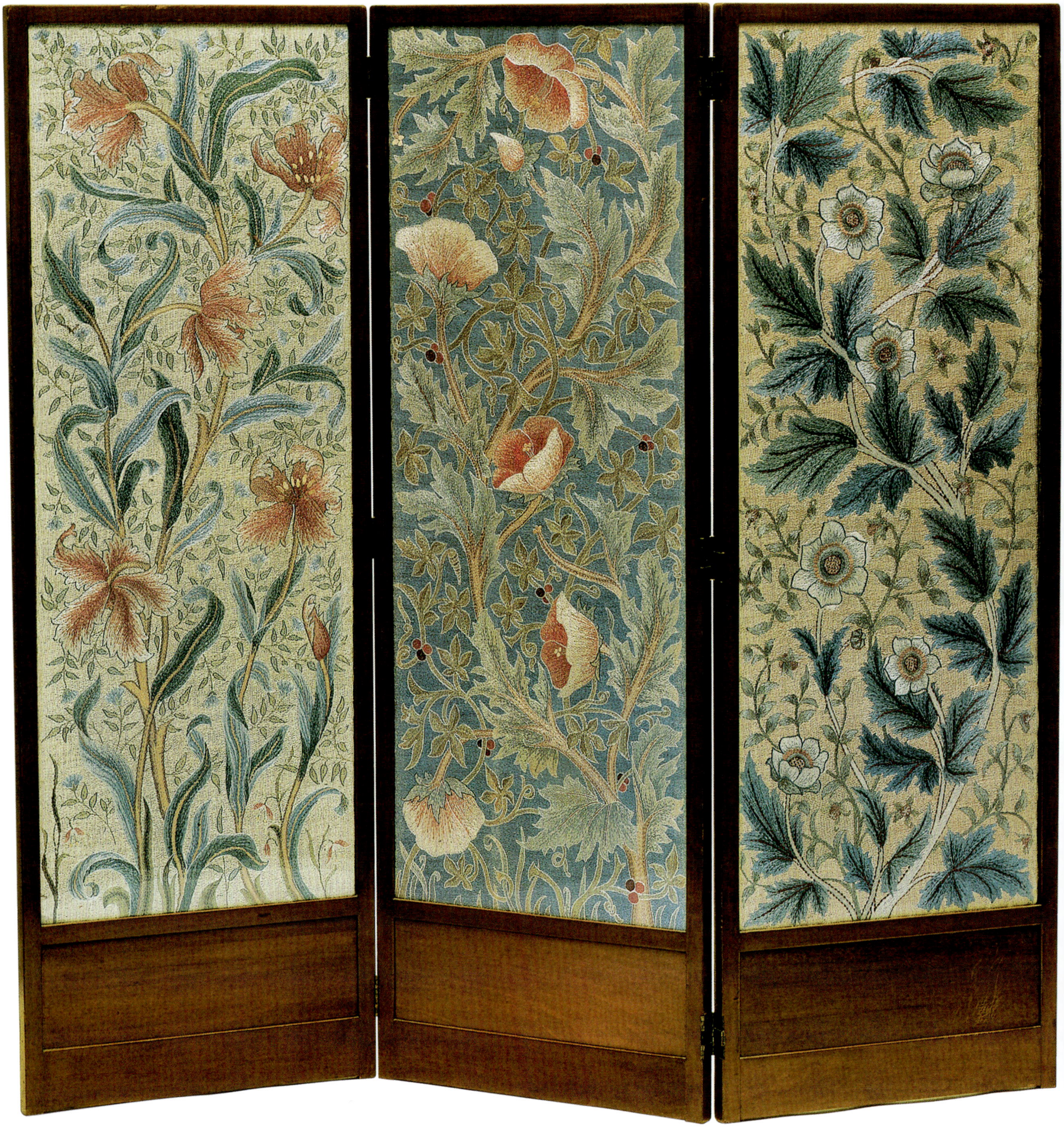

3 - Ashbee and the Reconstructed Workshop

"The crown and fulfilment of national life is a wise understanding and enjoyment of beauty." Charles Robert Ashbee, *A Few Chapters in Workshop Reconstruction and Citizenship*, 1894.

The Essex House in London, "A Guild and School of Handicraft", is another milestone on the road to industrial freedom – on the testimony both of its work and of its purpose as recorded in the writings of C. R. Ashbee, the founder and director of the Essex Guild. Mr. Ashbee's special plea was for a reconstructed workshop, a workshop so constituted that it may function at once as the state, the school, and the factory. Membership in it should constitute citizenship, apprenticeship in it should afford education, production in it should provide materials for use and exchange.

In the final essay in Mr. Ashbee's volume entitled *Chapters in Workshop Reconstruction and Citizenship* the idealist's gospel of work and the ideal of citizenship in a workshop are finely presented. In the matter of production – what, Mr. Ashbee asks, is it all for?

"This mere trifle of mine, of what use or beauty may it be, will it give anyone delight? Maybe not, maybe it is useless and unlovely, and will give no man pleasure. What then? Why just this, we are brought face to face with the ethics of production; the artist producer stands forth. This trifle of mine is a mere symbol, the thing itself is empty, vain; its goodness consists in the spirit put into it, and the doing it; its creation by us reflects a greater doing, symbolises a creation elsewhere, in which we are sublimely and unconsciously taking part. We talk of a piece of machine-made work as soulless – what a deal we mean when we say that! So let us continue to make our trifles, remembering always that they are symbols only. This, if you will, is the Idealist's Gospel of Work, and the strength of our continuance is the measure of our idealism. Artist and producer then, have the same ethics, and just as it is the individual touches of the artist that make the great work of Art, so it is the little human details impressed upon production that give it interest or character. This, in our vast mechanical system of industry and individualism, we have missed sight of. Individualism has lost us individuality. Individuality has gone out of industry, but it must be brought back again. The system has destroyed the things created, and in

John Henry Dearle (for the design) and **Morris & Co.** (for the production), screen, 1885-1910.
Glazed mahogany frame, with panels of canvas embroidered with silks in darning, stem and satin stitches, 162.9 x 166.2 x 2.8 cm.
Victoria & Albert Museum, London.

Chris Lebeau,
screen, 1905.
Batik on silk, mahogany frame.
Drents Museum, Assen.

Gustav Stickley, Craftman Workshops (for the manufacturing),
screen, c. 1905.
Oak, leather, linen *appliqué* on canvas.
Private collection.

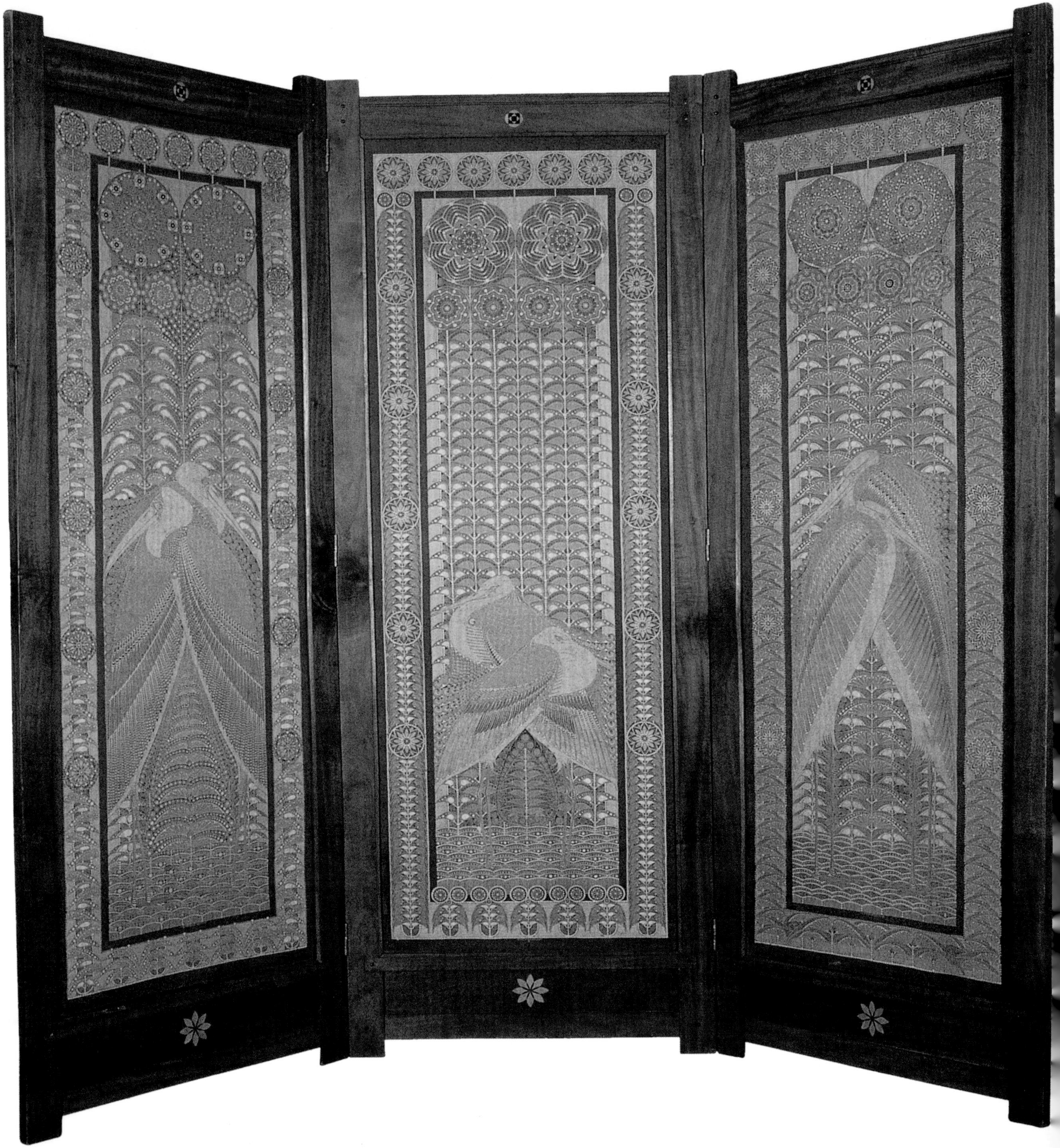

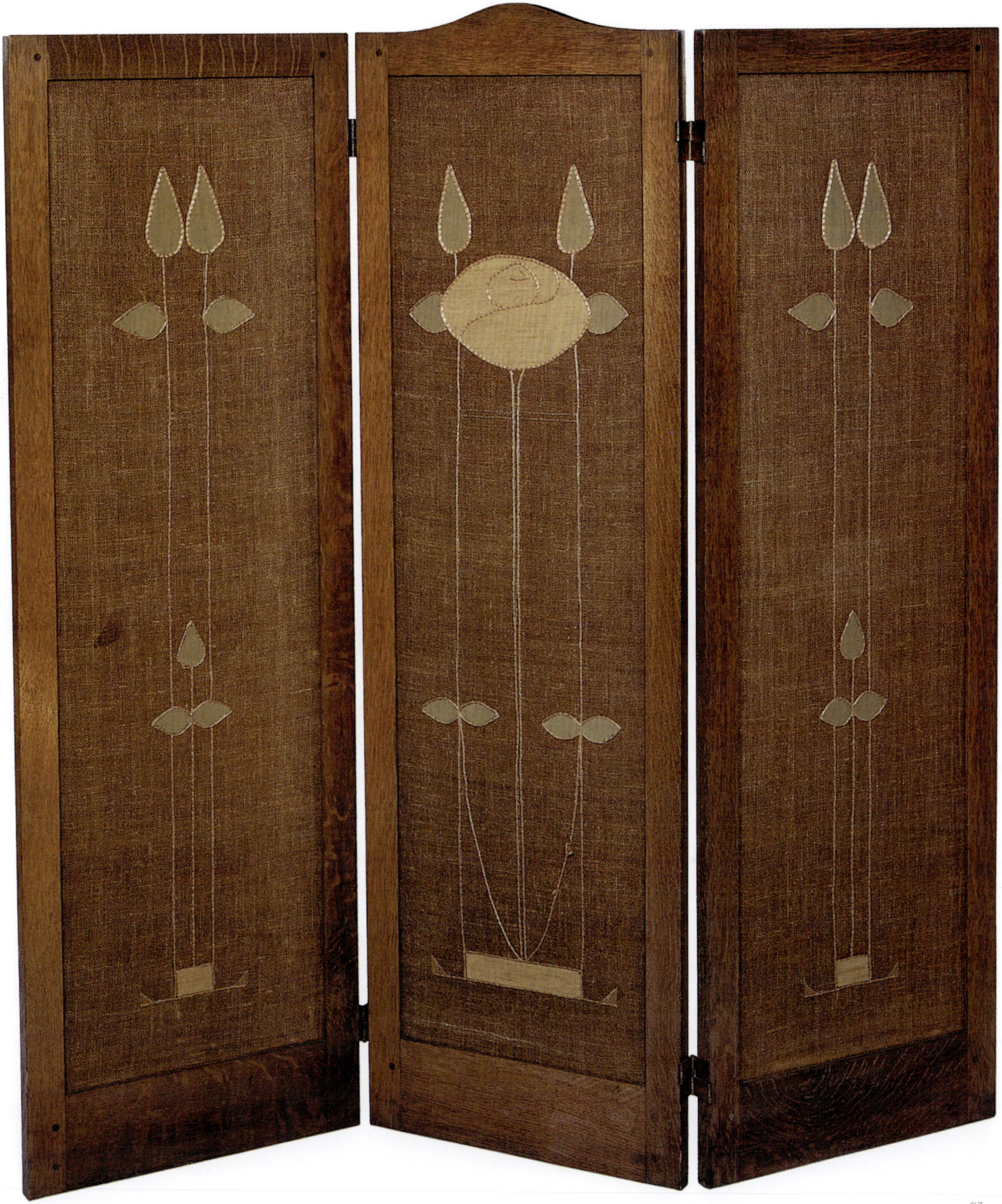

destroying the productions we destroy the producers. Lower the standard of the work and you lower the standard of the man."

But given individualism how shall sovereign individuals be united in a community? The "Workshop" gives the solution to this question also.

"The reconstructed workshop must have an intimate human relationship for its basis; here will be the faith of the little citizen of the future. So personal is this question, that it seems out of place in any consideration of the action of men together for any public purpose. But it is just because it is so personal that it is so important. As present, where men are bound together in production, their bond is one of chance, or of common enmity to an employer, and they become friends because they are shopmates. In the reconstructed workshop this will have to be inverted, and they will become shopmates rather because they are friends. Here, once again, is the unit; we come back to that. It is the unit, the individual, that we have got to touch.

Somewhat in this way might we state our belief: That moment when the hand of my friend was pressed in mine has expanded over my life, and become it. The reason why I choose you – what is it? Let us call it a twofold reason. First, because of the you in you; second, because of the you in me – the first in your own character and choosing; the second, the magnetic force of which I am the vessel; the first in your own making; the second intrusted to me by God. It is not new in itself; this, the feeling that drew Jesus to John, or Shakespeare to the youth of the sonnets, or that inspired the friendships of Greece, has been with us before, and in the new citizenship we shall need it again. The Whitmanic love of comrades is its modern expression, democracy – as socially, not politically, conceived – its basis. The thought as to how much of the solidarity of labour and the modern trade-union movement may be due to an unconscious faith in this principle of comradeship is no idle one. The freer, more direct, and more genuine relationship between men, which is implied by it, must be the ultimate basis of the reconstructed workshop. 'When I touch the human body,' said Novalis, 'I touch heaven!'

This relationship – human bond – as distinguished from the cash or other *nexus*, we have to study, to analyse, to find, if possible, the philosophic basis of, and we may learn in teaching it. We have to train ourselves and those we teach to lay high stakes on new personalities, to strive for infallibility of decision, and instant decision when a new personality comes. I look into your eyes, stranger; God grant me the power of instantly telling whether or not you are sent for me. A few times wrong, and we grow sensitive to right choosing; each right choice makes the next more certain. This magnetism of the human bond, too, is generative; you light me, and the fire grows within me; I spread it, and it grows again, till at last the whole air in which we move is charged with it. It runs into us, and through us, again and

Lucia Mathews,
screen, c. 1910-1915.
Painted and gilt wood,
182.8 x 203 x 2.5 cm
Oakland Museum, Oakland.

Morris & Co., **Edward William Godwin**, **Bruce Talbert**, **Peter Waals**, **Ernest Gimson**, **Alfred** and **Louise Powell**, **Ernest Gimson**, and the **Barnsleys**,
"Sussex" armchair, ebonized chair with cane seat, ebonized beech side chair, ladderback chair in beech, side chair of beech with holly and ebony stringing, between 1880 and 1910.
Private collection, Birkenhead.

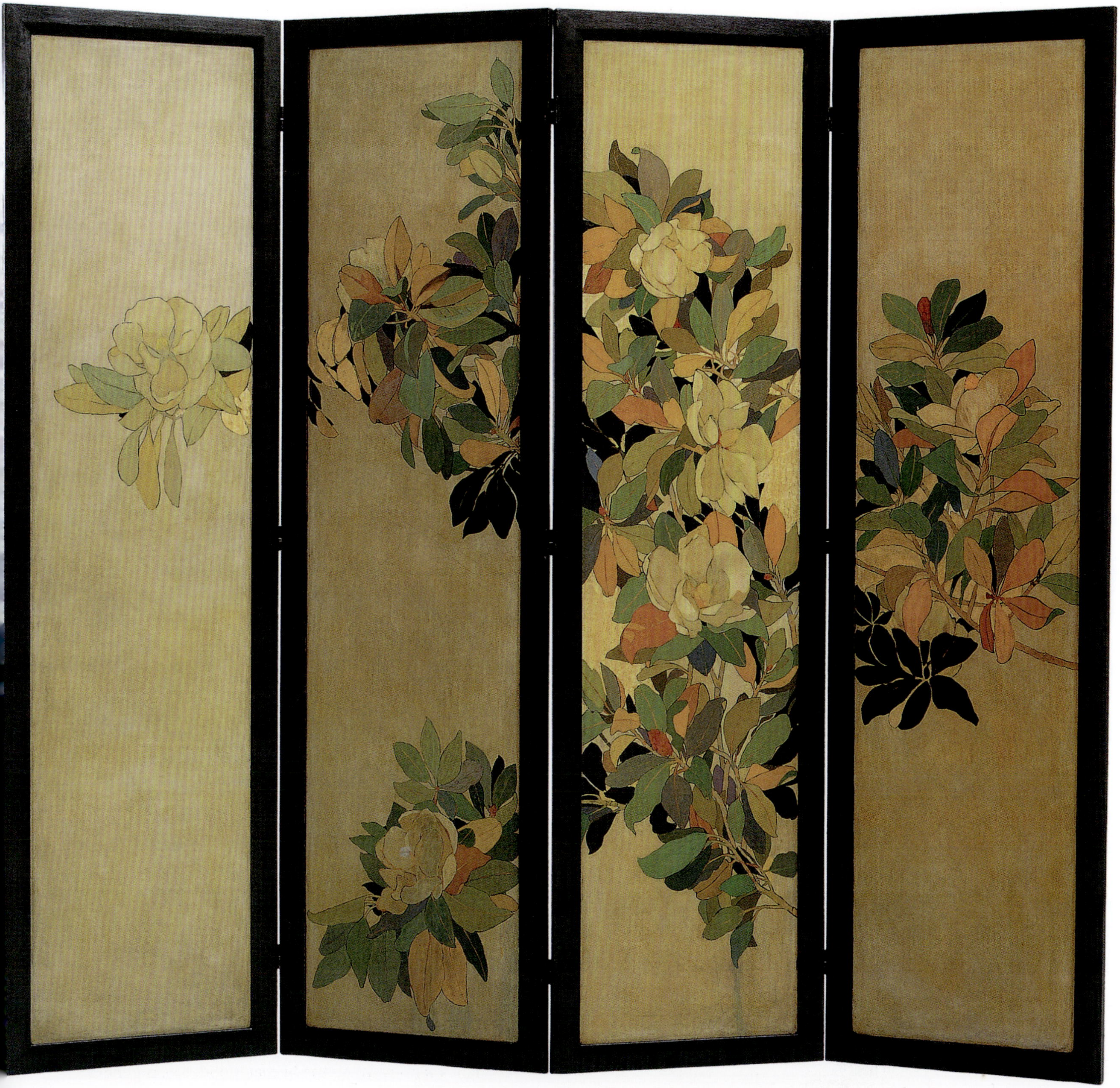

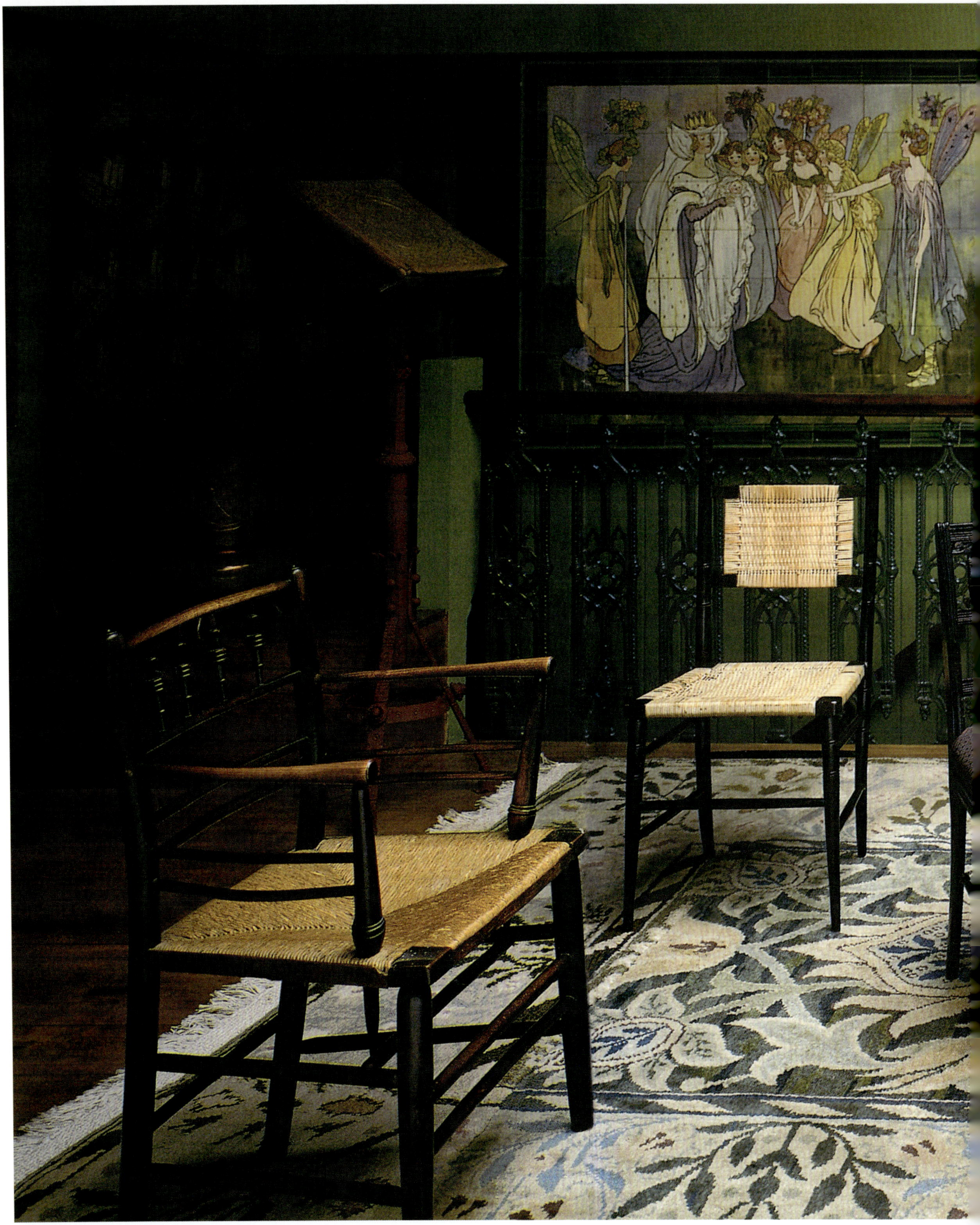

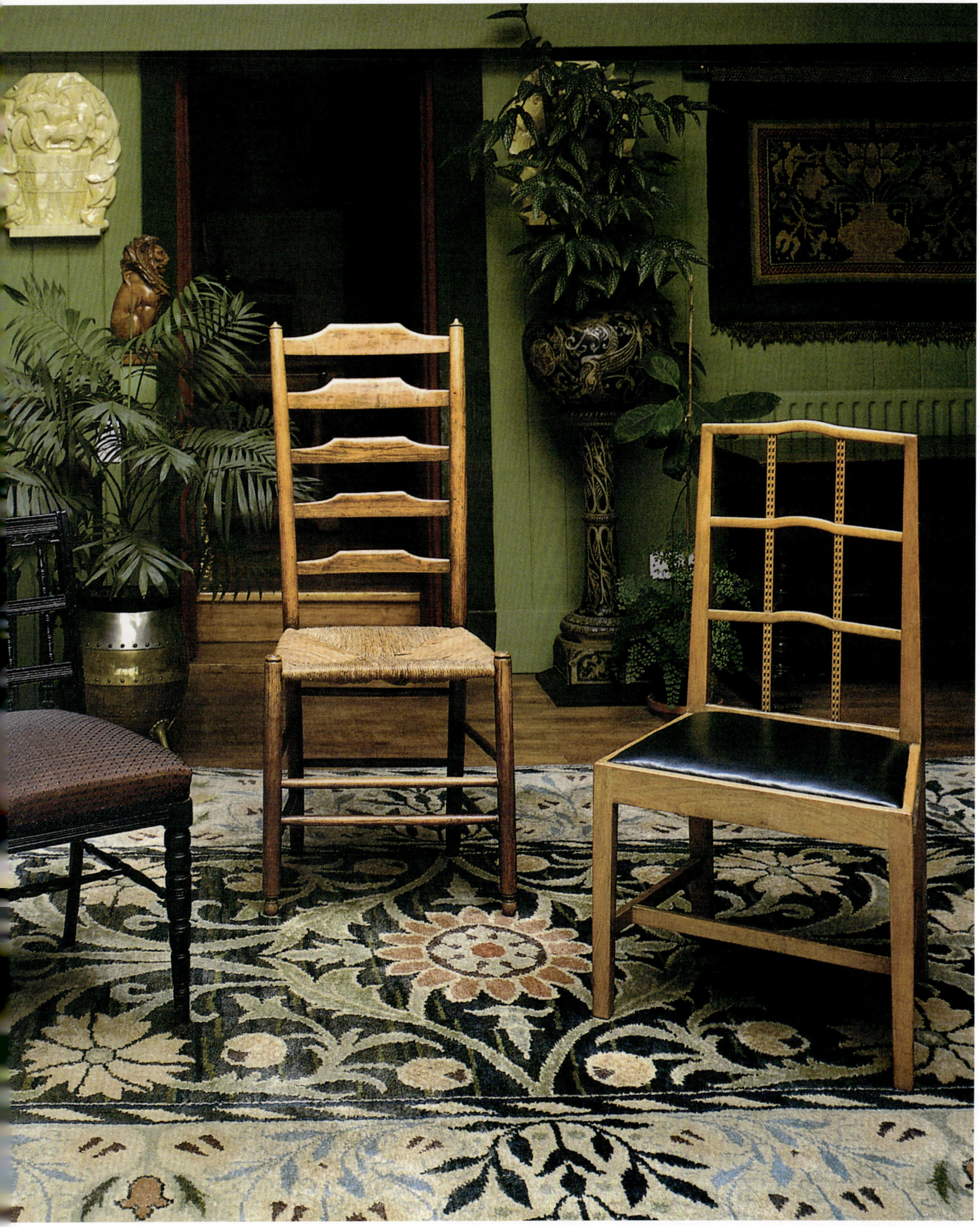

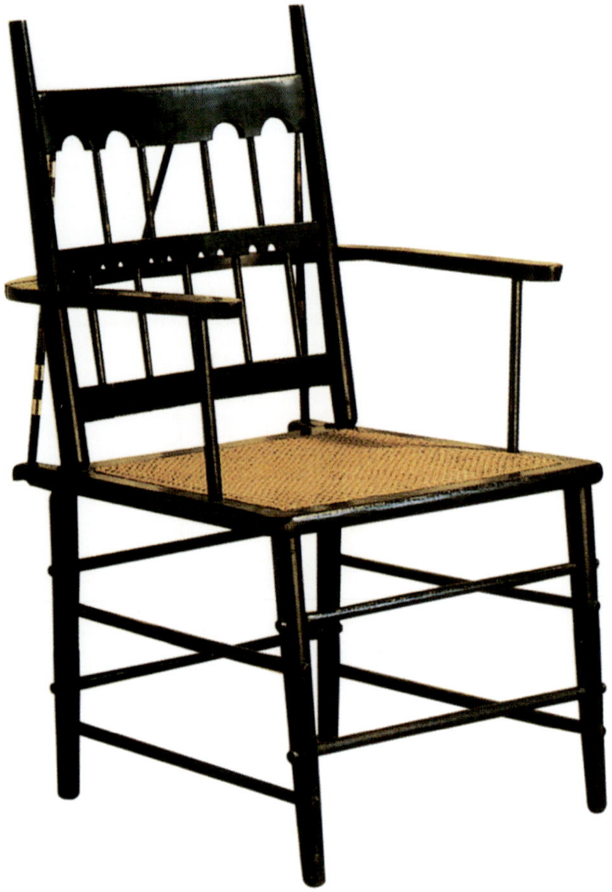

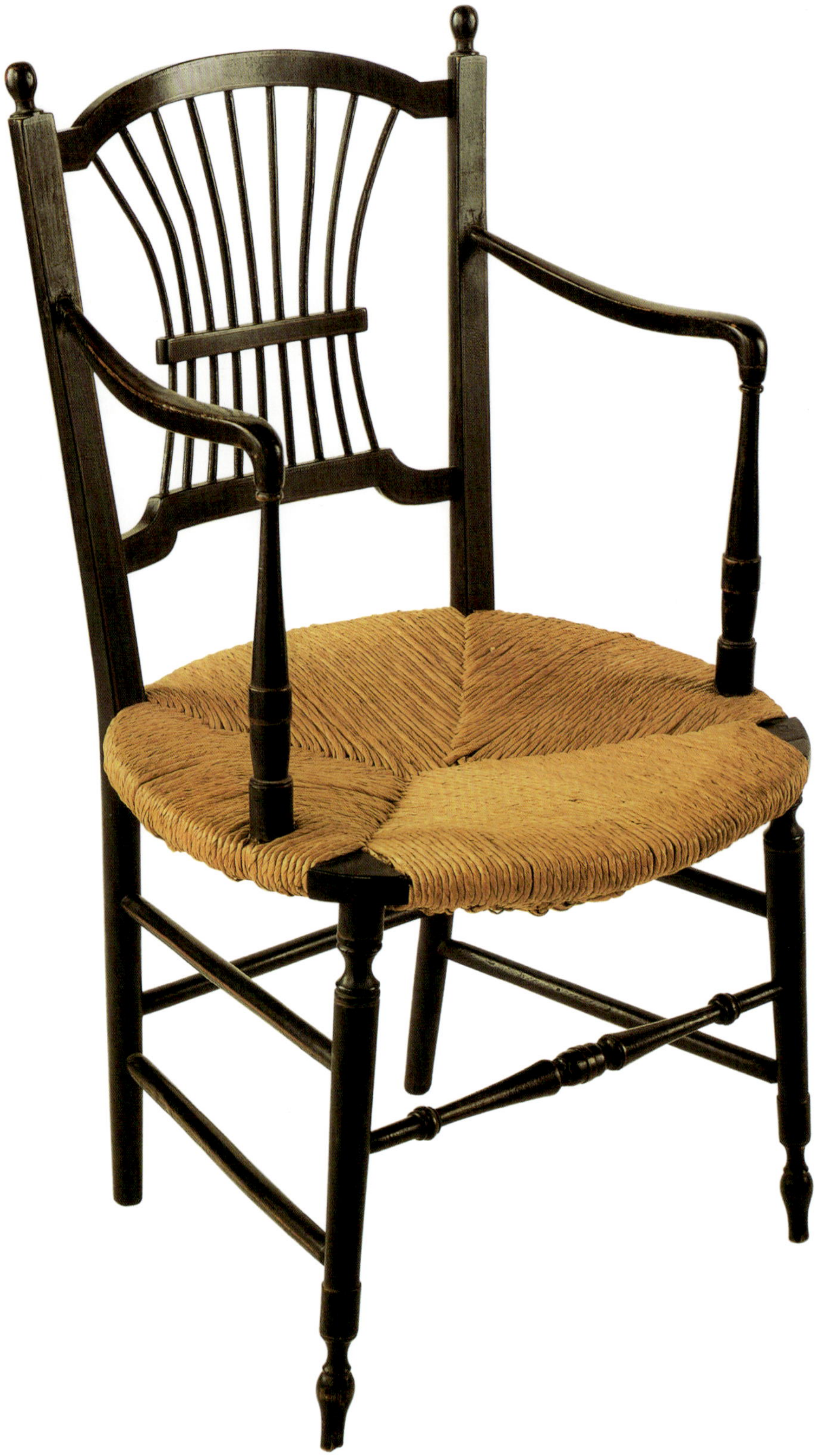

Philip Webb (for the design) and
Morris, Marshall, Faulkner & Co.
(for the production),
armchair, 1861-1862.
Ebonized wood with gilded bands,
99 x 41 x 43 cm.
Kelmscott Manor, Kelmscott.

Dante Gabriel Rossetti
(for the design) and **Morris & Co.**
(for the production),
The Rossetti Armchair, 1870-1890.
Ebonized beech, with red painted
decoration and rush seat,
88.8 x 49.5 x 53 cm.
Victoria & Albert Museum, London.

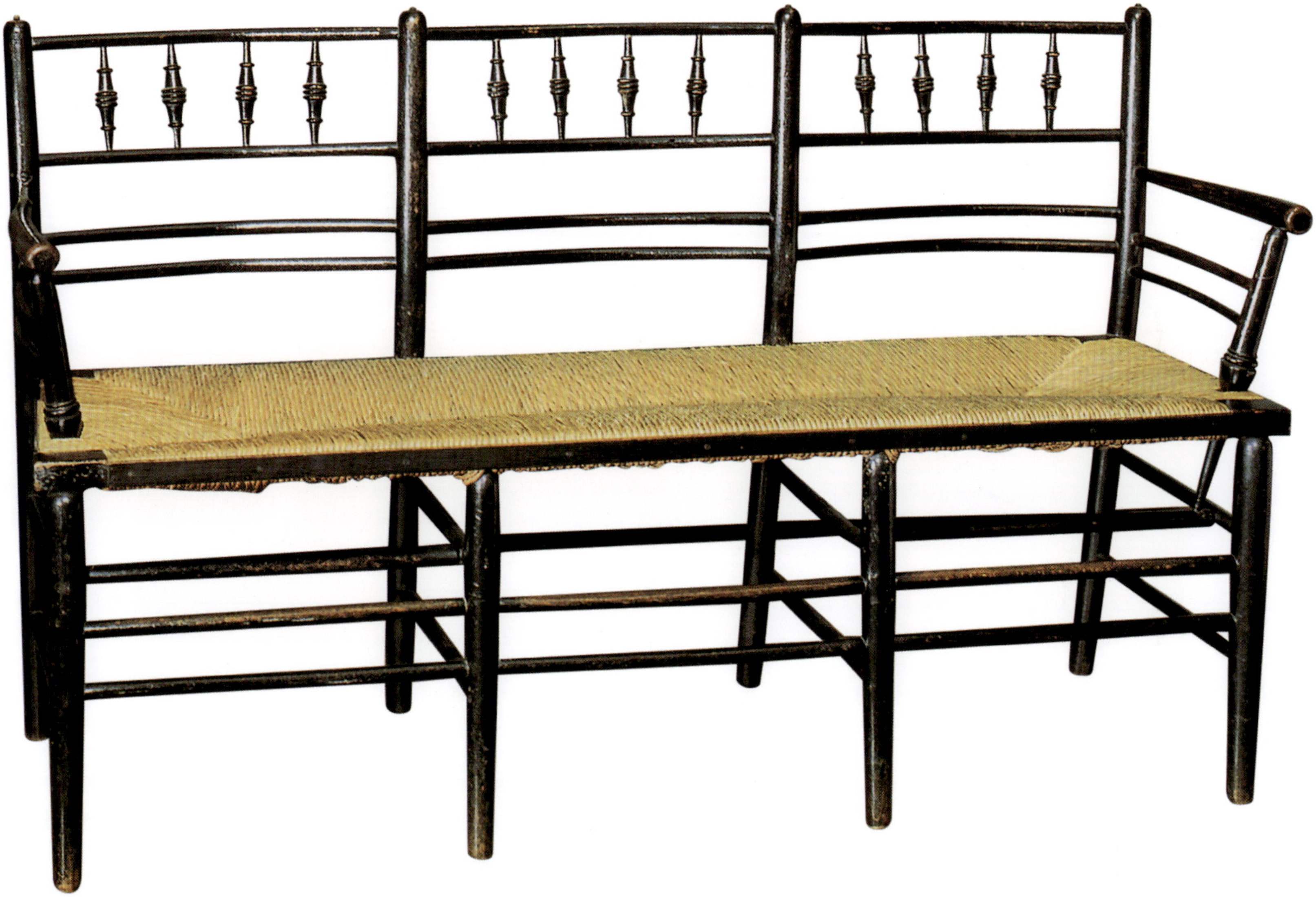

Morris, Marshall, Faulkner & Co.,
settee from the *Sussex* range,
c. 1865.
Ebonized beech and rush seat,
85.1 x 137.2 x 41 cm.
William Morris Gallery, London.

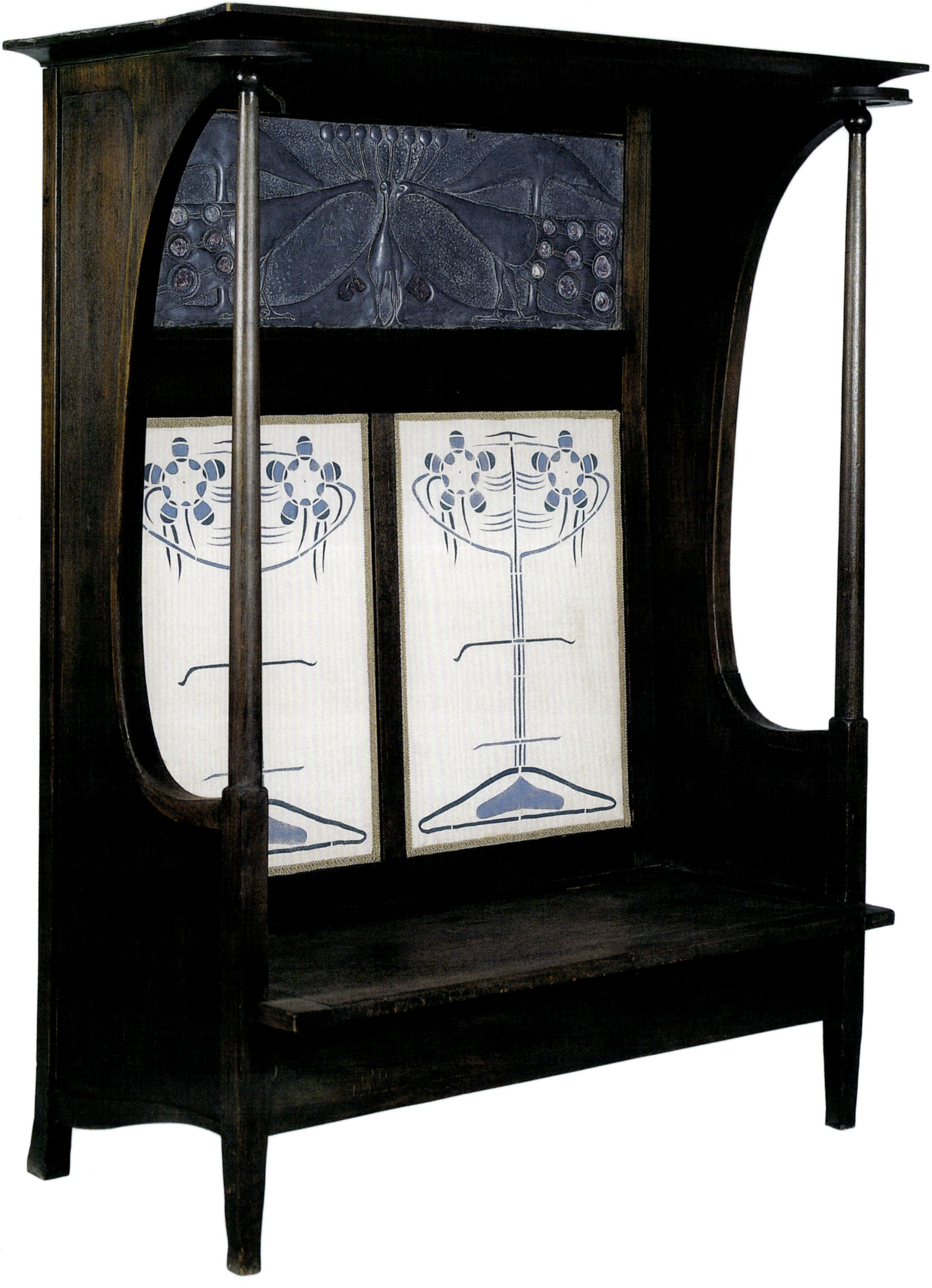

again; as we receive more we emit more, till our whole surroundings grow brilliant with light – that incomprehensible blue light in the vision of Heinrich von Ofterdingen."

From this ideal of citizenship – individuality on the basis of comradeship – the problem of education takes on meaning. Throughout his writings Mr. Ashbee insists upon connecting the teaching function with the workshop function. Teaching outside the workshop is too artificial, too remote from life, too abstract. "Our ideal is to create a school whose life shall depend upon what is the only living thing – the life of workmanship; a school whose future shall be bound up with the future of those who labour in it; a school, therefore, that shall be self-dependent and supported from within, not from without – the school of a movement." It is first necessary to co-ordinate the abstract and the concrete, to graft the humanistic onto the industrial. It is seen that every craft has its social, historical, literary, artistic, technical, and scientific aspect. Starting from the manipulation, say of metals in the workshop, the lines of interest run out in every direction and involve scientific and humanistic studies in their most vital bearings. Then art instruction must be transferred from the studio to the workshop. The studio is, in its nature, subjective and nonsocial. It fosters selfishness and a kind of refined sensuality. The workshop in its nature is objective and social. It cultivates the higher socialism. In the workshop those magnetic affinities that engender creative impulses spring up between men. Based on comradeship production is humanised. In the workshop questions of organisation and division of labour are solved on democratic grounds. The workshop, constructed on such grounds, renders schools of design and polytechnic institutions unnecessary. It is idle to teach design abstractly as an end in itself. "Design," says Mr. Ashbee, "is that element in any art and craft by which the whole hangs together, first constructively and then aesthetically." Design, therefore, must have reference to something – a building, a table, jewel, lamp, or book. A craftsman learns design by applying thought to materials. In polytechnic institutes instruction is again given outside the workshop by teachers who know little or nothing of practical craftsmanship. Instead of maintaining an industrial system whereby a few men become holders of great wealth, a part of which, forced by public opinion, returns to the public in the form of endowed technical schools, the query arises why cannot technical instruction be conducted within the system, and by the workers themselves? Some such conclusion as Mr. Ashbee reaches is forced upon us. "We must: convert Mr. Pushington's great house into a sort of industrial partnership whose future is invested in its producers, not its entrepreneurs, and we must utilise the sum which public opinion extorts from his munificence, not for the purpose of swelling big polytechnics, but of teaching in the workshop." "Suppose," says Mr. Ashbee further, "Mr. Pushington were to keep his £20,000. Suppose he were to spend the interest of it upon the educational development, in artistic matters, of the employes of Sky Sign & Co. Suppose he were to build a small hall, with benches, books, and appliances, useful and illustrative of the trade of Sky Sign & Co. Suppose he were then to say to Mr. Pennyworth: Now complete your knowledge by a more careful application to the tools

Charles Rennie Mackintosh,
settle, c. 1896.
Wood, linen and lead,
183 x 73 x 142.5 cm.
National Museums of Scotland, Glasgow.

William Morris,
pair of high-backed chairs, 1856.
Victoria & Albert Museum, London.

Philip Webb (for the design) and **Morris, Marshall, Faulkner & Co.** (for the production),
settee, c. 1865.
Oak wood with gilded gesso decoration.
Private collection.

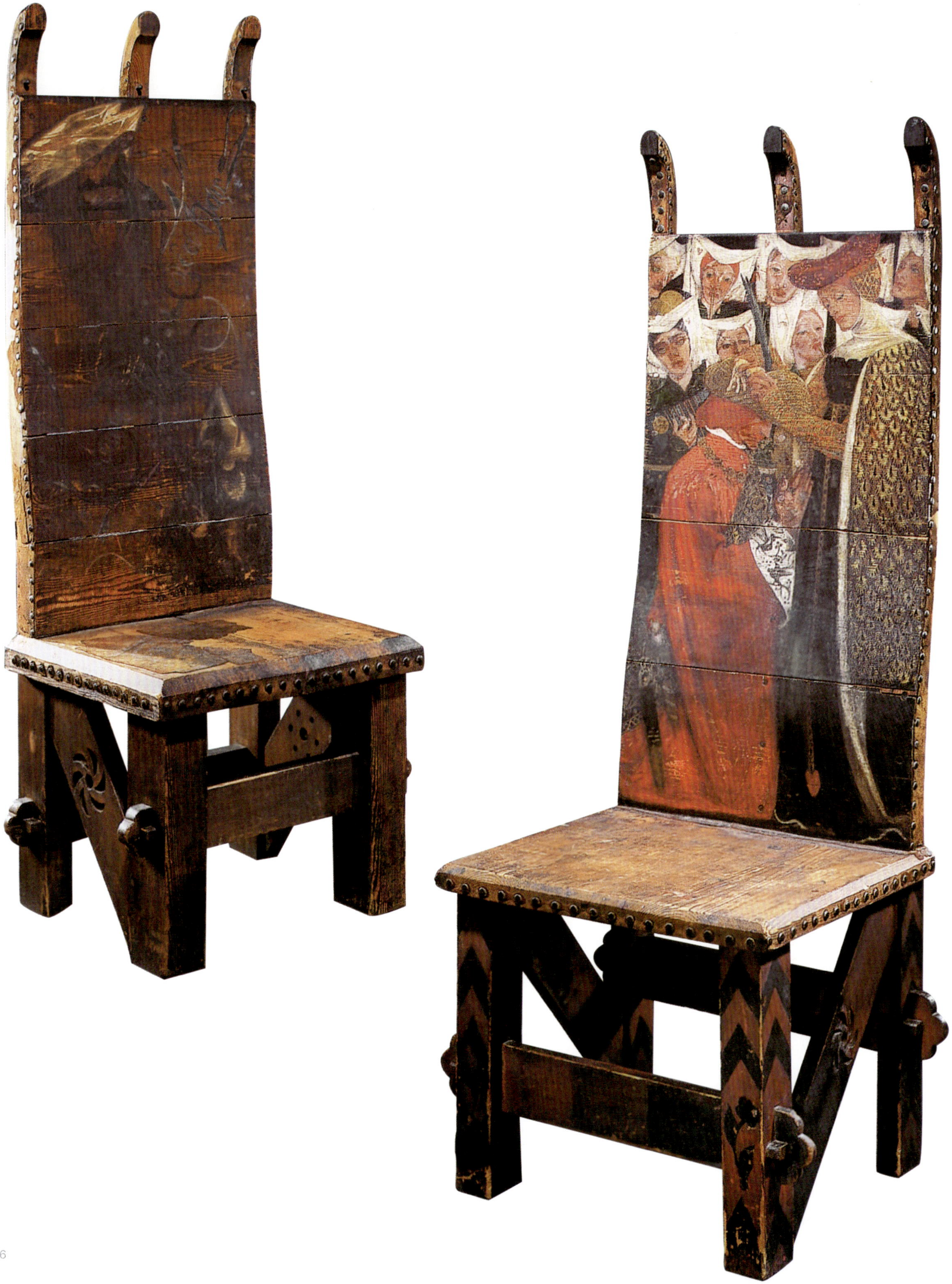

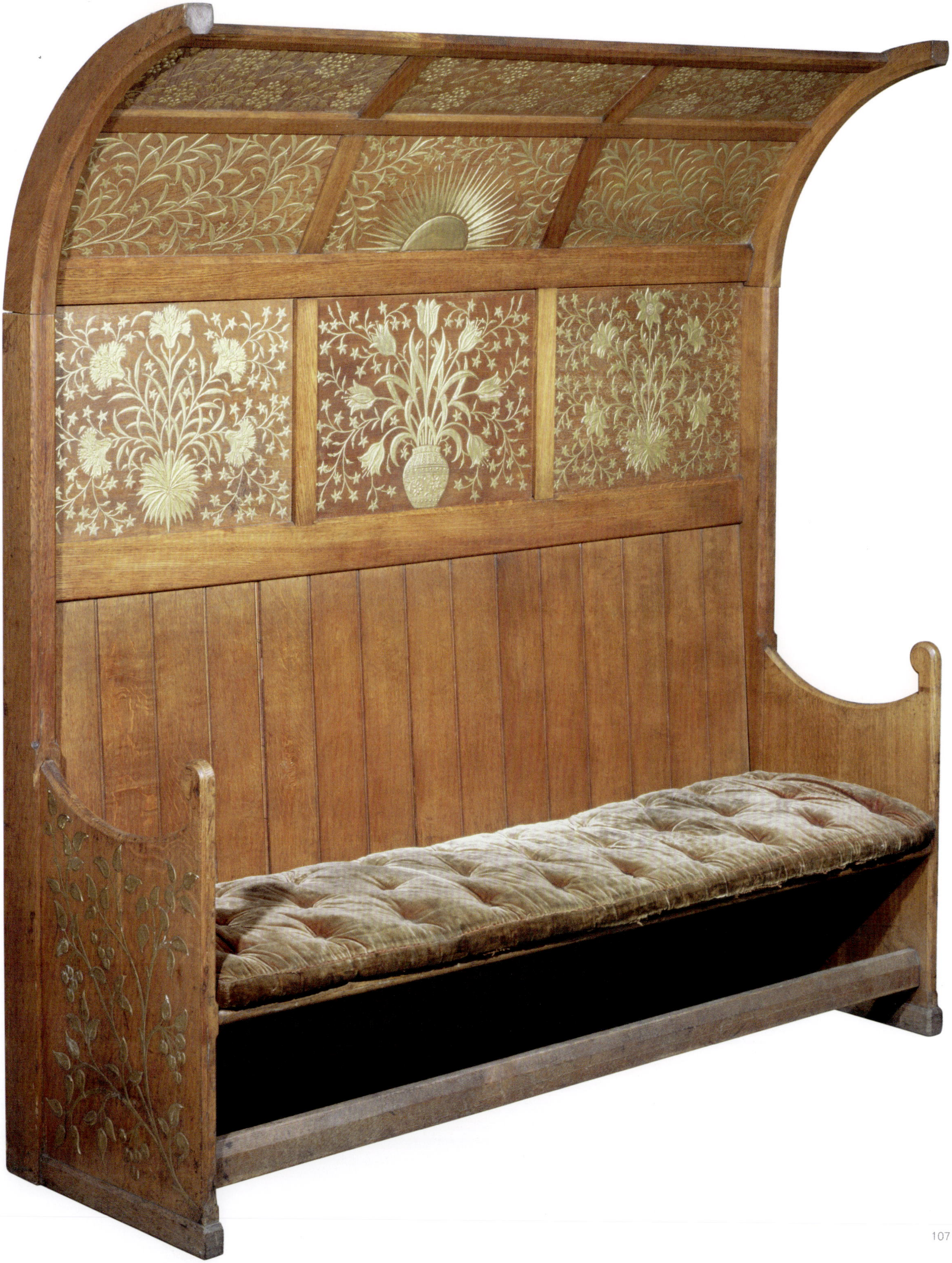

and concrete facts of design; and to Mr. Trudge, now come and improve not your technical skill, but master some of the theory of your trade, and learn how the whole hangs together. In addition, suppose he taught, in his school the small Pennyworths and the small Trudges the use of the tool and the use of the pencil alike, and got them in their boyhood to feel this relation of art to industry; got them to see the charm of a well-lit, wellhung hall of art and industry; got them to feel their own little relation to Sky Sign & Co., perhaps even insuring them a footing, after their pupilage in the school, in the historical house itself. There, it seems to me, would be a veritable polytechnic, and a genuine application of art to industry."

The workshop as factory, which shall be also a training school for citizenship and for occupations, is as yet but a vision offered to the future for realisation. The present factory, with its monarchic organisation, its commanders and bosses, its special designers, its divided workers, and as a whole, its commercial motives, will give way in time to the guild or small co-operative society, which shall be integral as to its work, human as to its motives, artistic as to its ends. By integral labour is meant that the workman must give his entire energy, physical, moral, and intellectual, to his work, and that all his faculties must touch his work at all points. By human motives is meant that the producers, and not the things produced, are to be valued and conserved. By artistic ends is meant that work must constantly tend towards imaginative production. "Art" is the "higher production", differing from "craft", which is technical production, and from "industry", which is mechanical production, only in the degree of personal creativeness involved in the process. Thus considered, art is the "crown and fulfilment of noble citizenship", and the ultimate function of the workshop, Among the aphorisms offered by Mr. Ashbee to guide our thinking on workshop reconstruction appear the following:

"The only hope for the development of the sense of beauty is among the artificially cultured class of artists and the artisan; the one conscious, the other unconscious."
"Under modern conditions of art, picture-painting is forced into an artificial prominence, and the constructional and decorative arts, the real backbone, have as yet no right recognition among us."
"The problems of machine production will have to be solved within the workshop. A sharp distinction will have to be drawn between what is produced by machinery and the direct work of man's hands, and the standard of artistic excellence must depend ultimately upon the pleasure given, not to the consumer but to the producer."
"At the present day, the social problem has prior claim to the artistic."

The Guild and School of Handicraft, where these ideas have been demonstrated, was founded by Mr. Ashbee, in 1880, as the result of a small Ruskin class conducted at Toynbee Hall. Mr. Ashbee notes:

Gustav Stickley,
fixed-back oak armchair, c. 1900.
Leather upholstery, h.: 108 cm.

Sir Edwin Lutyens,
dining room,
built between 1910 and 1920.
Mahogany paneling and an elaborate plasterwork ceiling.
Castle Drogo, Drewsteignton.

Sir Edwin Lutyens,
Mrs. Drewe's bedroom,
built between 1910 and 1920.
Castle Drogo, Drewsteignton.

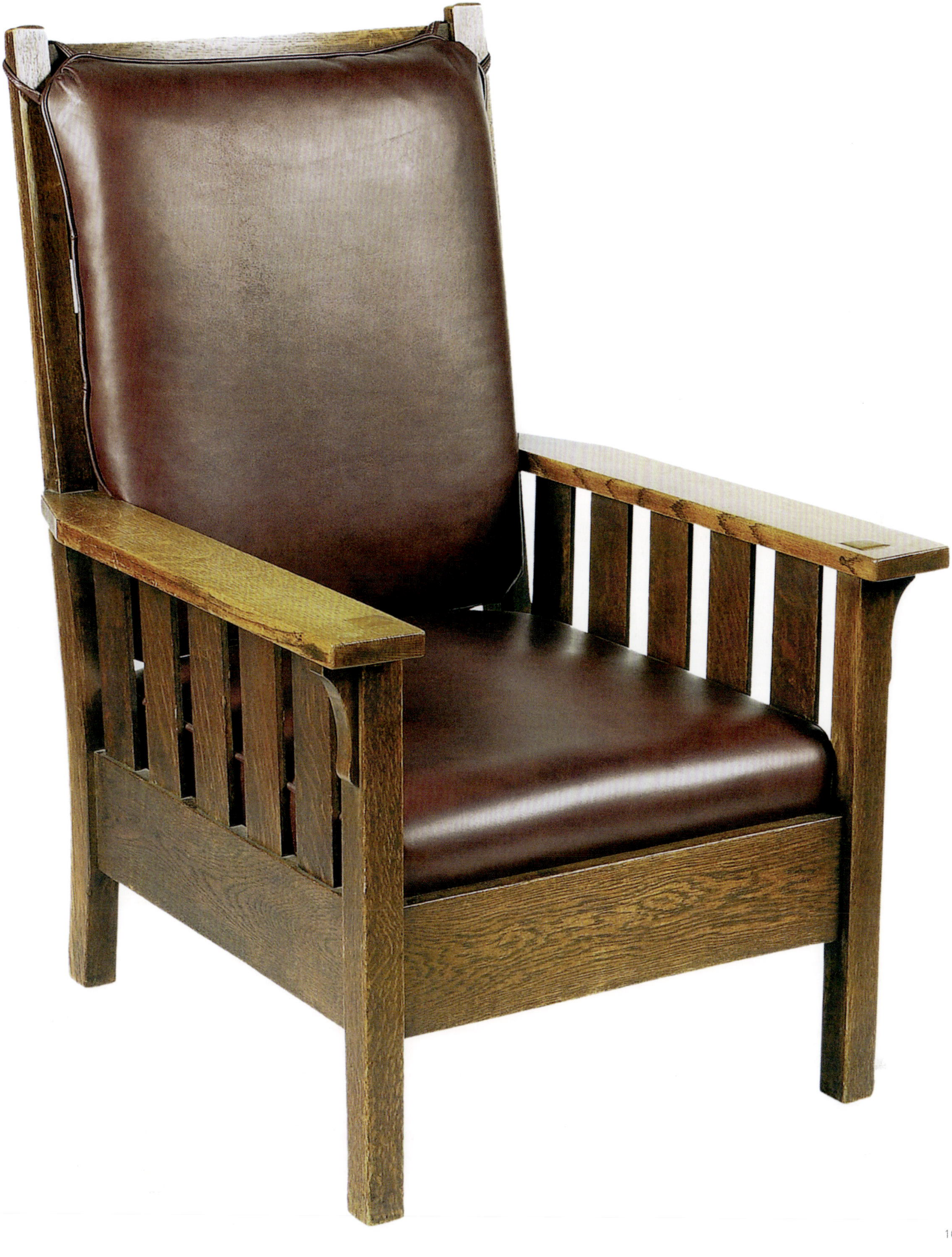

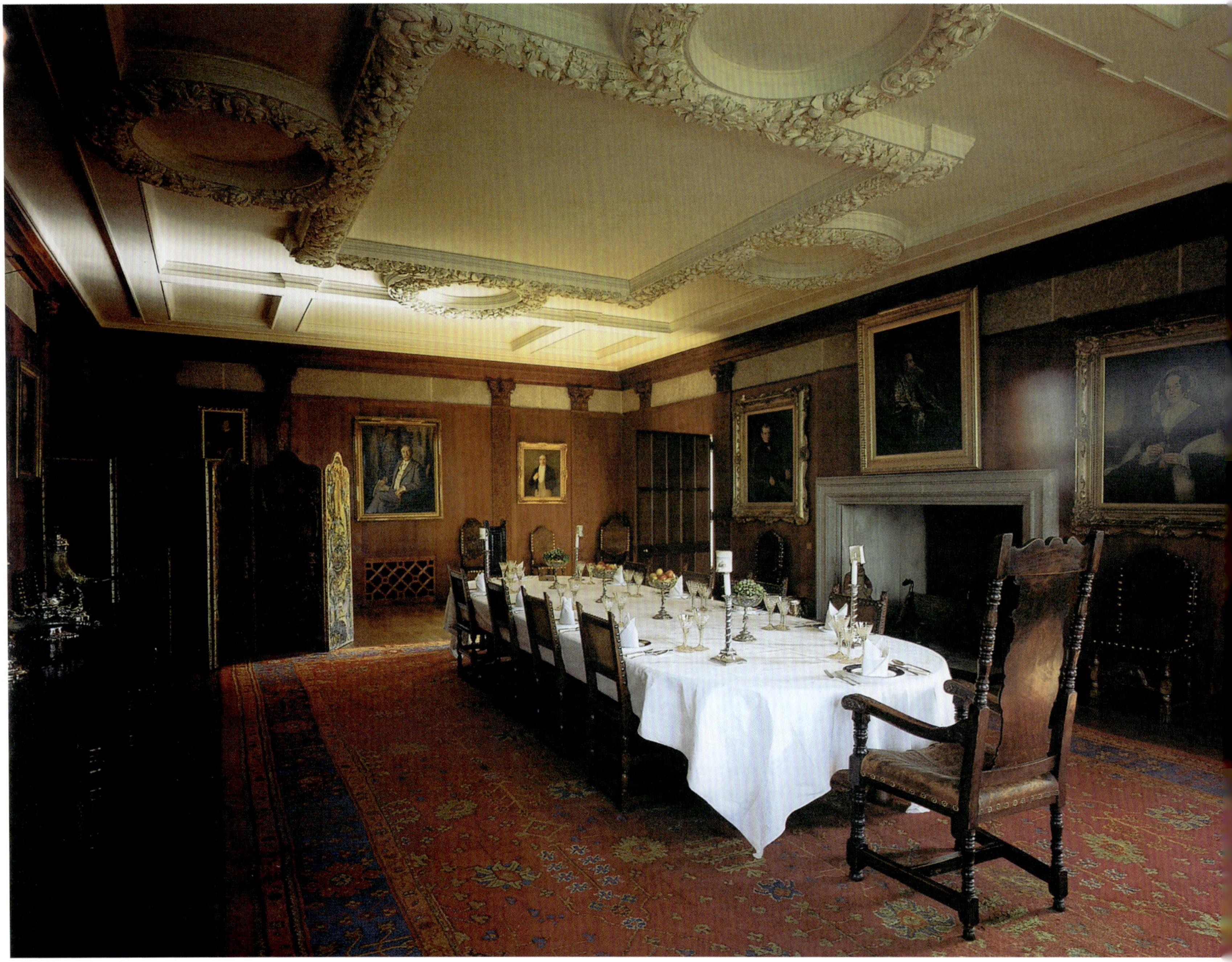

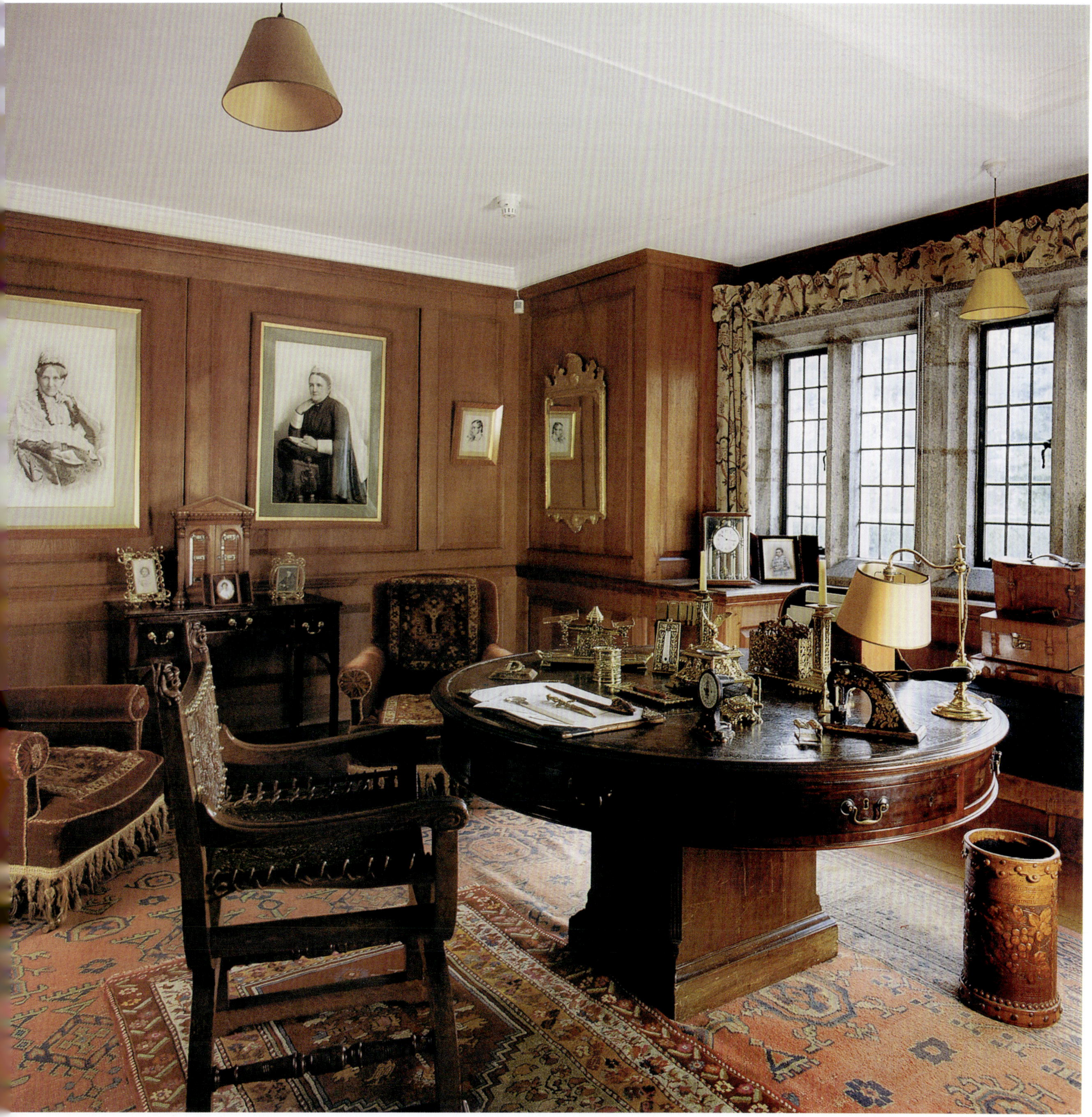

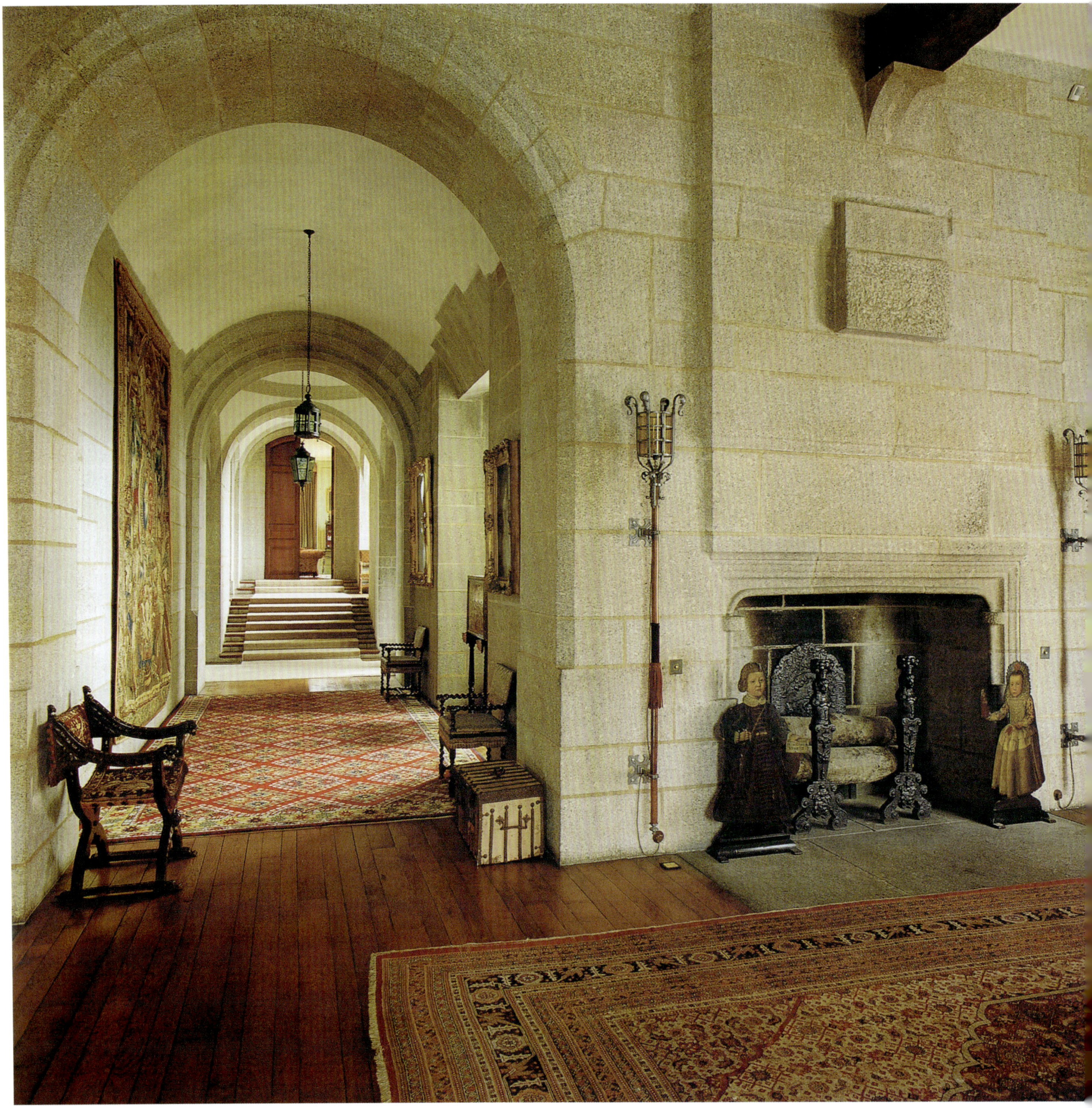

"The reading of Ruskin led to an experiment of a practical nature, and out of *Fors Clavigera* and the *Crown of Wild Olive* sprang a small class for the study of design. The class grew to thirty – some men, some boys – and then it was felt that design needed application to give the teaching fulfilment. A piece of practical work, which involved painting, modelling, plaster-casting, gilding, and the study of heraldic forms, gave a stimulus to the corporate action of the thirty students, and the outcome of their united work as *dilettanti* was the desire that permanence might be given to it by making it work for life and bread. From this sprang the idea of the Guild and School. Very undefined at first was the notion that a school should be carried on in connection with a workshop; that the men in this workshop should be the teachers in the school, and that the pupils in the school should be drafted into the workshop as it grew in strength and certainty. Wisdom pronounced the experiment, from a business point of view, as entirely quixotic, and precedent for it there was none.

The little Guild of three members to begin with, and the larger School of some fifty members was, however, started in its present form; the top floor of a warehouse in Commercial Street was taken for two years to serve as workshop and school-room combined; it was polychromatised by the pupils, and the Guild and School celebrated its inauguration on June 23, 1888. A kindly public gave the funds for supporting the School for two trial years; while the Guild, launching as an independent venture, announced its intention of taking up three lines of practical work: woodwork, metal-work, and decorative painting, and intimated the ambitious hope that it would one day take over the School, for which purpose, when formulating its constitution, it laid by a first charge on its profits. The little workship in Commercial Street saw many vicissitudes and unexpected developments. Strange new things had to be learnt, new conditions and new experiences. The introduction among its members of some of the leading trades-unionist workmen – an indispensable element in the solving of an industrial problem – gave to the Guild that peculiar character which has been the principal reason of its success so far. The marriage between the stolid, uncompromising, co-operative force of trades-unionism, and the spirit that makes for a high standard of excellence in English Art and Handicraft, has so far proved a fortunate one; and a younger generation is already beginning to tell of a life and tradition of its own. We look back now with wonder to the circulars issued in the days of the beginnings, and ask how far the original intention has been warped, and changed, and twisted; but the central ideas have been always maintained, that the movement shall be a workman's movement, that it shall be one for the nobility and advance of English Art and Handicraft, that it shall be developed not on the basis of mastership, in the ordinary sense, but co-operatively as an industrial partnership, and that the arts and crafts, united in the Guild, shall be the children of the mother art of architecture. This is the basis upon which all has been built up."

Sir Edwin Lutyens,
walls and arches in the entrance hall,
built between 1910 and 1920.
Granite.
Castle Drogo, Drewsteignton.

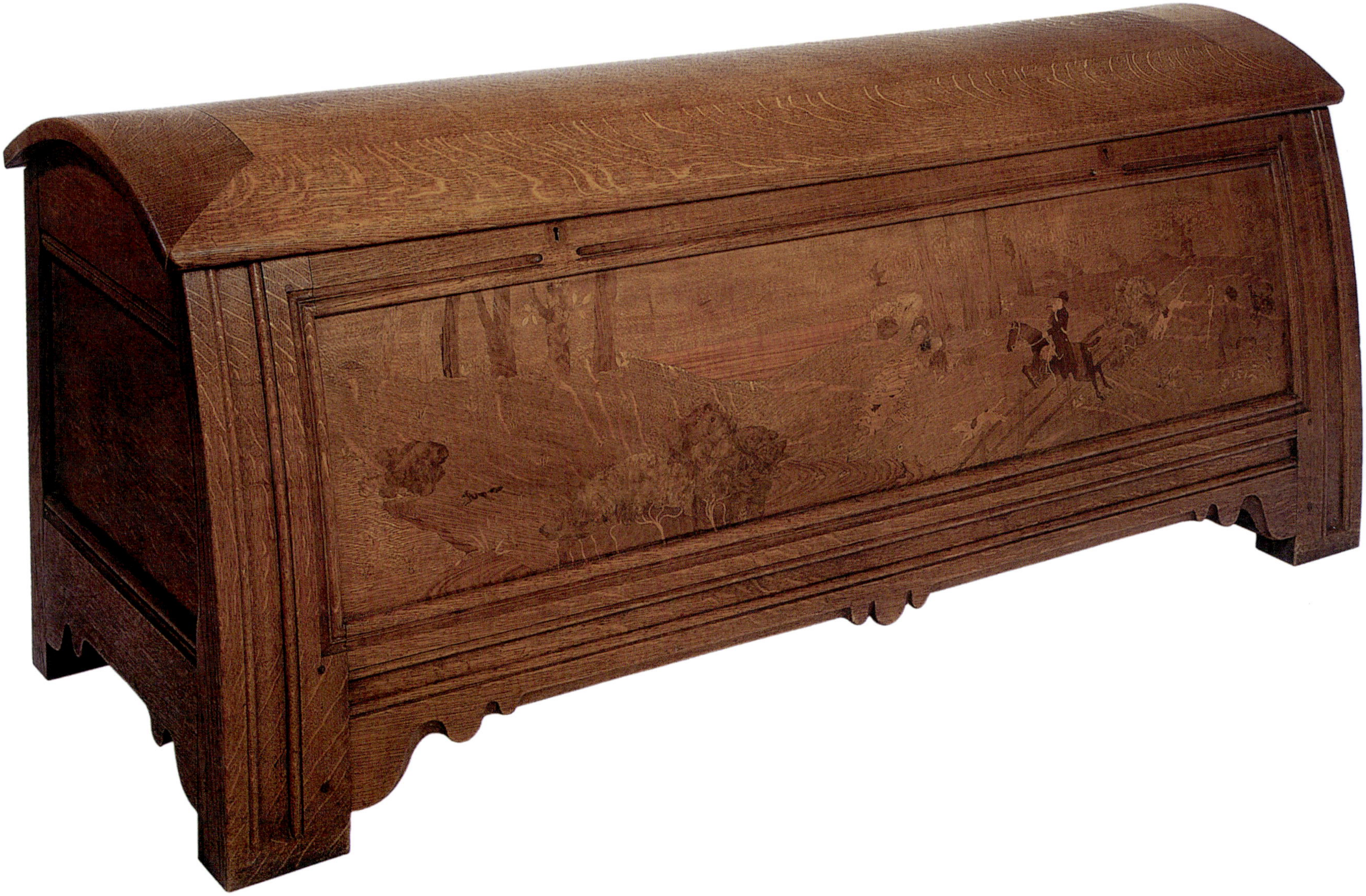

Robert Lorimer (for the design),
rug chest, designed in 1890,
made in 1899.
Oak, 72 x 172 x 61 cm.
National Museums of Scotland,
Edinburgh.

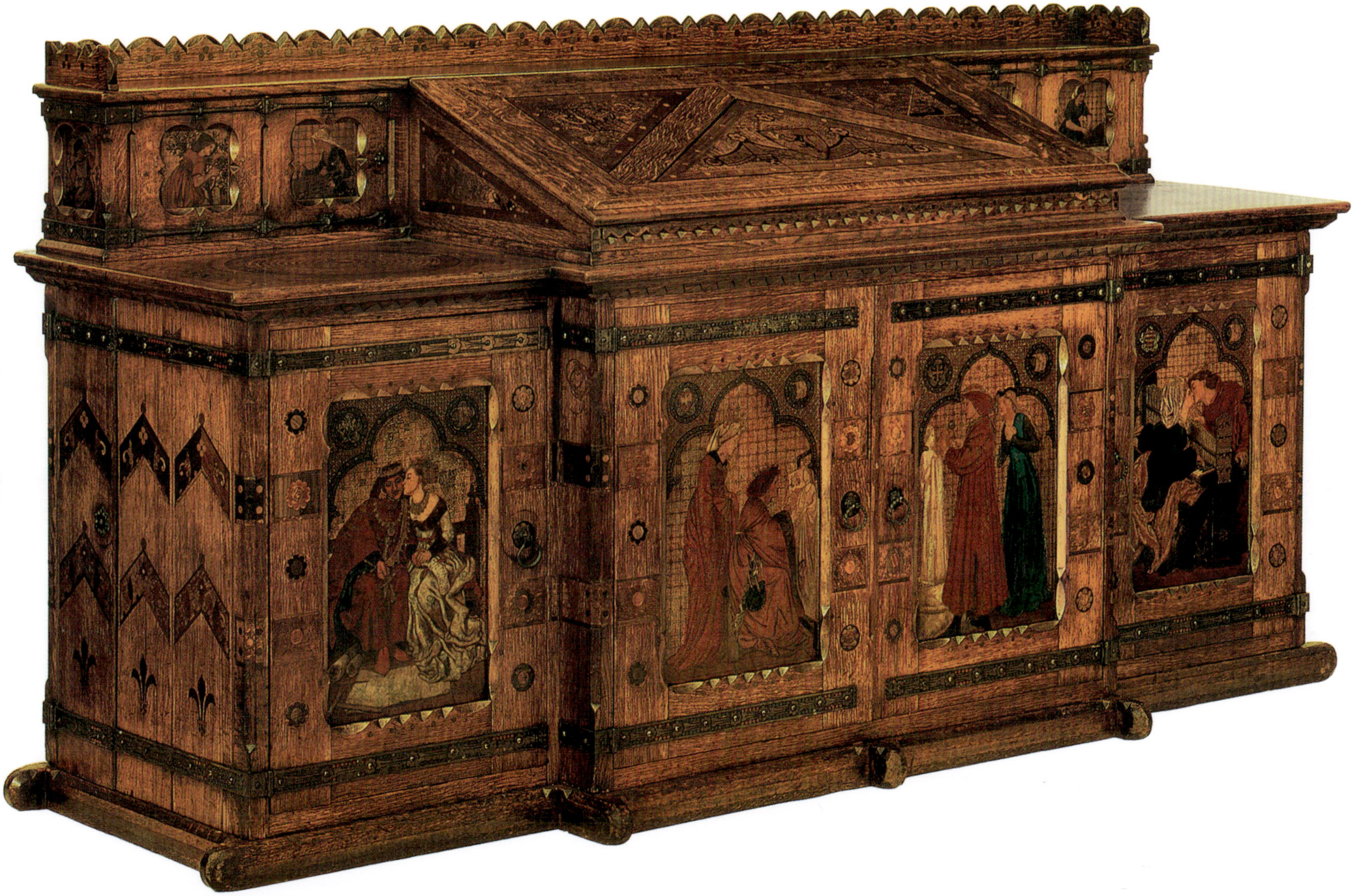

John Pollard Seddon (for the design) and **Morris, Marshall, Faulkner & Co.** (for the production), *King René's Honeymoon* cabinet, 1860-1862.
Cabinet decorated with oak, inlaid with various woods, with painted metalwork and painted panels, 133.4 x 252 x 87 cm.
Victoria & Albert Museum, London.

The original notice as to the objects of the Guild and School was as follows: "The Guild and School of Handicraft has for its object the application of Art and Industry. It is a Co-operative Society of Workmen, working out original designs, either of their own or such as may be submitted to them from without. In connection with, and dependent on it, is a School of about one hundred working men and boys. Its effort is to apply the Guild System of Mediaeval Italy to modern industrial needs, and to the movement for Technical Education."

The Essex House, located on the edge of Whitechapel, was a flourishing industrial institution, with the original principle of co-operation still in force, and the guild idea fully worked out, until 1907, when the guild was liquidated.

To the question of whether the Guild of Handicraft was not merely a business enterprise, Mr. Ashbee gave an answer which is characteristic of those who have to do with the new industrialism. He said:

"This is not the case. There are many of us in the Guild – I for one – who, if it were a mere business enterprise, would have no further interest in it. Mere business we could pursue more profitably elsewhere, and unencumbered with altruism. It is just because of the nature of its constitution, and in what it seeks to produce, that the Guild is a protest against modern business methods, against the trade point of view, against the commercial spirit." Then when asked if this did not mean the mixing of sentiment with business, he answered in the affirmative, and retorted: "The great businesses of England, could their histories be written, would often be found to have had in them some other than merely the pecuniary objective. They are voiceless for the most part because they have been built up by men that do not talk. But every now and then we catch a glimpse of the unexpected workings of these sentimental considerations. In one of the letters of the great house of Wedgwood, which old Josiah, the potter, founded in the middle of the last century, appears the following, written to Bently on whom he is urging the partnership: 'You have taste, the best foundation for our intended concern, and which must be our *primum mobile*, for without that, all would stand still, or better it did so.' And the great house still exists in the Midlands, for all the decay and taste that later and more commercial times may have brought with them. The point to be noted is that it was a sentimental consideration that inspired its founding, and that the founders knew how to apply the sentiment. And so I fancy with many of the great businesses, they would probable be found to have in them some quality of Idealism however slight, some sense of a need towards the raising of the standard of life, some inspiration of a better taste, a more useful purpose, however misdirected, some further object than the mere increase of the margin of profit, unconscious no doubt, but none the less present, the *primum mobile* in the words of that old business man and Idealist, which, if misapplied, would stand condemned as sentiment in business, but which, if rightly applied, becomes its justification, its first principle."

Bruce Talbert (for the design),
Gillow & Co. (for the production),
The Pet sideboard, 1873.
Boxwood panels, ebony borders.
Victoria & Albert Museum, London.

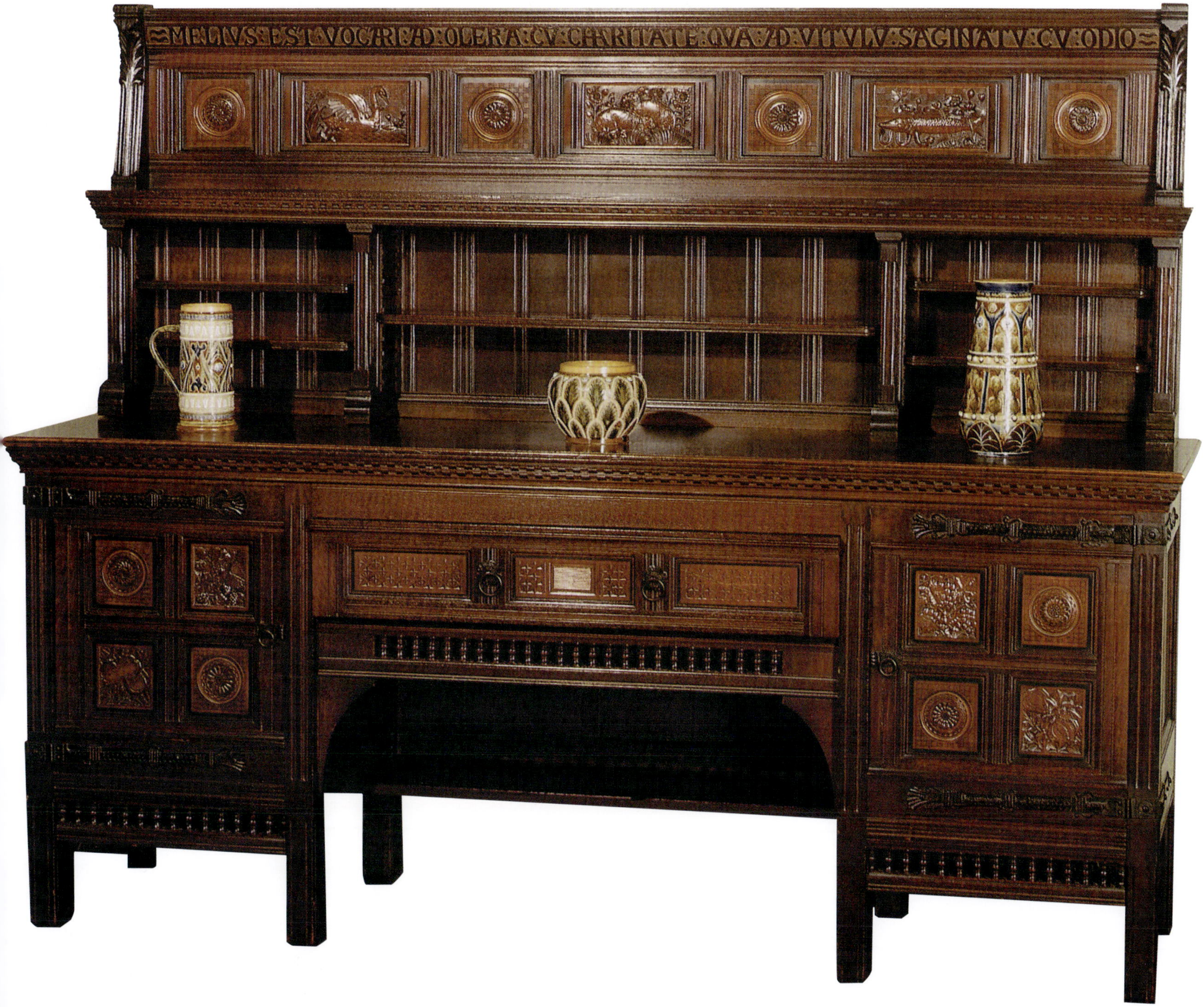
MELIUS EST VOCARE AD OLERA CU CHARITATE QUA AD VITULU SAGINATU CU ODIO

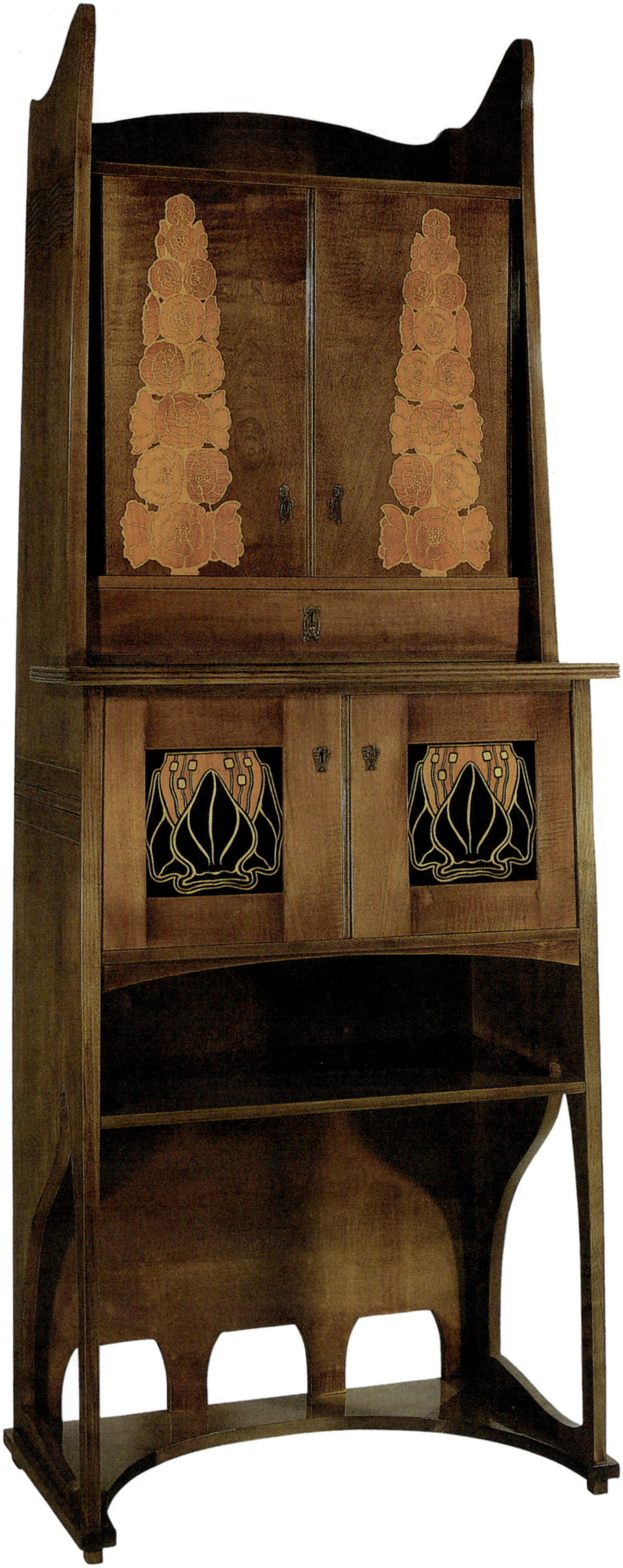

Joseph Maria Olbrich,
cabinet, 1900.
Maple wood inlaid with various exotic woods, 183 x 71 x 40 cm.
Museum Künstlerkolonie, Darmstadt.

William Burges (for the design),
chest on a stand for Tower House,
1875.
Tower House, London.

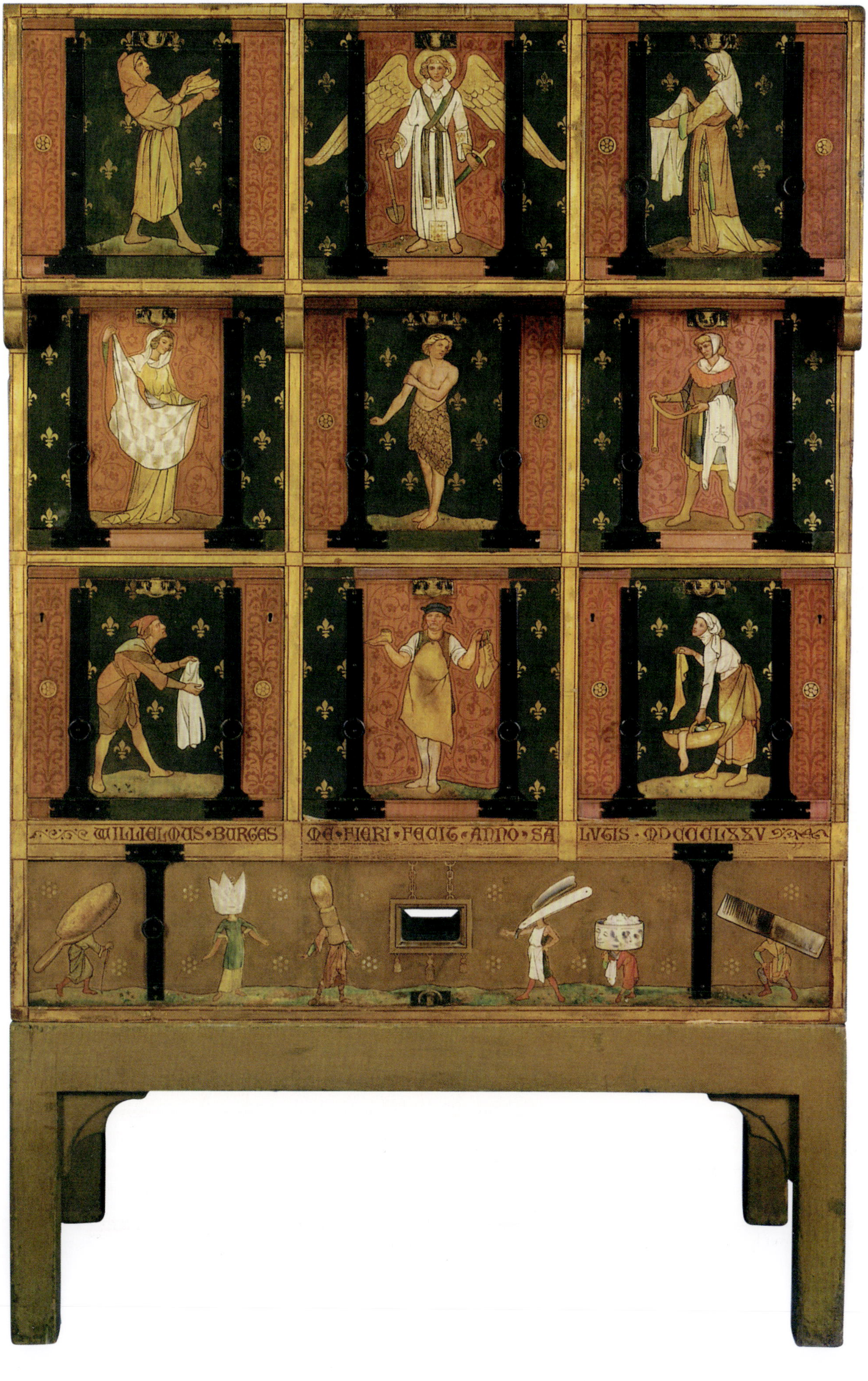
WILLIELMUS·BURGES ME·FIERI·FECIT·ANNO·SA LUTIS·MDCCCLXXV

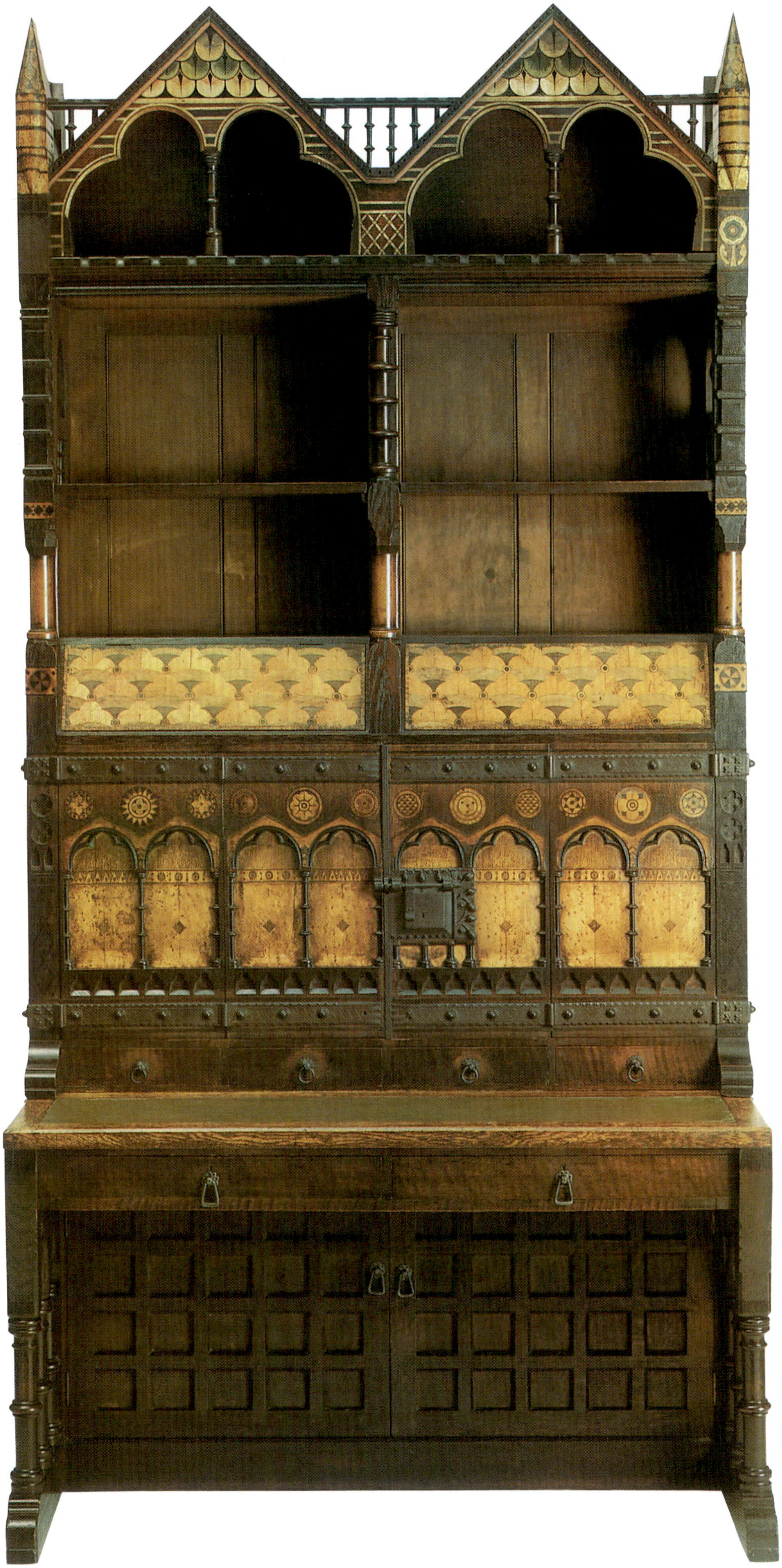

From these and other sayings it will appear that Ashbee continues the traditions of Ruskin and Morris in attempting to humanize business and industry.

Rookwood: An Ideal Workshop

"The social question," said Mr. Ashbee, in his fifth aphorism, "has prior claim to the artistic," The world slowly adjusts itself to the truth of this statement. The question of art is altogether a question of social reform. Art must grow out of the life, if the life is not so ordered that art will appear as its crown and fulfilment it is idle to foster and upbuild it. To give it independent development is to preserve the empty form and overlook the informing and vitalising spirit. Those who prate most of art are not the true promoters so much as the thinkers, the social reformers, who are trying to reach a status of true liberty, to destroy slavery of every kind, to humanise industry, and to introduce other motives into production than the commercial and mechanical ones. Hence the Arts and Crafts movement, with its principle of co-operative individualism, is brought into harmony with some of the deepest thought tendencies of the times; with such books as George's *Progress and Poverty*, Kropotkin's *Farm, Field, and Factory*, Tolstoy's *The Slavery of Our Times*, Edward Carpenter's *Angels' Wings*, and *Towards Democracy*, Whitman's *Leaves of Grass*, Crosby's *Plain Talk in Psalm and Parable*, and the writings of Bolton Hall. For when the present system is outworn, and a more just and equal order is established, the order for which these writers are labouring, industry will be the crown of life, and art the crown of industry. Art on any other terms than the contentment of a well-ordered and consistent life is undesired and undesirable.

So long as the factory is organised to the end of making profits for some owner and director, an issue of production in art is practically impossible. The wage slavery of the factory forbids art; the machine forbids it; competition forbids it; the methods of designing and executing by division of labour are against it. The factories that are so constituted that their products rise to the plane of art may be counted on the fingers of one hand. These few, conducting business within the present system, but with higher motives, may be referred to as indicating also the tendency toward workshop reconstruction. Chief among the factories that undertake production from the instinct for beauty – and which enjoy also commercial success – may be counted the Rookwood Pottery at Cincinnati. Instituted as a private industrial experiment by Maria Longworth Storer in 1880, it grew to a position of public importance and of far-reaching influence. The aspects of its organisation and work that bear upon our present theme may be briefly considered. Three factors evidently conspired to make the Rookwood Pottery what it was – the founder, the workmen, and the public.

Richard Norman Shaw,
cabinet: bookcase and writing desk, 1861.
Oak, inlaid with satinwood, rosewood, walnut, bird's-eye maple and oak, partially painted, with steel hinge, 280 x 142 x 79 cm.
Victoria & Albert Museum, London.

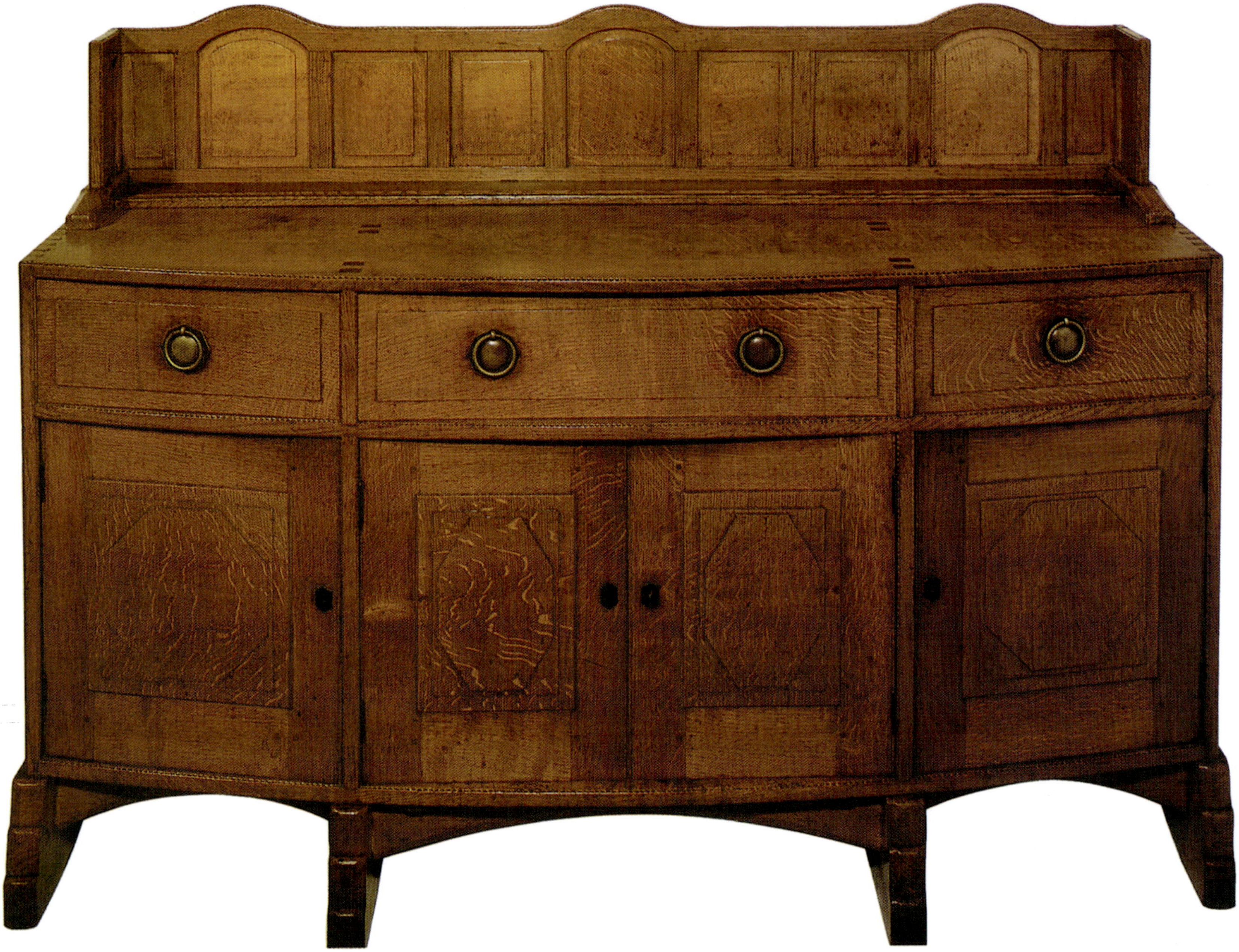

Sidney Barnsley,
sideboard, 1924.
Oak.
Cheltenham Art Gallery & Museum,
Cheltenham.

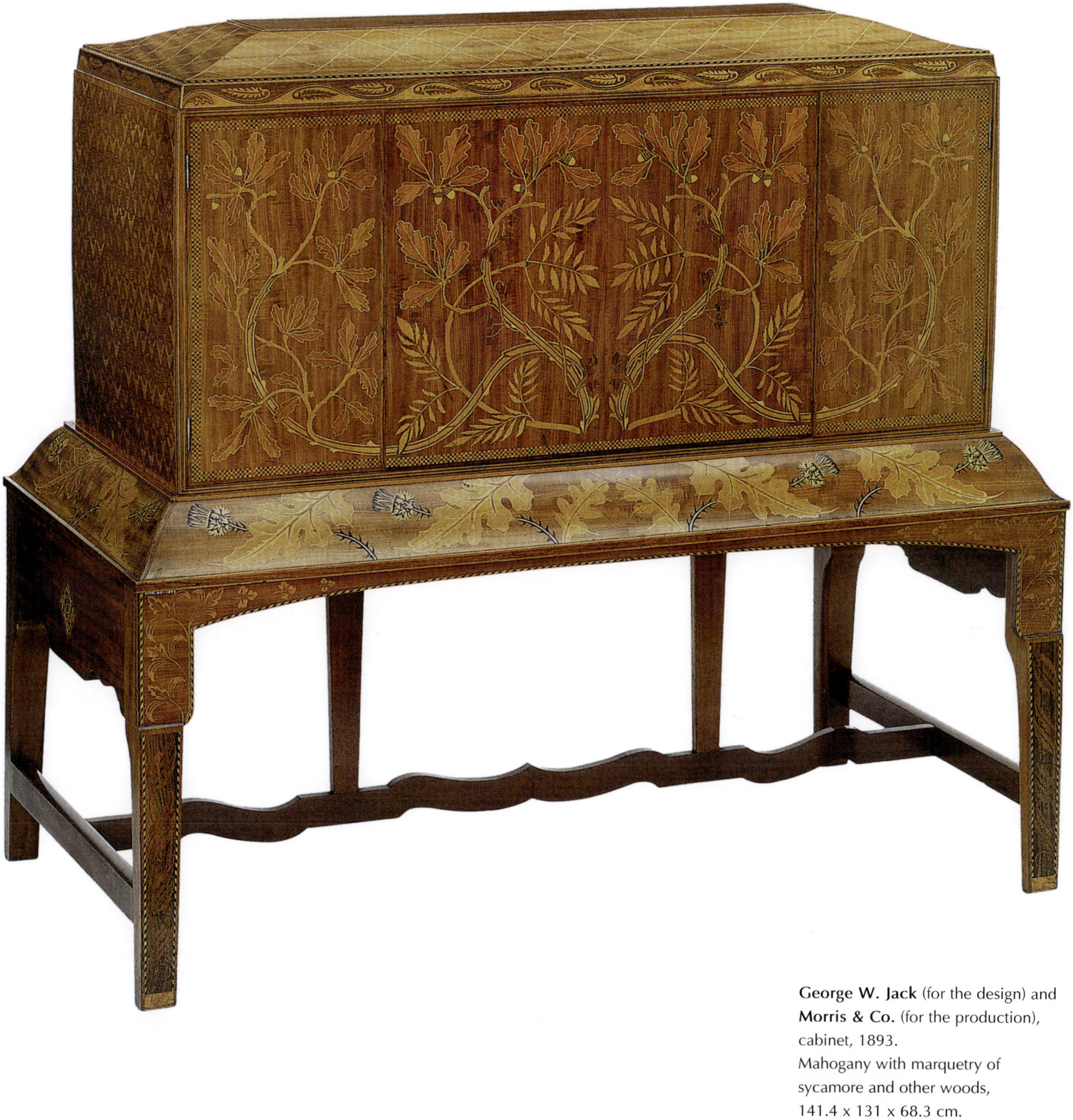

George W. Jack (for the design) and **Morris & Co.** (for the production), cabinet, 1893.
Mahogany with marquetry of sycamore and other woods, 141.4 x 131 x 68.3 cm.
Victoria & Albert Museum, London.

The Rookwood Pottery had – so to speak – a soul. A woman's intelligence and affection went into its creation. It was established upon a person. Upon this fact all other features of the factory depended. The motive that controlled the enterprise from the beginning was the desire to produce a perfect product. Below this must have been the intention to perform a social service in perfecting a given product. But perfection is fugitive – how could they secure it in a workshop involving many hands and minds?

Though the management of the business centred in a board of directors, the fullest possible freedom was given to the workmen; they were encouraged to experiment, to express their own individuality, and to increase their culture by study and travel. The spirit of the factory was one of co-operation and good fellowship. Mr. Taylor, the genial director, called himself "the arbiter", expecting initiation from his associates. From the first any problems were solved as they arose from the inside. The factory consequently had its traditions, and its products represented organic growth. Its art was as indigenous as that of the first potter. The principle of construction was to adjust design sympathetically to shape and material. No printing-patterns were permitted, and no copying or imitation allowed. Division of labour was practiced sufficiently to ensure technical skill but not to the extent of destroying unity of design. This one fact, unity of design, that for which Rookwood is especially noted, is itself evidence of the unity of the workers, their absorption in a common purpose. Let discord enter or dissatisfaction be felt, or let the pride of any worker assert itself, or the authority of the director be unduly exercised, and the effect is recorded at once in the product. The problem of uniting a workshop of large membership would seem to be solved here by the cultivation of human sympathy – that delicate something that is the source of all high endeavor.

But the pottery was not merely a workshop; it was in a sense a school of handicraft, an industrial art museum, and a social centre. The craftsmen, creating and initiating on their own ground, constantly improve in skill and character. By the employment of apprentices the workshop could be at once transformed into a school. A portion of the building was devoted to exhibition. By means of lectures, and other entertainments at the pottery, the public participated in some degree in the enterprise, and by reaction shaped the product. Here were all the elements needed for the ideal workshop – a self-directing shop, an incidental school of craft, and an associative public. Standing high on the edge of Mount Adams, an attractive building in a fair environment – the building an interesting example of Early English architecture, with roof of tile and walls of cement decorated by scratchwork – it was a model factory. Its motive, its management, its principles of work, its fine artistic production – all distinguished it from contemporary factories. With only slight changes, by the development of forces already implicit, such a workshop as the reformers have dreamed of could be here and now created.

Peter Behrens,
dresser, c. 1902
Stained and painted wood.
Private collection.

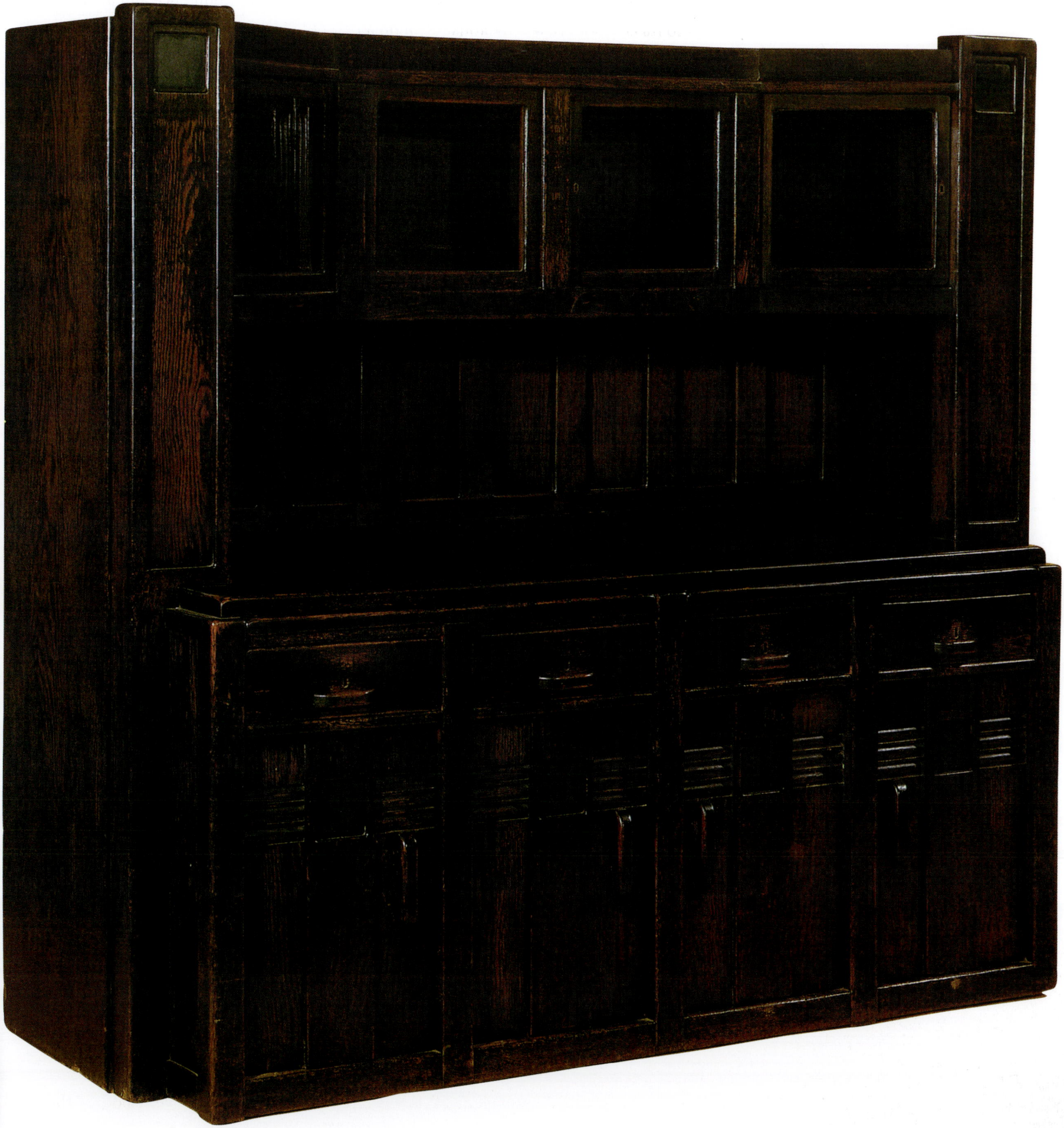

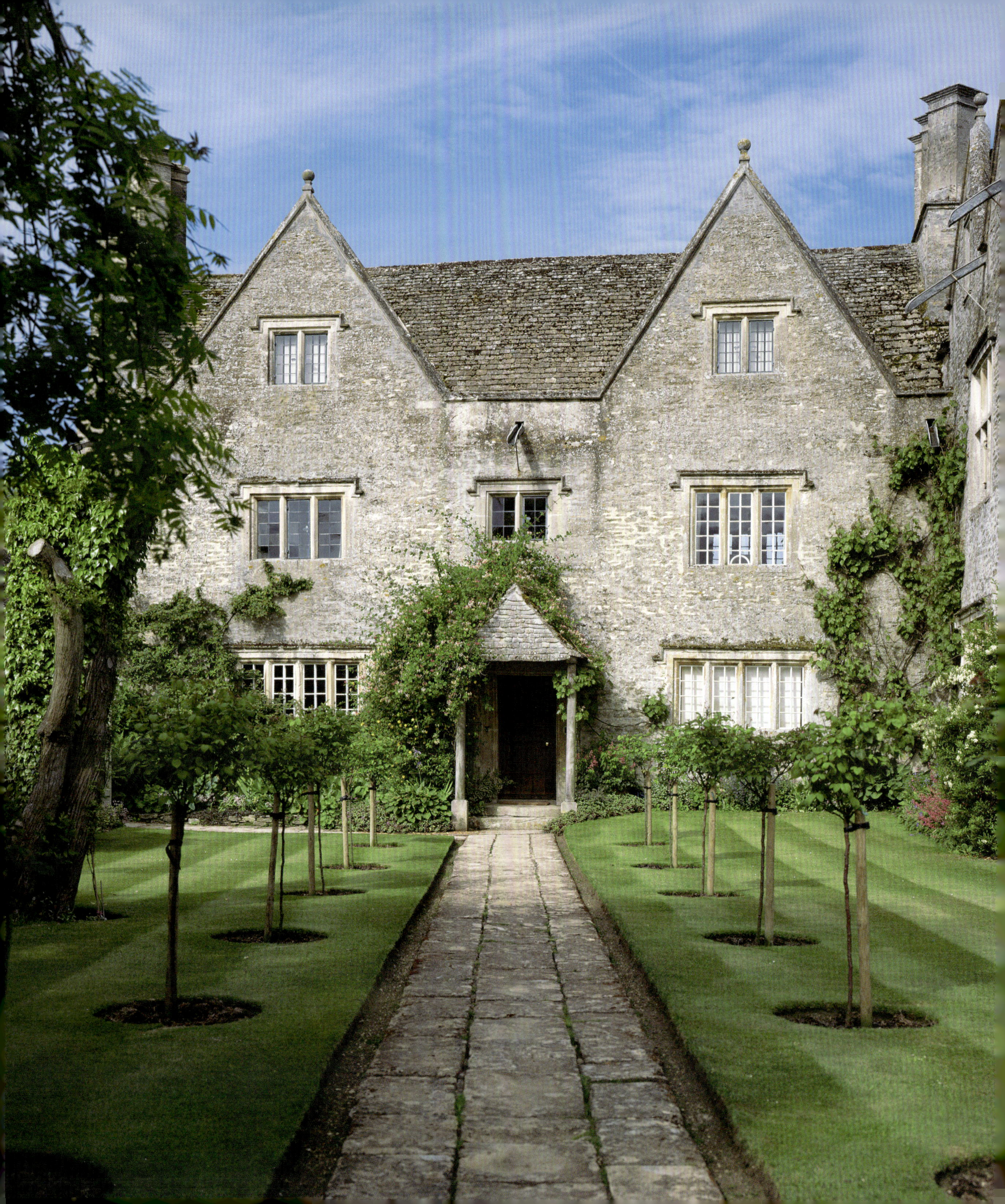

4 - The Development of Industrial Consciousness

"I do not want art for a few any more than education for a few, or freedom for a few."
William Morris, *The Lesser Arts*, 1877.

At the beginning of the twentieth century, the Arts and Crafts movement was the industrial phase of the modern evolution of individuality. For several centuries the conditions of life tended to produce a general uniformity of civilisation within the bounds of large social groups. The Arts and Crafts were to change this uniformity.

Different definitions of art were formulated by Morris and Tolstoy. Let the terms be noted and their import fairly considered. "By art I understand," said Morris, "the pleasure of life." Such a definition at once universalises art and individualises it. For pleasure is, or may become, universal, but when universal it is least uniform. Let all men share in art; let: all, that is, do what gives them pleasure, or do that which gives pleasure to others, and the individuality of the maker and user is forthwith outdrawn and exercised. The uniform machine-made products of the present day – uniform because impersonal and for the "average" – are made without pleasure and produce no pleasure; they spring from pain, and if not actively painful to the user, yield but little satisfaction. The workers are pained because they must subdue themselves to the system, must hold in abeyance their own affections and thoughts and imaginings, must become an impersonal machine serving another impersonal machine. The theologians have never imagined a more painful hell than the actual factories economists have constructed, wherein a man is hopelessly engaged in the performance of one never-ending and abhorrent task. In distribution also the goods thus made are dissevered from personality. Of necessity the consolidated factory, making uniform wares by wholesale, labours for no one individual, but for an abstract average individual – a person who has of course no real being. When the consumer finds in the goods he has purchased no real fitness, no response to his needs, no appeal to memory or associations, no real adjustment between the body and its garments, he can experience no genuine pleasure or rational satisfaction – in most cases the shoes actually pinch his feet, and the clothes constrain some part of the body. The fault is not with the materials, nor with the form – considered abstractly – and not in workmanship nor the style; still

Kelmscott Manor.
Built in 1570.

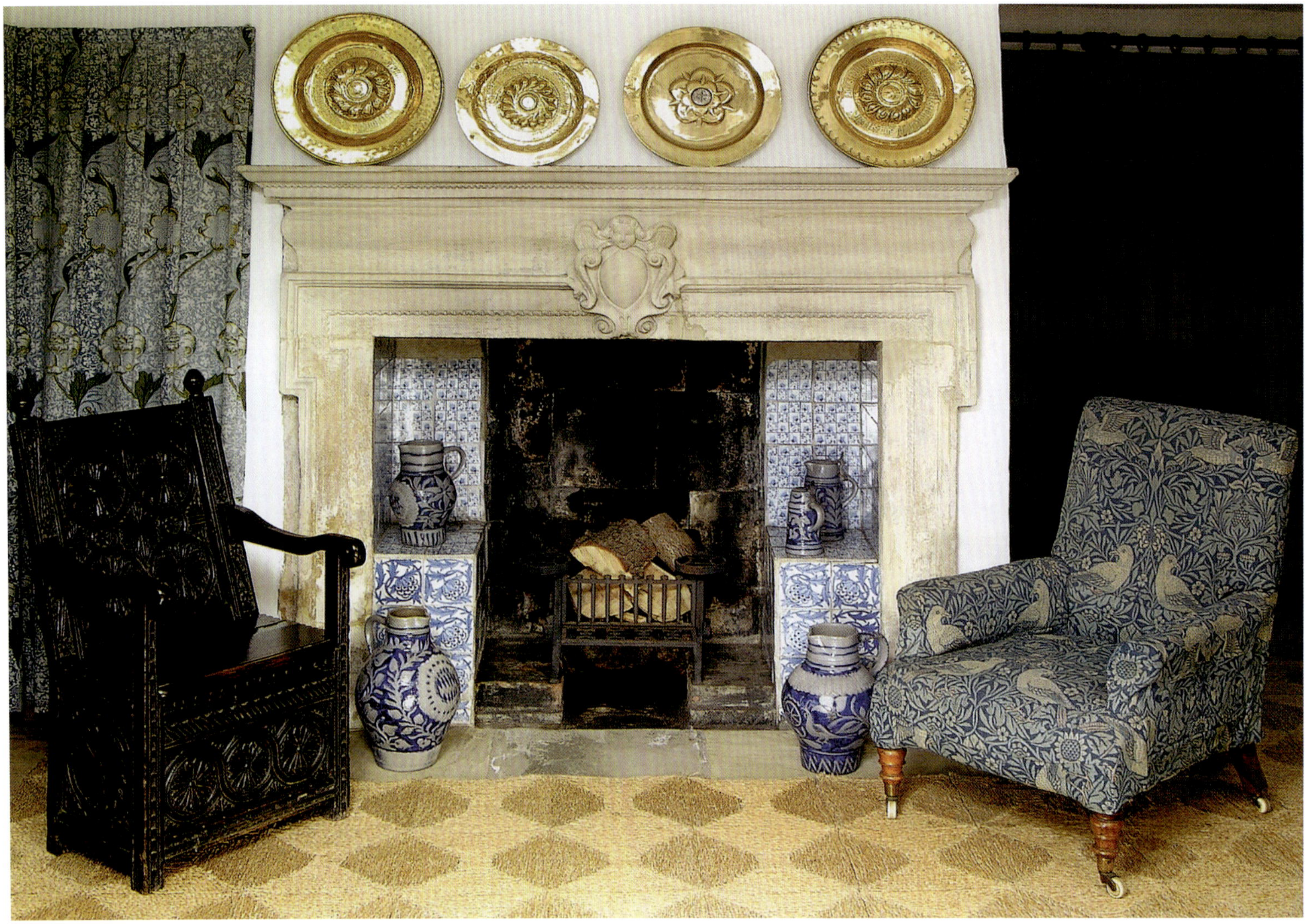

William Morris and **various designers**,
The Green room, c. 1883.
Kelmscott Manor, Kelmscott.

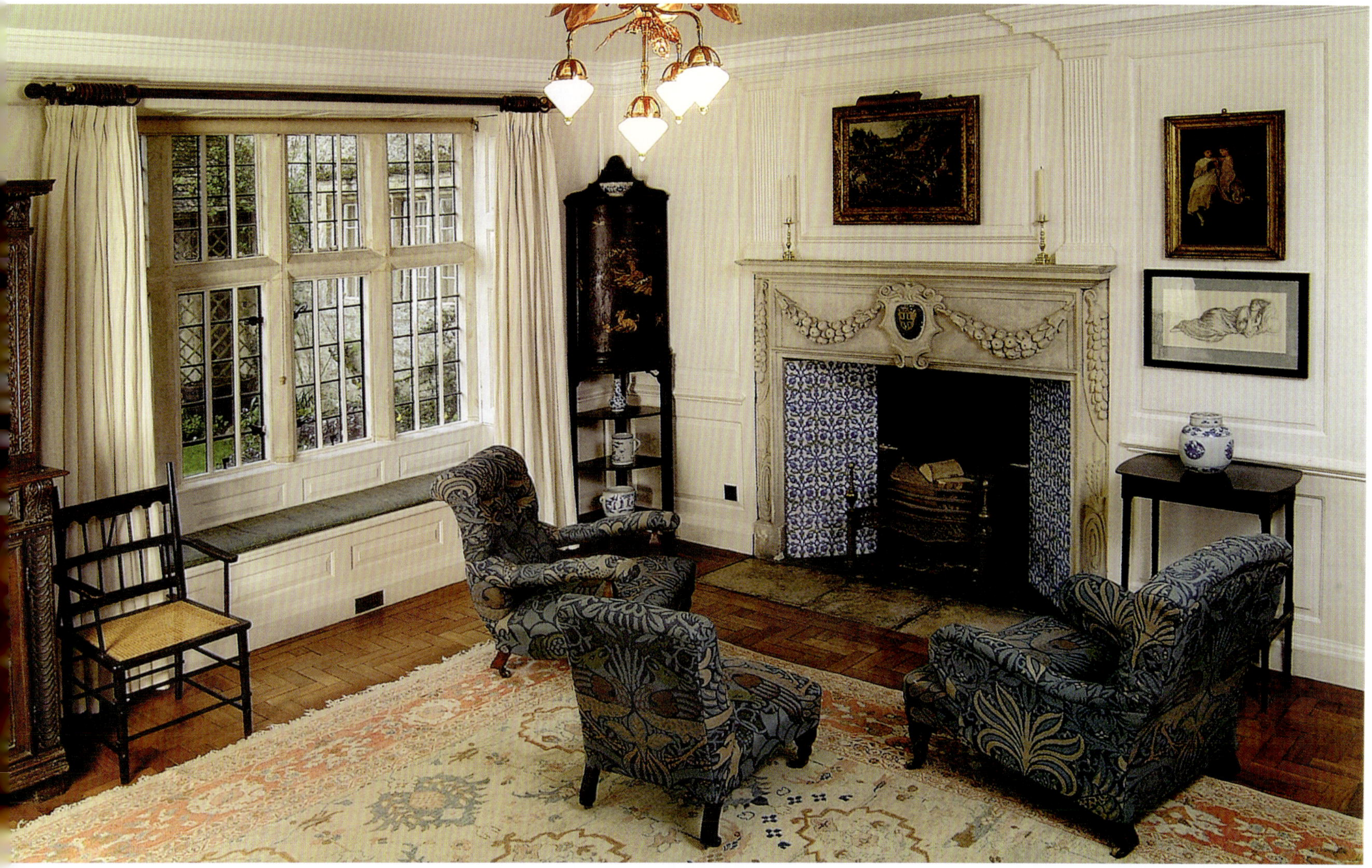

Various designers,
The Paneled room, 1871-1896.
Three chairs upholstered in *Peacock and Dragon* woven wool, the painting over the fireplace is *The Tulip Garden* by Pieter Brueghel the Younger.
Kelmscott Manor, Kelmscott.

there is no pleasure to the user. Unless goods that are costly, perfect in their workmanship and tasteful in their design, serve an individual need, they are inappropriate, and in reality ugly and painful. If on the other hand the article evidences the maker's pleasure, his affection for his work, his play of memory and intelligence and faith, or if it is constructed with reference to another's need, and represents some claim of the soul for outer garment; if the work be individualised, it becomes to that degree a work of art, a part of the pleasure of men's lives, the source of happiness. When once the habit of pleasurable labour is established, then it will be possible for all to take a pleasurable interest in the details of life, to feel ourselves a part of nature, and thoughtfully and without distraction note the course of our lives amidst the events that make up the whole of humanity. Then art will be synonymous with life, and the very activity of life will be an artistic activity. As life is now, under the compulsion of uniformity, it is anxious, inhuman, inartistic, empty. It will thus be seen that Morris's definition of art is social in its bearing. It implies the modern necessity of building up the ornamental part of life, its pleasures of every nature, on the basis of work undertaken cheerfully, with the consciousness of helping ourselves and our fellows.

In his volume *What is Art?* Tolstoy offers a definition that accords closely with that of Morris, though perhaps with a wider view of what constitutes social well-being. Tolstoy's treatment of the theme is consciously revolutionary. He abandons the current theories of beauty, the theories that make beauty something " fine", abstract, exclusive, perceiving that as long as the world upholds such theories art will tend more and more to separate itself from life, and lead a poor, thin existence with the privileged and esoteric cults. As a matter of social justice it is necessary to re-establish art among the people, and restore to toil its natural solace. The definition of art founded upon the current metaphysics of beauty is a class definition, and is intended to preserve the upper classes in their special privileges of culture and "taste". After centuries of exclusiveness art has become perverted, is devoid of natural and spontaneous feeling, and is generally incomprehensible, and in truth "decadent". To bring art back to the people, and make it universal in its appeal, we are required to start an entirely new definition, and to understand art not as a possession for a select minority, but as a means toward human perfection and the brotherly union of mankind. The inaccuracy of previous definitions arises from the fact that in them art is considered as an end in itself, or as a means of pleasure to a specially equipped class of persons; whereas the true view is to consider art as one of the conditions of human life, a means of intercourse between man and man. "The activity of art," Tolstoy says, "is based on the fact that a man, receiving through his sense of hearing or sight another man's expression of feeling, is capable of experiencing the emotion which moved the man who expressed it." From this fact the definition of art is deduced: "Art is a human activity consisting in this, that one man

Anonymous,
The Tapestry Room (view to the south).
Kelmscott Manor, Kelmscott.

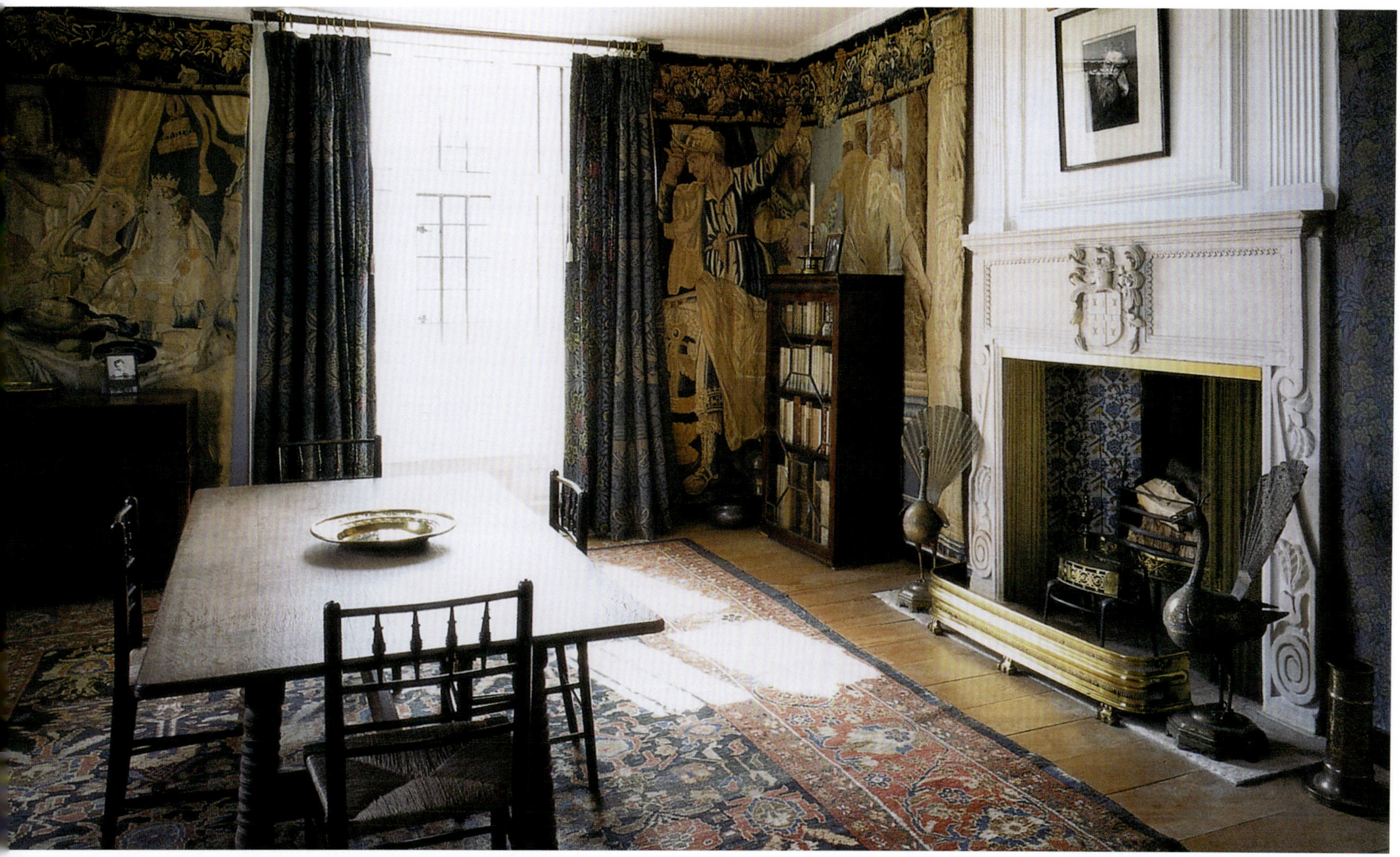

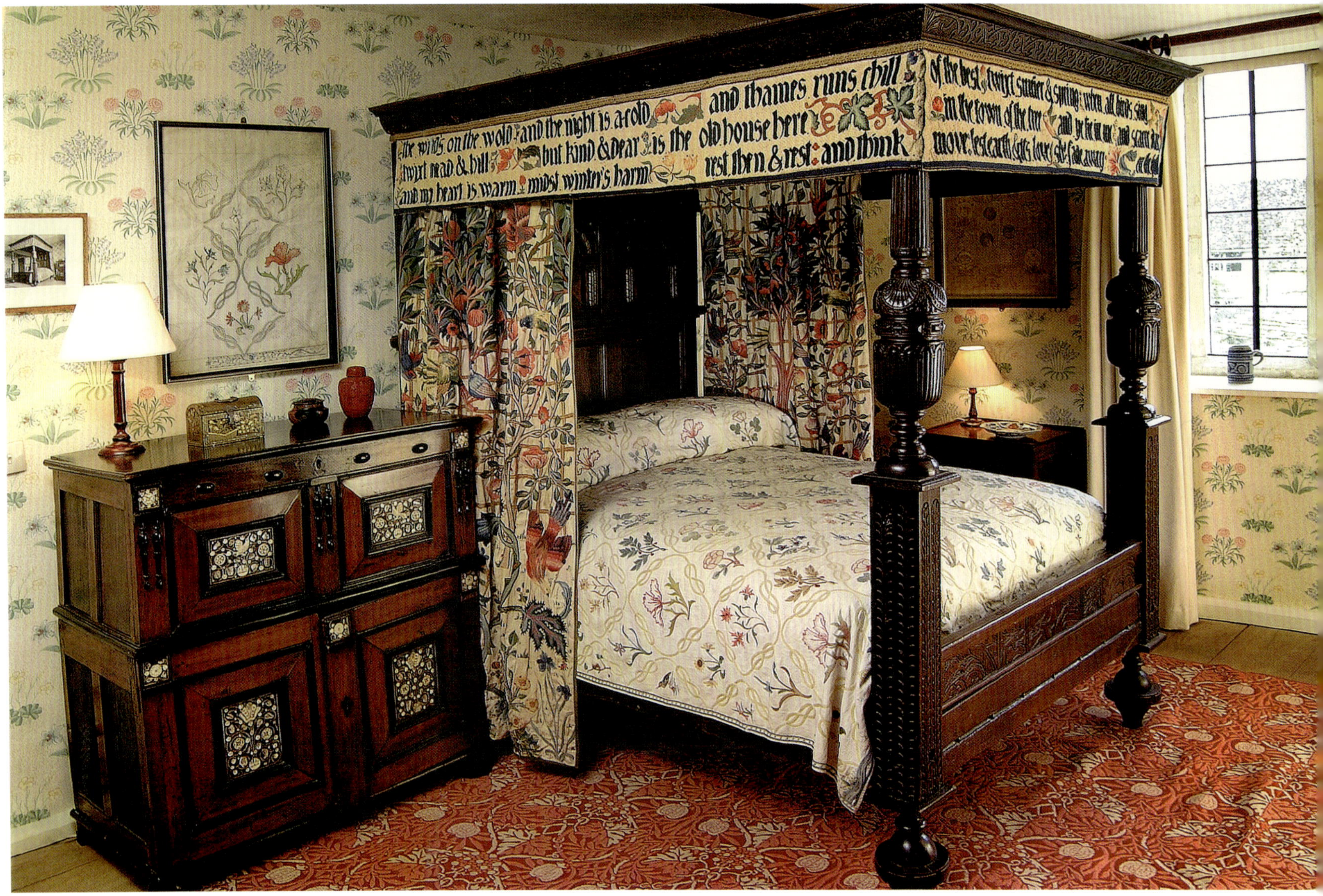
the winds on the wold and the night is a-cold and thames runs chill
twixt mead & hill but kind & dear is the old house here
and my heart is warm midst winter's harm rest then & rest and think
of the best twixt summer & spring when all birds sing
in the town of the tree

consciously, by means of certain external signs, hands on to others feelings he has lived through, and that other people are infected by these feelings, and also experience them". It follows from this that the purpose of art is to create the sense of kinship: "Art is a means of union among men, joining them together in the same feelings, and indispensable for the life and progress towards well-being of individuals and of humanity." The activity of art is, therefore, a general activity, as widely diffused and as common as speech itself. Art and speech are indeed the two organs of human progress; by speech we convey thoughts, by art we interchange feelings. Of course with perverted ideas of art, and on the supposition that the art of the upper classes is the whole of art, it has come about that only a small fraction of the people make any use of art or even understand it. And this fact of exclusiveness in art points to a social condition wherein the masses of the people are in virtual slavery to the privileged classes.

The question of art becomes then at once a social question, and Tolstoy, like Morris, requires a complete revolution of the social system, and an entire change in the ideals of life. Morris's definition of art in terms of pleasure, and Tolstoy's in terms of infection, have practically the same ground, and reach essentially the same conclusion: an art that is common to all, yet one that admits the freest play of individuality.

Two definitions of education were enunciated by prominent educators, that represented the advance in educational theory corresponding to the stage reached by Morris and Tolstoy, in their definitions of art, and displayed like these the subtle forces in modern life working for democracy. "Education," said Francis W. Parker, "is expression." "Education," says John Dewey, "is life." These definitions or descriptions of education point to the rejection by modern thinkers of those theories that, like the older definitions of art, grew up from the social order of feudalism, and maintained the cultural classes in their positions of privilege. Feudalistic education had learning for its motive and discipline for its method. The priestly and noble classes alone possessed the key of knowledge, the capacity of translating the symbols of learning, and imposed upon the world the tyranny of culture. Secure in their special privileges, these classes enforced on their underlings the forms of obedience drawn on the model of the military, and by this means suppressed the disposition on the part of any one to assert his own nature and live his own life. In whatever school today the stress of education is placed upon learning and intellectual culture, in the manner and by the discipline prescribed by authority, in that place the forces of an earlier system are surviving. But wherever the emphasis is withdrawn from teachers and books and examinations, and placed upon the child, regarded as a living personality with a character to develop, his

William Morris, **May Morris** (for the hangings) and **Jane Morris** (for the bed cover),
William Morris' bedroom, c. 1891.
Seventeenth-century oak four-poster bed with poem written by Morris in 1891.
Kelmscott Manor, Kelmscott.

Charles Sumner Greene and **Henry Mather Greene**,
the stairs in the David B. Gamble house (detail), 1908-1909.
101 x 189.9 x 101 cm
The David B. Gamble House, Pasadena.

Richard Norman Shaw (architect),
main staircase, 1883-1884.
Carved oak, highlighted by carved lion newel posts holding light standards.
Cragside House, Garden and Estate, Rothbury.

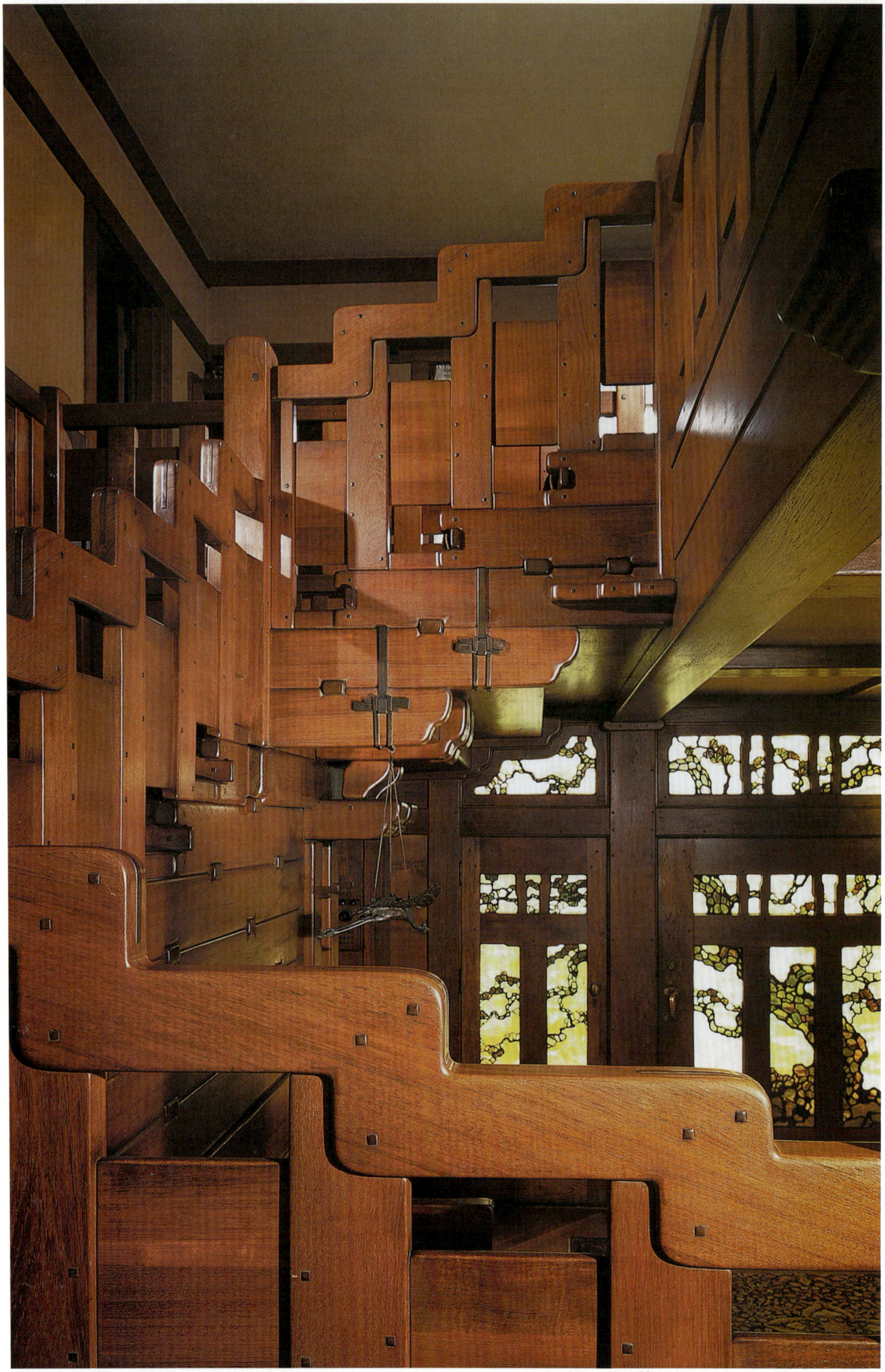

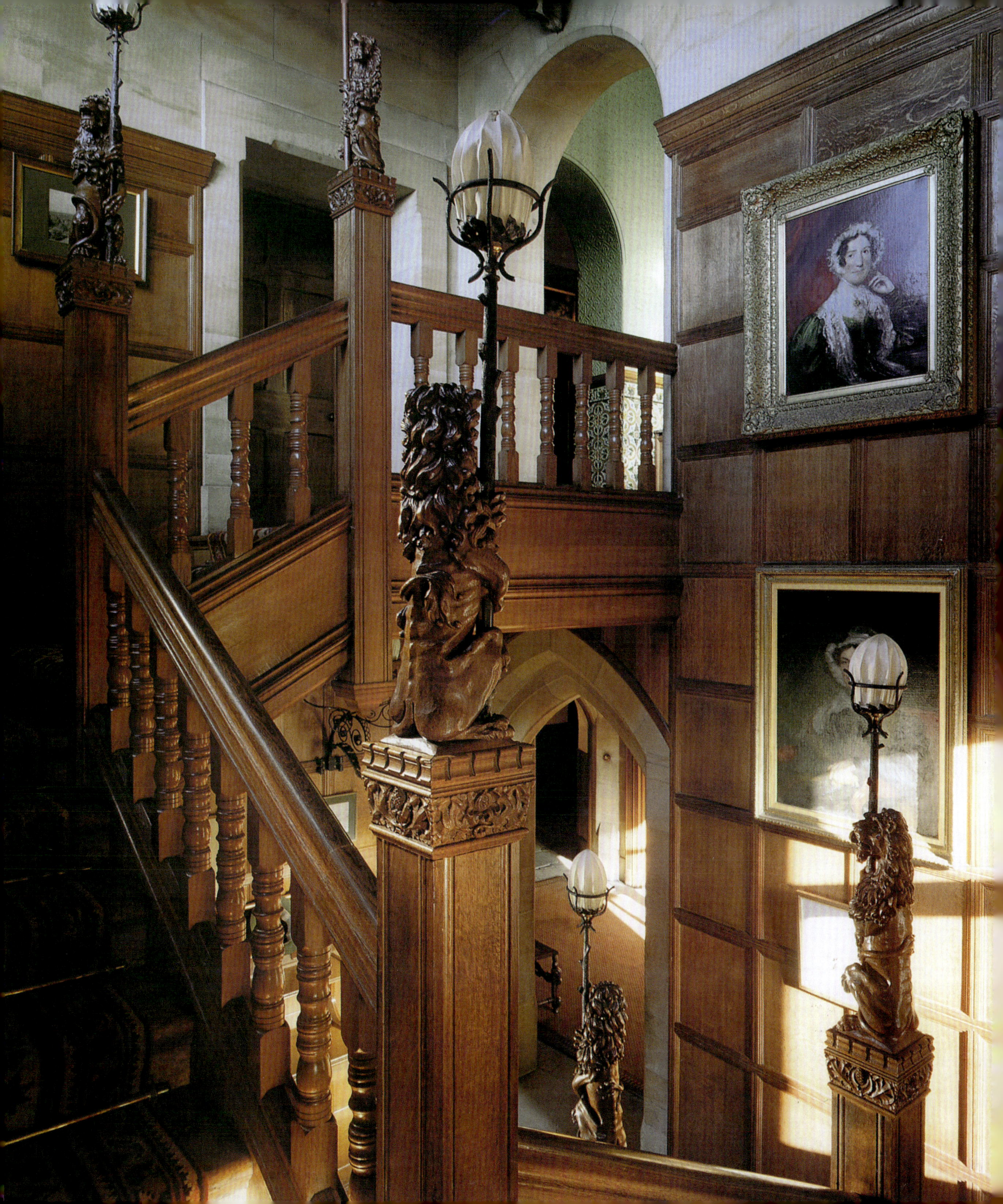

ends to seek, and his social relations to realise, there are the evidences of the new spirit in education.

Of necessity the new educators, like Morris and Tolstoy in their spheres, are in the broad sense of the term socialists, and their hands reach out not merely to educate the child in terms of self-activity, but to shape society so that the newly formed individuality may not be thwarted and destroyed by environment. If the man in his industrial activities is not permitted to exercise his individuality, it is folly to educate the child in freedom. If education be expression, the child's self-activity cannot stop at the boundary of schoolyards. If education is life, then the general life must be so shaped as to be in itself educative. In short, the new education, precisely in the way of the new art, makes culture coincide with life, and as the new art promises to destroy the professionalism and commercialism of the special artist, so the new education will eventually dispense with school-systems, all external machinery, even with teachers as they are now known, and will erect school-houses on an entirely new model. I think probably a building modeled on the idea of a workshop, wherein the life activity of the young will be developed at the freest yet with the most intimate relationship with all other social factors.

A greater revolution cannot be conceived than that taking place today in the schools. The movement in education is one phase of a general emancipatory movement which has for its purpose the complete democratisation of the modern world. Morris and Tolstoy foretold the democratisation of art, which means the association of art and life. The new education promises the association of education and life. In reality art and education are modes of the same activity, and they properly coincide in the larger synthesis we call life.

Considering the converging lines of all these tendencies, I see no reason why the workshop will not become at once the school and the factory. But this would mean an industrial revolution. It would mean that the workshop would aim to minister to the well-being of the workers, and not merely to make wares for sale. It would mean that men and women would take pleasure in their work, that their work was in line with their ideals. It would mean that through their work they would be attached to the past of life, and be brought into contact with their fellows. But a humanised workshop has yet to be developed. Before industrialism can join with art and education it must pass through a long evolution, be disciplined by suffering, and tried by success. It is the part of the twentieth century to reconstruct the workshop, and to train for citizenship in an industrial country.

Richard Norman Shaw (architect), dining room, 1883-1884
Cragside House, Garden and Estate, Rothbury.

But with the absorption of the higher type of mind in industrial pursuits bad conditions are destined to pass away. Industry will be moralised and intellectualised. Already those who have acquired great wealth by means of the

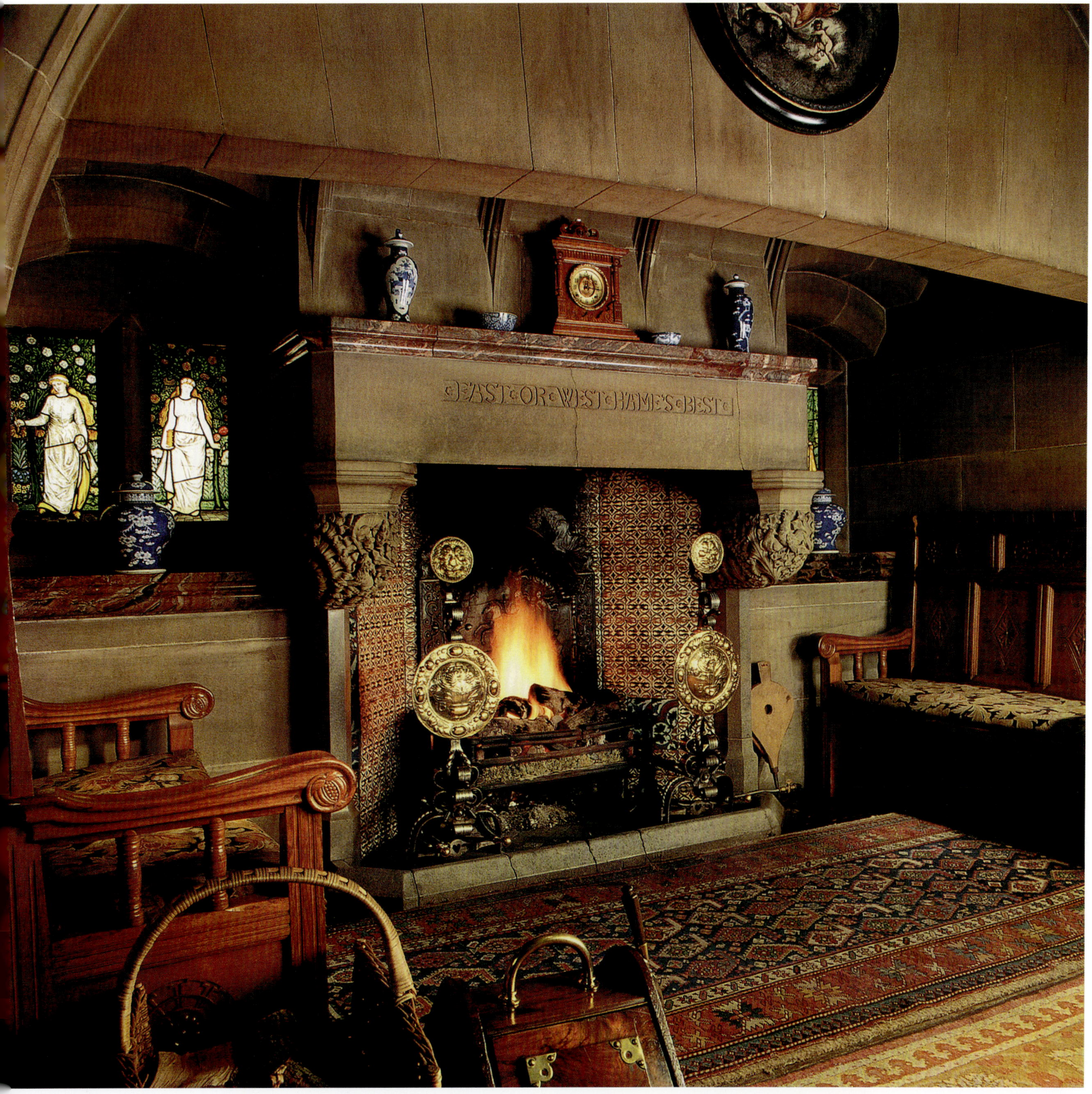
EAST OR WEST HAME'S BEST

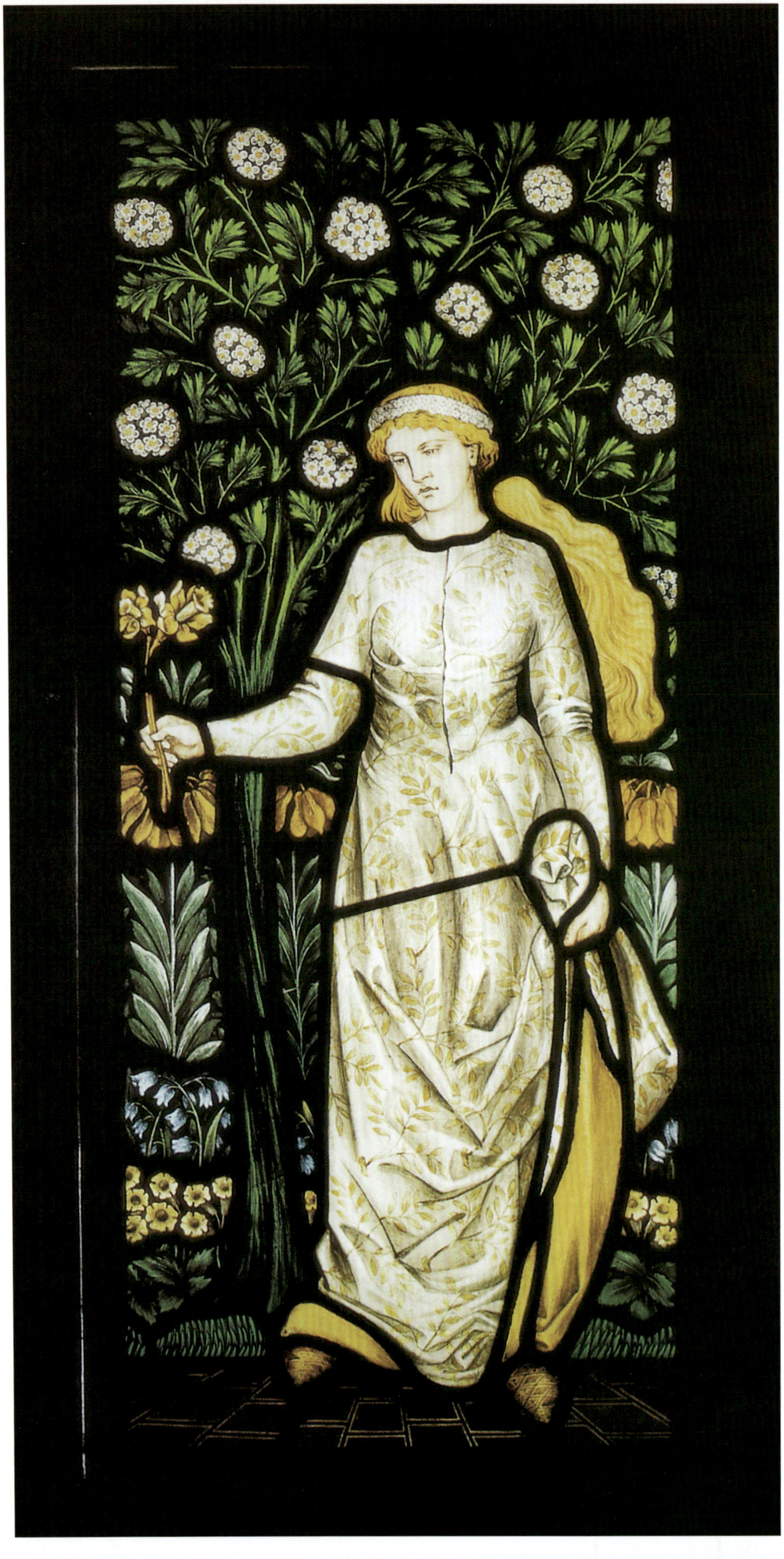

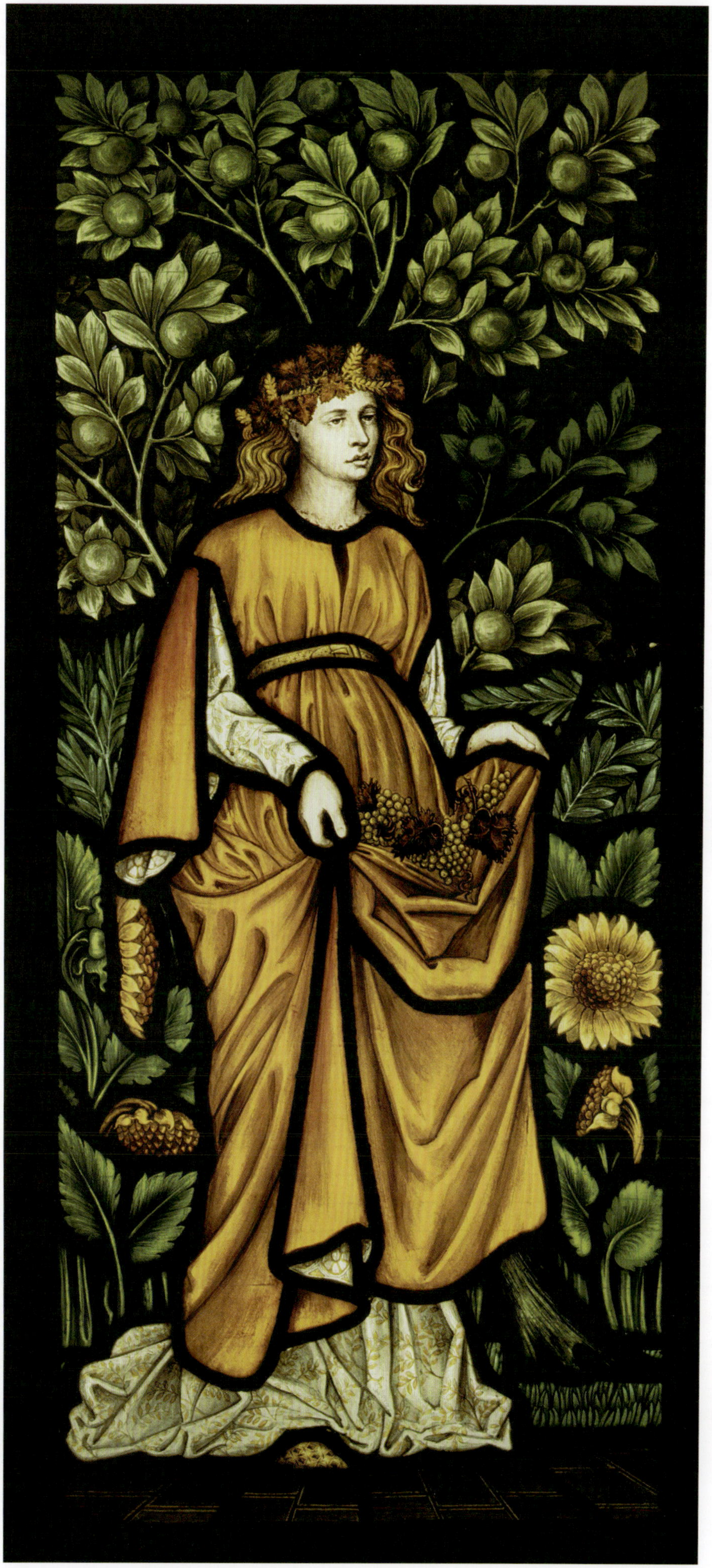

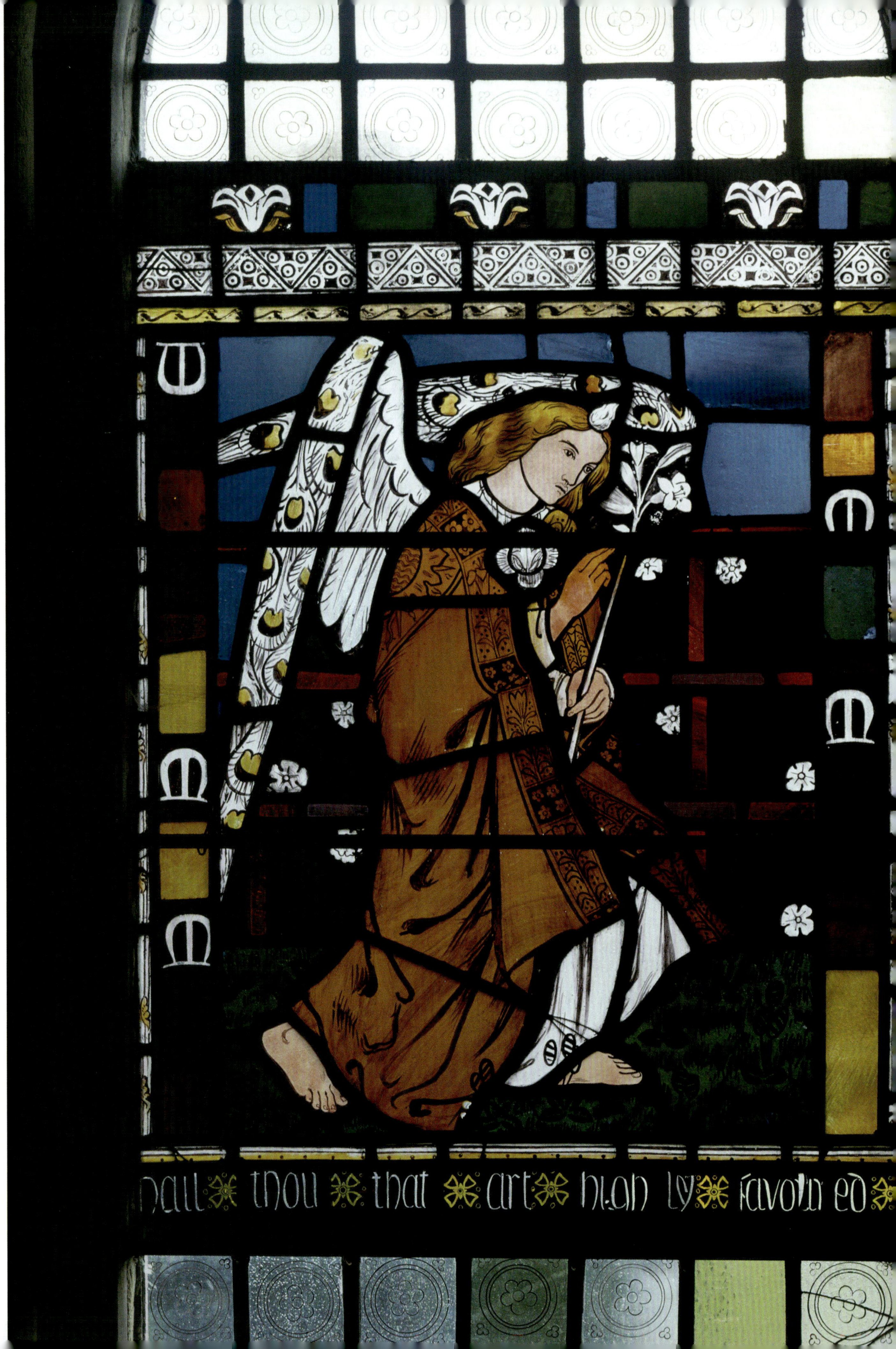
hail thou that art high ly favour ed

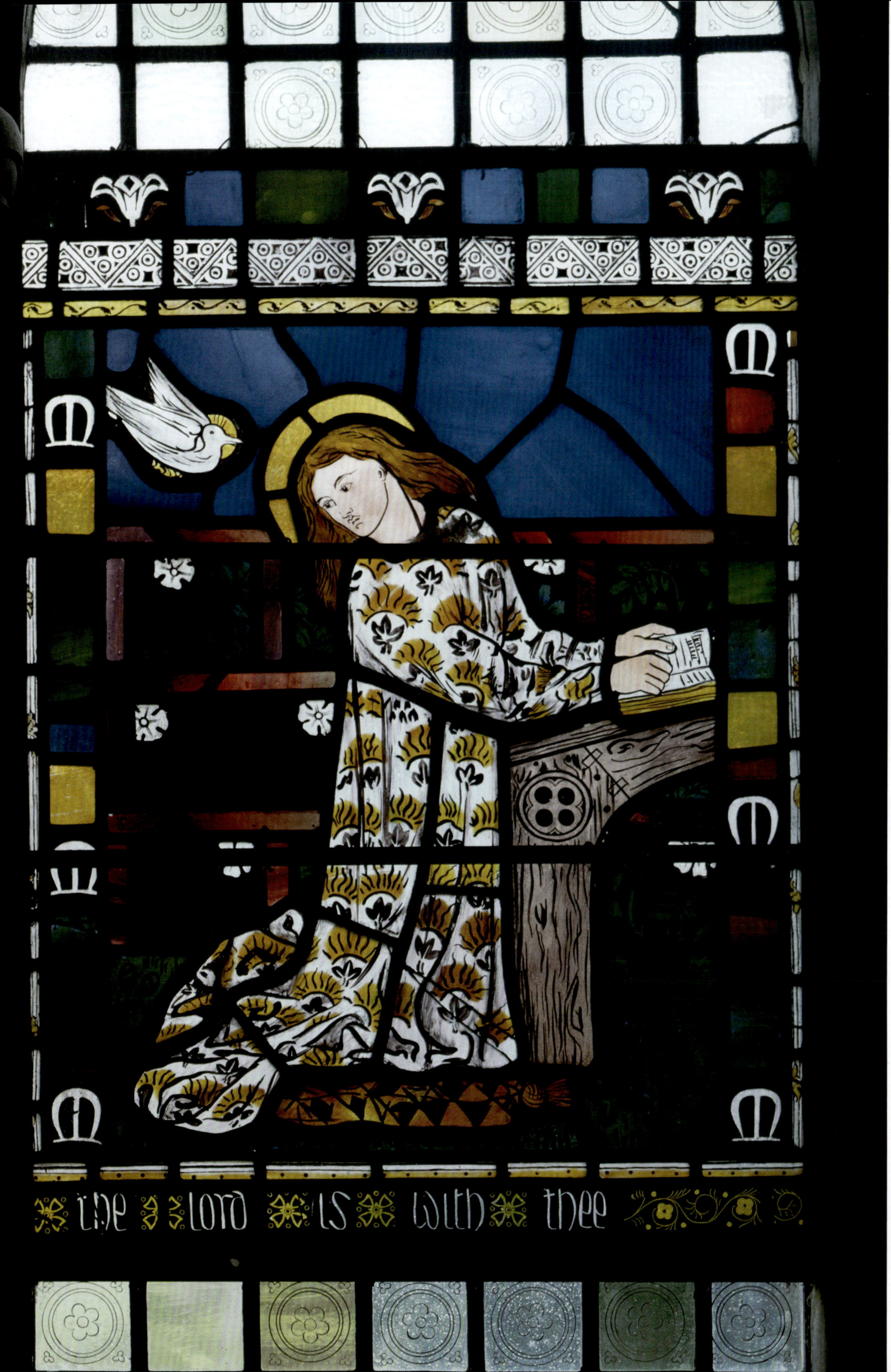
the lord is with thee

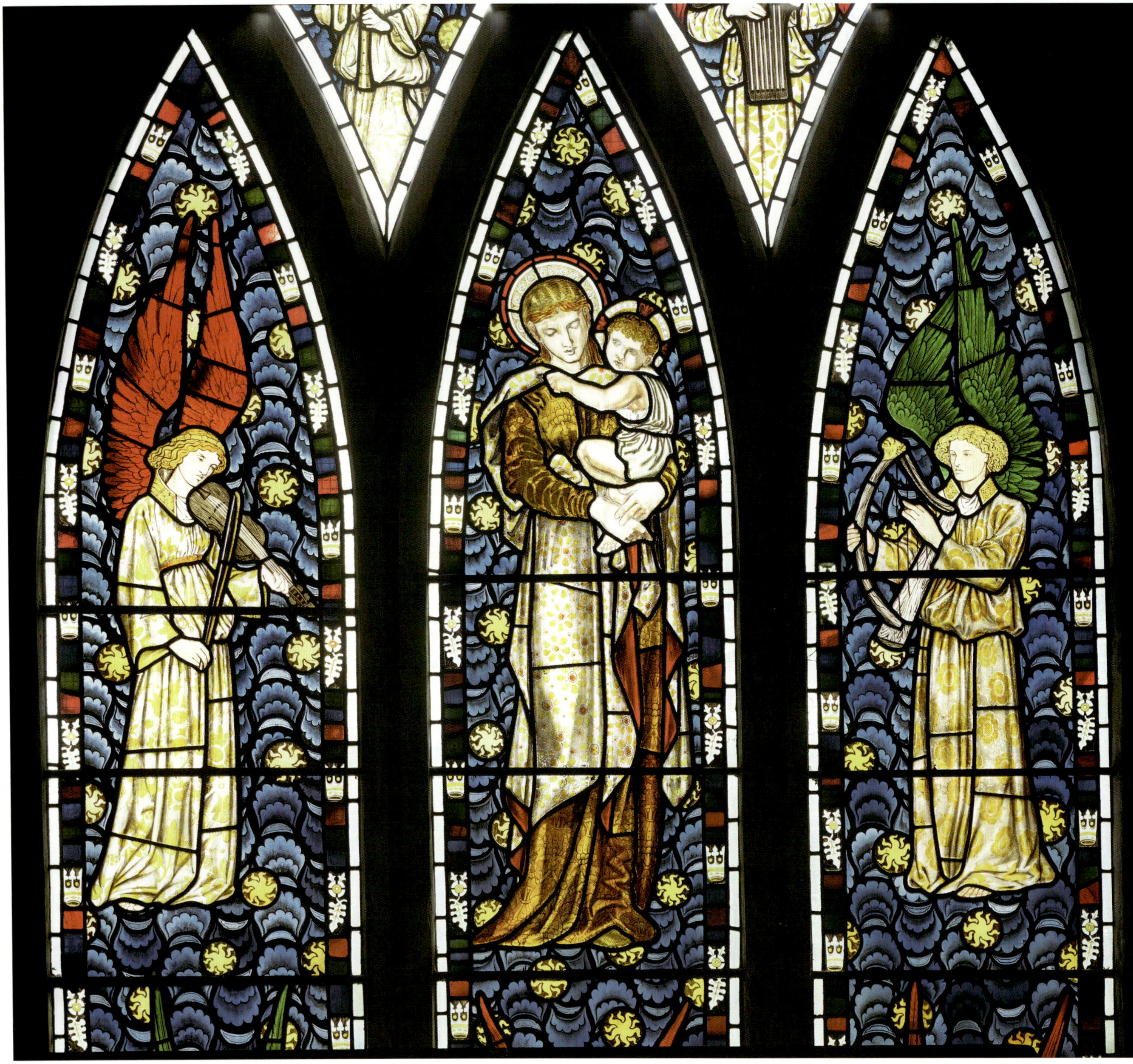

present system are seeking to know their duty in regard to that wealth. Humanise the system still further, and not only the wealth will be moralised, but the entire system as well. But the more hopeful sign of change is taking place in the workshops outside the system. In these independent workshops the elevation of work is steadily taking place. If a great poet like William Morris can find a more secure satisfaction in his workshop than in his library, if a large-minded lawyer like J. Cobden-Sanderson can find a fuller exercise of his faculties in book-binding than in law-practice, there must be some exceptional resources in work as yet quite unsuspected by the majority of mankind. Infuse these larger minds into industrialism, and it will follow that the system will be purged of many of its evils, and that work will change its character till it yields the highest pleasure.

Two modes of economy are combining to release for the higher individual work vast numbers of industrial agents; the machine and the "trust". The machine is a device for transforming potential or unapplied energy of the universe into practical energy with the least possible intervention of the human hand. The perfect machine is the automatic machine. Science and invention promise the construction of machines for certain purposes so simple and efficient that the human hand may be wholly withdrawn from their manipulation. The organisation of industry and the organisation of the organisation effect a similar economy of persons. The great organiser, building with men as the machinist with iron, brings into being a self-directing, self-supporting system. Mr. Carnegie is quoted as saying that if all his money and materials were taken away from him, he could regain them all if his organisation were left intact. With the further removal of friction by the co-ordinating of systems by the trust, the work of the world is conducted with the least possible expense of energy.

Put these facts together and we have, first, the general tendency on the part of all to be active in some sphere, but this is met by the opposite tendency to eliminate persons from the organised systems of production. It is not likely that either of these tendencies will change; men and women will continue to love to work, and the machine and the trust will but increase their economy. There is but the one outlet into the field of individual work, the field that affords the greatest opportunity for free labour, where work is undertaken as a satisfaction to personality and as a pleasure.

The emancipation of labour is accomplished by changing the character of labour. No one desires to be free from work, but to be free and self-directive in his work. The machine in doing the drudgery of the world is undoubtedly an instrument for the furthering of industrial liberty. Voluntary co-operative individualism is the goal toward which the whole industrial world is now tending.

William Morris,
Spring, 1873.
One of four panels of stained glass in the inglenook fireplace in the Dining Room of Cragside.
Cragside House, Garden and Estate, Rothbury.

William Morris,
Autumn, 1873.
One of four panels of stained glass in the inglenook fireplace in the Dining Room of Cragside.
Cragside House, Garden and Estate, Rothbury.

William Morris,
The Annunciation, 1861.
Stained glass window.
All Saints Church, Selsey.

Morris, Marshall, Faulkner & Co.,
Musical Angels (detail of the upper-half of the Angels window), 1869.
Stained glass window.
St. Michael's Church, Tilehurst, Reading.

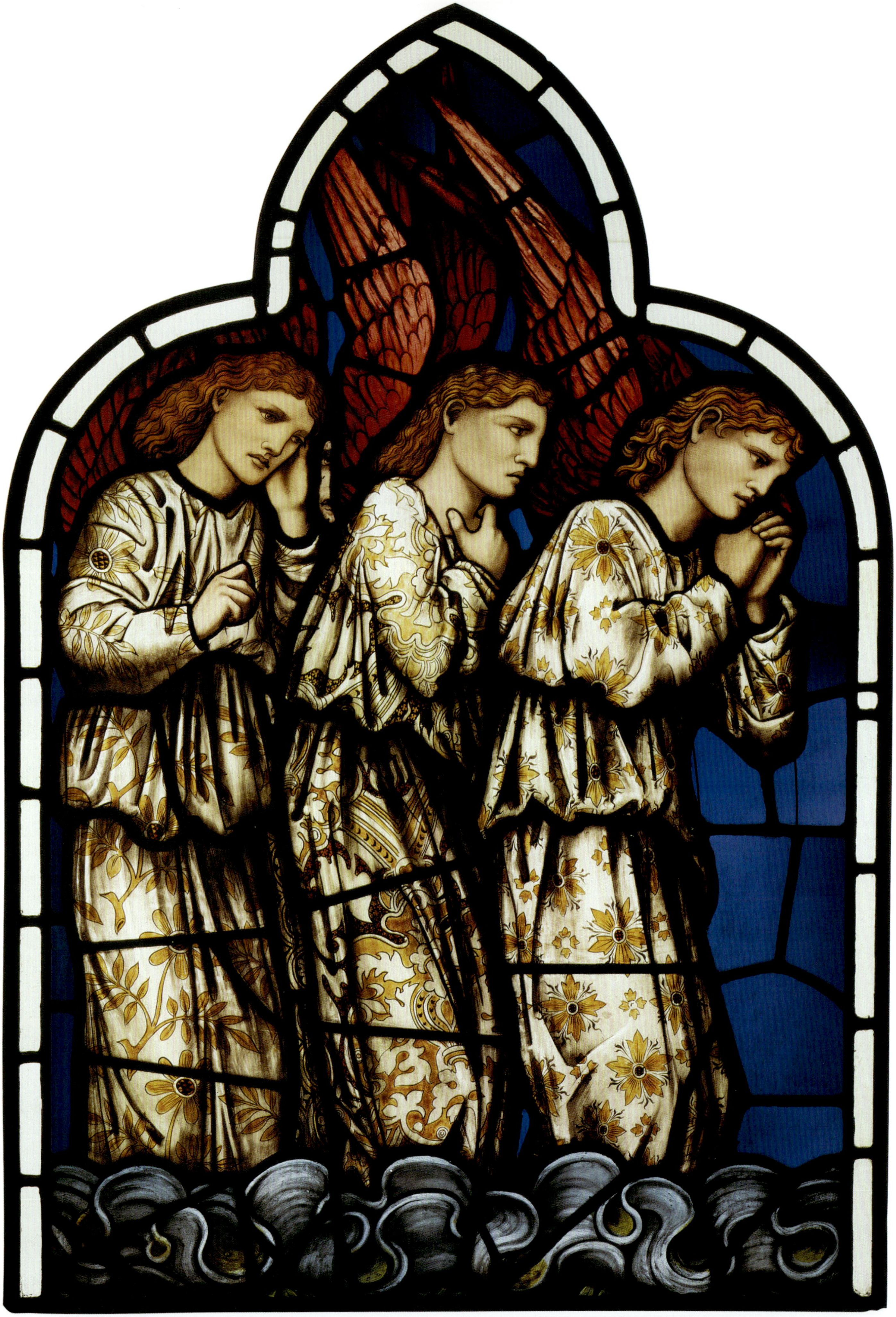

Major Artists

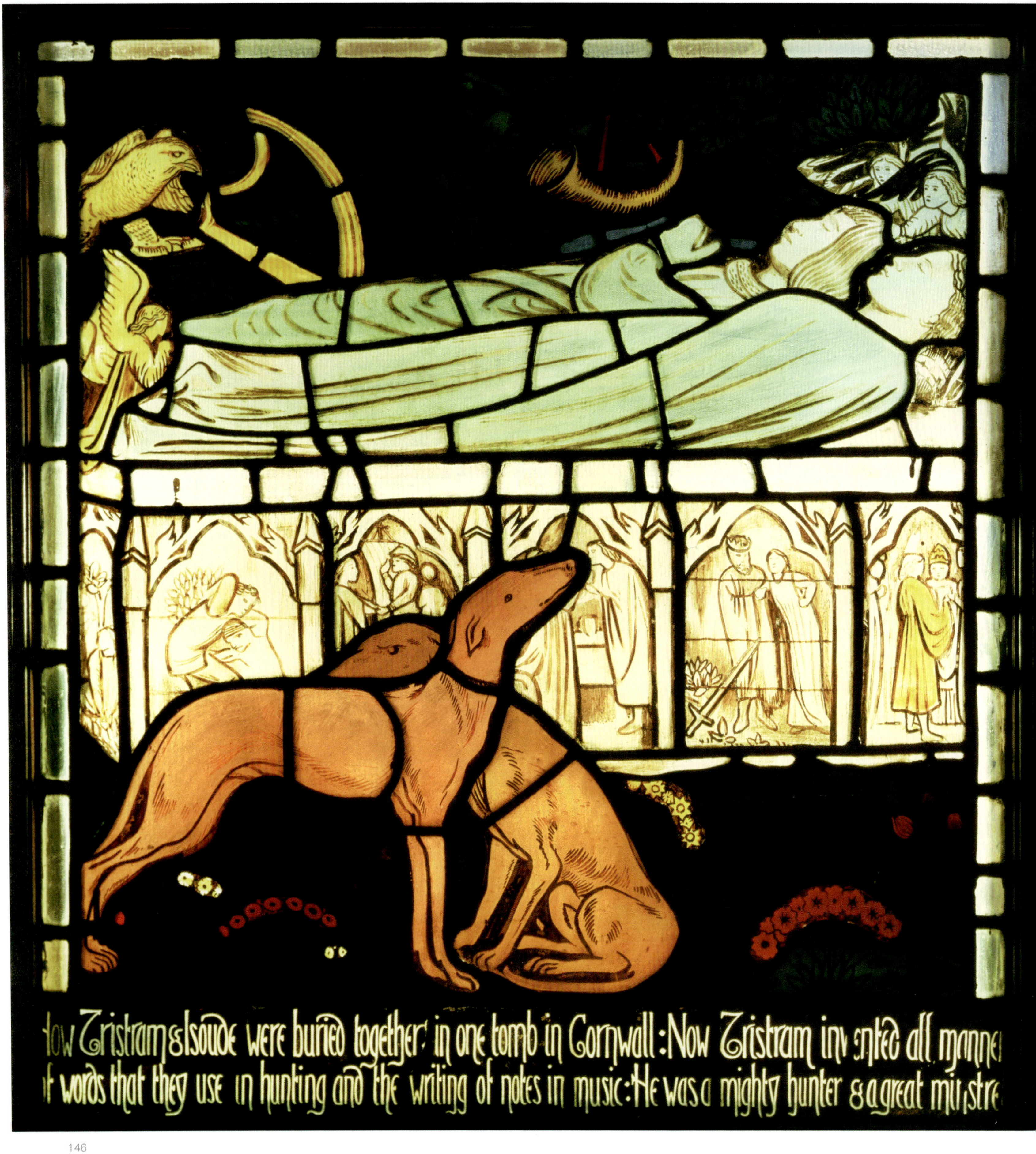
ow Tristram & Isoude were buried together in one tomb in Cornwall : Now Tristram inv ented all manne
f words that they use in hunting and the writing of notes in music : He was a mighty hunter & a great minstre

John Ruskin
(London, 1819 - Coniston, 1900)

John Ruskin was a talented and influential English critic of art, architecture, and society and a gifted painter. His social theories were the main source of inspiration for the Arts and Crafts movement. Born in London in 1819, he was the only child of a prosperous wine importer, John James Ruskin, and of a piously Protestant mother. He was educated at home, where he was given a taste for art by his father's collection of contemporary watercolours. He later went to Oxford University for five years of erratic studies but still won the Newdigate Prize for poetry. Ruskin's family background not only provided him with the means for his extensive travels to see paintings, buildings, and landscapes in Britain and continental Europe but also gave him an understanding of the newly rich middle-class audience for whom his books would be written.

During his formative years, painters such as J.M.W. Turner and John Constable were at the peak of their careers. In 1833, Ruskin discovered the work of Turner whom he met and befriended, and whose late work he soon defended and explained in his writings. Turner – who was a member of the Royal Academy – had been attacked by neoclassical critics for failing to represent the "general truth". In 1843, Ruskin went on to publish the first volume of *Modern Painters*, one of his major works that would eventually consist of five volumes and occupy him for the next seventeen years. In a prose style peculiarly well adapted to the discussion of the visual arts, he argued that modern landscape painters were superior to neoclassical Masters who, according to him, lacked of attention to natural truth. Ruskin's first major achievement was to bring the assumptions of Romanticism to the practice of art criticism and to the understanding of the public who was thus introduced to the possibility of enjoying and collecting art. By this time, he had become the most famous cultural theorist of his days.

At the end of the second volume of *Modern Painters*, he wrote about the painters of the Gothic Middle Ages (especially Giotto, Fra Angelico). He believed these medieval religious artists could provide an inspiring model for the art of the modern age. This enthusiasm was one reason that Ruskin was so ready to lend his support to the Pre-Raphaelite Brotherhood, a group of young English artists formed in 1848, including John Everett Millais and Dante Gabriel Rossetti. However, medievalism was even more important in the field of architecture, where the Gothic Revival was a direct expression of the new Romantic spirit. In 1848, he married Euphemia (Effie) Gray, and they went on a honeymoon tour of the Gothic churches of northern France. The couple met Millais in 1851 and the three of them went to Scotland in 1853, where the painter – who fell in love with Effie – made sketches for the famous portrait of Ruskin standing amongst rocks and streams.

Dante Gabriel Rossetti or **Edward Burne-Jones** (for the design) and **Morris, Marshall, Faulkner & Co.** (for the production),
Three Angels, 1870.
Stained glass window removed from the East window of St. James' Church. Brighouse, West Yorkshire (now demolished), Bradford Museums Galleries and Heritage, Bradford.

Edward Burne-Jones,
The Tomb of Tristan and Iseult the Fair from the Story of *Tristan and Iseult.*
Stained glass window from the Music Room.
Harden Grange, Bradford Museums Galleries and Heritage, Bradford.

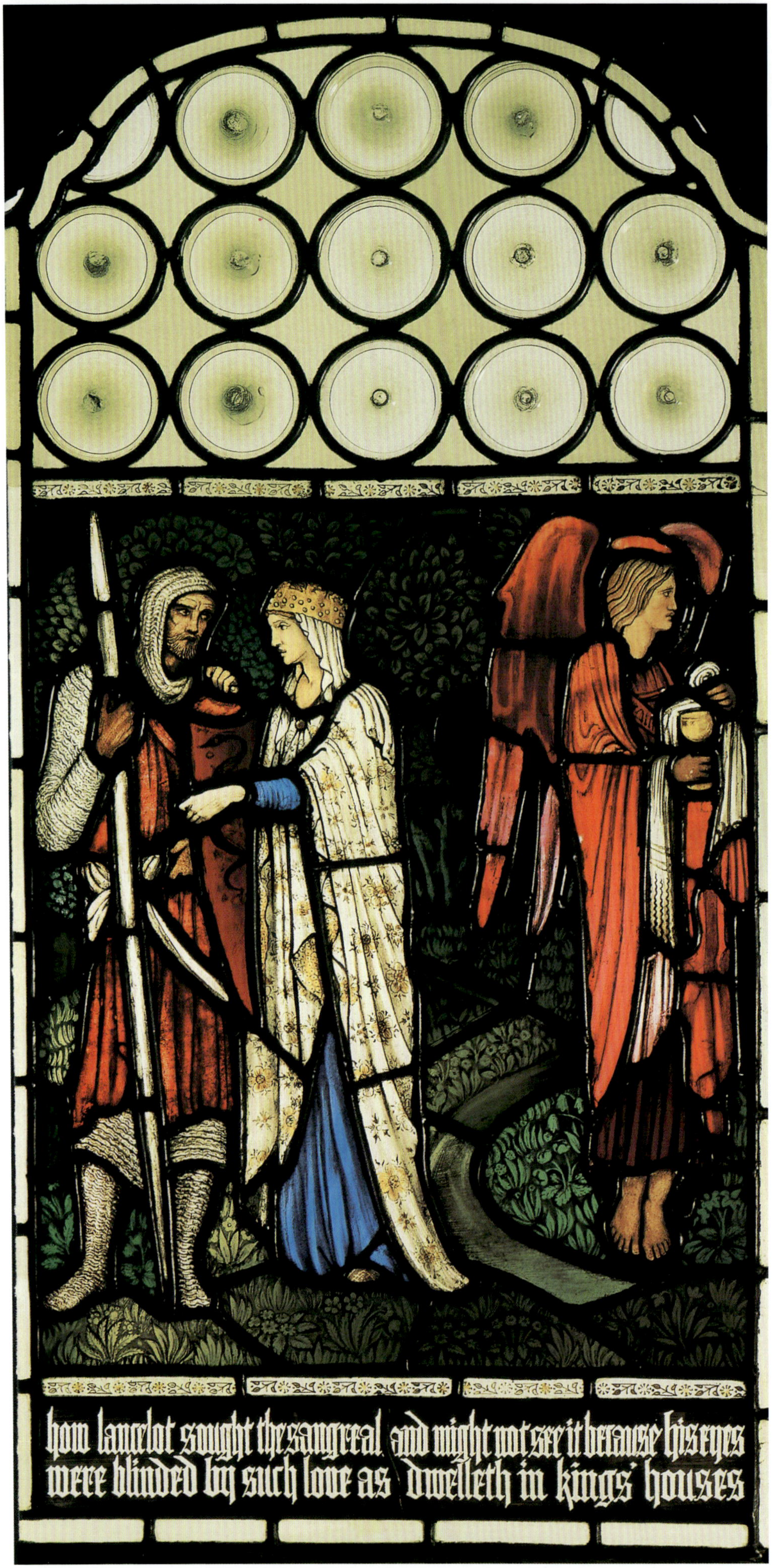
how lancelot sought the sangreal and might not see it because his eyes
were blinded by such love as dwelleth in kings' houses

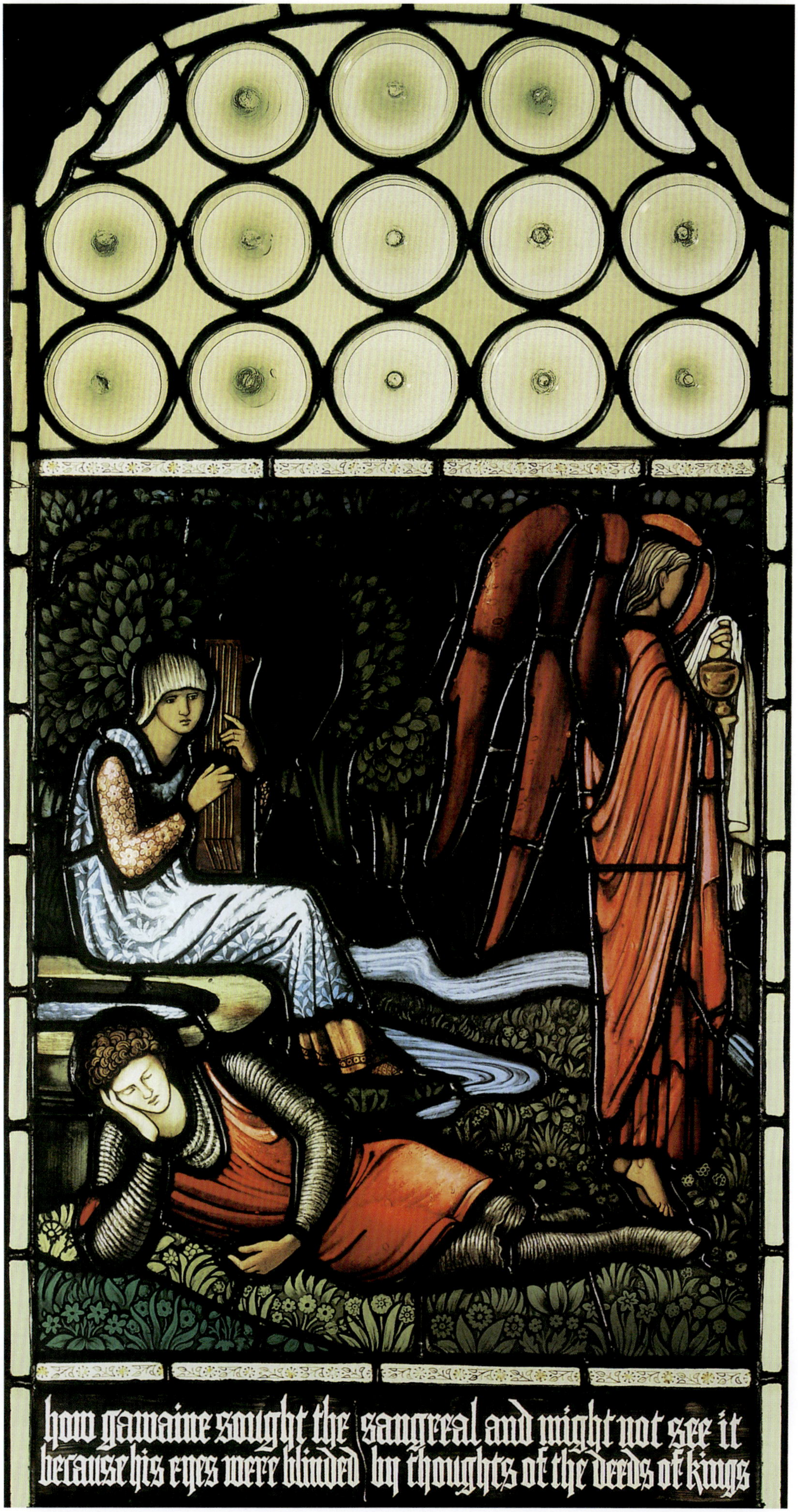
how gawaine sought the sangreal and might not see it
because his eyes were blinded by thoughts of the deeds of kings

Ruskin afterwards began to write his first major book on architecture, *The Seven Lamps of Architecture*, in 1849. The book lays down seven moral principles to guide architectural practice, one of which, "The Lamp of Memory," articulates the scrupulous respect for the original fabric of old buildings that would inspire William Morris and, through him, the conservation movement of the twentieth century. Ruskin went abroad again, this time to Italy, to do research on the Venetian architecture. When he came back, he published *The Stones of Venice* in three volumes, one in 1851 and two more in 1853, where he wrote that art and architecture are, necessarily, the direct expression of the social conditions in which they were produced.

The Stones of Venice was one the nineteenth century's most influential books. Ruskin's celebration of Italian Gothic encouraged the use of foreign models in English Gothic Revival architecture. His writing played a key part in establishing the view that the architectural style of Venice and was particularly appropriate for buildings in modern Britain (which he would later regret).

Ruskin also believed that Gothic architecture allowed a significant degree of creative freedom and artistic fulfilment to the individual workman. In this statement lay the roots of Ruskin's rejection of mechanisation and his distaste for standardisation which made him an inspiration for the Arts and Crafts movement of the later nineteenth century.

During 1850s came a turning point in Ruskin's life; he gradually abandoned art criticism to focus on his social writings. His friend Turner died in 1851 and he became the chief artistic executor of his will. In 1854, his marriage to Effie Gray was dissolved on grounds of his "incurable impotency" which has led to much speculation, including a contentious disgust for pubic hair. Effie Gray was then free to marry the painter Millais.

Under the influence of the historian and essayist Thomas Carlyle, Ruskin wrote *Unto This Last* where he developed theories about social justice which were an inspiration for the British Labour Party.

His father's death in 1864 had left Ruskin a wealthy man. He used his wealth to promote idealistic social causes, notably the Guild of St. George, a pastoral community first planned in 1871 and formally constituted seven years later. During this period, he was unhappily in love with a woman 30 years his junior, Rose La Touche, who finally rejected him in 1872 and died soon afterwards. These events plunged Ruskin into despair and he began to show signs of serious psychological illness. In 1871 he bought Brantwood, a house in the English Lake District (now a museum of his work) and lived there for the rest of his life.

Ruskin's appointment as Slade Professor of Fine Art at Oxford in 1870 was a welcome encouragement at a troubled stage in his career, and in the following year he launched *Fors*

Edward Burne-Jones (for the design) and **Morris & Co.** (for the production), *Lancelot and the Quest for the Holy Grail*, 1885-1886.
Stained glass window, 46 x 33 cm.
Victoria & Albert Museum, London.

Edward Burne-Jones (for the design) and **Morris & Co.** (for the production), *Gawain and the Quest for the Holy Grail*, 1885-1886.
Stained glass window, 46 x 33 cm.
Victoria & Albert Museum, London.

William Morris,
King Arthur and Sir Lancelot, 1862.
Stained glass window.
Bradford Museums Galleries and Heritage, Bradford.

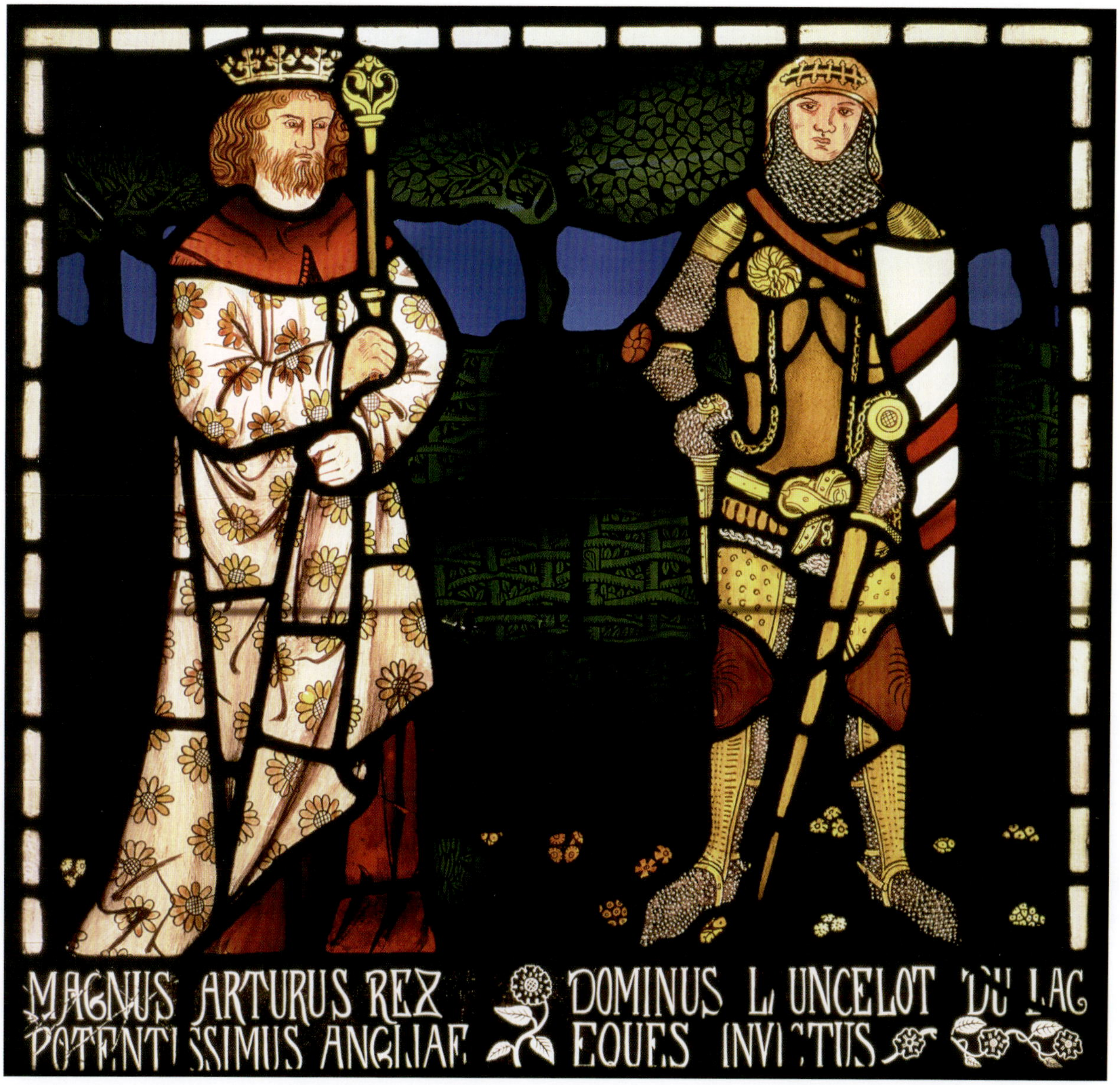

Clavigera, a one-man monthly magazine in which, from 1871 to 1878 and 1880 to 1884 he developed his cultural theories. Ruskin finally wrote his last major work, his autobiography, *Praeterita* (1885–1889). Unfinished, partial (it omits, for example, all mention of his marriage) and chronologically untrustworthy, it provides a history of the growth of his distinctive sensibility. Ruskin died in 1900 in the Lake District.

Since then Ruskin has gradually been rediscovered. His importance as a thinker about ecology, and the conservation of buildings and environments, about Romantic painting, and art education, and about the human cost of the mechanisation of work became steadily more obvious. The outstanding quality of his own drawings and watercolours (modestly treated in his lifetime as working notes or amateur sketches) was increasingly acknowledged, as well as his role as a stimulus to the flowering of British painting, architecture, and decorative art in the second half of the nineteenth century.

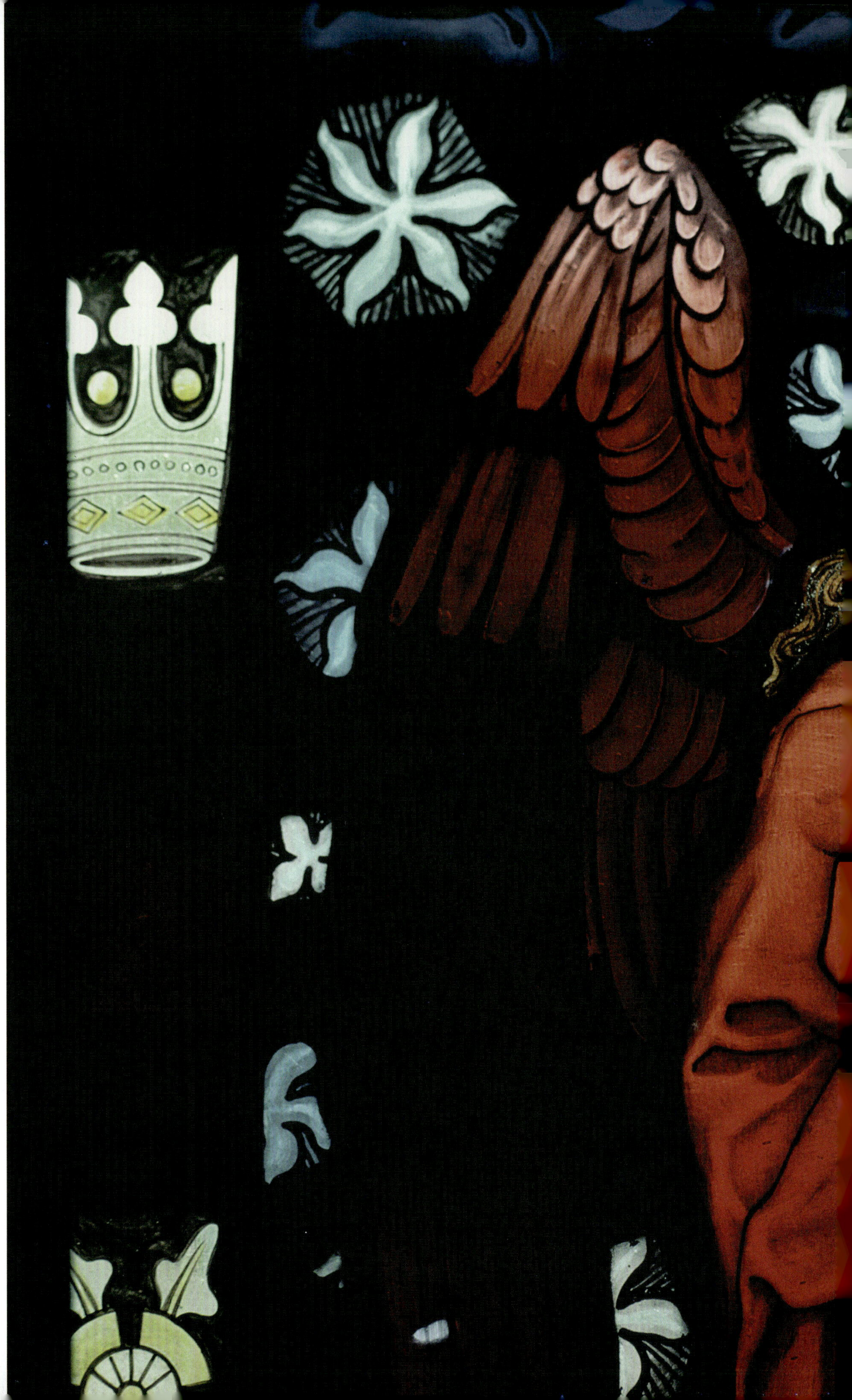

Edward Burne-Jones
(for the design)
and **Morris & Co.**
(for the production),
Musical Angels (detail), 1882.
Stained glass window.
Church of St. Peter and St. Paul,
Cattistock.

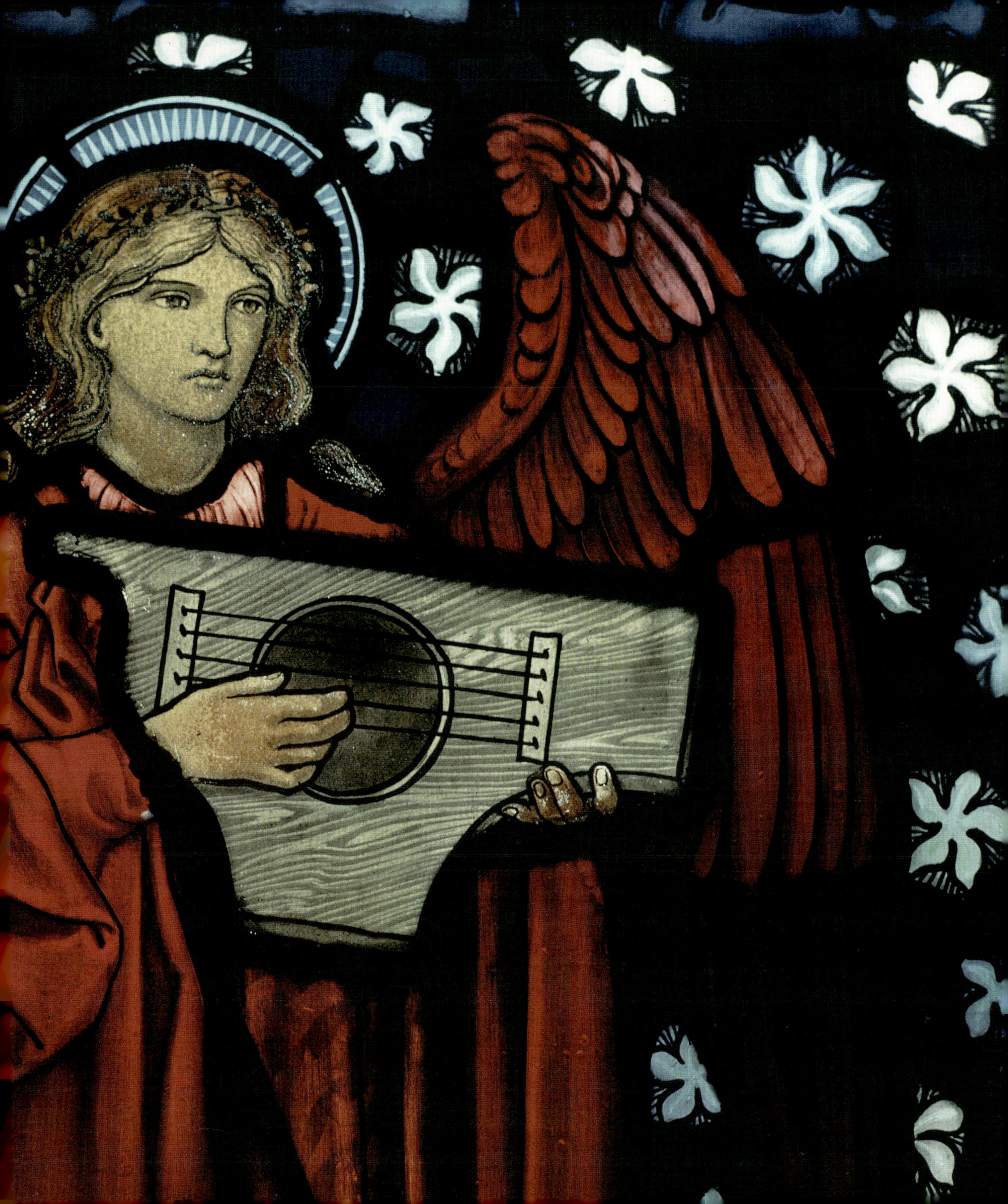

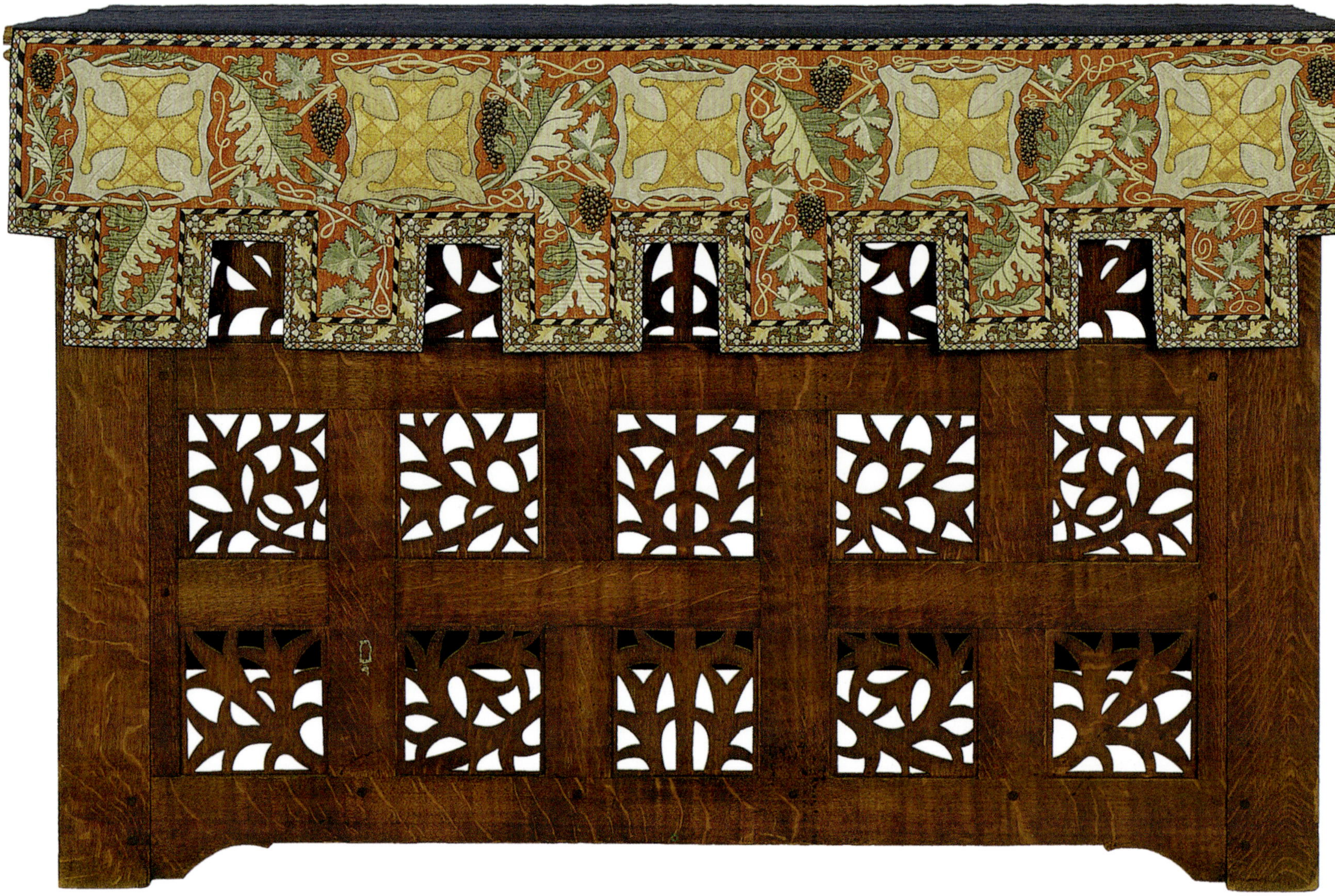

Philip Speakman Webb
(Oxford, 1831 - Worth, 1915)

Philip Speakman Webb was an architect and one of the most important members of the Arts and Crafts movement.

He was born on 12th January 1831 in Oxford. His father was a doctor and his grandfather was Thomas Webb, a medalist. Webb was quite unhappy during the start of his education in a grammar school located in Aynho in Northamptonshire. In 1846, when he was only fifteen years old, his father died, leaving Webb free to make his own decisions. He thus began as an apprentice under John Billing, an architect in Reading, Berkshire. He then went to Wolverhampton where he was an assistant to a firm of builder-architects. After this period, Webb moved to London where he was to become a junior assistant in the office of the eminent Gothic Victorian architect, George Edmund Street. The latter had just relocated his offices in London, he had previously been in Oxford. In Street's London office he met William Morris, who stayed in the practice for nine months in 1856. They were to become life-long friends as well as partners.

Webb stayed with Street until 1858 when he decided to open his own practice at twenty-seven years old. In the late 1850s, Webb toured France with Morris and Charles Faulkner. Together, they visited cathedrals and were especially struck by French tapestries. This journey influenced their view on the Gothic Revival and on art in general.

A year later, as a young architect, he designed the Red House in Bexleyheath, Kent, for his friend William Morris. In his buildings and notably the Red House, Webb would not hesitate to put together contrasting material. For example, one thinks of the Red House in bare brick on the outside and white interior walls as a contrast.

In 1904, the German Scholar Herman Muthesius described Webb's building as, "the first private house of the new artistic culture, the first house to be conceived as a whole inside and out, the very first example in the history of the modern house". Morris wanted his house to be a "palace of the arts" and thanks to Webb, this was made possible. Although the Red House was only the first building entirely designed by Webb, he insisted that the subsequent projects he carried out were done in the same fashion. He wanted that the owners of the houses share his ideals of artistic and yet practical homes. This typically Arts and Crafts belief was to guide all his projects throughout his life. He was once quoted saying: "I never begin to be satisfied until my work looks commonplace".

Philip Webb (for the design)
and **John Garrett & Son**
(for the production),
altar table and superfrontal,
1896-1899.
Oak, linen embroidered with silks by
May Morris, 94.7 x 145.7 x 66 cm.
Victoria & Albert Museum, London.

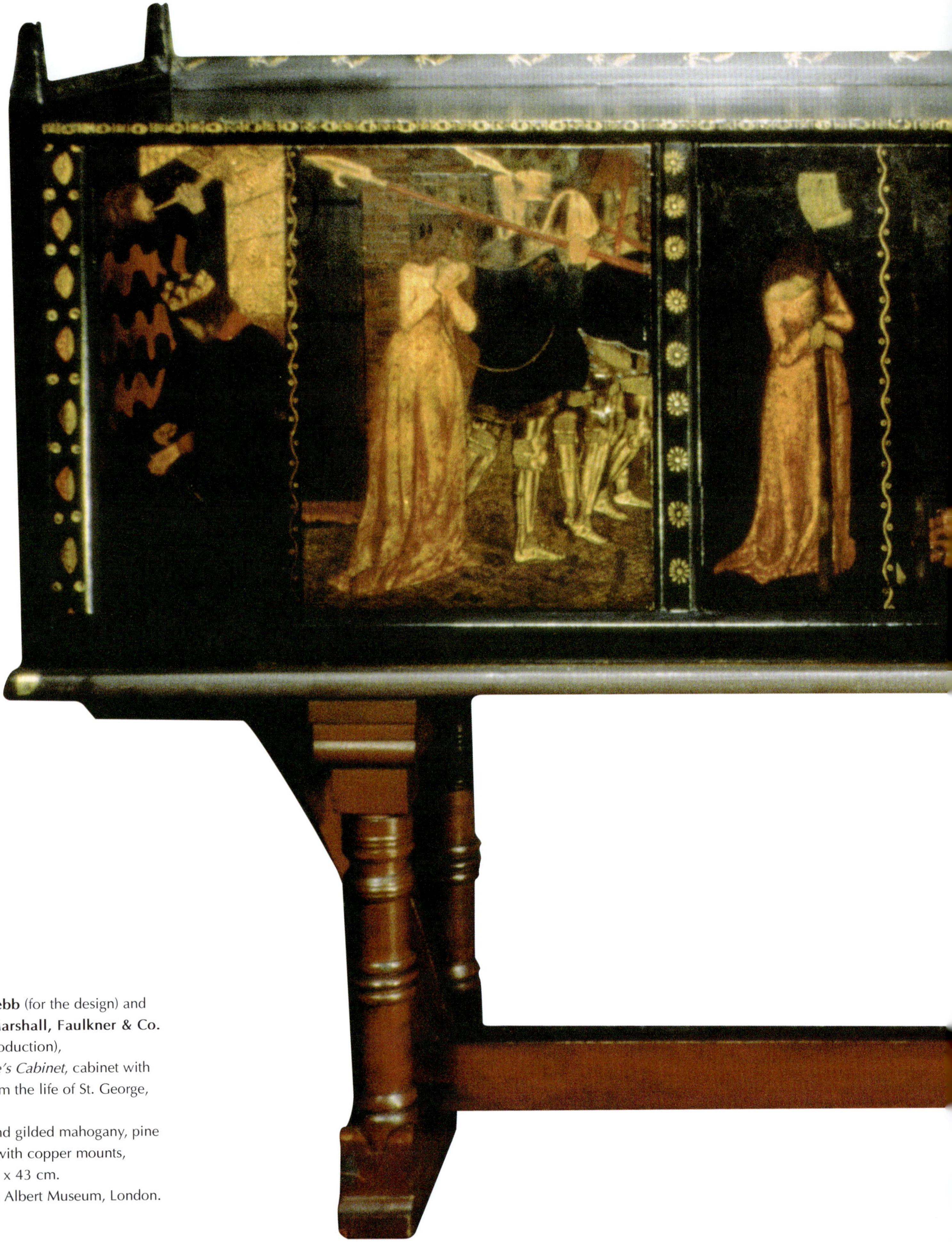

Philip Webb (for the design) and
Morris, Marshall, Faulkner & Co.
(for the production),
St. George's Cabinet, cabinet with
scenes from the life of St. George,
1861.
Painted and gilded mahogany, pine
and oak, with copper mounts,
111 x 178 x 43 cm.
Victoria & Albert Museum, London.

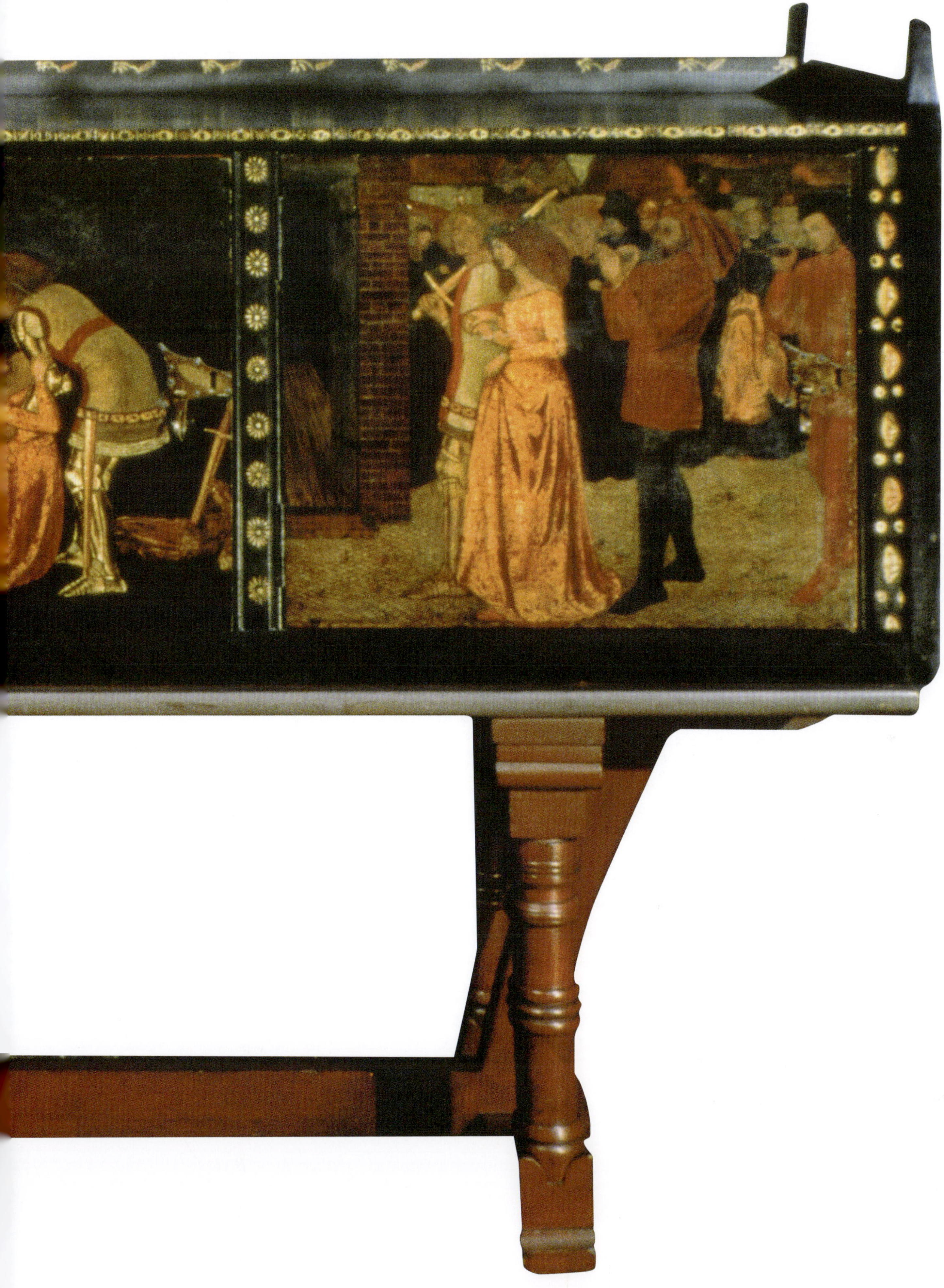

In 1861, Webb participated to the creation of the firm Morris, Marshall, Faulkner and Co. "Art Workmen in Painting, Carving, Furniture and the Metals". The firm was specialised in stained glass, carving, furniture, wall paper, carpets and tapestries. Webb designed furniture for the firm and for Morris and Rossetti personnally. Webb's furniture demonstrate the artist's complete understanding of the Arts and Crafts principles as well as a certain sophistication and a touch of medievalism.

In 1868, he designed and supervised the construction of no.19 Lincoln's Inn Fields, London and no. 1 Palace Green, London, for George Howard (later the ninth Earl of Carlisle). George Howard was himself an artist and a patron of Webb's work. He was also a close friend of his as well as of Burne-Jones and Morris. Howard owned an estate in Cumbria near Brampton called Naworth Castle. Webb was commissioned to restore much of the interior of the castle, including the library, drawing room and the former Protestant chapel, which became Howard's private library. He also built two more houses on the same estate: Four Gables and Green Lane House. Still in Brampton, in 1878, Webb was asked by Charles Howard MP and George Howard to build Saint Martin's Church. He used an unusual building scheme, as the church is square. The stained glass windows were designed by Burne-Jones and produced by Morris & Co.

In 1877, Webb founded with William Morris the Society for the Protection of Ancient Buildings in Queen Square, Bloomsbury which still exists today. The founding members were interested in the survival of ancient and historical buildings. The original spirit of those buildings is endangered by restorations that are not properly done. The aim of the SPAB is to repair not restore, and maintain the buildings in good condition while informing the public of the importance of their legacy. Webb also joined Morris's Socialist league in 1885 and became its treasurer.

In 1886, Webb build the country house Clouds in Wiltshire for Percy Wyndham, a British politician, intellectual and collector and his wife, Madeline. The house was severly damage by fire in 1889. Today it is a drug rehabilitation centre.

Between 1892 and 1894 Webb designed and build the Standen house for a properous London solicitor, James Beale, his wife Margaret and their seven children. Webb firmly believed in the principles of the SPAB as he always based his architectual works on actual existing buildings. Typically, the Standen house was an ancient farmhouse, dating from 1450. Instead of tearing it down and rebuilding a new one on the site, he used the old farm and a barn as a basis for his work. The yeoman's house of the medieval times still stands and the picturesque site is therefore preserved.

Philip Webb (for the design) and **Morris, Marshall, Faulkner & Co.** (for the production), sideboard, c. 1862.
Ebonized wood with painted and gilt decoration and panels of stamped leather; brass and copper hinges and handles, with incised decoration, 195 x 197.5 x 66 cm.
Victoria & Albert Museum, London.

Philip Webb (for the design) and **Morris, Marshall, Faulkner & Co.** (for the production), side table.
Oak, with turned legs and stretchers, drawer with brass drop-handles, 73.6 x 167 x 60.9 cm.
Private collection.

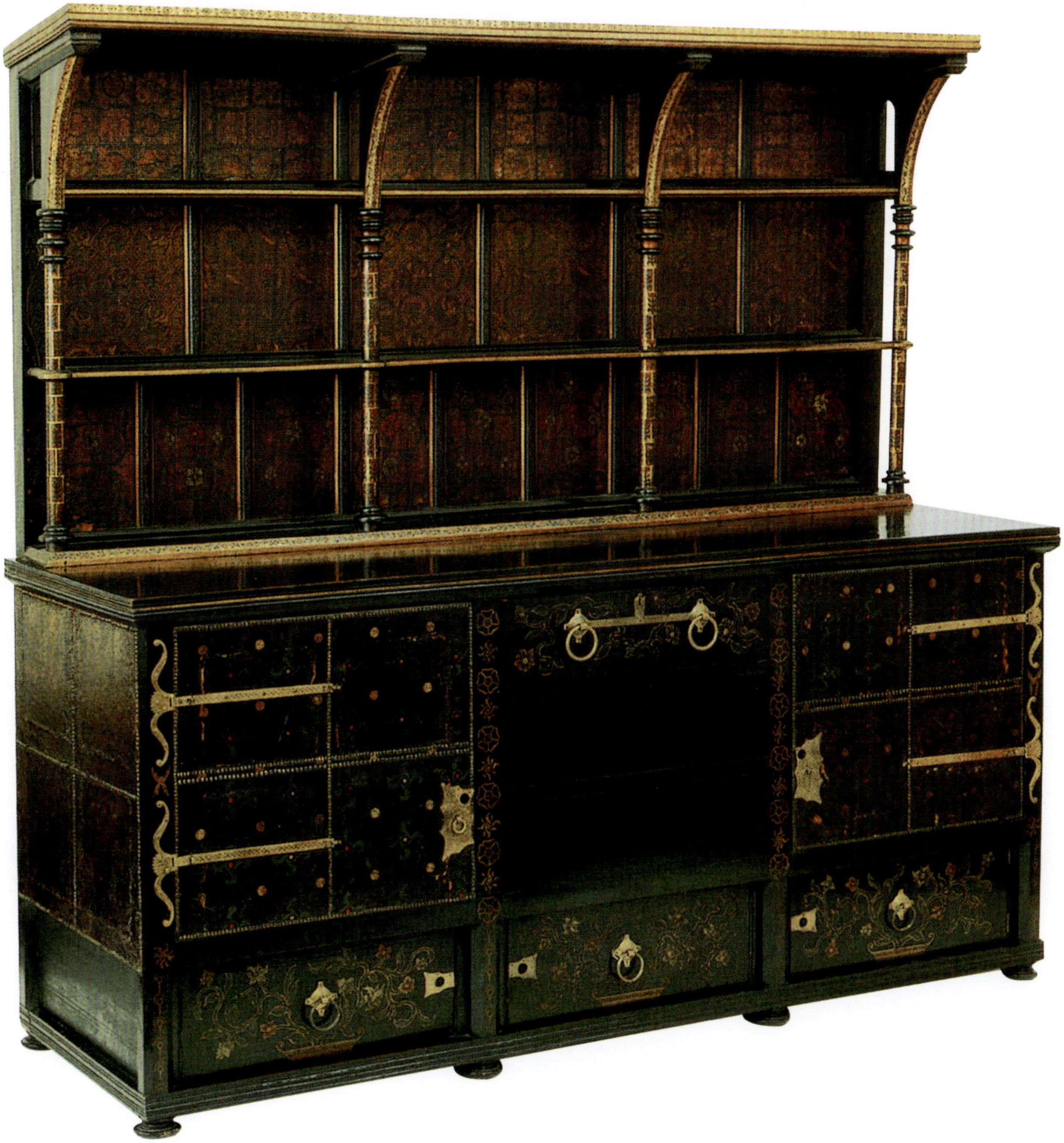

Webb was not interested in having a major and busy practice. He never took apprentices, for example. Instead, he had a limited number of participants and could focuse on individual Arts and Crafts homes. He would occasionally hire a couple of junior assistants. His clients were mostly wealthy individuals who agreed with his strong views on artistic yet practical homes. During the 1880s George Jack, a junior assistant, took care of a number of Webb's design after the latter had retired in 1901. Webb moved from London into the country in Worth, in Sussex, where he lived until his death in 1915.

Contrary to his friend, William Morris, Webb never published his philosophy of architectural design of work but his influence can be seen in various furniture pieces and stained-glass windows. In 1935, William Lethaby, another famous architect wrote a book on his life.

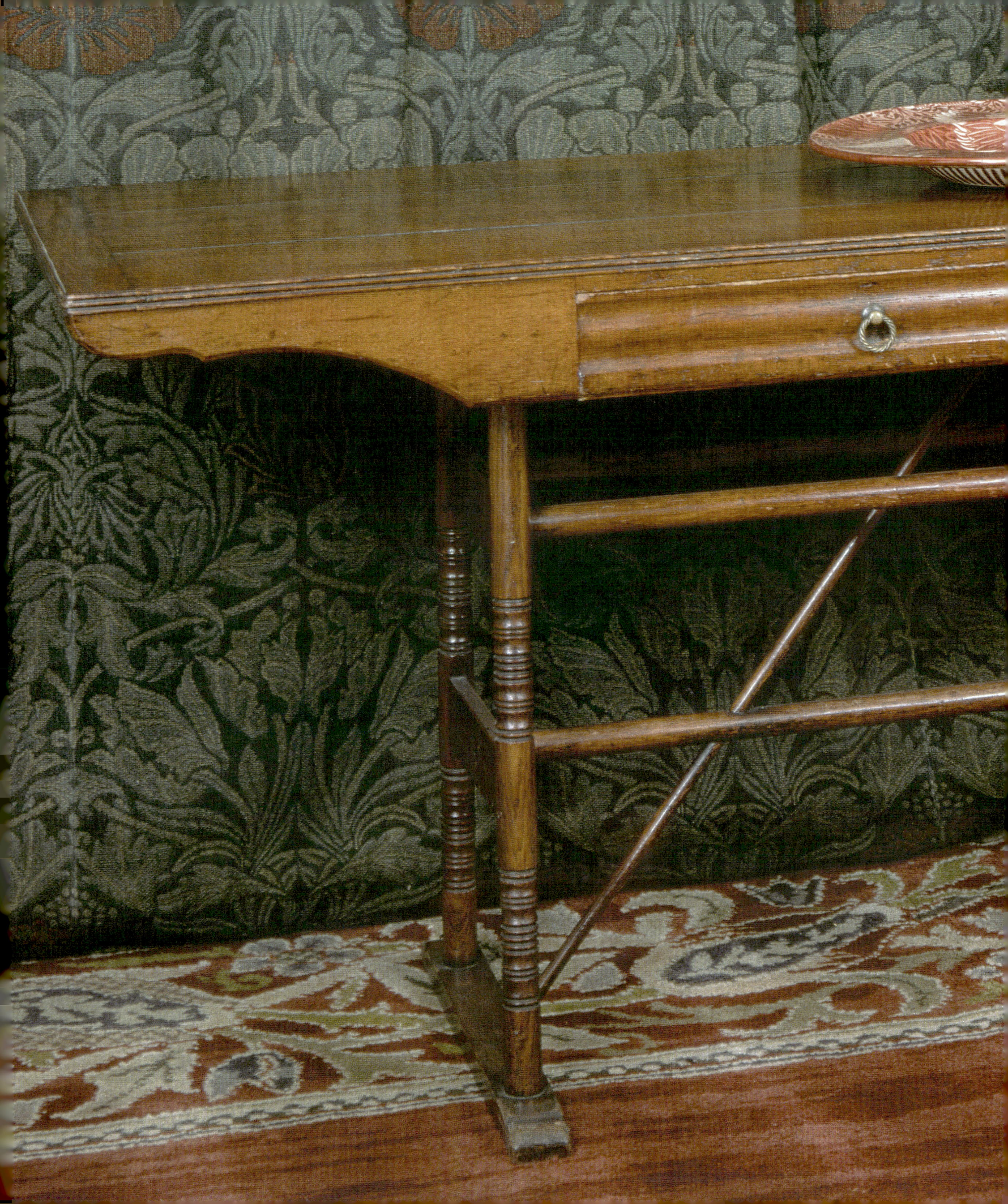

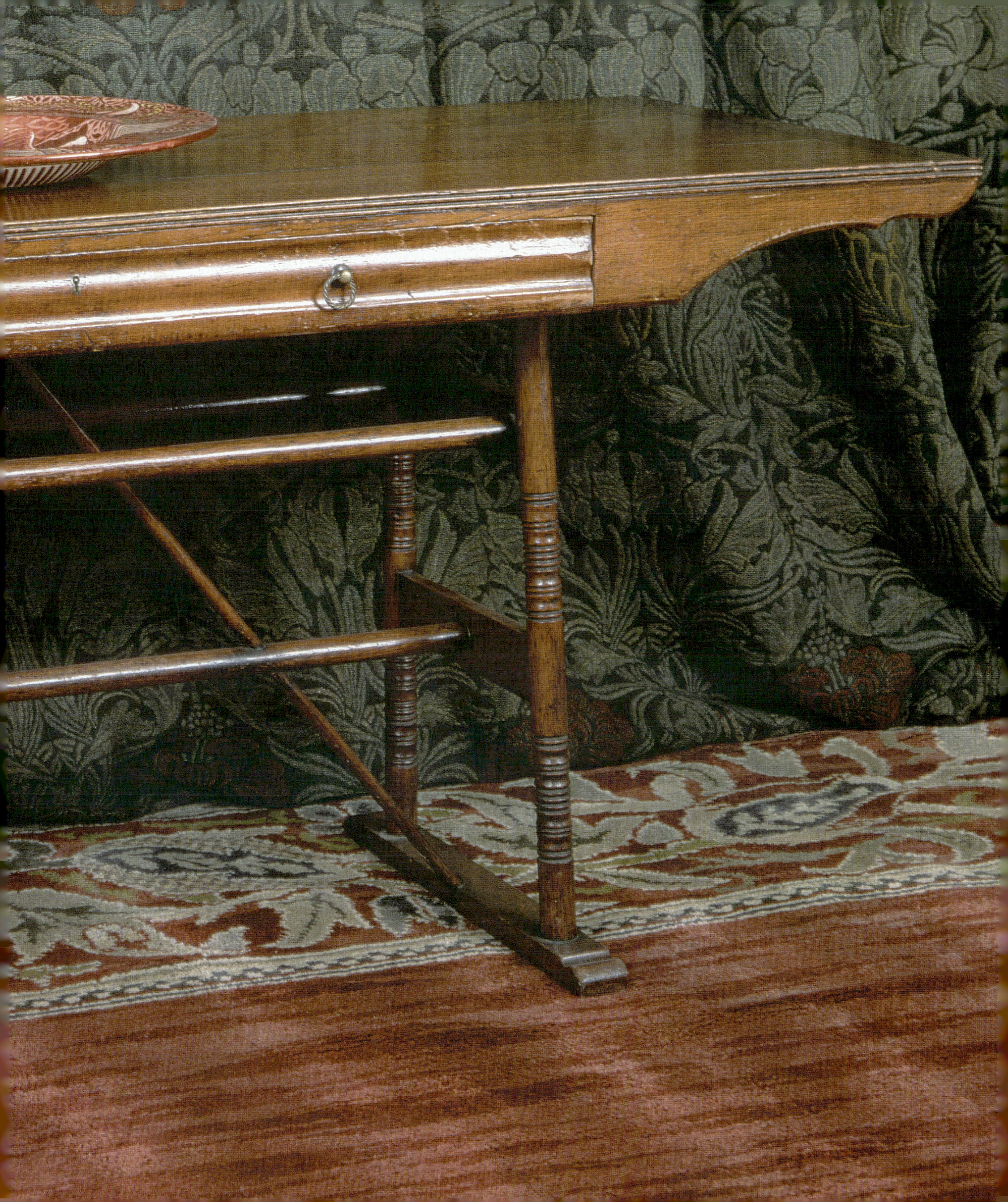

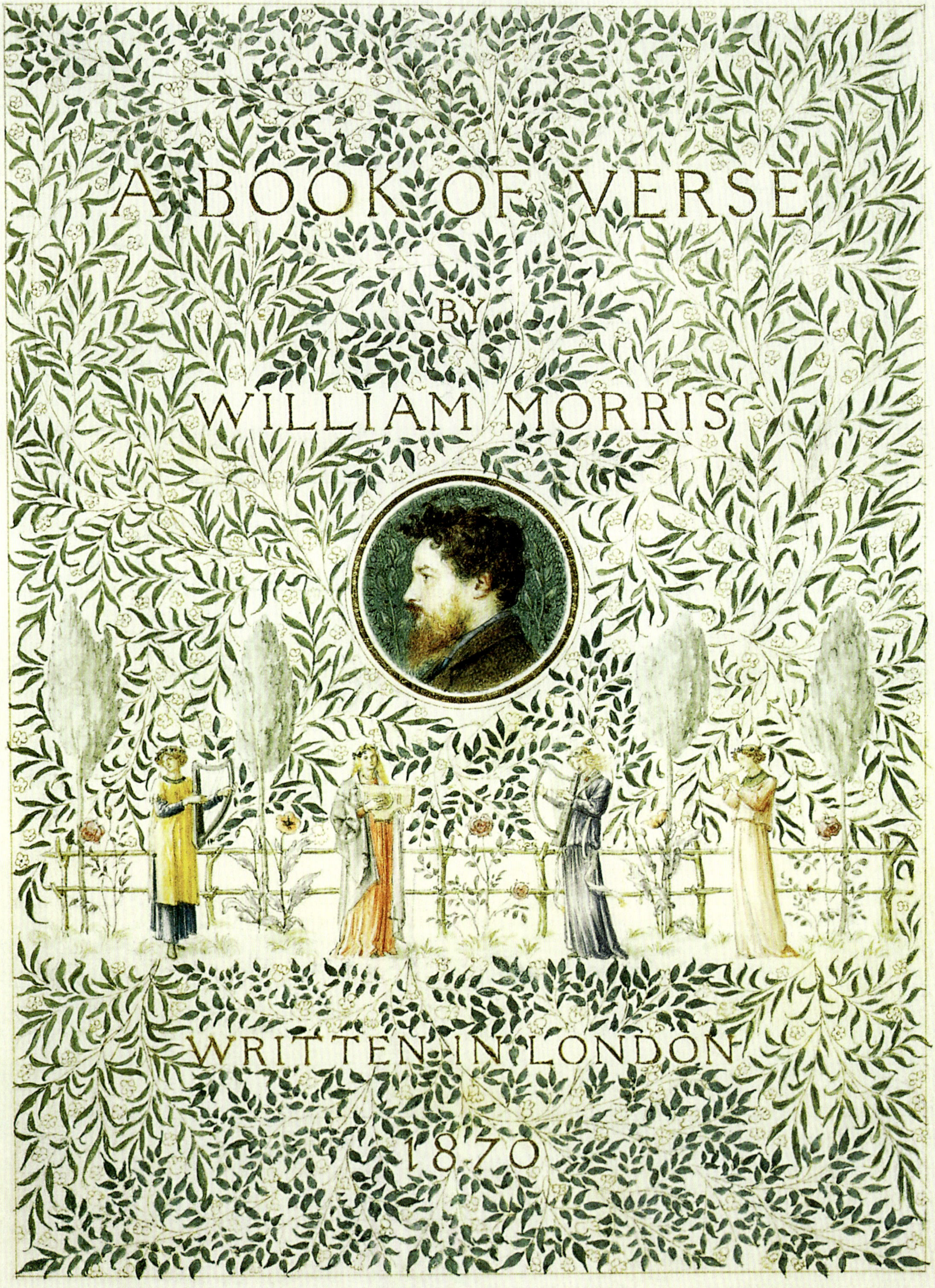
A BOOK OF VERSE
BY
WILLIAM MORRIS
WRITTEN IN LONDON
1870

William Morris
(Walthamstow, 1834 - Kelmscott, 1896)

William Morris was among the most creative artists associated with the Arts and Crafts movement Britain has ever produced. The extent and depth of his achievements make him a unique figure in the history of art and design. He was a revolutionary interior designer and book printer, a famous and prolific poet, a weaver, embroiderer, dyer, calligrapher, a convinced socialist and architectural preservationist.

He was the third of nine children of William Morris, a rich Lombard Street broker, and his wife Emma. He learned to read very early, and at four years old he was already familiar with all of Sir Walter Scott's novels. He studied with his sisters' governess and went to school for the first time at nine years old. In 1848, after his father's death, William entered Marlborough College, where he was influenced by the Oxford Movement within the Church of England.

In 1853 he went to Exeter College in Oxford where he met and befriended Edward Burne-Jones. They both intended to become clergymen and belonged to a circle of aesthetes fascinated by an idealised vision of the Middle Ages, whose purpose was to "lead a crusade and a holy war against the contemporary era". The members of this small group called themselves a brotherhood and read books together on theology, ecclesiastical history, and medieval poetry, as well as Tennyson's poems and the writings of Ruskin which influenced his conceptions of art.

In 1855, still accompanied by Burne-Jones, he took a tour of the great Gothic cathedrals of northern France, and the two friends abandoned the priesthood to fully devote themselves to art.

In early 1856 Morris began an apprenticeship with the Gothic Revivalist architect George Edmund Street, during which he met his future collaborator Philip Webb. At the same time, he founded *The Oxford and Cambridge Magazine* and met Rossetti, who incited him to immediately abandon architecture for painting and made him participate, in 1857, in the decoration of the Oxford Union Library's walls.

This was also the year that Morris met the woman who would be his wife and muse, Jane Burden. She was also one of Rossetti's preferred models. In 1858 he published his story The Defence of Guenevere, which is now considered one of the most beautiful Victorian poems. The next year he married Jane Burden, and they moved in Kent into the Red House designed

William Morris,
A Book of Verse, 1870.
Front page.
Victoria & Albert Museum, London.

William Morris,
Odes of Horace, 1874.
Illustrated page of the manuscript.
Bodleian Library, University of Oxford, Oxford.

William Morris, Charles Fairfax Murray, Louise Powell and **Graily Herwitt,**
The Story of Frithiof the Bold, c. 1873.
Watercolour and gilding on paper, 40.1 x 53 cm (open book).
Paul Getty Library, Wormsley.

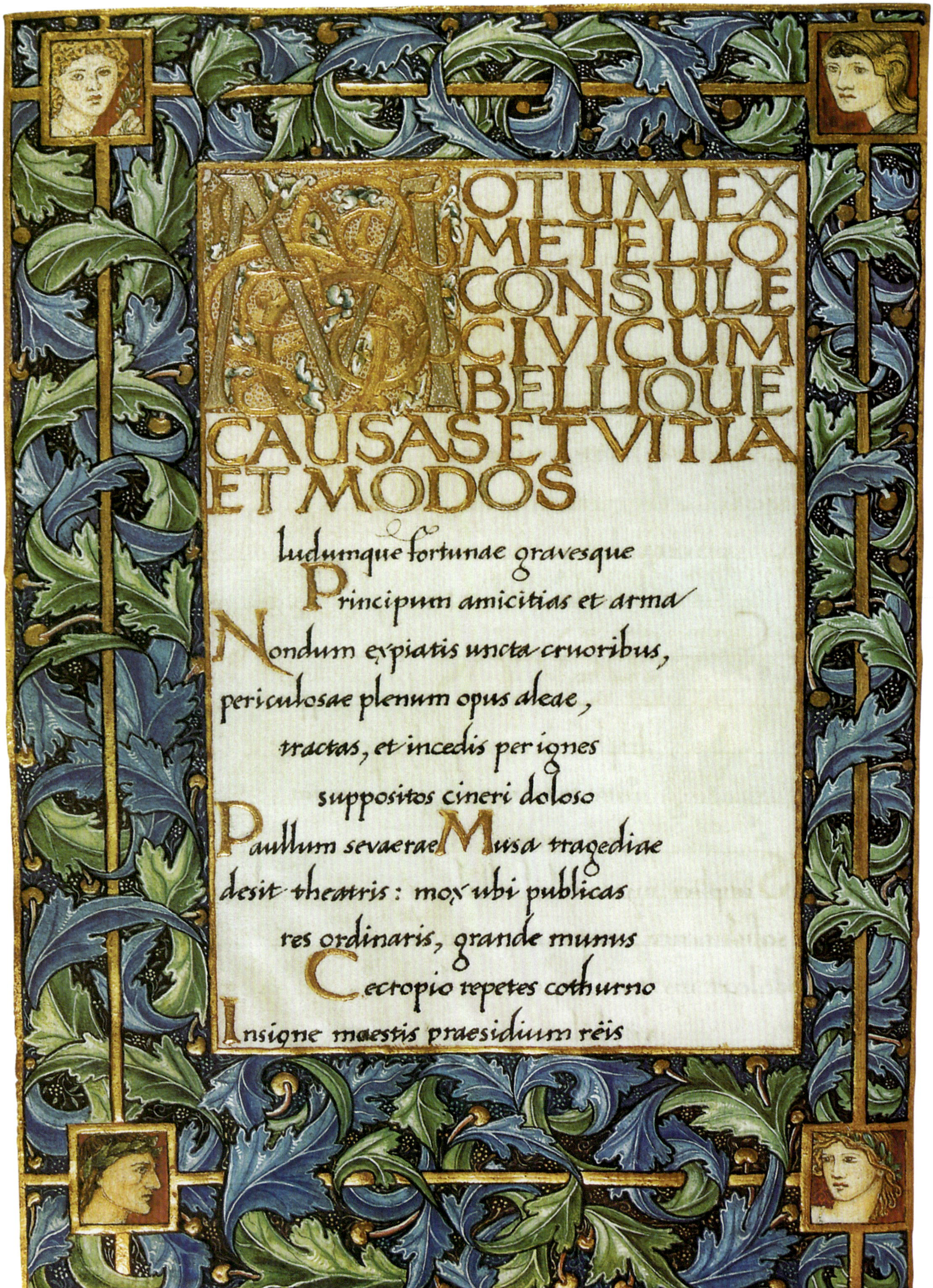
MOTUM EX
METELLO
CONSULE
CIVICUM
BELLIQUE
CAUSAS ET VITIA
ET MODOS
ludumque fortunae gravesque
Principum amicitias et arma
Nondum expiatis uncta cruoribus,
periculosae plenum opus aleae,
tractas, et incedis per ignes
suppositos cineri doloso
Paullum sevaerae Musa tragediae
desit theatris: mox ubi publicas
res ordinaris, grande munus
Cecropio repetes cothurno
Insigne maestis praesidium reis

THE STORY OF FRITHIOF THE BOLD

CHAP. XIII

NOW weareth away the mid-winter, and when spring cometh, the weather groweth fair, the wood bloometh, the grass groweth, and ships may glide betwixt land and land.

So on a day the king says to his folk: "I will that ye come with us for our disport out into the woods, that we may look upon the fairness of the earth."

So did they, and went flock-meal with the king into the woods: but so it befell, that the king and Frithiof were gotten alone together afar from other men, and the king said he was heavy, and would fain sleep: then said Thief: "Get thee home, then, lord, for it better beseemeth men of high estate to lie at home than abroad."

"Nay" said the king "so will I not do." And he laid him down therewith, and slept fast, snoring loud. Thief sat close by him, and presently drew his sword from his sheath, & cast it far away from him.

A little while after the king woke up, and said: "Was it not so, Frithiof, that a many things came into thy mind een now? but well hast thou dealt with them, and great honour shalt thou have of me. Lo now, I knew thee straightway, that first evening thou camest into our hall: now nowise speedily shalt thou depart from us; and somewhat great abideth thee."

39

Said Frithiof: "Lord king, thou hast done to me well, and in friendly wise; but yet must I get me gone soon, because my company cometh speedily to meet me, as I have given them charge to do."

So then they rode home from the wood, and the king's folk came flocking to him, and home they fared to the hall and drank joyously: and it was made known to all folk that Frithiof the Bold had been abiding there through the winter-tide.

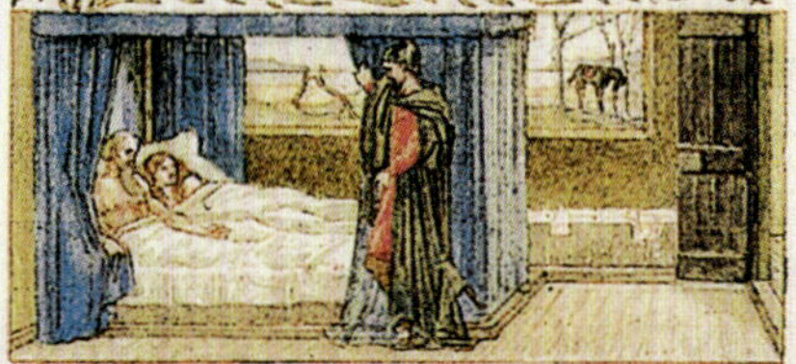

CHAP. XIV

EARLY of a morning-tide one smote on the door of that hall, wherein slept the king and queen, and many others: then the king asked who it was that called at the hall door; and so he who was without said: "Here am I, Frithiof; and I am arrayed for my departure."

Then was the door opened, and Frithiof came in, and sang a stave:

Have great thanks for the guesting
Thou gavest with all bounty;
Dight fully for departure
Is the eagles' feeder now;
But Ingibiorg I mind thee
While yet on earth I dwell;
Live gloriously! I give thee
This gift for many kisses.

40

for them by his friend Webb. After fitting out the house, Morris decided in 1861 to establish a decorating business of "fine art workmen" included founding co-partners Peter Paul Marshall and Charles Faulkner, Webb and the artists Burne-Jones, Ford Madox Brown, and Rossetti. Morris and Burne-Jones were the firm's principal designers but the entire Pre-Raphaelite community worked there, along with Arthur Hughes and William De Morgan. This group of artists who turned their attention to designing objects to decorate homes, helped elevate the decorative arts to the level of fine art. The firm gradually expanded as it found commercial success with the innovative patterns for wallpaper and textiles for which Morris is now famous (especially "Jasmine" in 1872 and "Marigold" in 1875).

In parallel with his decorating work, Morris began studying Old Norse in 1868, and with Eiríkr Magnússon (an Icelandic linguist) he published his first translations of Icelandic sagas, *The Saga of Gunnlaug Worm-Tongue* and *The Story of Grettir the Strong.* Between 1868 and 1870 he published the four parts of *The Earthly Paradise*, a series of poems based on classical and medieval sources.

After these accomplishments in decoration and literature, Morris became interested in politics. For him, the Socialist movement seemed to be the only solution to the problems of Victorian society, particularly the complications emerging from the Industrial Revolution.

In 1871 Morris and Rossetti became co-proprietors of Kelmscott Manor in Oxfordshire. Rossetti was very close to "Topsy", his nickname for William, and Jane Morris, with whom he had an affair. In 1874 Morris took sole possession of Kelmscott without Rossetti, and for purely commercial reasons became the sole owner of the firm, known thereafter as Morris & Co.

Though he was becoming more and more involved in politics, he found time to travel to Iceland twice in 1871 and 1873, and to publish *Sigurd the Volsung and the Fall of the Nibelungs* in 1875. In 1877 he founded the Society for the Protection of Ancient Buildings, to fight against the drastic methods of restoration used in Great Britain, and gave his first public lecture, "The Decorative Arts". In the same year, he left the Social Democratic Federation and founded the Socialist League. In 1884 Morris wrote numerous essays on socialism that were read throughout England and Scotland.

In the last decade of his life Morris added the profession of book printer to his already remarkable range of occupations. In 1891 he founded the Kelmscott Press (named after his former house) in Hammersmith, which published the *Kelmscott Chaucer* in 1896. This book was typeset by Morris and illustrated by Burne-Jones, and is an outstanding example of Morris' ideas. He was skilled at combining beauty and utility in everyday objects, and though he was a poor painter, he helped to promote the Pre-Raphaelite ideal

William Morris,
Burnet, 1881.
Wallpaper.
Victoria & Albert Museum, London.

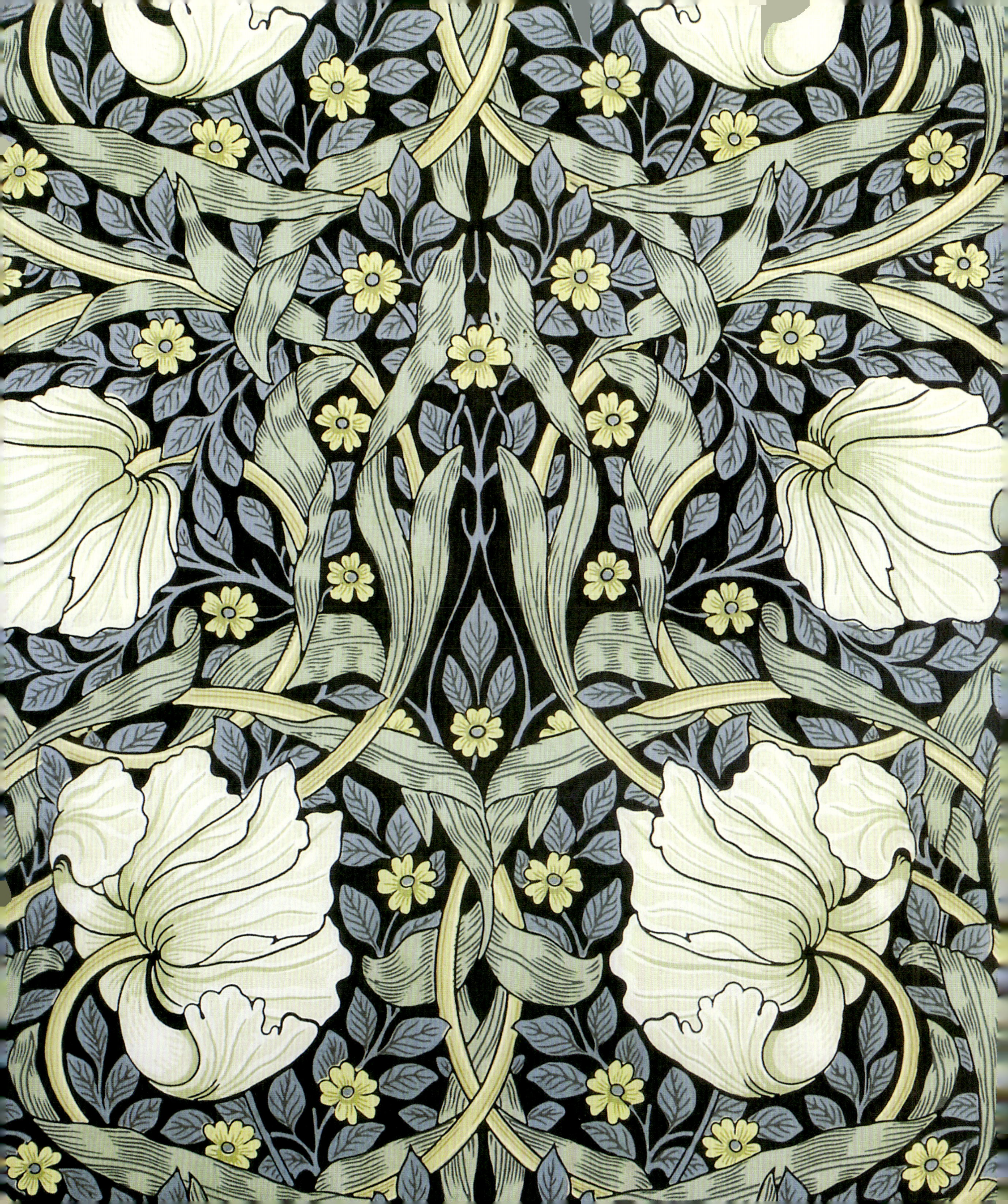

HAST thou longed through weary days
For the sight of one loved face,
Hast thou cried aloud for rest,
Mid the pain of sundering hours,
Cried aloud for sleep and death
Since the sweet unhoped for best
Was a shadow and a breath —
O, long now, for no fear lowers
O'er these faint feet-kissing flowers
O, rest now; and yet in sleep
All thy longing shalt thou keep.

Thou shalt rest, and have no fear
Of a dull awaking near,
Of a life for ever blind,
Uncontent and waste and wide.
Thou shalt wake, and think it sweet
That thy love is near and kind
Sweeter still for lips to meet;
Sweetest, that thine heart doth hide
Longing all unsatisfied
With all longing's answering
Howsoever close ye cling

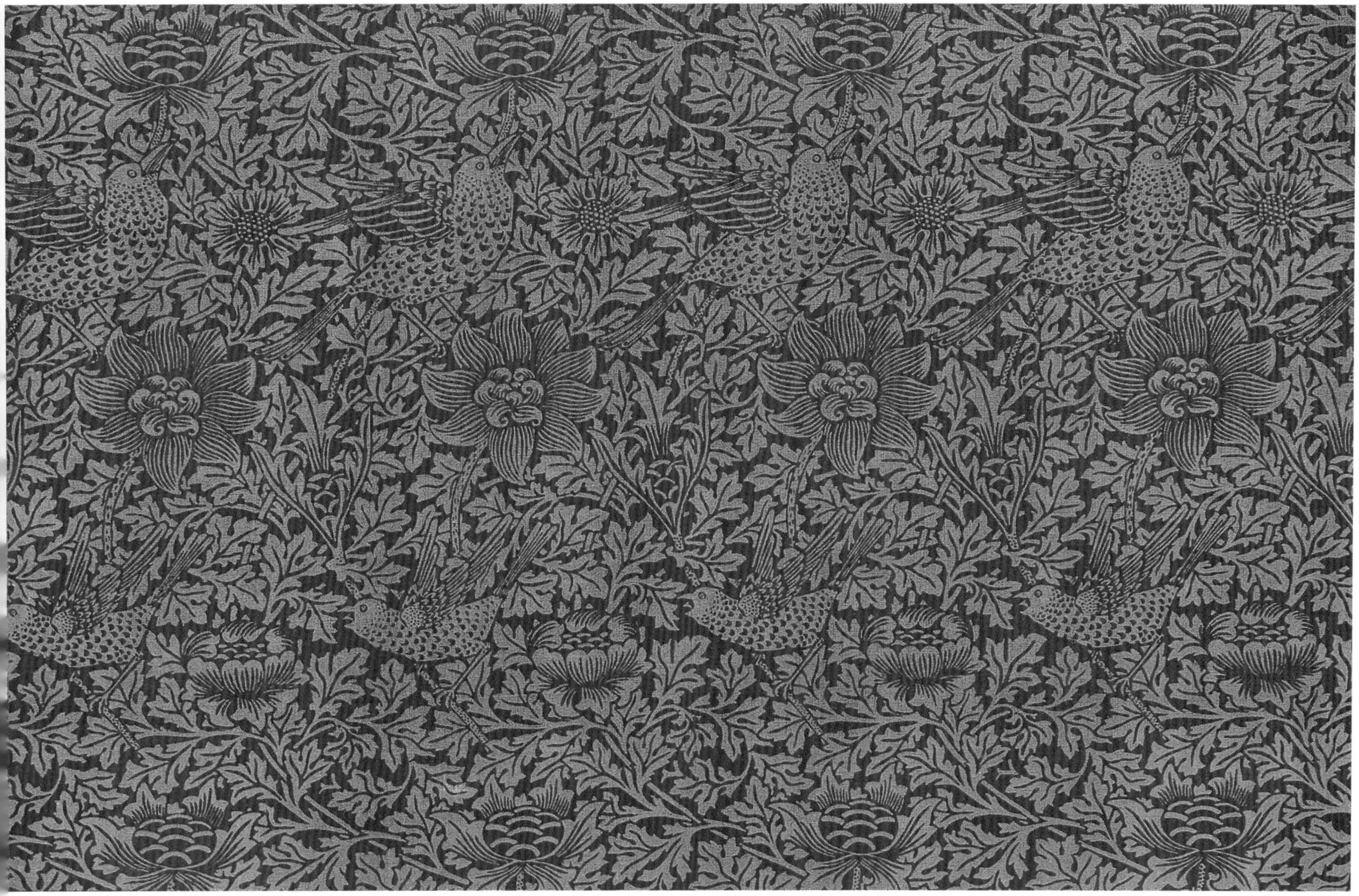

of beauty through his work. All aspects of the books were conceived by Morris, from the typography and ornamented initials and borders to the page layout, format, and bindings, and were printed on handmade paper on a hand-press. He fought for a more beautiful world, a return to the aesthetics of the Middle Ages, and a more demanding attitude towards the art objects that surround us.

After he returned from a last sea voyage to Norway, he died in 1896 and was buried in the cemetery of Kelmscott village beneath a simple gravestone designed by Webb. Morris's art, his ideals, and his lifework paved the way for generations of artists who followed him in his pursuit of what he called "the beauty of life".

William Morris,
Detail from *Love Fullfilled,* a poem from *A Book of Verse,* 1870.
Written and illuminated as a gift for Georgiana Burne-Jones.

William Morris,
Bird and Anemone, 1881.
Furnishing fabric. Dyed cotton ground, with a block-printed pattern in red madder dye, 62 x 46 cm.
Victoria & Albert Museum, London.

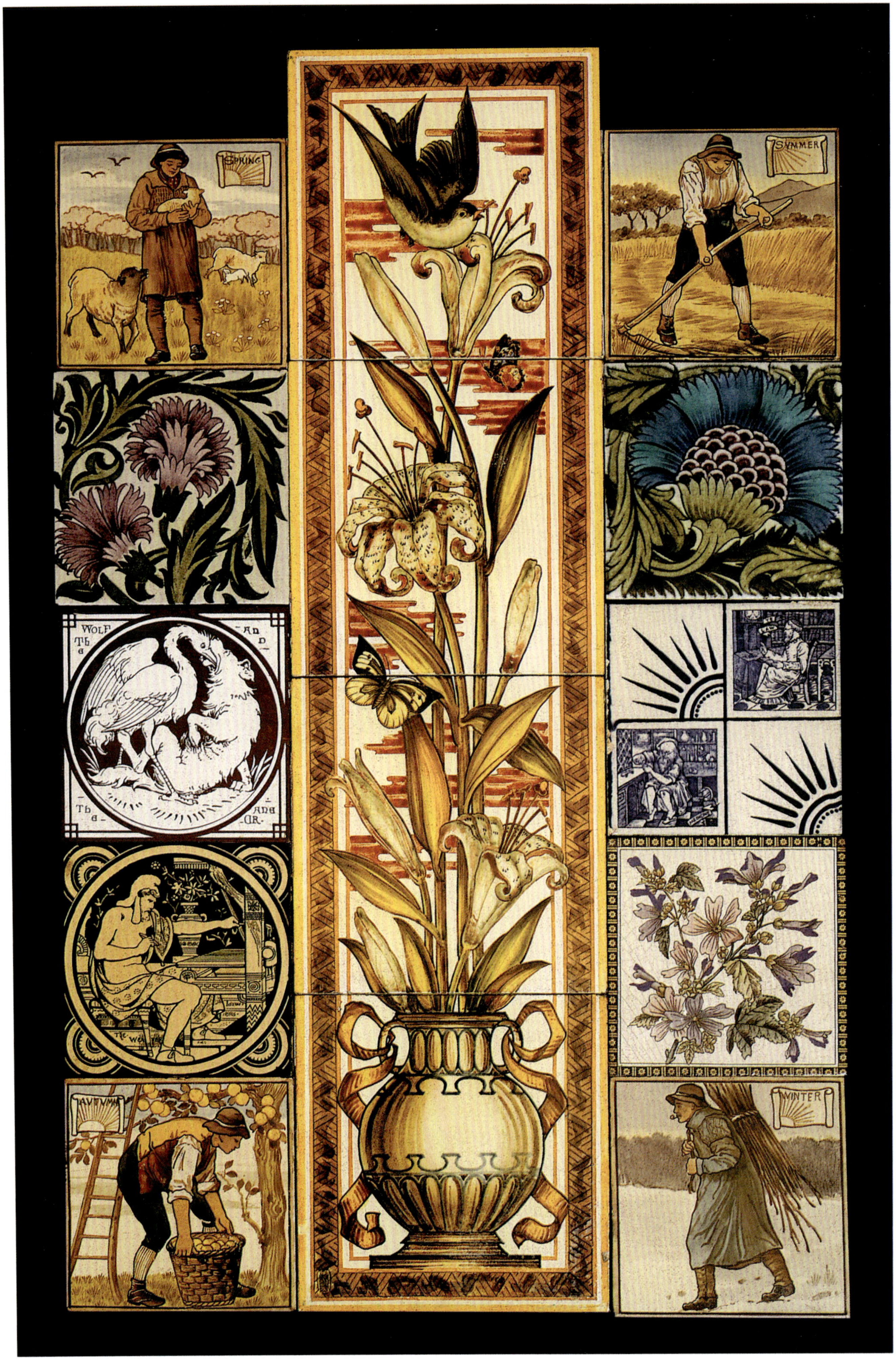
SPRING
SUMMER
AUTUMN
WINTER

WILLIAM FREND DE MORGAN
(LONDON, 1839 - 1917)

William Frend De Morgan was a key figure in the Arts and Crafts movement. He was a potter and a tile designer as well as an inventor and writer. He was born in London on 16th November 1839. His father, Augustus De Morgan, was a famous English mathematician and logician. He also was the first professor of mathematics at the newly founded University College London. His mother, Sophia Elizabeth Frend, herself the daughter of a mathematician, was a writer and a suffragette; she also fought for prison reform with Elizabeth Fry, the famous English prison reformer and philanthropist. The De Morgans had a large circle of intellectual and artistic friends where they lived in Chelsea. His brother, George Campbell De Morgan, was on the contrary a young man of the highest scientific promise, whose name would long be connected with the London Mathematical Society of which he was one of the founders. He tragically died in 1867 leaving his family, especially his father, devastated. Both Augustus and Sophia Elizabeth had a taste for innovation. He had introduced the abstract approach to algebra and she was militating for the rights of women and prisoners. William was brought up in a stimulating and progressive household, and instead of pursuing the lineage of mathematicians, he decided to focus his attention on the arts.

In 1859, De Morgan entered the Royal Academy Schools where he specialised in Fine Arts. The institution did not fulfill his thirst for innovation though as it offered more conventional subjects such as sculpture or painting. He studied alongside Simeon Solomon, a follower of the Pre-Raphaelites, who remembers De Morgan as an "entirely uncommonplace young man; tall, thin, high forehead, aquiline nose and high squeaky voice". His fellow students nicknamed him "Mouse". The stained glass artist, Henry Holiday, who knew Burne-Jones and William Morris, introduced De Morgan to the latter around 1863. This encounter marked a turning point in De Morgan's career as soon after he focused on stained glass and the decorative arts. At first he experimented on the fabrication of tiles and stained glass. William Morris had not encountered great success with his own tiles, and De Morgan offered to take up that part of the creative business. However, it must be stated that De Morgan, contrary to general belief, never became a partner of Morris & Co. However, they worked alongside for many years, De Morgan gradually creating his own tiles and his own style. Morris would sell De Morgan's products and was inspired by De Morgan's designs. They remained lifelong friends.

In 1871, Augustus De Morgan, who had suffered from ill-health from 1867 onwards, died on the 18th of March. The following year, William De Morgan moved to a larger

Minton's (for the "Four Seasons", the "Wolf and the Crane"), **W. B Simpson and Sons** (for the central panel), **William de Morgan** (for the flower designs) and **Wedgwood** (for the blue and white tiles), collection of tiles.

William Morris, *Tulip and Trellis*, 1870. Hand-painted in blue and green and tin-glazed earthenware tile, 15.3 x 15.3 cm. Victoria & Albert Museum, London.

William Morris (for the design) and **Architectural Pottery Co.** (for the production), four *Pink and Hawthorn tiles*, 1887. Slip-covered, hand-painted in colours and glazed on earthenware blanks, 15.5 x 15 cm. Victoria & Albert Museum, London.

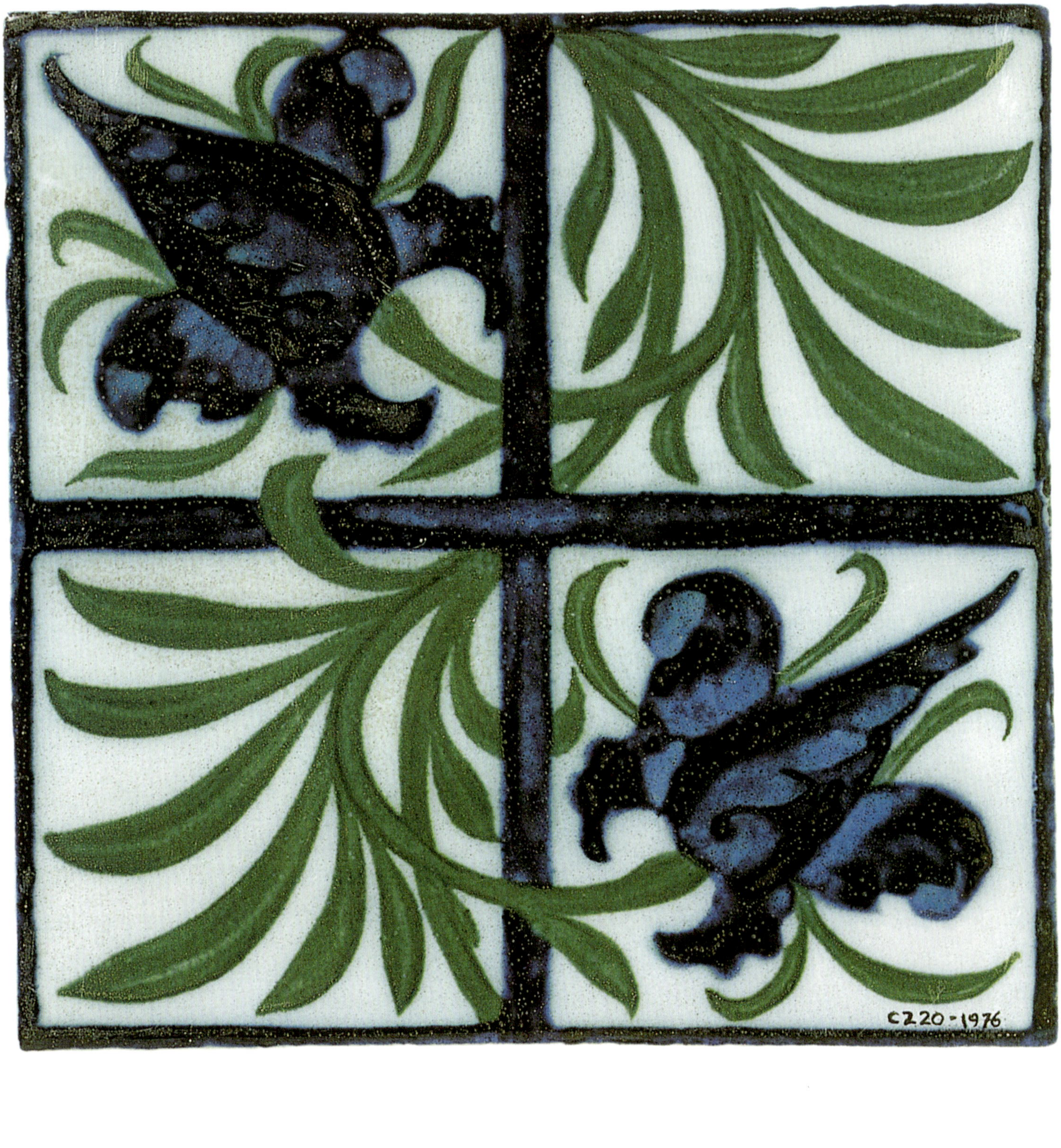
C220-1976

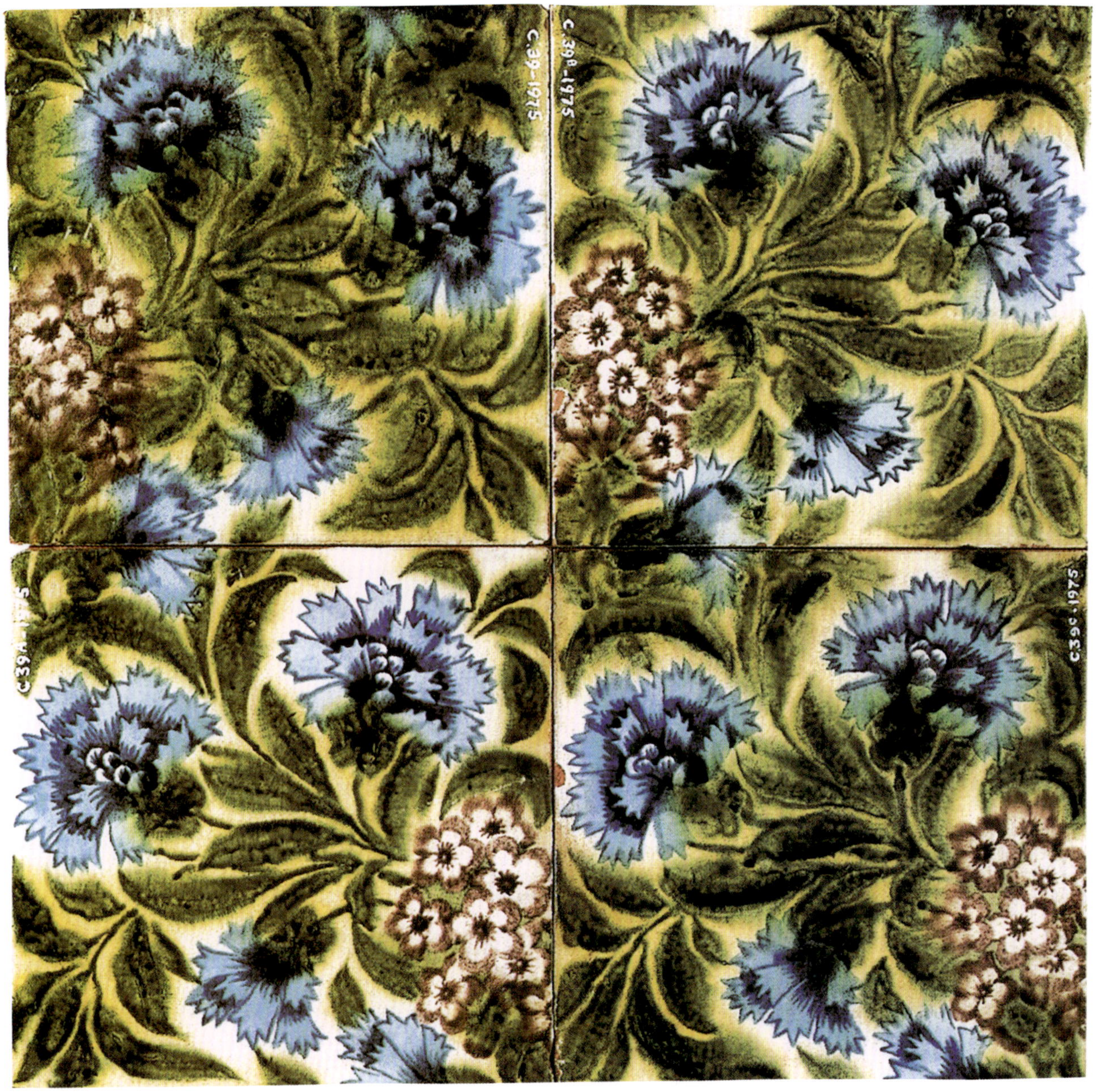

studio in Chelsea, as he had burned down his previous dwellings in Fitzroy Square with an experiment that went out of control. He didn't paint on ready-made tiles, but made them himself. In Chelsea, he founded his own firm where he supervised the production of decorated tiles and ornamental pots. While overseeing the production of his firm, De Morgan continued his experimentations along with the creation of new material to make tiles and in the early 1870s he brought lustreware back in fashion, reviving this type of ceramics that were over five centuries old. This technique was quite dangerous and required caution. It had been abandoned for it required too much work, but not only did De Morgan re-introduce it into Britain's nineteenth-century tile production, he also perfected it. The lustreware technique and the designs De Morgan used both came from the Middle East where he found his inspiration.

In 1882, when the tile production increased widely, De Morgan moved to a larger workshop not far from that of Morris near Merton Abbey. His team produced vases, bowls and dishes. Moving closer to Morris brought about a renewal in De Morgan's design and he refined his designs of plants and animals.

In 1887, William De Morgan married the artist Evelyn Pickering. Born in 1855, Evelyn Pickering was sixteen years younger than William De Morgan. She had studied at the Slade School of Art, the art school of University College London, under the direction of Edward Poynter. Her work was very much influenced by her uncle, the painter Roddam Spencer Stanhope. Surprisingly, William and Evelyn had a lot in common. They shared a thirst for knowledge and great sense of humour. Evelyn was quite wealthy which helped the pottery as this business, although successful, required a large cash flow.

To stabilise his workshop further, the business was moved in 1888 to Sands End in Fulham. There, De Morgan started a partnership with the architect Halsey Ricardo which was to last until 1898. During this period of new creative energy generated by a new location and the new partner, De Morgan began serving on the committee of the Arts and Crafts Exhibition Society as well as showing his own works at the exhibitions.

His health was starting to fail though and he divided his time between England and Italy where the winters were warmer. He and Evelyn loved their life there; she could paint and he could work on new designs. Evelyn already was familiar with the country since her uncle Stanhope, who was occasionally their host, had taken her on trips when she was younger.

Even if those stays in Italy were good for his health and moral, eventually the workshop came to suffer from De Morgan's long absences. With no one to direct them since his partner Ricardo had quite a lot going on for himself, production slowed considerably to the point where their partnership was dissolved in 1898. The friendship between De

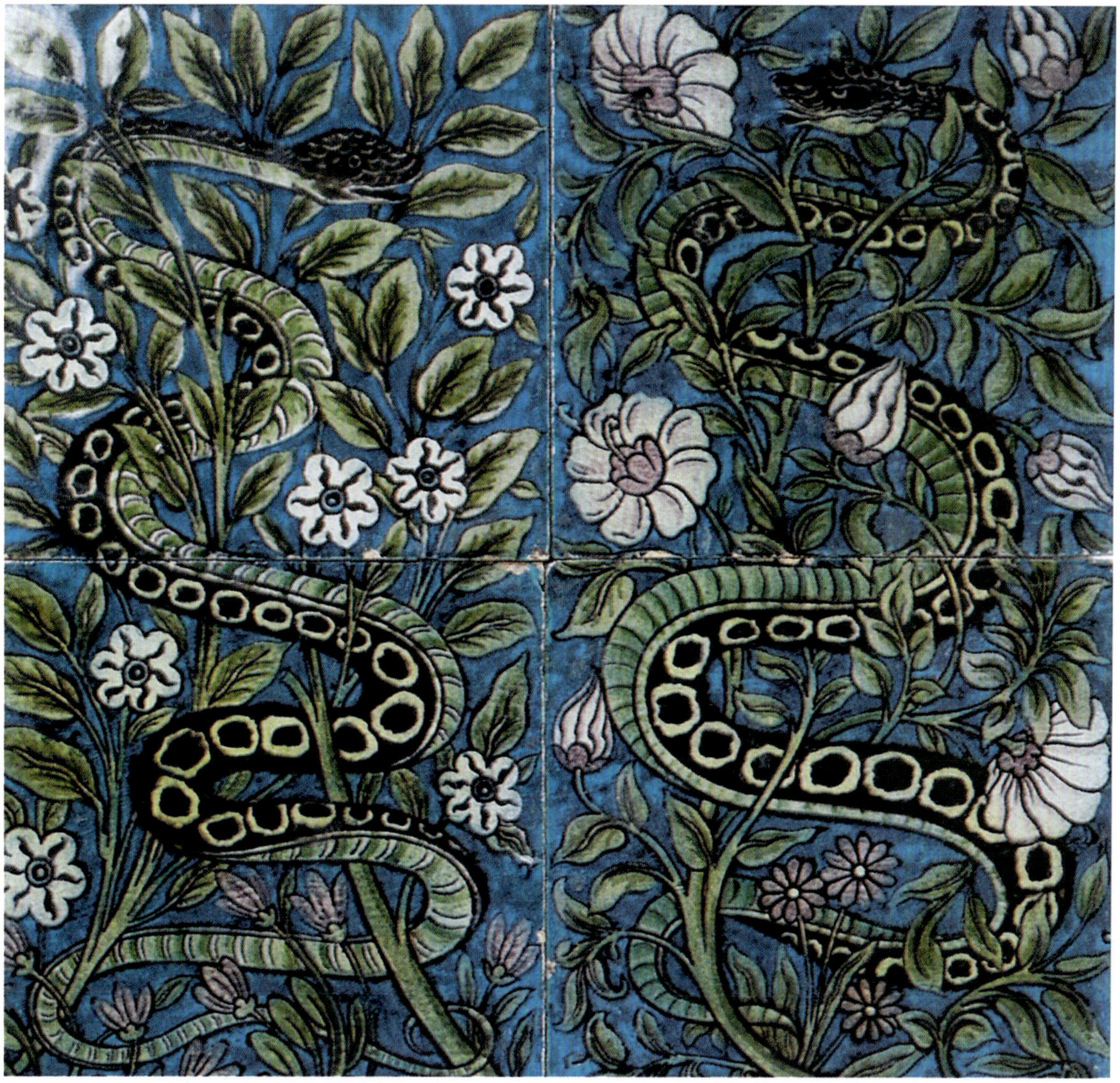

Morgan and Ricardo overcame this, however. De Morgan tried to take up another partnership with a few employees but the costs were too high to maintain. After a few years of persistence, the firm went into voluntary liquidation in 1907. His work as a potter was always highly praised but never provided enough money.

De Morgan decided to put his creative energy into writing and his life took a radical turn. Indeed De Morgan became a successful novelist. He wrote a first novel called *Joseph Vance* published in 1906 which was then followed by *Alice-For-Short* in 1907 and *Somehow Good* in 1908. They were all bestsellers. At over sixty-five, De Morgan had reinvented himself and encountered more success as a novel writer than as the avant-garde potter he used to be. He died of influenza in 1917. He is recalled today as a potter more than a novelist. However his creative enthusiasm allowed him to do more than tiles and books. He also worked on equipment for pottery, on bicycles, on telegraph codes and warfare strategies.

William De Morgan,
four-tile panel, c. 1890.

Various designers,
tile panel, 1876.
Slip-covered and hand-painted in various colours and glazed, on earthenware blanks,
160 x 91.5 cm.
Victoria & Albert Museum, London.

William De Morgan (for the design) and **Sands End Pottery** (for the production), panel, between 1888 and 1897.
Buff-coloured earthenware, with painting over a white slip,
61.4 x 40.5 cm.
Victoria & Albert Museum, London.

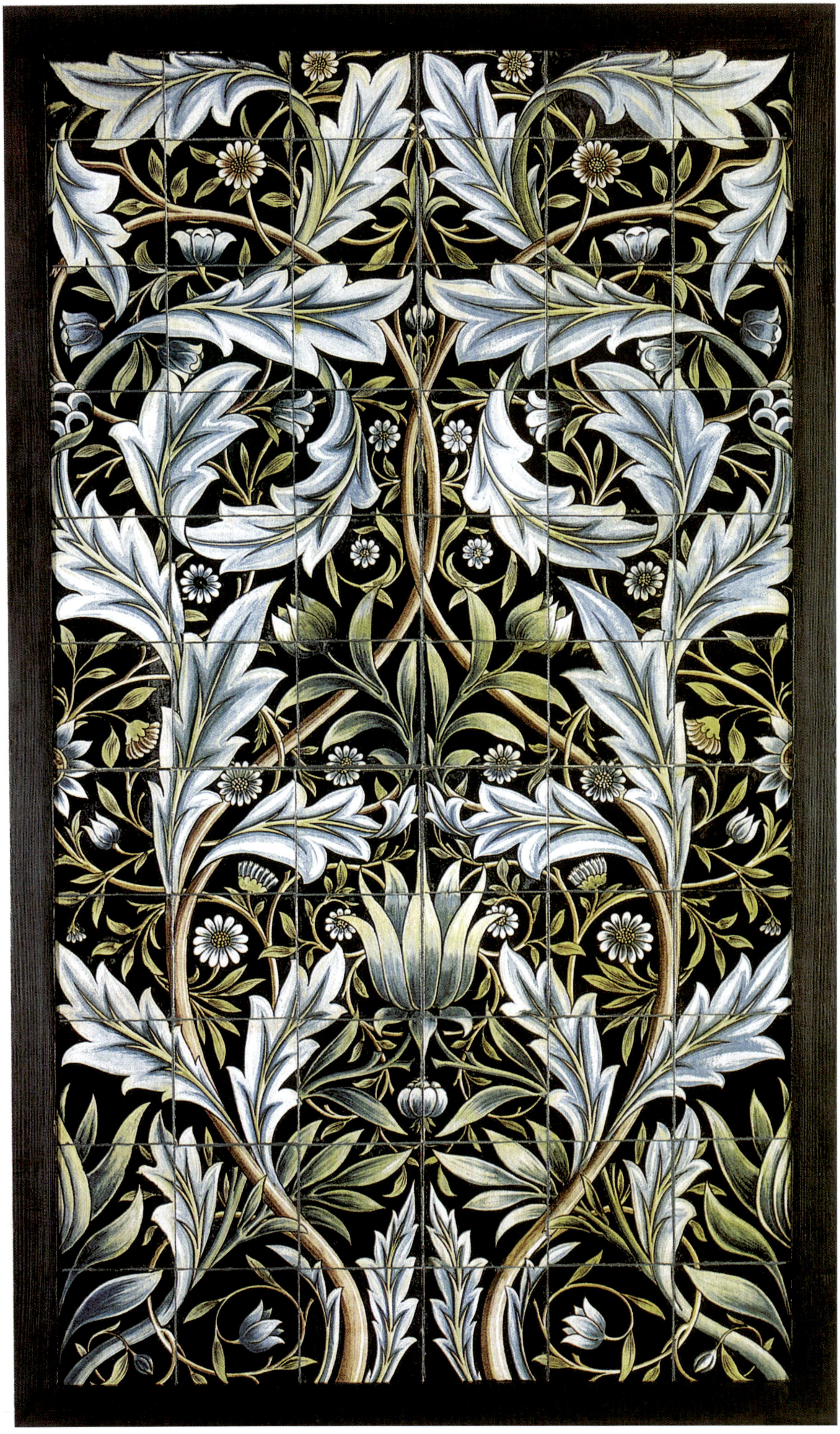

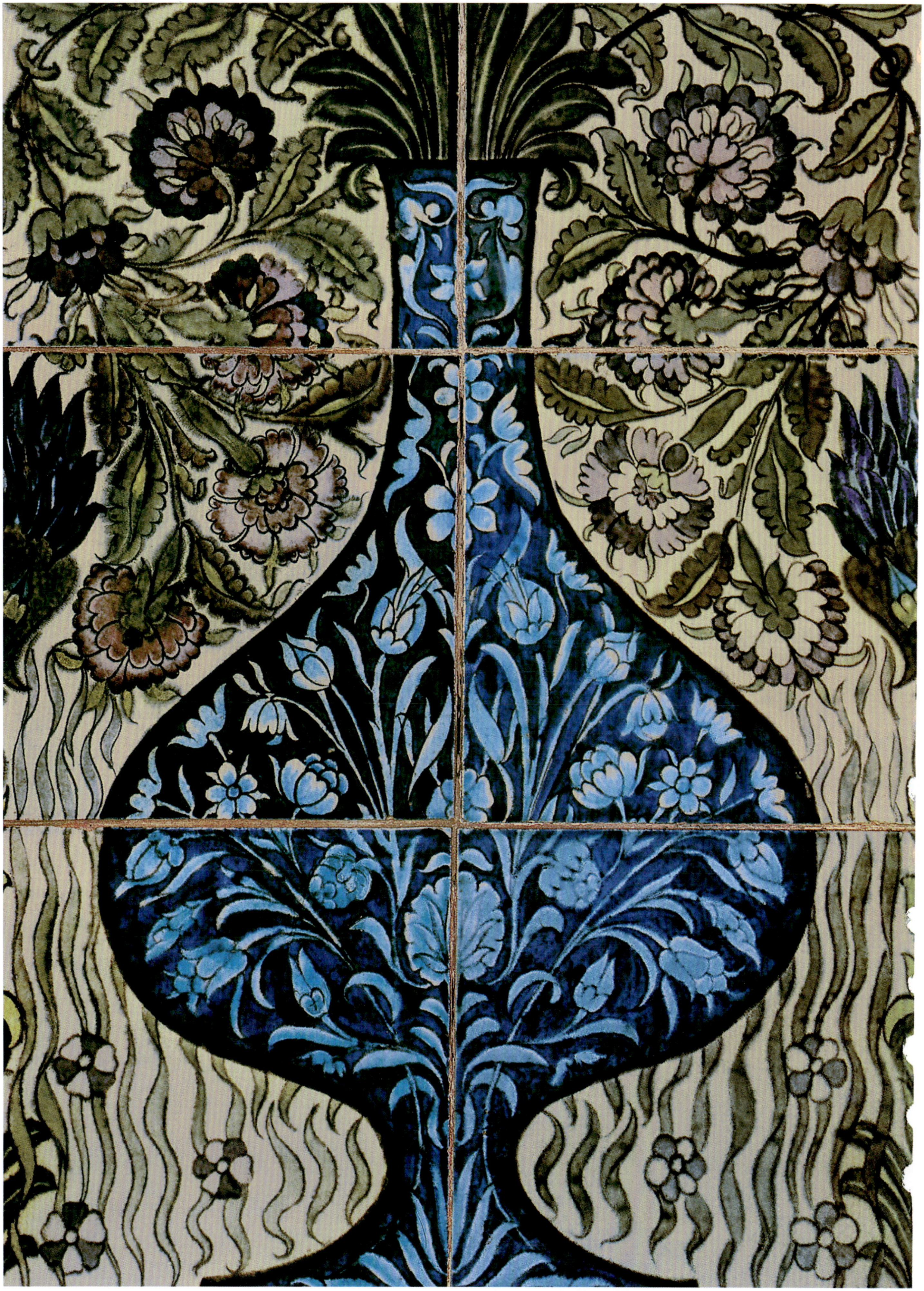

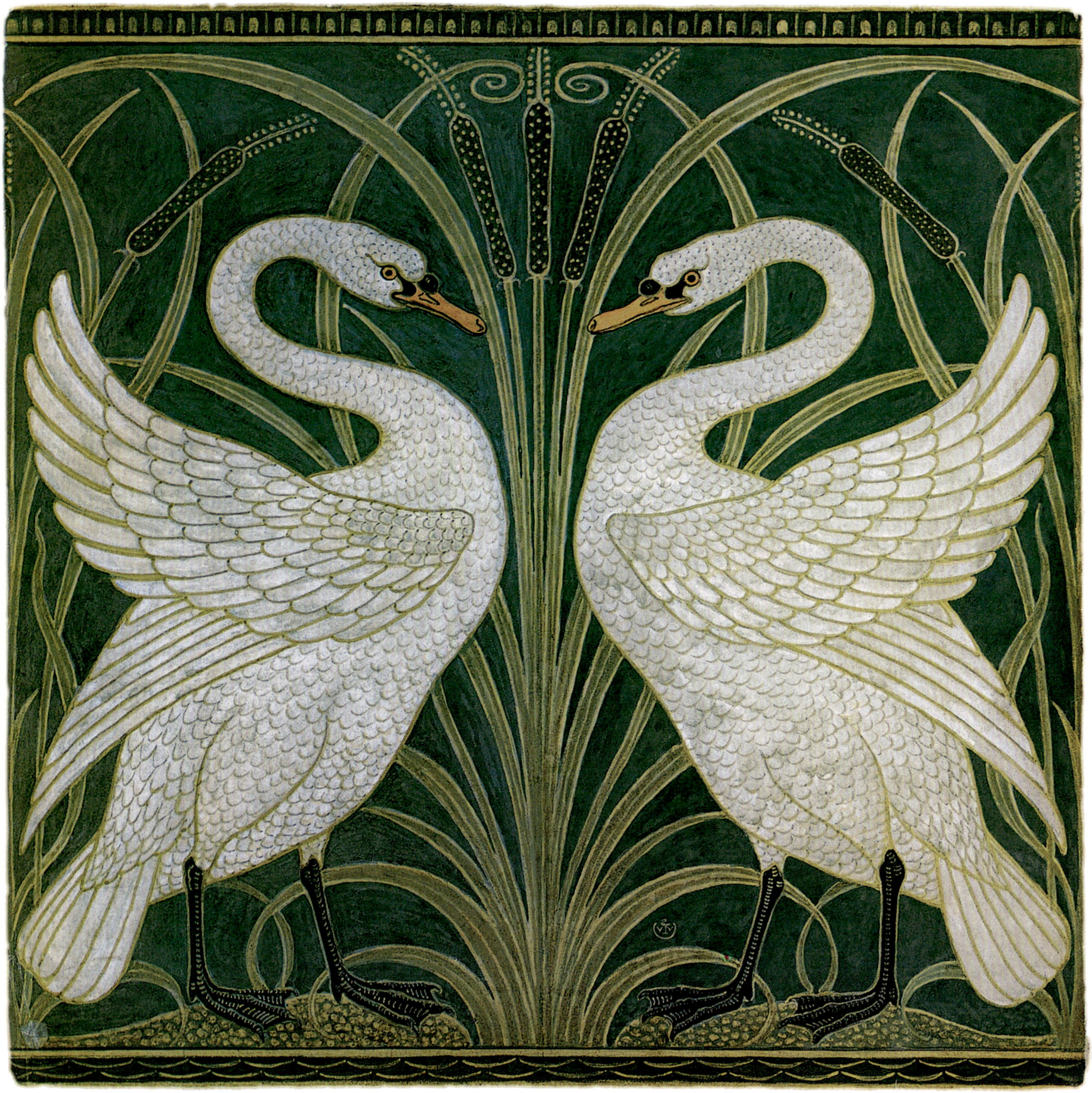

WALTER CRANE
(LIVERPOOL, 1845 - HORSHAM, 1915)

Walter Crane was a British painter of portraits, figures and landscapes and is remembered as the most important of all the children's book illustrators. He also produced ceramic tiles and other decorative objects in the line with the Arts and Crafts movement.

Walter Crane was born in Liverpool in 1845. He was the third of five children to Marie and Thomas Crane who was a portrait painter and miniaturist.

Crane became known at a young age as an accomplished artist, as some of his illustrations came to the attention of the art critic John Ruskin and William James Linton, one of the best wood engravers of his time.

In January 1859, when he was thirteen, Crane entered his three-year apprenticeship to Linton. He studied there the contemporary works of the Pre-Raphaelites Rossetti, Millais and Burne-Jones as well as the Italian old masters. He was also greatly influenced by the writings of John Ruskin concerning beauty and utility in works of art and concerning the dignity of the craftsmen.

Crane later worked with Linton on book projects, and after the wood engraver moved to the United States, he learned the printing techniques and subsequently worked closely with the printers of his work.

After the three years of his apprenticeship were completed, Crane tried to live on his works and attended art classes at Heatherley's Fine Art School at night. This school, founded in 1845, is probably the oldest independent art school in London and is among the few art colleges in Britain that focus on portraiture, figurative painting and sculpture.

His work at this time consisted largely of vignettes, landscapes, and groups of people in society dress for the covers or chapter headings of books. Crane had learned how to

Walter Crane,
Swans, wall paper design, 1875.
Gouache and watercolour,
53.1 x 53 cm.
Victoria & Albert Museum, London.

William Morris,
Cherwell (named after an Oxfordshire district), 1887.
Pattern for printed velvet.
Private collection.

Walter Crane (for the design),
Jeffrey & Co. (for the manufacturing),
Cockatoo and Pomegranate, 1899.
Hand-printed wallpaper.
Whitworth Art Gallery, Manchester.

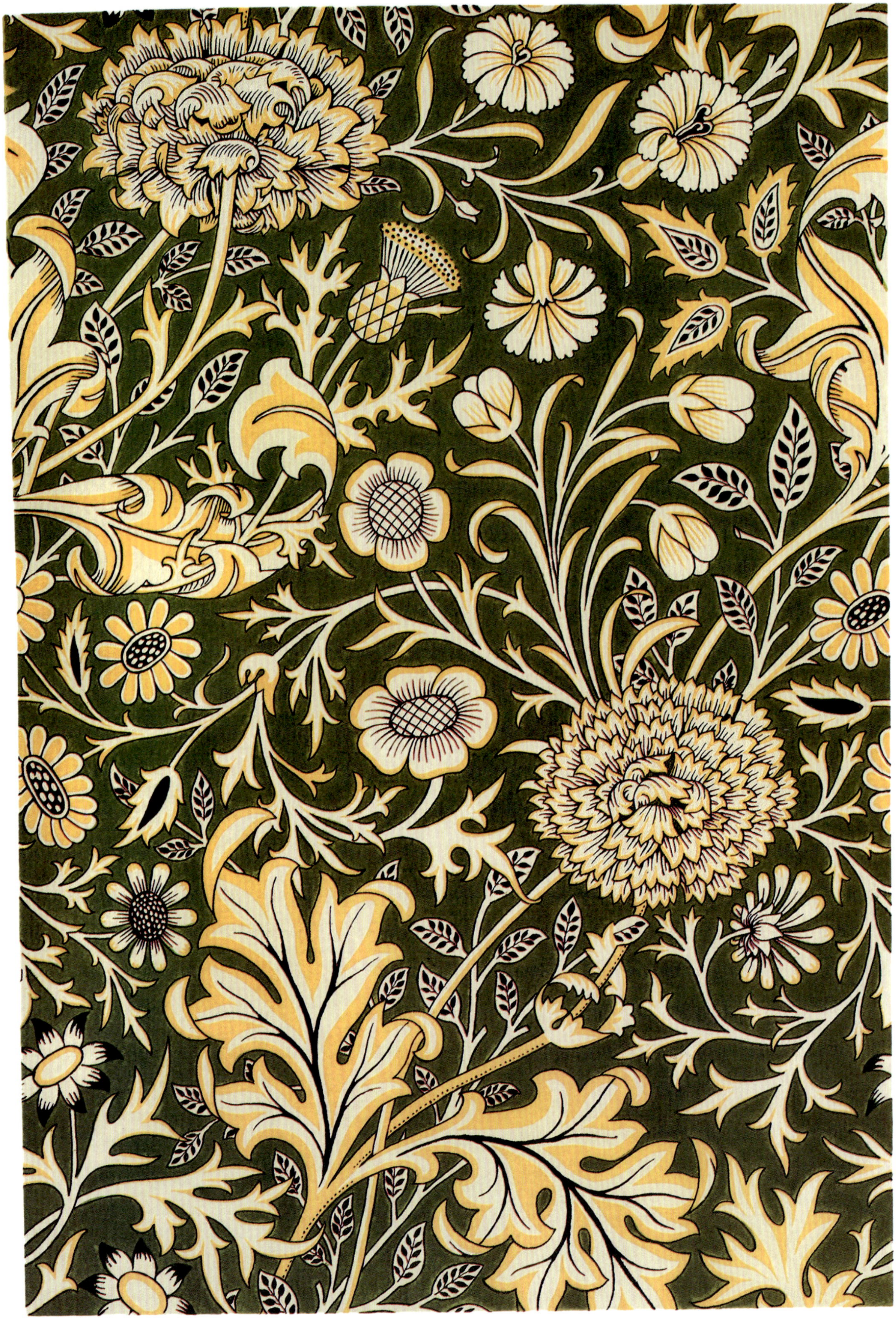

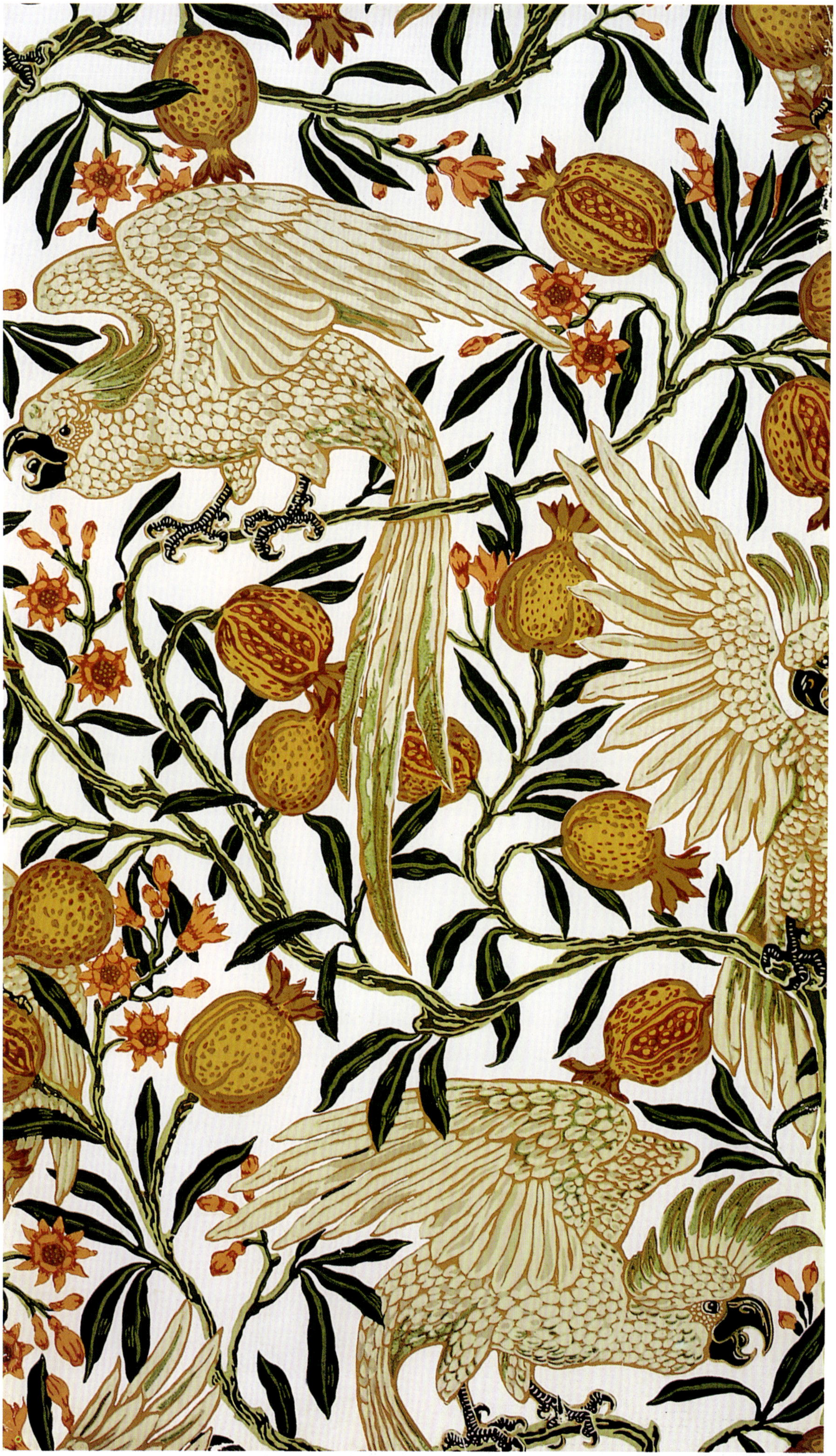

simplify the details in his images, which would characterise his picture books, and would show off the colour that made them unique.

The influence of the Pre-Raphaelites' paintings is obvious in his early work such as *The Lady of Shalott.* Crane's picture was exhibited at the Royal Academy in 1862, but later the Academy refused his more mature work. However, the Grosvenor Gallery, founded in London in 1877, and a rival to the Royal Academy, displayed Crane's work as well as the work of artists outside the British mainstream.

In 1863, Crane met the printer Edmund Evans, with whom he was to do much of his most creative work. He began by drawing the covers of cheap, sensational novels for Evans. Then, in 1865 he began a series of colourful inexpensive picture books, the six-penny toy books of nursery rhymes. In 1865-1866, his first series of toy books (which reached around fifty titles over the subsequent thirty years) was published. His soon renowned illustrations helped influence the look of nineteenth-century British children's literature. A new series, beginning with *The Frog Prince* (1873), shows the influence both of Florentine fifteenth-century painting and Japanese colour prints that helped him develop his style.

We don't know much about Crane's private life, except that he married Mary Frances Andrews in 1871 and that their marriage lasted until she died in 1914.

From the early 1880s, initially under Morris's influence, Crane supported concretely the young Socialist movement by contributing weekly cartoons to the socialist periodicals *Justice* and *The Commonweal.* Like Morris himself he wanted to bring art into the daily life of all classes. Thus, he devoted attention to designs for textiles, for wallpapers, and to house decoration. He was also concerned about the condition of art education and manufacture.

He gave much time and energy to the work of the Art Workers Guild established in 1884 by a group of young architects associated with the ideas of William Morris and the Arts and Crafts movement.

In 1888, he also founded the Arts and Crafts Exhibition Society of which he was the first president. The society mounted Arts and Crafts national – in England – and international exhibitions. Notably, William Morris, Edward Burne-Jones, and Philip Webb were included in the founding members of this Society.

Crane later collaborated with William Morris (in 1894) at the Kelmscott Press on the page decorations of *The Story of the Glittering Plain*, a fantasy novel by Morris. He

Walter Crane,
Hammersmith Branch Socialist League (Membership Card for Henry Halliday Sparling), 1890.
Ink on paper, signed by Emery Walker and William Morris,
11.4 x 7.6 cm.
Private collection.

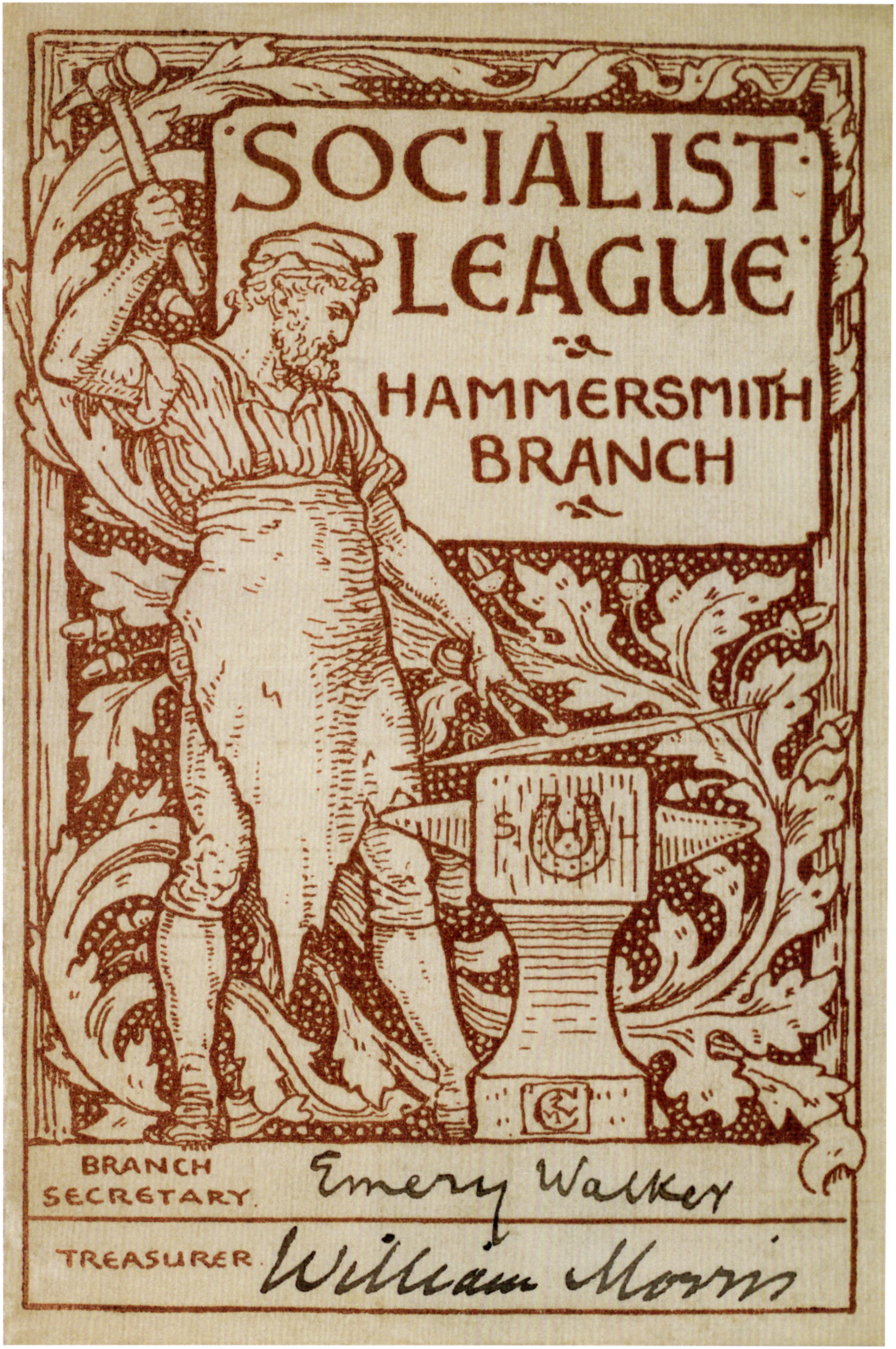
SOCIALIST LEAGUE
HAMMERSMITH BRANCH
BRANCH SECRETARY Emery Walker
TREASURER William Morris

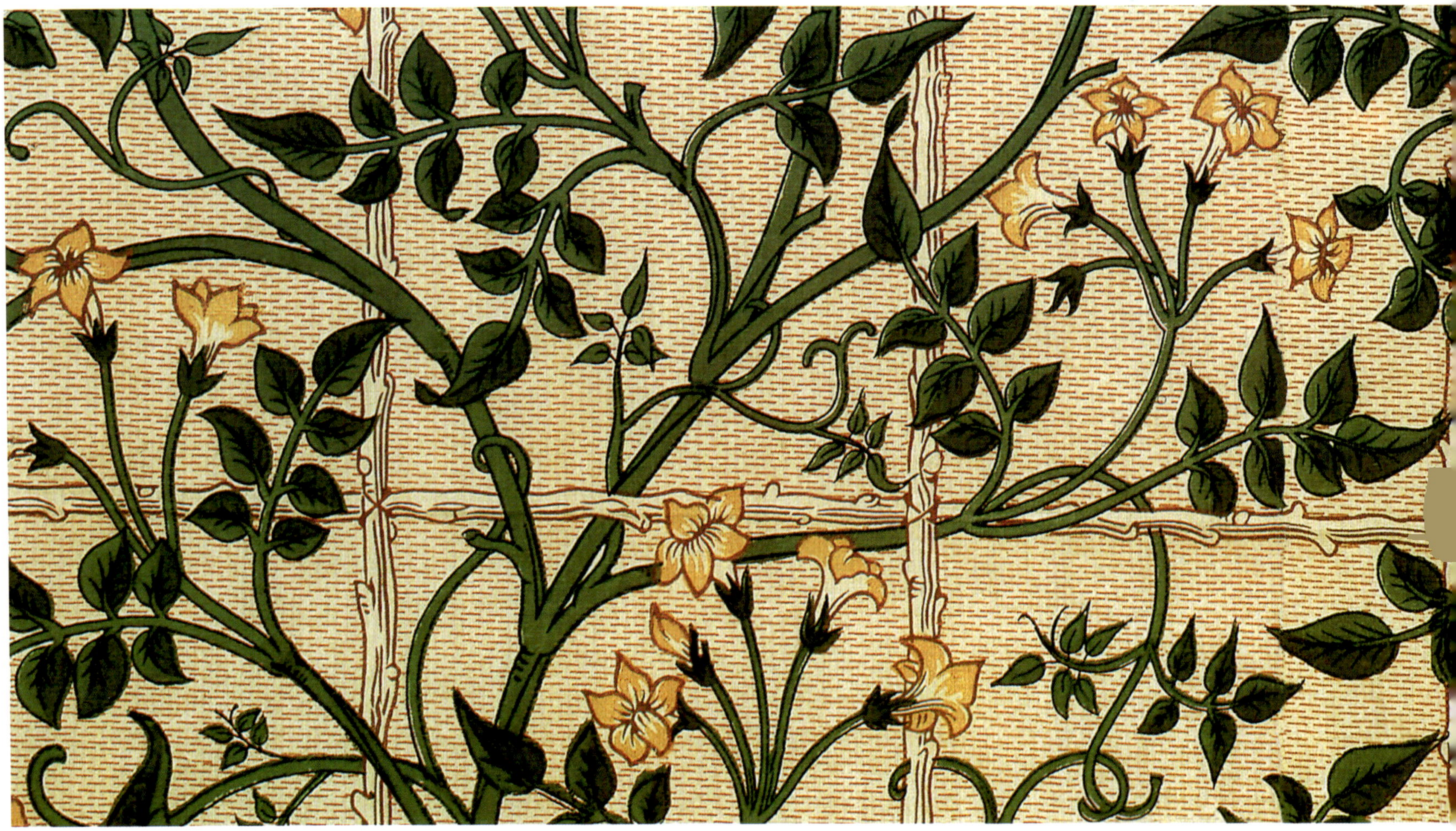

designed the wood-engravings that would illustrate the book on the model of fifteenth-century German and Italian woodcuts. William Morris had founded the Kelmscott Press in 1891, in West London, in order to produce examples of improved printing and book design, using traditional methods of printing and craftsmanship, in line with the Arts and Crafts movement.

Crane's involvement in decorative design was a high point in his career since the textiles and wallpapers he designed became internationally popular. He worked for Jeffrey & Co. (the leading producers of Art Nouveau style wallpapers in turn of the century Britain) from 1875. He also worked for Maw and Co. (the largest tile company in the world by 1900), Pilkington (a glass manufacturer)

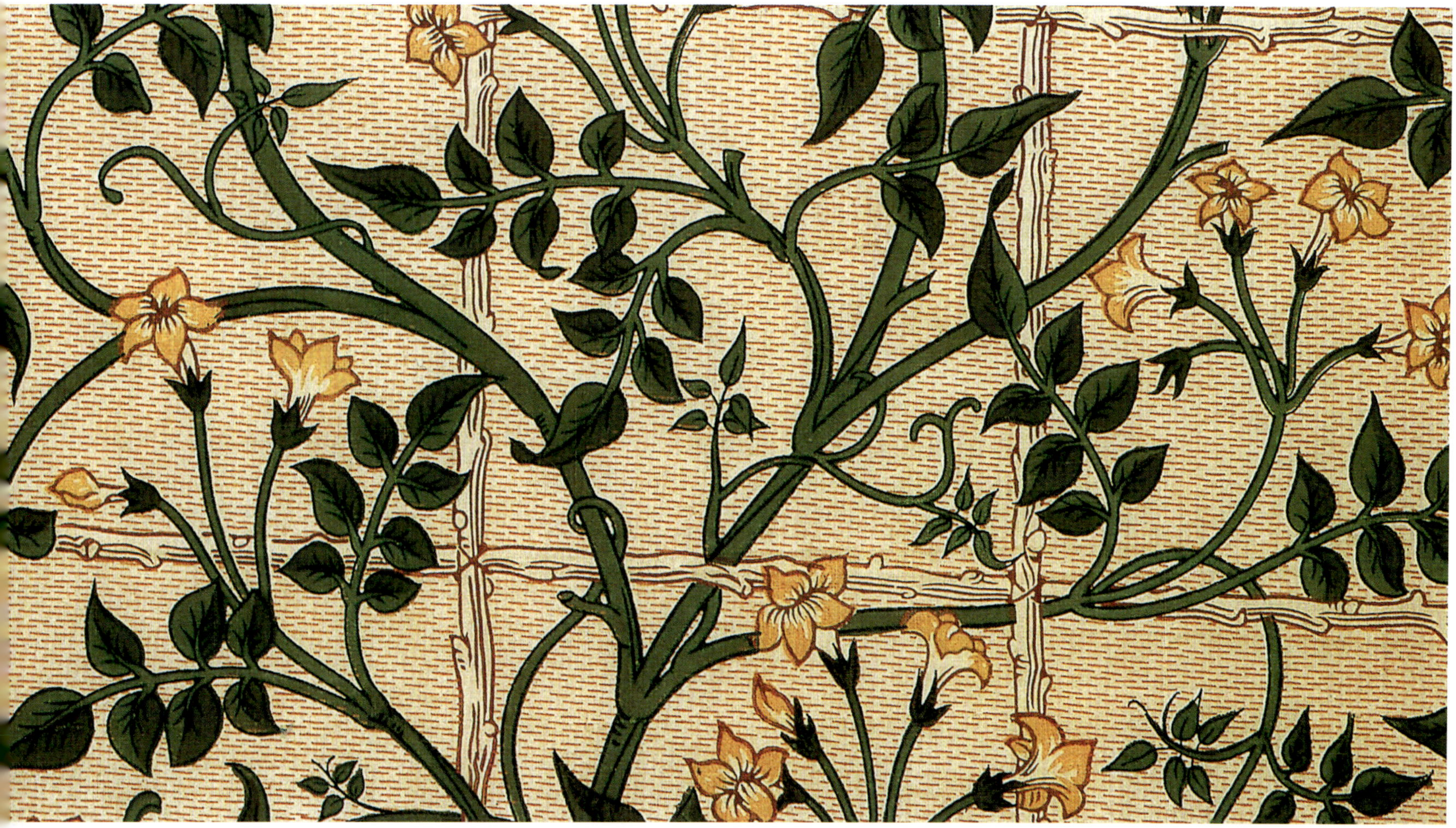

and for Wedgwood (the famous china company). Crane was much involved in art education. He was art director first of the Manchester School of Art from 1893 to 1896 (his lectures there where published with illustrated drawings), then of the Reading College from 1896 to 1898 and was finally appointed – for a short time – Principal of the Royal College of Art in 1898 (the national art and design college, founded in 1837). He also wrote important books on decoration and design, including *The Decorative Illustration of Books* (1896) and *Line and Form* (1900).

Walter Crane died in 1915 in Horsham, Sussex. For his varied work, he applied the principle that in decorative design "the artist works freest and best without direct reference to nature, and should have learned the forms he makes use of by heart."

William Morris,
Jasmine Trellis, 1868-1870.
Block printed on cotton,
22.9 x 94 cm; pattern repeat,
45 x 45.5 cm.
Victoria & Albert Museum, London.

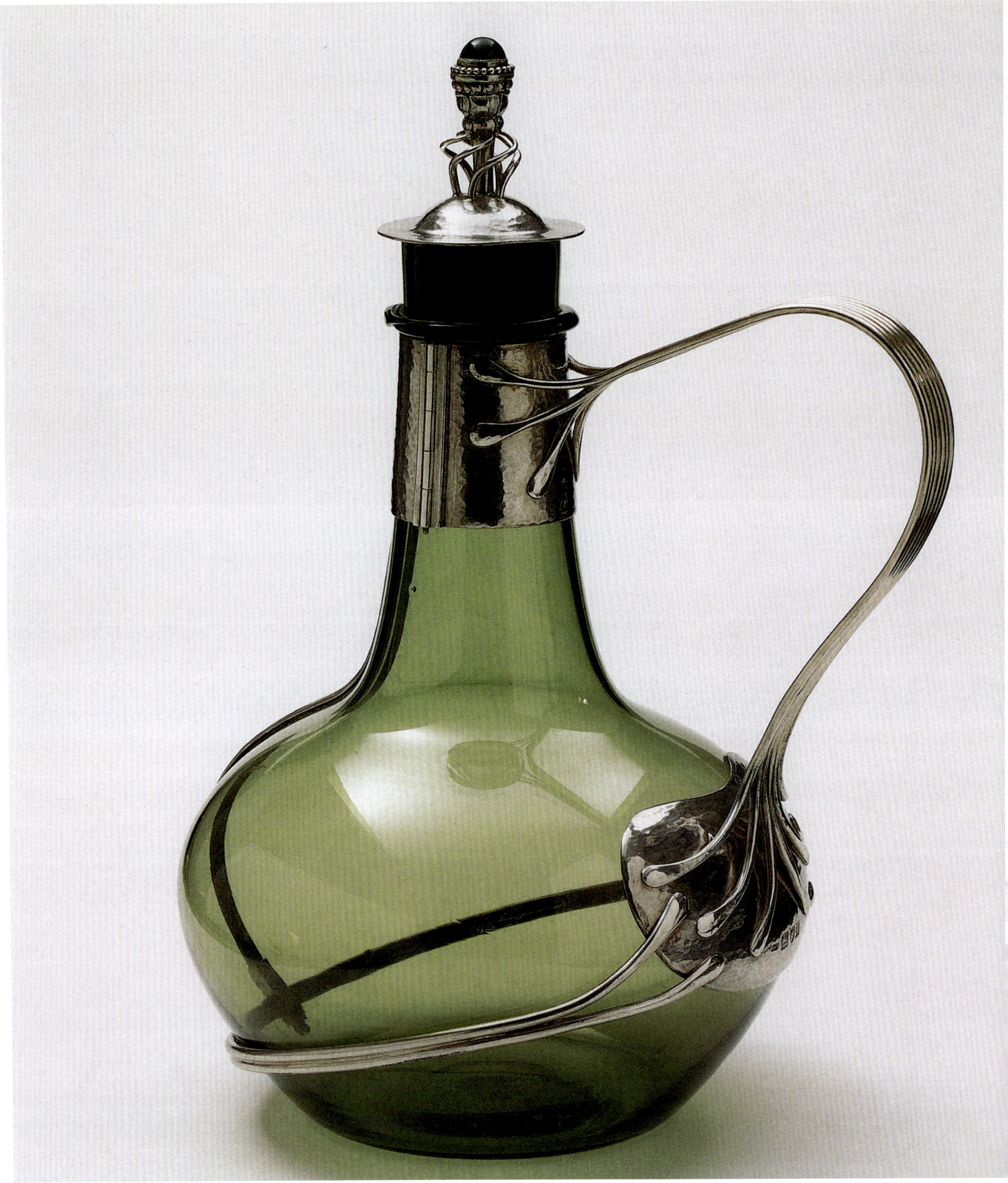

Charles Robert Ashbee
(London, 1863 - Sevenoaks, Kent, 1942)

Like other members of the Arts and Crafts movement, Ashbee was active in various domains. He was firstly a designer but he also later became a writer, architect and a social reformer. Born in London in 1863, Ashbee was the son of the businessman Henry Spencer Ashbee who happened to be a bibliophile specialising in erotica. His mother was Jewish and a suffragette, and all his sisters were progressive as well.

Ashbee was educated in Wellington College and King's College, Cambridge where he studied history. During his studies, he was very much influenced by the writings of John Ruskin and William Morris. He embraced the principle of the creative workshop and the independence of the worker. Ruskin and Morris particularly stressed the importance of the welfare of workmen, and this especially appealed to young Ashbee who was engaged in social work at Toynbee Hall. This institution made a strong impression on our young artist.

Located in Whitechapel in the East End of London, Toynbee Hall was the original house of the settlement movement and offered social services for the lower classes. They provided shelter and education thanks to the members of the community. Graduates, being the future elite of the nation, would also take care of the poor. By experiencing closeness to poverty, the future leaders became aware of social issues and this way the system would gradually shift towards a fairer one. Prestigious individuals went through Toynbee Hall such as Clement Atlee, Prime Minister of Great Britain from 1945 to 1951, the eminent economist William Beveridge and Robert Ashbee among others. While working in Toynbee Hall, he also studied under the direction of the architects Thomas Gardner and G. F. Bodley who was active in the movement of the Gothic revival.

Through Ruskin and Morris's influence and his work in Toynbee Hall, Ashbee was determined to pursue his work in humanising British industry. With this in mind, Ashbee created in 1888, while still active in Toynbee Hall, the Guild and School of Handicraft in the same neighbourhood. While the school only lasted until 1895, the Guild flourished. The Guild was a workshop combining the principles of the Arts and Crafts as well as the social aspects Ashbee had learned with his social work. Five workmen constituted the small staff that begun the Guild of Handicraft under the supervision of Ashbee. They made furniture and worked with metal. The year following the creation of the workshop, they participated in the second exhibition of the Arts and Crafts Exhibition society as members of the co-operative of craft workers in leather, wood, metal and jewellery. In 1891, the Guild moved to Essex House still in the East End while a retail shop was implanted in the West End so

Charles Robert Ashbee (for the design), **the Guild of Handicraft** (for the manufacturing), decanter, c. 1904-1905. Green glass with silver mount and a chrysoprase set in the finial, 23.5 x 13 cm. Victoria & Albert Museum, London.

Charles Robert Ashbee (made by **the Guild of Handicraft**) and **Charles F. A. Voysey** (for the interior painting design), *Lovelace* escritoire, c. 1900. Oak outside, stained dark green, with interior of painted poplar and pierced wrought-iron hinges backed with morocco leather, 147.3 x 123.2 x 61 cm. Private collection.

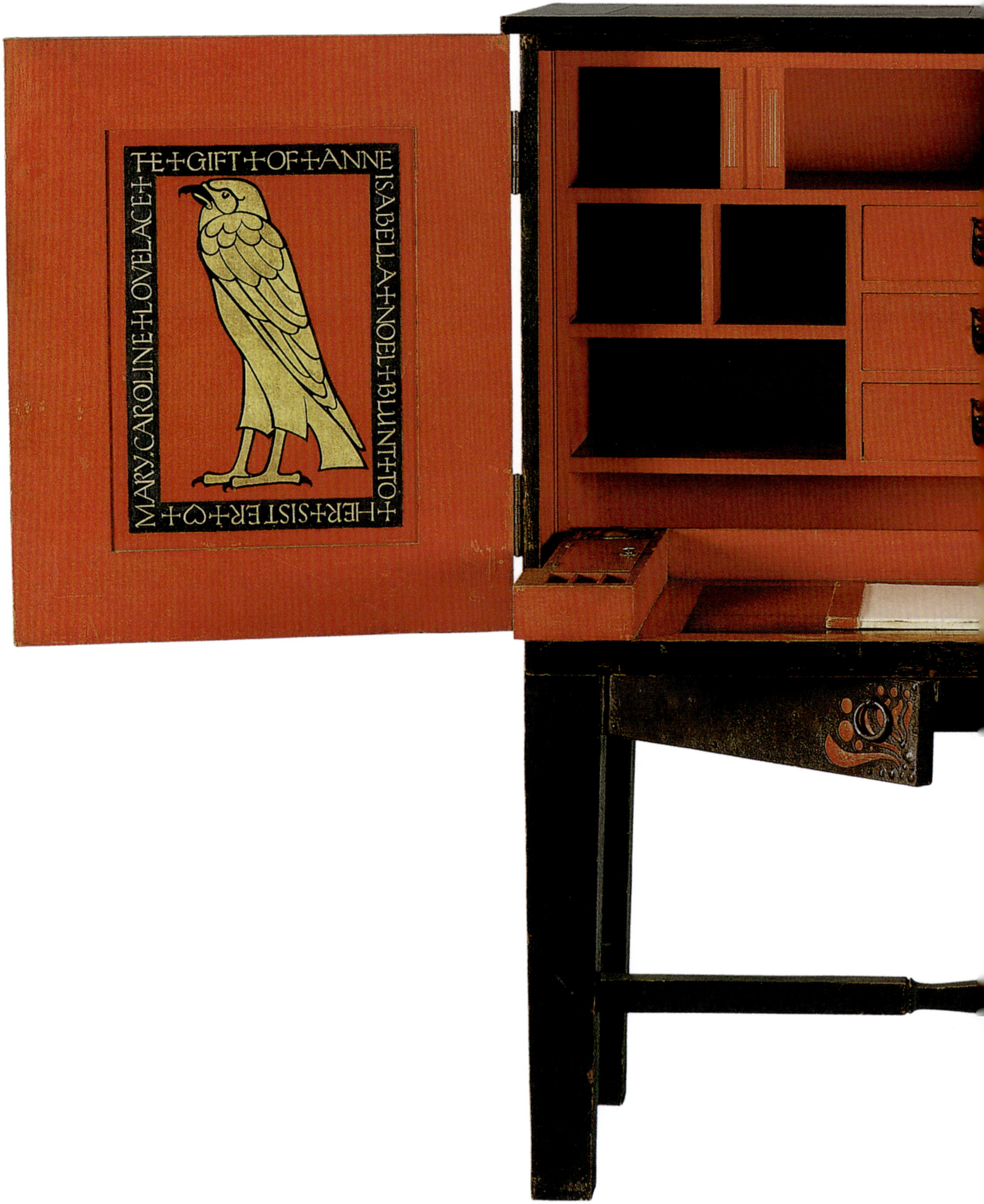
TE + GIFT + OF + ANNE
ISABELLA + NOEL + BLUNT + TO
+ HER + SIST ER + ω +
MARY. CAROLINE + LOVELACE +

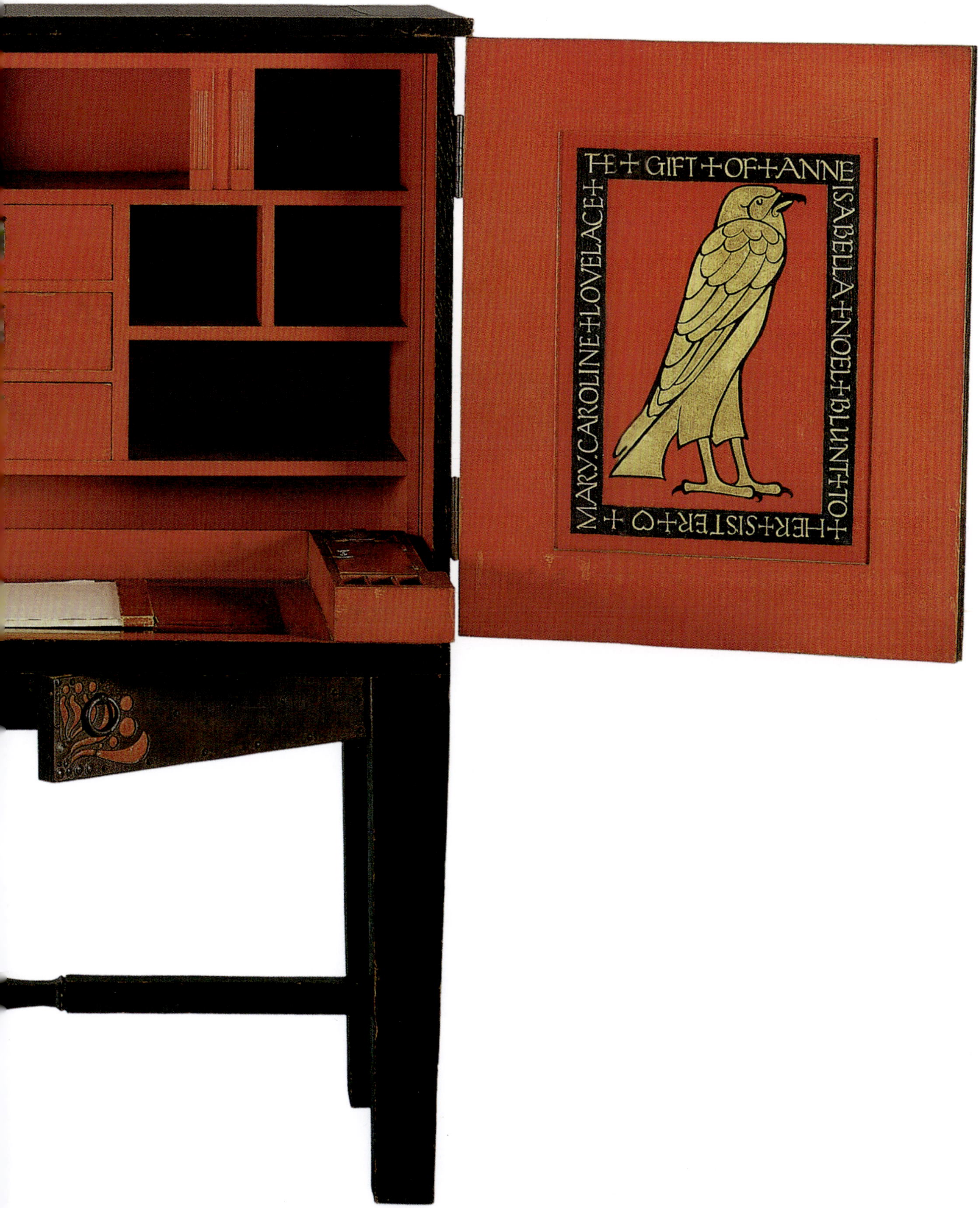
THE + GIFT + OF + ANNE
ISABELLA + NOEL + BLUNT + TO
HER + SISTER +
MARY CAROLINE + LOVELACE +

it would be more accessible to the patrons of the Guild. In the new workplace, the workshop was able to expand the work to jewellery, silverwork and enamel. In 1894, he started the survey of the historical monuments of London which constantly threaten to collapse and required restoration. This reminds us of the Society for the protection of ancient buildings founded by Morris and Webb.

The year 1898 was a landmark in Ashbee's life as he married Janet Forbes, the daughter of a wealthy stockbroker. It must be noted that Ashbee preferred men over women, but as homosexuality was illegal, he married Janet while telling her about his sexual preferences. Predictably, the marriage was somewhat unstable but after thirteen years of extramarital affairs on both parts, they finally had four children, all girls, together. That same year he opened the Essex House Press as he hired the former staff members of William Morris's Kelmscott Press as well as recovered the material and equipment to found his own Essex House Press. Between 1898 and 1910, the Essex House Press released over seventy publications. Still in the year 1898, the Guild was registered as a limited company with enlarged capital. Ashbee's ideal workshop was finally taking off and setting a successful example.

In 1900, Ashbee made a little parenthesis to the Guild when he met the world-famous architect Frank Lloyd Wright. The latter was to publish his executed works in Germany and asked Ashbee to write the preface of the book. This shows how much Ashbee was connected to the architectural world and that he had not forgotten his first centre of interest.

In 1900, the Guild of Handicraft constituted thirty workers and was well in business. Two years later, the workshop moved to Chipping Campden within the Cotswold district, making the small market town a centre for the Arts and Crafts movement. Chipping Campden was an industry-free area, thus corresponding to the ideals of Ashbee and Arts and Crafts in general: having an area free of any industrial stigmata. The implantation of the workshop brought about notable changes to the town like the renovation of local buildings and more work. The locals gladly patronised the workshop. However, the production level dropped from 1905 onwards and the limited company, which had been registered in 1898, went into voluntary liquidation. During the last two years of the company, the workers had carried on making products even though no orders were coming in. The Guild however lasted until 1919 with fewer members and a considerably reduced production.

The Guild was a unique experiment for its members were not only co-workers; they also spent a tremendous amount of time together outside the workshop. It was essential for Ashbee that the workers of the Guild understood each other and appreciated one another. This would bring harmony to the workshop and thus the work would be better.

Mackay Hugh Baillie Scott, *Manxman* piano, designed in 1896, made in 1902-1903.
Ebonized mahogany, carved wood, pewter, mother-of-pearl, marquetry of stained woods, silver-plated handles and hinges, 116.8 x 136 x 62.4 cm.
Victoria & Albert Museum, London.

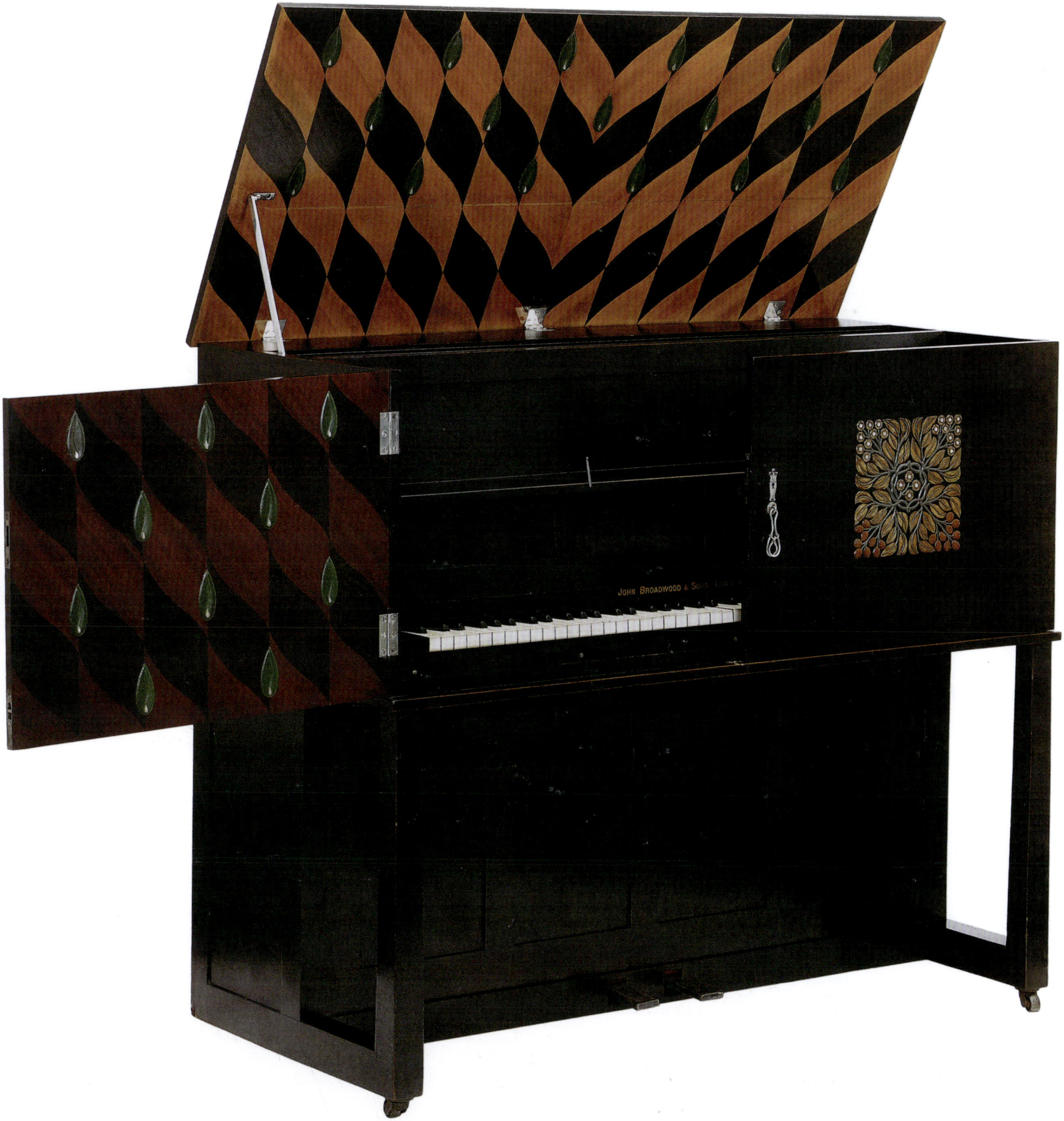
JOHN BROADWOOD &

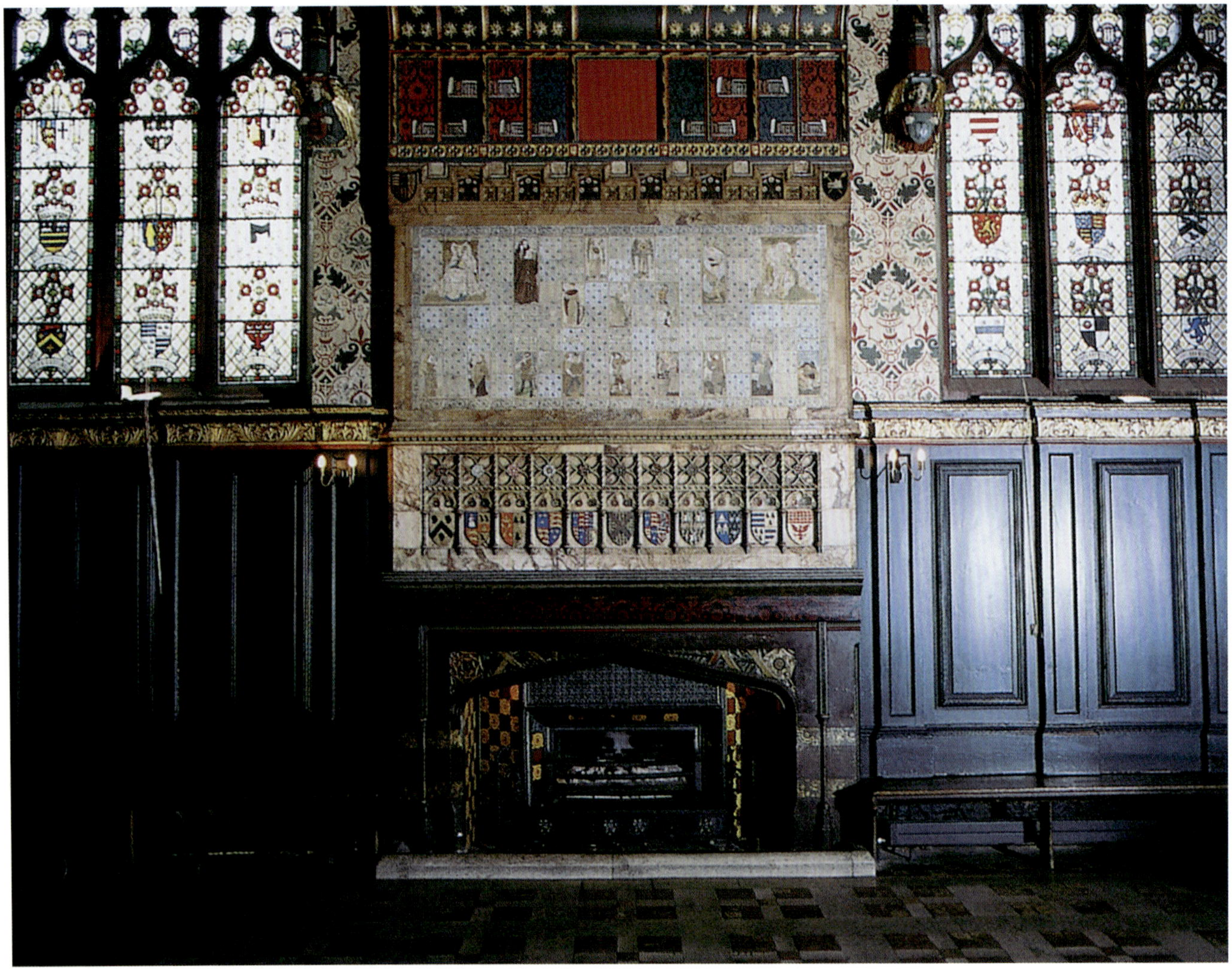

Like Morris, Ashbee fully controlled the production of the Guild and designed pieces himself. The forms he used were simple and powerful. He also designed houses and built seven houses on Cheyne Walk in Chelsea, London around 1898. With an appropriate design, Ashbee combined a modern, simple and overall genuine touch.

After the Guild was forced to cease all activities in 1919, Ashbee's career came to a turning point. It was then that he was appointed Civic Adviser to the city of Jerusalem. He was in charge of rebuilding the city and protecting the ancient buildings and historical monuments. His extensive knowledge in urbanism and his love for the preservation of ancient buildings were particularly useful for this task. He lived in Jerusalem to carry out this most ambitious project from 1919 to 1923, and he resigned from his post in 1922. Thereafter, he went back to England and retired in Godden Green in Kent.

Through the way he designed and led his business and life, one can say that Robert Ashbee was a true craftsman dedicated to his arts and times. Throughout his life, whether it be success or failure, he always carried on with great faith in his times and doings.

Anonymous,
fireplace, 1863-1864.
Queen's College Hall,
Cambridge.

William Morris,
Minstrel, 1872-1874.
Stained and painted glass,
71 x 43 cm.
Victoria & Albert Museum, London.

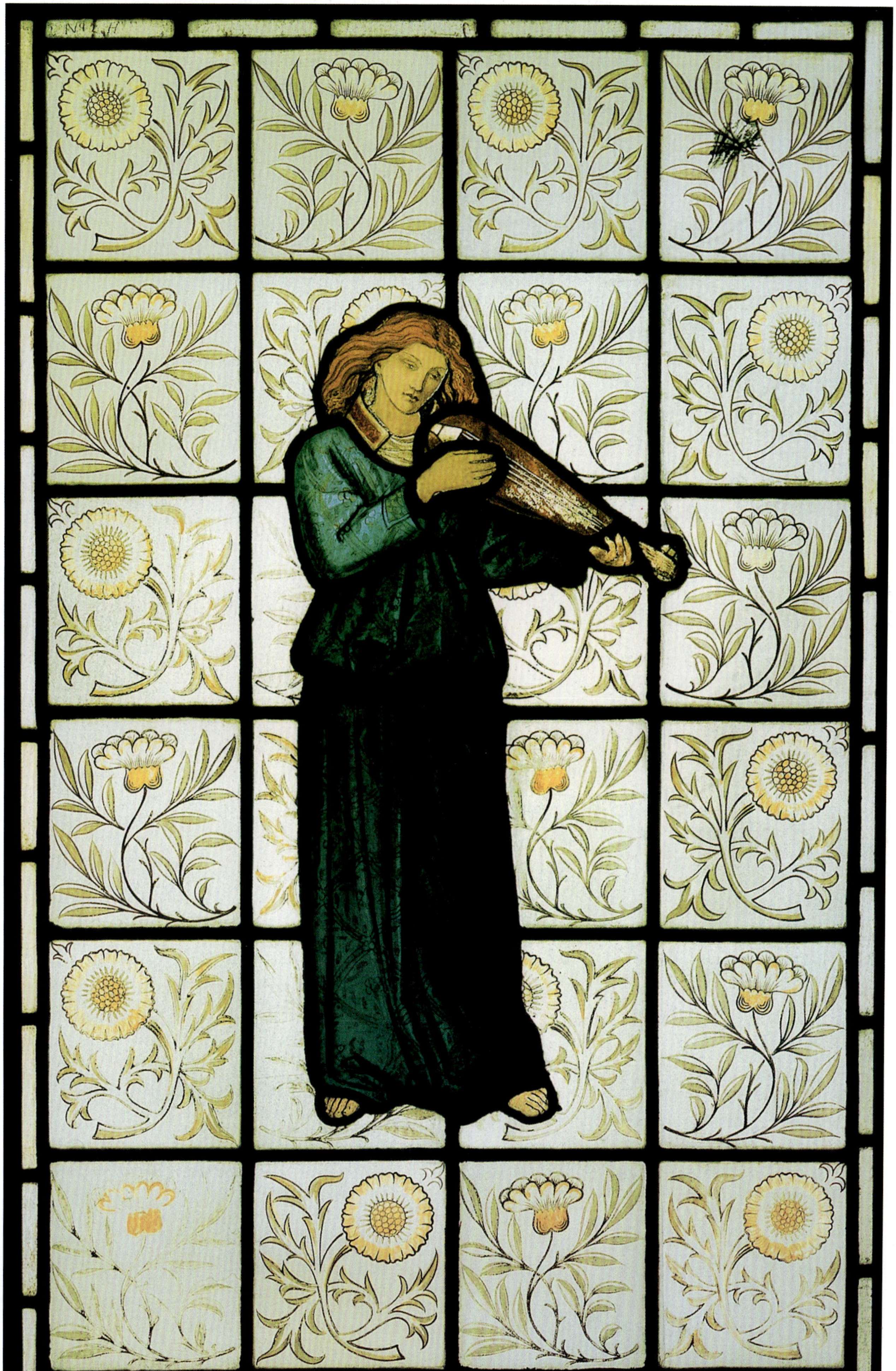

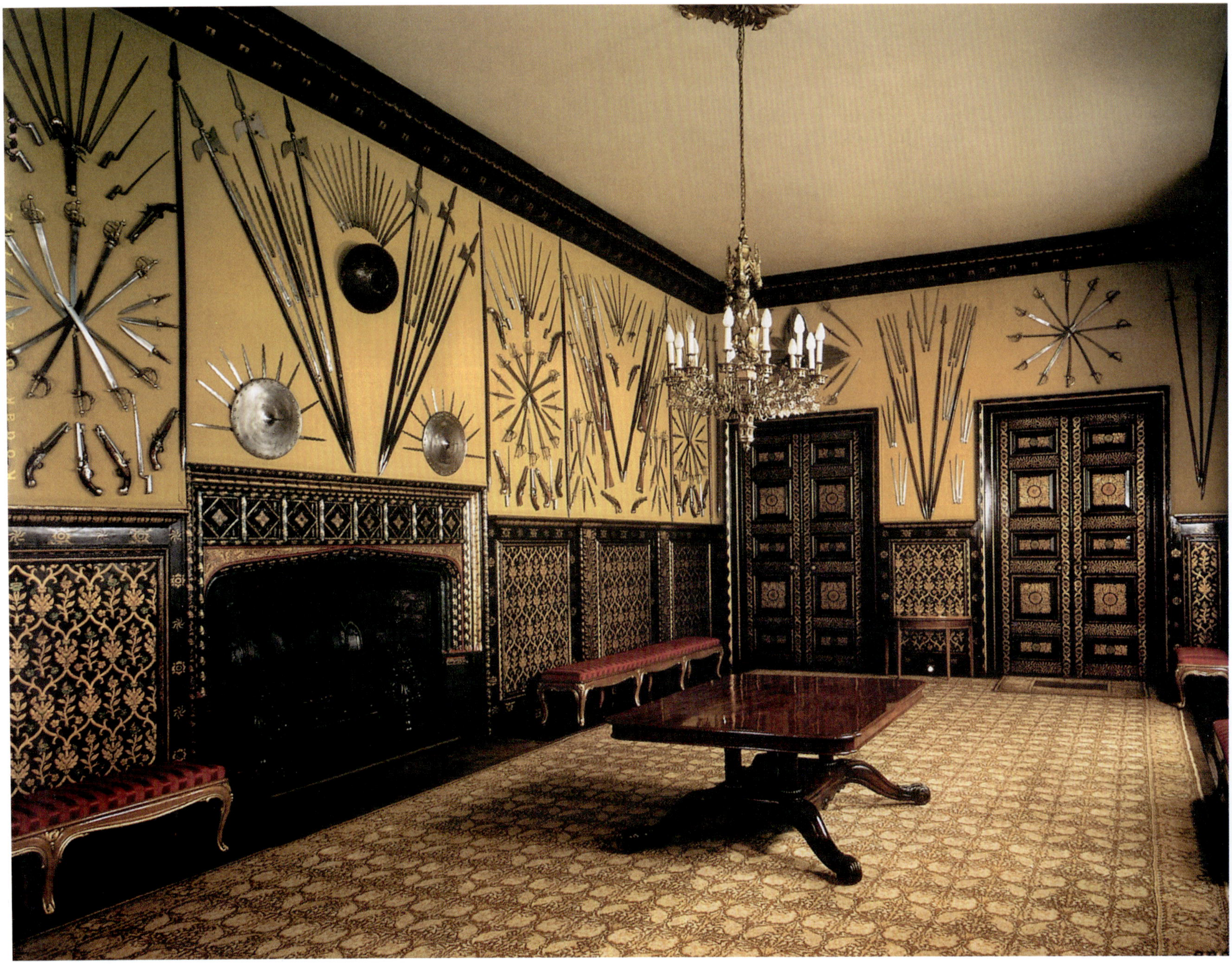

BIBLIOGRAPHY

Anscombe, Isabelle.
Arts and Crafts Style, London: Phaidon, 1991.

Anscombe, Isabelle and **Charlotte Gere**.
Arts and Crafts in Britain and America, London, 1978.

Arts and Crafts Exhibition Society.
Arts and Crafts: Essays by Members of the Arts and Crafts Exhibition Society, with a preface by William Morris, London, 1899.

Ashbee, Charles Robert.
A Few Chapters in Workshop Reconstruction and Citizenship, and an Endeavour towards the Teaching of Ruskin and Morris, London, 1894.

Carlyle, Thomas.
Past and Present, 1843.

Clutton-Brock, Arthur.
William Morris, New York: Parkstone International, 2007.

Coleman, Brian D.
Historic Arts and Crafts Homes of Great Britain, Utah, 2005.

Collingwood, William Gershom.
The Life and Work of John Ruskin, London, 1893.

Crawford, Alan.
C. R. Ashbee: Architect, Designer and Romantic Socialist, New Haven and London, 1985.

Cumming, Elizabeth and **Wendy Kaplan**.
The Arts and Crafts Movement, London: Thames & Hudson, 1991.

Exhibition catalogue.
Museum of Fine Arts, Boston, 1987.

Haslam, Malcolm.
Arts and Crafts Carpets, London, 1991.

Kaplan, Wendy.
"The Art that is Life", The Arts & Crafts Movement in America, 1875–1920,

La Sizeranne, Robert (de).
The Pre-Raphaelites, New York: Parkstone International, 2008.

Livingstone, Karen and **Linda Parry**.
International Arts and Crafts, London: V&A Publications, 2005.

Miller, Judith.
Arts and Crafts, London: Dorling Kindersley Limited, 2005.

Parry, Linda.
Textiles of the Arts and Crafts Movement, London: Thames & Hudson, 1988.
William Morris Textiles, London, 1983.

Peck, Herbert.
The Book of Rookwood Pottery, New York: Crown Publishers Inc., 1968.

Ruskin, John.
Modern Painters, 5 vol., London, 1851-1860. *The Seven Lamps*, London, 1909.
The Stones of Venice, 3 vol., London, 1851-1853.

Anonymous,
armoury, 1863-1864.
Queen's College Hall, Cambridge.

INDEX